Branding Trust

AMERICAN BUSINESS, POLITICS, AND SOCIETY

SERIES EDITORS
Andrew Wender Cohen, Shane Hamilton, Kimberly Phillips-Fein, and Elizabeth Tandy Shermer

Books in the series American Business, Politics, and Society explore the relationships over time between politics, society, and the creation and performance of markets, firms, and industries large and small. The central theme of this series is that culture, law, and public policy have been fundamental to the evolution of American business from the colonial era to the present. The series aims to explore, in particular, developments that have enduring consequences.

A complete list of books in the series is available from the publisher.

Branding Trust

Advertising and Trademarks in Nineteenth-Century America

Jennifer M. Black

PENN

University of Pennsylvania Press

Philadelphia

Published by
University of Pennsylvania Press
Philadelphia, Pennsylvania 19104-4112
www.upenn.edu/pennpress

Printed in the United States of America on acid-free paper

10   9   8   7   6   5   4   3   2   1

Hardcover ISBN: 978-1-5128-2500-8
eBook ISBN: 978-1-5128-2499-5

A catalogue record for this book is available from the Library of Congress.

For TJB

Contents

Introduction

The Value of a Label

The winter of 1843 had been especially harsh for Daniels Carpenter. The War of 1812 veteran had been down on his luck for nearly a decade and had been working in a thread factory for the past three years, struggling to make ends meet in Foxborough, Massachusetts. As a gripping nor'easter blanketed the region in snow that March, Carpenter received word that he was being sued for counterfeiting cotton threads in the state of New York. Before the year was over, he would be named in two additional suits: one in the federal court in Boston and a second in the state of New York.[1] Reflecting on his situation, he might have wondered how he had gotten here. In many ways, Carpenter's experience had been typical for young white men growing up in the generation after the American Revolution. After the war, he had built a successful commercial farm, producing straw for the region's hat factories. The booming American economy seemed boundless and, as a young man, Carpenter took every opportunity to get ahead. But the 1830s had been exceptionally difficult, leaving him scrambling to get by. Carpenter had attempted to diversify his income by investing in a thread factory, but dumb luck had him signing the papers just as the economy crashed in 1837. Thankfully, he was able to sell his interest in 1839 and retain a position for himself.[2] Three years later, Carpenter spotted an opportunity that offered redemption.

The threads sold by his employer in Foxborough had struggled to compete with the more popular lines imported from England—the British were, after all, well-known for their textiles, and the public was willing to pay a premium price for the high-quality products. Scrutinizing the labels for Taylor's Persian Thread, Carpenter probably marveled at the symbolic importance of such a small piece of paper. Remarkably, this round label turned a banal spool of thread into a luxury commodity: The women about town asked for it by name in the dry goods stores, making it hard for local manufacturers to break into the market. But Carpenter had an idea. He had heard of a lithographer in Boston who would take commission orders for reproductions of commercial labels. If Carpenter could get counterfeit labels printed in Boston, he could attach them to threads produced by a local mill in Foxborough. Of course, the lithographer would have to be highly skilled to reproduce the visually distinct Taylor labels, and he would need to be discreet.

The plan had come together surprisingly easily in 1842. Carpenter used his connections to procure labels and cases of unmarked threads. He then secured a commission agent in Boston, and another in New Jersey, who helped him funnel his fraudulently labeled goods through wholesalers and into retail stores in Boston and New York. The labels he scored from the lithographer matched the Taylor trademarks perfectly, and the popularity and reputation of the Taylor products made it easy to sell his fakes at a discount price. If everything had gone smoothly, Carpenter could have made thousands of dollars—surely enough to rebuild his farm. But as the snow drifted down in March 1843, Carpenter realized he had been caught, and he resolved to mount a strong defense in court.

Carpenter's story weaves together two key threads at the center of this book: the growing importance of trademarks and reputation to America's commercial market, and the centrality of visual designs and images—including labels—in communicating to the public. Tracing these interconnected story lines, *Branding Trust* explains the cultural work of advertising media in constructing personal connections between producers and consumers over the course of the nineteenth century. It examines the complex interactions among advertising professionals (whom I call "admen"); their clients, which included manufacturers, merchants, wholesalers, and others, all of whom the admen called "advertisers"; and the public.[3] As many of these exchanges took place in print, printers and newspaper editors also played an important role in mediating and shaping advertisers' interactions with the public. Likewise, visual and material culture assisted manufacturers and advertising professionals in communicating their classed and often racialized identities, which they used to build rapport with potential customers, and ultimately boost sales. These practices prefigured so-called modern branding techniques.

Carpenter's story tells us that historians ought to be looking at the early nineteenth century to better understand these developments. The story of branding and trademarks in the United States did not begin in the Gilded Age and Progressive Era but rather in the Age of Jackson, when economic instability and dreams of social mobility created opportunities for fraud, while the absence of widespread federal regulation allowed those frauds to thrive. The chilling ease with which Carpenter orchestrated his counterfeit scheme helps to explain why many Americans, especially those in the middle class, worried so much about status and appearances in this period. One's economic stability might only be one big con—or one poor investment—away from bankruptcy. As advertisers attempted to address consumer fears about commercial accountability, they incorporated language and visual cues that demonstrated education and gentility, drawing from the middle-class culture of character and respectability. Trademarks became a central, symbolic component of these strategies. From the 1830s forward, advertisers used such tactics to establish a *visual rhetoric* of trust and legitimacy and to cultivate meaningful relationships (both real and imagined) with the consuming public.

Trademarks are part of the branding process, and contemporary specialists generally distinguish between trademarks and brands in several ways. A *trademark* is a symbol or device that helps to distinguish one product from others like it in the market. Trademarks have a long history dating back to ancient Greece, and traditionally functioned to indicate a product's origin and ensure accountability toward consumers. With the growth of international trade in the early modern period, trademarks emerged to ensure the distribution of name and reputation alongside the wider distribution of products. Yet, as various economic actors and competitors clashed in the market, the exclusive right to use a trademark became contested ground. In the United States, the evidence suggests that the battle over trademarks' meanings and value took place in two key arenas: in the legal sphere (courts, legislatures, and legal treatises) and in the retail marketplace (especially dry goods stores). Over time, British and American courts gradually recognized the merchant's name, commercial identity, and reputation as property rights that deserved legal protection.[4] At the same time, advertisers and admen developed and reworked theories of branding that would associate trademarks with identity and reputation.

While the trademark is a visual symbol that can be materialized in print, the brand is abstract. A *brand* encapsulates the range of characteristics and attributes associated with a particular product, corporation, or other well-known public or commercial identity. Today, practitioners recognize that advertising and public relations campaigns help to cultivate a brand's identity, which often hinges on the firm's public image, its social values, and its potential to speak to consumers in terms of emotional attachment, lifestyle, and status.[5] Brands must be meaningful, distinguishing the product from competitors' products through the promise of higher quality or other advantages. Some scholars argue that brands help enable firms to charge higher prices for their goods or to facilitate the profitable introduction of related goods or product lines under the same parent brand (such as new cereals under Kellogg).[6] Historically, trademarks have become the vehicles through which the brand is communicated to the public, working in conjunction with advertising campaigns to distribute and publicize brand identity. In this way, the trademark serves a linguistic (hence, semiotic) function, providing a shorthand for the complex set of attributes constructed around the brand.[7]

As this book demonstrates, trademarks gain and maintain their meanings through repeated social use, gradually building and accumulating brand identity over time. It can be instructive, therefore, to think of the meanings behind a trademark through Walter Benjamin's theory of the aura. Like the celebrity of a famous work of art (its "aura"), the aura of a trademark is consecrated through social interaction and the field of vision. Repeated demonstrations in print help to create the aura of a trademark (which we might also call its symbolic meaning, or "brand") in a dialogic process between producer and consumer, mediated by visual communication.[8] Text and image thus work together in advertisements to create the symbolism behind trademarks. For the viewer, the trademark becomes a conjuring symbol, prompting memory recall of all the associations one has made with it in print, as well as personal experiences, secondhand information, and the constructed cultural meanings crafted by advertisements. When the trademark is reproduced in print and witnessed in myriad spaces and pages, its aura grows in the cultural sphere. More and more people recognize it, its symbolic associations, and its referents (the brand, product, company, or any combination of these three). Over time, trademarks grew into a logo-based language—a hieroglyphic set of graphic signifiers—with both universal symbolism and idiosyncratic meanings rooted in individual experiences. As a visual register for the brand and its reputation (and, in turn, expected future profits), the trademark is a highly valuable and marketable asset. Yet without the symbolic meanings, reputation, and expected profits accruing from the brand, the trademark has little monetary value.

Like the history of trademarks, the process of creating brands actually has a deep history stretching back to the colonial period in the United States—a story that this book aims to clarify. Advances in advertising practice emerged incrementally and through experimentation, beginning in the Early Republic. Successful tactics took time to disburse throughout the varied networks of newspaper men, printers, sales agents, manufacturers, retailers, and nascent advertising professionals—all of whom contributed to the discourse on building brand identity in the United States. While these actors did not consistently use the term "branding" to describe what they were doing, they concretely understood the economic imperative of maintaining one's commercial reputation—what specialists today would call "goodwill."[9] As a legal concept, goodwill first arose in British common law in the sixteenth century. It can be defined as an intangible asset linked to brand loyalty and the future profits a corporation could expect as a result of such loyalty.[10] Today, a company's goodwill value factors heavily into acquisition decisions and corporate mergers, and it motivates the maintenance of product lines associated with brands such as Nabisco even after their corporate takeover by large companies like Kraft Foods or Mondelēz International.

Understanding the cultural, legal, and industrial roots of the concept of goodwill helps to explain why firms fought so hard to protect their commercial reputations; as an intangible asset, goodwill quantified brand value. It allowed (and continues to allow) firms to monetize reputation, and it was a consistent factor in infringement cases in the nineteenth century.[11] Firms worked hard to earn consumers' trust, which they hoped would translate into higher profits. Whether we use nineteenth-century businessmen's terms describing this practice (maintaining a positive reputation), assign the early twentieth-century term (goodwill), or consider the practice by its contemporary name (either branding or building brand loyalty), gaining consumers' trust has been the goal of advertising since the beginning.

While this book aims to illuminate this deep history of the evolution of branding and trademark use in the United States, it also offers an explanation as to why the Gilded Age has tended to monopolize historical understandings of this story. Some of the earliest histories of American advertising have also had the longest reaching effects on historians' understanding of this industry and its role in ushering in the modern consumer society that would reign in the twentieth century. Perhaps the most comprehensive and influential book in this literature is Frank Presbrey's *History and Development of Advertising* (1929). An advertising expert who came of age in the early twentieth century, Presbrey traced, in encyclopedic detail, the progression of advertising tactics from Europe in the early modern period to the United States in the early nineteenth century, through the economic transformations in the Gilded Age that seemed to lay the groundwork for mass consumption. In telling his story, Presbrey emphasized the economic and institutional factors that helped integrate the American national market after the Civil War, including expanded distribution channels, a shift from bulk goods to packaged consumable goods, and the loss of face-to-face interaction between producers and consumers.[12] Importantly, this assumption—that before the last quarter of the nineteenth century most American consumers knew and engaged directly with the producers of the commodities they used—has often been cited as a primary factor motivating the use of trademarks. Trademarks emerged, according to this narrative, to supplant the loss of face-to-face exchange as the distance between producers and consumers grew and the scope of trade in the United States expanded to a national level.

Presbrey traced the well-known products of his own time to the innovation of large, multinational corporations headed by clever entrepreneurs, who established the brands that would carry America's consumer culture into the twentieth century. In so doing, he set a model for later scholarship that would similarly focus on the genius of a select few entrepreneurs and firms.[13] Like others of the interwar generation, Presbrey saw his contemporary moment as moving away from the values and culture of the Victorians; he criticized the old newspaper advertising as "cluttered," favoring instead the clean, restrained designs that characterized the work of his peers.[14] From Frank Presbrey's vantage point as an industry insider in the 1920s, the dramatic technological and economic changes of the Gilded Age and Progressive years must have seemed predetermined to bring the triumphal rise of America's modern mass-culture society. Though some critics would later dispute this teleological view, Presbrey's narrative of entrepreneurial and agency-led change has largely prevailed in the history of advertising.[15]

Presbrey drew heavily from biographies and institutional histories written by his peers and other industry experts, and thus his views were not so different from the generation of advertising professionals that had preceded him.[16] The narrative of progress that drove American society at the end of the nineteenth century led the admen of the 1890s to hold up their own efforts as the most modern, innovative, and efficient, just as Presbrey would do a generation later. Before the 1890s, businessmen seemed to have neither the means nor the motive to advertise on a national scale.[17] It's not hard to understand why the nineteenth-century narrative of progress resonated so loudly then, and perhaps continues to resonate with scholars today. New railroad lines, new resources from the West, and booming industry had fueled the expansion of the American economy after 1870. The Civil War had sparked an explosion in journalism, while technological improvements and new bulk mailing rates facilitated cheaper circulation prices and wider distribution areas for both newspapers and magazines. Larger advertising sections helped to pay for these expanded periodicals; as a result, the advertising industry appeared to explode in the last quarter of the century. By 1900, several agencies counted multiple offices throughout the United States and even abroad, including N. W. Ayer & Son (est. 1869); J. Walter Thompson (est. 1871); Lord & Thomas, later Foote Cone & Belding (est. 1871); George Batten Co., later BBDO (est. 1891); and the Bates Agency (est. 1893).[18]

Advertising firms such as George P. Rowell & Co. (est. 1865) and J. Walter Thompson wrote their own histories in the early twentieth century, claiming to have pioneered the brand-marketing strategies that ushered in modern consumer culture. From their vantage point, professional advertising agencies had won greater authority for manufacturers by appealing directly to consumers, while advertising itself had helped to socialize Americans to the consumption ethos.[19] Per capita incomes rose in the United States, precipitating a new form of conspicuous consumption. For the consumer, shopping transformed into an experience characterized by flashy packaging, more colorful advertisements, and louder and more frequent appeals from distant manufacturers clamoring for the consumer's attention. Department stores popped up in large and small cities across the United States, while new mail-order catalogs expanded the availability of goods to rural families at the end of the nineteenth century.[20] Finally, regulatory changes around 1900 seemed to spark innovation in trademark design and advertising, even though lawmakers were only responding to social and political pressures in crafting new laws that would accommodate and regulate existing business practices.[21] But, for Presbrey and later scholars, the disruptive impact of the American Civil War had thrown all of these Gilded Age developments into high relief and obscured the seeds of change earlier in the century.

In fact, by the mid-eighteenth century, Americans had already demonstrated an interest in acquiring luxury goods that would convey status and wealth. From its earliest years, the American market was simultaneously local and international, characterized by face-to-face exchange as well as by impersonal consumption and trade with unknown actors and through intermediaries. While artisans developed their trades and catered to local demand in the growing colonial cities, merchants engaged in long-distance trade through British imperial channels to bring a host of foreign goods to the American market. Contrary to Presbrey's assumptions about the Gilded Age, Americans engaged in long-distance exchange and consumption from the colonial period. This early culture of consumption in the American colonies laid the groundwork for economic transformation and industrialization after the Revolution.[22] In the Early Republic, technological improvements brought large-scale manufacturing to the American Northeast, intensifying a "Market Revolution" already under way. Such changes multiplied the volume of long-distance trade, enabling more specialized firms to thrive and intensifying their reliance on logos and trademarks to distinguish their wares.[23] Drawn by the promise of economic opportunity, an influx of migrants from the countryside and abroad flooded the developing cities along America's East Coast. While the young women and immigrants who arrived gained employment as low-paid laborers in the developing factories, aspiring young white men found clerkships in the commercial sector. As the United States expanded across the continent after 1804, migrating merchants brought their connections to regional, eastern, and international markets with them and helped new shop owners join this existing trade network before 1860. Together, these developments established the framework that would guide the integration of America's national market in the nineteenth century.[24]

This rapid economic growth before the Civil War triggered a series of booms and busts, especially because the American economy depended on a healthy flow of credit. Banks assisted this flow of credit by printing paper money and lending to reputable merchants, which enabled the latter to buy, sell, and trade goods with suppliers and consumers, who also used credit to buy, sell, and trade. One gained access to credit by maintaining a strong reputation for integrity and honor, especially in repaying one's debts.[25] In the words of one historian, business in pre–Civil War America "depended extensively on personal trust": Banks and others trusted individuals when they granted credit, trading partners trusted each other when buying and selling on credit, and employers trusted their clerks not to steal material goods, money, and trade secrets.[26] When it worked well, the credit system kept the economy in working order, but at best the system was uneven and prone to fractures and missteps. Several periods of rapid credit expansion and speculation, followed by inflation, economic downturn, and business failures punctuated the antebellum years. Perhaps the most notorious came with the Panics of 1837 and 1839, which saw the closure of several long-standing American firms and the financial ruin of thousands. Over the next several years, Americans like Daniels Carpenter expressed widespread uncertainty in the market while worrying about their own financial solvency.[27] Under the deflationary pressures of the 1840s, the market value of commodities, land, and other assets fell by 40 percent, while unemployment rose sharply and wages declined.[28] Americans demanded, bought, and consumed less during such economic depressions, which meant competition among merchant, jobber, and manufacturing firms was fierce.

Such changes disrupted the hopeful, egalitarian outlook bequeathed by the Revolutionary generation, and fostered new modes of thinking about class distinction and new anxieties about social standing, particularly among socially mobile whites.[29] Daniels Carpenter and other aspiring white middle-class men experienced these changes acutely. The expanding footprint of northeastern cities thrust populations together in ways that increased anonymity among urbanites, while the traditional modes of identity formation tied to artisanal production and the consumption of luxury goods seemed to be melting away.[30] Given the period's economic instability, the threat of financial ruin seemed to loom around every corner. How could one determine whom to trust? To alleviate this problem, intellectuals and tastemakers turned to standards of character, adapted from the aristocratic gentry of the Old World but modified to align with the ideals of American republicanism. This new culture of character combined guidelines about proper manners and etiquette from the early modern period with more recent conversations about "taste." As a platform for social distinction, this culture stressed one's ability to demonstrate virtue, transparency, and integrity, but it contributed to the myth of America's classless society by ignoring the structural constraints that prevented disadvantaged groups from participating and by maintaining the fiction that anyone could access social mobility.[31]

By the 1830s, cultural authorities had constructed a complex rubric that defined an ideal middle-class identity in terms of transparent self-display (both in appearance and behavior) and honest communication (visually, verbally, and through written language). These ideals rang true for both private and commercial dealings among white individuals across the North and South. Etiquette manuals, fashion magazines, and advice literature institutionalized strict codes of dress, conduct, and correspondence, instructing socially mobile men and women how to behave appropriately to their station and helping them socialize their children into this culture. An iconography of gentility emerged in this literature, structuring a "sentimental typology" that indicated one's character to others, both in the parlor and on the street.[32]

But it is important to point out that this culture of character was always exclusionary, in that it erected barriers to entry based on education, race, and other factors. Popular culture and public discourse often used the rubrics of proper etiquette to assess the civic worth of people of color, of immigrants, and of the working classes, ridiculing their inability or unwillingness to adhere to the dictates of good character. In this way, the rubric of character reinforced existing racial hierarchies and contributed to the assumption that to be "American" was to be a member of the white middle class.[33]

In many ways, the white middle-class obsession with outward demonstrations of class and character largely grew out of the economic circumstances of the antebellum period and of cultural responses to those circumstances. With rapid industrialization came the opportunity for social advancement, but population growth and migration meant more competition in the cities, especially for higher paying jobs. The economic uncertainty that characterized American life in this period prompted an underlying anxiety among the emergent middle classes, who uneasily jettisoned the eighteenth-century standard of a propertied independence to accept (for themselves or for their spouses) wage-paying jobs in the growing commercial sector. Success in commerce and manufacturing depended on credit and trust—both one's ability to gain credit and the trust of potential trade partners and one's skill in ascertaining the trustworthiness of others. Importantly, the middle classes learned how to present themselves carefully within these codes of gentility and how to read the symbols of gentility in others by scrutinizing dress, behavior, and language. The capitalist marketplace facilitated these expressions of identity, prompting individuals to adorn their homes and their bodies with objects and fabrics that would further express taste and propriety. In these ways, individuals in the Early Republic and antebellum period turned to metaphors of sight and seeing when calculating social differences; demonstrations of taste and character were often located in the field of vision and visuality.[34]

Yet, my goal is not to examine the processes or objects involved in building individual identities, as this is well-covered territory among social and cultural historians of the United States.[35] Rather, I aim to trace how advertisers and advertising professionals used such cultural knowledge to appeal to consumers' identities and how those appeals changed over time. For advertisers throughout the nineteenth century, the task of communicating one's character hinged upon careful performances of class in print. Advertisers sought public patronage much like merchants and others sought lines of credit from various lenders. Both efforts required displaying one's character and class in order to secure a commercial transaction; both efforts required one party to gain the trust of another in order for the transaction to be successful. Consumers in the early nineteenth century encountered an increasingly wide array of disposable goods in the retail marketplace, particularly in urban dry goods "emporiums," such as A. T. Stewart's in New York. In the face of multiplying choices at the point of sale, consumers needed more information to guide their purchase decisions.[36] How did manufacturers and marketing professionals attempt to resolve the information asymmetries that developed in this expanding marketplace? This is a primary question explored in this book.

Dry goods stores became an arena for such negotiations because of the prevalence of fraud in the nineteenth century, which stemmed from free-market ideologies and inadequate trademark regulation before 1870. The political economy that prevailed from the Early National period into the latter half of the nineteenth century drew from the Revolutionary generation's philosophy privileging individualism and the legal concept of *caveat emptor* (buyer beware) over widespread federal and state regulation.[37] Lawmakers and the courts often expressed ambivalence about expanding the reach of federal power—especially into industry—preferring to leave such work to the states. From the mid-1830s through the 1860s in particular, the United States Supreme Court upheld the rights of the states to license and tax out-of-state commercial firms in ways that privileged in-state firms.[38] Yet, it would be inaccurate to suggest that the federal government was somehow "weak" in these years; at key moments, the regulatory impulse swelled among state and federal lawmakers, often in response to specific disasters, such as steamboat accidents. Nineteenth-century public policy stemmed from the ideals of the founding generation, especially their faith in individual virtue and their commitment to self-discipline and innovation to further the common good. Many lawmakers preferred to restrict the destructive tendencies of self-interest by disciplining the market through various regulatory mechanisms, while those at the federal level often yielded autonomy to the states.[39] In short, lawmakers used regulation as a tool to promote moral commercial activity, prescribing appropriate market activity by restraining inappropriate activity. In the arena of trademark protections, it soon became clear that maintaining the public good required federal action.

Lawmakers had good reason to be concerned about commercial morality at the time: The antebellum marketplace has been described as a chaotic, undisciplined environment where entrepreneurs and con men mingled promiscuously with middle-class shoppers, working-class laborers, and elite factory owners. Among the public, anxieties swelled as newspapers frequently reported on bankruptcies, business failures, and commercial fraud. Newspaper editors warned consumers to be vigilant against dishonest secondhand dealers and mock auctioneers, who swindled unsuspecting and naïve city visitors by the dozen.[40] At the same time, merchants had to sharpen their skills when judging the trustworthiness of customers standing at the shop counter, given the frequent circulation of counterfeit bank notes. Hustlers and swindlers cleverly took advantage of America's decentralized currency to flood the market with fraudulent notes, and successful counterfeiters knew how to deploy the codes of middle-class respectability to ensure their fake notes would pass for genuine.[41]

A host of legal and institutional structures developed to alleviate these concerns about social and commercial legitimacy in the first half of the nineteenth century; many of these structures hinged upon cultural understandings of honor and creditworthiness. The nation's first bankruptcy protection law (1841) appropriated the standards of trustworthiness enshrined by the white middle class as the framework for debt forgiveness. Importantly, the law's framers saw honesty and transparency as a path to restoring confidence in the nation's financial system following the crippling economic panics of the late 1830s.[42] Likewise, as the credit-reporting and insurance industries matured, they developed criteria for assessing an individual's liability as a credit or an insurance risk, drawing on cultural assumptions about proper moral behavior and assessing an individual's business skills, experience, punctuality, thrift, and avoidance of vice. As American society transitioned out of the nineteenth century and into the twentieth, popular understandings of morality and individual worth would eventually change, but definitions of creditworthiness, insurability, and "business character" remained fairly constant.[43] These brief examples demonstrate the interconnected nature of economy and culture, especially the influence of the antebellum culture of character on American business. Nascent economic and commercial institutions transformed cultural ideals about character into determinants for economic benefits related to social mobility, cementing subjective notions of virtue and individual worth into the institutional structures of American capitalism.

Legal protections for trademarks also evolved out of these contingent understandings of character. In a series of lawsuits stretching from the early 1840s through the end of the nineteenth century, state and federal courts in the United States issued expanding protections for trademarks as a form of property, and, in the process, they normalized white middle-class ideas about morality and unfair or dishonest trade. Judges applied moral language that drew from cultural notions of good character, building up common-law precedents that subsequently fueled a range of congressional debates about how to protect American commerce (and the public) from dishonest traders. As the advertising industry matured in the second half of the nineteenth century, admen established guidelines for ethical business practice that also drew from older understandings of virtue and commercial honesty. In 1905, federal trademark law synthesized these currents in common law and business practice: It recognized the property value of trademarks as visual symbols of reputation and goodwill by defining ethical commercial practice in opposition to the dishonest frauds that sullied the character of the American market. The modern branding regime of the twentieth century grew out of these developments. By 1927, Frank Schechter, a leading scholar on trademark law, noted with certainty that the most important function of a trademark was not to distinguish goods at the point of sale but to symbolize reputation and merit.[44] The deeply thoughtful and sophisticated strategies antebellum advertisers used to publicize their goods had set the wheels in motion that would bring about America's modern consumer society.[45]

This book expands and transforms the histories of branding and advertising practice, as well as those of commercial honesty and fraud in the United States, by tracing the cultural dialogue linking producers, consumers, and advertising middlemen from 1830 through 1920. The complex interactions among these groups were contingent upon changing cultural ideals about ethical commercial behavior, virtue, and trustworthiness, while their interactions were mediated through, and drew sustenance from, advertisements and the courts. To reconstruct these interactions, this study disaggregates the advertising industry both spatially and categorically, assessing various practices, assumptions, and rules according to each sector.[46] *Branding Trust* expands the sphere of examination beyond well-known entrepreneurs and advertising agents to include printers, newspaper editors, designers, industry experts, judges, consumers, counterfeiters, and others.

In doing so, this book reveals that the evolution of branding as a practice was not a hegemonic development spiraling outward from the largest advertising agencies. Instead, it was a collaborative and diffused practice with multiple points of innovation and contingency, involving both structural trends in industry and cultural ideas filtered through individuals. Advancements came unevenly throughout the nineteenth century, with several earlier pockets of innovation springing up before the large structural changes of the 1890s and the rise of America's large multinational corporations. Examining the network interactions among various, seemingly disparate actors, illuminates how modern consumer culture has developed and been mediated through these multiple entities and across great distances.[47] *Branding Trust* traces the impact of these interactive networks on American consumer society and trademark law.

Methodologically, this book offers a roadmap for decoding and understanding the visual and textual languages that advertisers used to signal their character and class—in short, their legitimacy and trustworthiness—to the public. Much of this development hinged upon the visual construction of reputation, on the one hand, and the visual experiences that contributed to a new mode of interaction between producers and consumers in the nineteenth century, on the other. In order to understand the social and cultural functions of advertising, we must acknowledge that visual media are more than simple illustrations of past ideas; they have the potential to influence human behaviors and instigate change.[48] In his pathbreaking studies of advertising in the interwar years, for example, Roland Marchand demonstrates how advertisements visually communicated to the American public and shaped standards of individual achievement, national belonging, and corporate responsibility.[49] Taking a cue from Marchand and others, the chapters that follow contextualize and deconstruct advertising media in order to identify their meanings and trace the changing scope of those meanings over time. In these ways, this book contributes as much to the study of visual culture as it does to the fields of US business and cultural history.

Part of this method includes treating the images as *objects*, to better understand how advertising images were produced, circulated, consumed, and received (if possible), and their lasting impact. Just as advertising trade cards circulated among consumers in a variety of ways, advertisements in newspapers and other printed materials circulated, too. The trademarks that appeared on product labels and packaging applied additional layers of meaning to this commercial material culture, and, like print ads in the public sphere, these objects were circulated, exchanged, and saved, and often became the focus of intense informal and legal debates. Wherever possible, I offer evidence that documents consumers' actual responses to the advertisements discussed in the text in order to further support my analyses. For example, many Gilded Age individuals compiled scrapbooks using advertising ephemera, which can be read through particular lenses to get a sense of the user's privileging of information and imagery, as Chapter 4 demonstrates.[50] Yet, few individuals left behind straightforward, written reflections on the advertisements they saw in print and in public spaces. In such cases, historians can triangulate reception by applying an iconographic and semiotic reading to the images; by looking at long-term trends in advertising design; and by reviewing contemporary experts' advice and recollections on which strategies proved successful with their clients. These methodologies, along with lessons drawn from material-culture scholars, inform the visual and cultural analyses throughout the book.[51]

Situating advertisements as both visual media *and* symbolic material objects, the chapters in this book identify some of the most potent symbols used in American advertising, reconstructing the function and meaning of advertisements through their vehicles for reception (such as newspapers, magazines, catalogs, almanacs, and albums). This book demonstrates that, over the course of the nineteenth century, advertisements contributed to a shared visual experience that defined the relationship between producers and consumers as one of perceived trust and accountability in addition to the market relations of capital exchange. The roots of these developments lay in the antebellum period, when printers and others experimented with a range of visual strategies to attract the viewer's eye.

Chapters 1 and 2 trace the influence of middle-class culture on the commercial behavior of admen, advertisers, and jurists. Using the moralized language of character, merchants demonstrated their own classed identities, attempting to draw in middle-class consumers through rhetorical codes that the public would understand. Focusing their efforts on consumer-oriented appeals, early advertising agents, such as Volney Palmer, devised strategies to express virtue and character through print, thus establishing foundational tactics for the advertising industry as it matured in the decades that followed. At the same time, the judges hearing the first trademark-infringement lawsuits in state and federal courts scolded defendants like Daniels Carpenter for their dishonest frauds. For Carpenter and the other men indicted for trademark infringement in the antebellum years, the fluctuating legal boundaries of legitimate and illegitimate commerce could mean riches or ruin. The plaintiffs in trademark-infringement cases often crafted their complaints using the same rhetoric of character that saturated white middle-class culture and American advertisements. As common-law and legislative protections against trademark infringement developed from the 1840s through 1870, the legal benchmarks of honest commercial practice intertwined with middle-class standards of transparency. This development was as much about demarcating the boundaries between lawful and unlawful competition as it was about valuing the time and labor spent in building one's commercial reputation with the public. A positive reputation carried with it the potential for expanded credit lines, greater trust from the public, and increased profits. Through advertisements, manufacturers, merchants, and others built their public reputations; thus, protecting one's reputation by prosecuting trademark infringement went hand in hand with advertisers' efforts to cultivate rapport with the public.

Yet, as economic growth expanded after 1840, the further integration of the national and international markets meant that individual firms faced wider competition for their market share. Advertising strategies shifted and adapted to these changing economic and social conditions: Just as advertisers had learned to use language to signal character in print, they collaborated with printers to leverage visuality as another layer of appeal. Chapters 3 and 4 turn to printers' efforts to craft increasingly elaborate and entertaining advertising designs from 1830 to 1900. Following an early ban on advertising imagery in the penny press, urban newspaper advertisers grew more creative in their use of negative (i.e., white) space; new fonts; bold, italics, and capital letters; and small woodcut images.[52] Interestingly, rural newspaper editors and printers outpaced the development of pictorial advertising in the big-city papers of New York City, demonstrating tremendous innovation despite limited resources.[53] As the nineteenth century progressed, printers began to anticipate viewers' reactions to ads through the visual paradigms, design strategies, and media they used to communicate with consumers. By the early twentieth century, commercial illustrators had learned to craft a multisensory experience in magazine advertisements, which anticipated the reader's use of the physical object.[54] In each of these cases, artists and printers sought to manipulate their media to improve audience reception: They shifted advertising strategies to increase consumer appeal and (hopefully) product sales. Though the Gilded Age seemed to explode with commercial pictures, newspaper printers had pioneered strategies to appeal to consumers through interesting, entertaining images gradually and incrementally from the 1830s forward, a progression that was only briefly interrupted by wartime mobilization at mid-century.

Outside of the newspapers, entertainment aesthetics increasingly defined printed advertisements during and after the Civil War, as Chapter 4 shows. Capitalizing on existing public fascinations with chromolithography and album-keeping, postwar printers bolstered the desirability of advertising trade cards as collectibles by adopting sentimental icons of children, flowers, and other objects from the antebellum cult of sincerity. Significantly, the spectacular print media that characterized the Gilded Age had been modeled after ephemera that circulated in a culture of personal expression much earlier in the century. In their desire to entertain the public through advertisements, printers appropriated and commodified sentiment to sell more goods.[55]

While the "chromo craze" was still underway in the Gilded Age, merchants and advertisers continued to rely on established modes of appeal, adapting the older rhetorical modes of demonstrating character to fit their evolving goals. Chapters 5 and 6 trace the persistent importance of the principles of integrity and transparency in the business world through the end of the century. While many advertisers continued to use older methods of demonstrating one's class and character to establish rapport with the public, others developed new tactics to achieve the same goals, such as inviting customers to visit the factory (a demonstration of transparency), referencing established credit lines and institutional history (to show longevity and financial solvency), and creating visual representations of company sincerity. The goals of demonstrating character and attracting the viewer came together in a new advertising invention in the 1870s: the trade character. Transitional figures, such as Lydia Pinkham, illustrate the communicative power of trademarked images that fused personal appeal with celebrity and virtue, paving the way for subsequent characters such as the Quaker Oats man.

Returning to trademarks and the law, Chapter 6 points to the ways in which moralized language continued to permeate the legal discourse about trademark protections and fair competition, especially in terms of protecting a company's goodwill. These ideas fused with advertising practice and the visual symbolism of the trademark in the 1905 federal trademark law. Framed within the context of Progressive desires to protect American consumers, this law built upon nearly a century's worth of legal discourse about "fair" competition, the importance of transparency in commercial behavior, and the need to secure one's commercial reputation. Moreover, efforts to safeguard a firm's market share by protecting its reputation and goodwill had laid the groundwork for what later practitioners would call "branding." By the first decade of the twentieth century, advertising professionals had formalized the tricks of their trade and demonstrated their abilities to craft reputation and goodwill *artificially* for new firms such as the National Biscuit Company. Admen had found the strategies to infuse the brand with public trust, lawmakers had encoded an inherently visual symbol of reputation (the trademark) with moral symbolism, and the 1905 law would, in turn, provide the foundation for future trademark protections in the United States.

Though the 1920s has often been held up as the birth of "modern" advertising by historians and practitioners, advertising professionals had learned how to navigate public relations over the previous century, developing proven strategies to grow profits by appealing to consumers on their own terms. In so doing, they institutionalized a step-by-step process for building and maintaining goodwill with the public—the necessary ingredient for protecting one's reputation, winning a larger market share, and growing profits. To appeal to consumers, early advertisers attempted to win public favor in the best method they knew how: They demonstrated their class and character in printed advertisements that would speak to like-minded members of the middle class. As market competition increased, printers and advertisers devised new and novel ways of attracting the viewer's eye, coupling visual strategies with rhetorical strategies first to grab the reader's attention and then to gain his or her confidence. At the same time, manufacturers learned the necessity of safeguarding one's intellectual property in order to maintain one's reputation in public—in short, they formulated ways to protect their brands from infringement. These developments are only visible when the historian takes a longer view of the nineteenth century, looking for patterns of continuity and transformation between the antebellum and the post-bellum periods. Rather than compartmentalizing legal history, cultural history, economic history, and visual culture, *Branding Trust* integrates the study of these typically disparate fields to emphasize their interdependence and shared influences in the nineteenth-century United States. Advertisers' efforts to demonstrate character, protect trademarks, and present entertaining novelties in print came together by the end of the nineteenth century, cementing the legal importance of trademarks and goodwill together with the entertainment aesthetics of visual appeals. This visual rhetoric of trust and legitimacy, established through trademarks and advertising imagery, has become a central component of American capitalism today.

CHAPTER 1

Epistolary Advertising

Commercial Morality in the Early Advertising Industry

In the half century following the American Revolution, the mid-Atlantic cities of Philadelphia and New York experienced profound transformation. New transportation and communication technologies carried goods and information from the cities to expanding markets across the Eastern Seaboard and the Midwest, while an influx of immigrants from the surrounding rural areas and abroad expanded these cities beyond their colonial footprints. In New York, for example, the population had grown fivefold between 1790 and 1830, making it the nation's largest city.[1] These social and economic changes shifted urban experiences dramatically.

Chronicling her time in Manhattan in the 1840s, abolitionist Lydia Maria Child observed, "It is sad walking in the city. The streets shut out the sky, . . . [and] amid these magnificent masses of sparkling marble, hewn in prison, I am alone. For eight weary months, I have met in the crowded streets but two faces I had ever seen before."[2] Child's reflection captured a sense of the cruel anonymity that had descended upon the city, punctuated by a dramatic realization of the social ills that capitalist industrialization brought. Wandering through the Battery neighborhood in February 1842, Child noticed, with irony, that one homeless mother sat on a stoop beneath a grand department store window, where "large vases of gold and silver" were on display. Child shuddered at the stark contrast between the luxuries for sale in this "commercial palace" and the "homeless outcast . . . shivering beneath their glittering mockery."[3] The city appeared to chew up and devour such individuals, before spitting them out and condemning them to destitution and misery.

The city's dangers also threatened visitors who came from the country: Newspapers regularly printed stories of countryfolk falling prey to swindlers, mock auctioneers, and morally bankrupt criminals. In July 1845, for example, the *New York Herald* recounted a story about a "verdant youth" from New Hampshire by the name of John Brown, who had arrived in the city only a day earlier. "Floating before his bewildered eyes were the fair sights, bewitching and voluptuous forms, and gorgeous descriptions of the wealth, beauty, and fashion of this vast metropolis," the article noted. Brown walked down Broadway, "lost in admiration at its splendor," but he was soon pounced upon by an auctioneer on Chatham Street. Only after a "violent struggle" did Brown escape the "den of the thieves," his meager savings clutched in his hand. Recounting his tale as a caution to others, the editors of the paper remarked with disappointment that "there are no legal means for the prosecution of these scoundrels."[4]

As these accounts demonstrate, the new visual and social experiences of the antebellum city sparked anxieties about the city's vast possibilities, both for wealth and ruin. Economic uncertainty ruled the day: The Panic of 1837 had rattled the financial stability of both the nation and the middle class, while the populism of Jacksonian democracy and growing labor agitation brought social and political unrest.[5] Given the period's financial panics, economic depressions, devalued currencies, and persistent threats from loan sharks and swindlers, the assets on which middle-class status rested must have seemed to be in constant danger of liquidation. Living in the city at this particular moment threw all of this economic uncertainty into high relief. In the space of just a few blocks, one could witness, as Lydia Maria Child did, not just the glittery splendor of industrial growth— the towering marble structures that housed city government, large commercial banks, and trading houses; the spacious department stores whose vast displays of abundance called passersby to worship at Mammon's feet—but also the depressing struggles of the city's working classes, crammed into emerging tenement districts known best for their filth, vice, and crime. As more and more immigrants poured into the city, their presence heightened middle-class anxieties about the dangers of the working class, especially for those whose economic positions wavered precariously between solvency and destitution.[6] For a class deeply concerned about categorizing economic and cultural differences, it must have been disconcerting to realize that everything seemed to operate in shades of gray.

In this urban climate of deceptive appearances, the American advertising industry took shape. The cultural, social, and economic changes witnessed by the antebellum city—and chronicled by the stories of Lydia Maria Child and John Brown—prompted a new form of advertising modeled upon the cultural conventions of genteel performance. Advertisers adapted existing practices, such as presenting letters of recommendation, and developed new commercial vocabularies modeled after middle-class notions of respectability and industriousness to reach middling sorts who would appreciate such ideas. Through all of these strategies, advertisers demonstrated their focus on appealing to the public as consumers, though that framework was often exclusionary. By addressing their readers in this way, advertisers contributed to the archetype of the white middle-class consumer, and forged strategies that would facilitate a reciprocal identification between producers and consumers in print media, through visual and linguistic means. Importantly, advertising strategies helped normalize the moral standards upheld by the white middle class in two key ways. First, such strategies cemented these moral standards as part of conventional business practice. Second, as business conventions evolved over time, they did so in discourse with legal standards for commercial morality in intellectual property disputes, especially those surrounding trademark infringement. Business conventions and legal standards for commercial morality became mutually reinforcing as the nineteenth century progressed, thus further normalizing the moral standards of character proselytized by the antebellum white middle class.

The Culture of Character

America's culture of character evolved from economic and cultural factors first established in the early to mid-eighteenth century. British industrialization and the increasing globalization of trade in the colonial period triggered both social mobility and class consciousness among artisans and middling sorts in the American colonies, precipitating the beginnings of a consumer revolution. As the century progressed, Americans purchased more luxury goods, and by 1750 merchants began to emphasize the importance of fashion by linking their goods to the latest styles from Paris and London, especially in advertisements. By the time of the Revolution, a growing contingent of Americans expressed their classed identities through the goods they purchased, wore, and displayed in their homes.[7] Over time, the emulative impulse bequeathed by British society challenged the new nation's commitment to republican principles of material equality (for some, at least). As a result, Americans in the Early Republic attempted to identify criteria, apart from monetary wealth, that could establish one's status. They settled on the concept of "character," which blended Christian morals of honesty and integrity with the republican ideals of civic virtue and responsibility. Middle-class tastemakers developed a strict rubric for proper etiquette, language, and dress, which would, they argued, demonstrate one's character to others. An education rooted in religion and the liberal arts promised to lay the foundation for one's strong adult character, while appropriate consumer choices would help reinforce the principles of refinement and respectability through the objects and clothing one bought and wore. Relative economic equality and expanded access to luxury goods helped to democratize consumption so that, by the 1820s, bourgeois respectability became accessible to a wider segment of the American population.[8]

Importantly, vision and visuality mediated these coded identity performances at home, on the city streets, and in print. Building from the Enlightenment faith in the power of visual observation to find scientific truths, tastemakers argued that outward appearances could reveal inner truths about a person's character.[9] In the parlor, members of the middle class surrounded themselves with artworks, furniture, draperies, and accessories to demonstrate their taste and refinement. Guidebook authors reminded audiences that such objects would help cultivate a family's appreciation for restrained beauty, high culture, and good character, while displaying those same qualities to visitors who entered the home.[10] Self-proclaimed etiquette experts coached their audiences to don "unobtrusive" frocks and suits, as this mode of "sentimental dress" would "purely translate the inner character into outward forms that could be read by anyone."[11] Textiles and clothing should coordinate color schemes and patterns, authors noted, which would show one's creativity without gaudiness. Clothing was supposed to fit well, but it should not be too tight, lest one be accused of sexual impropriety. Manners and etiquette rules reinforced these principles of restraint, while literary magazines such as *Godey's Lady's Book* offered illustrated fashion plates and provided advice on how to reconstruct the ensembles at home.[12] Through these modes, America's middle class learned that one's true character could be read on the body itself.

This emphasis on visual displays of refinement and character further extended to the printed word and language use, particularly in one's correspondence. Since the colonial period, letter writing had been a culturally important mode of demonstrating one's education and status. Instructional guidebooks and etiquette experts from the 1760s onward represented letter writing as a foundational component of character formation: In studying the language and forms of their class, middling men and women cultivated their own genteel sensibilities and separated themselves from the uneducated working classes below. Writing thus became a primary mode of displaying one's education (through proper use of form and grammar) and character (through penmanship and phrasing). Formal and informal education, including self-instruction, helped disburse genteel manners and composition etiquette first from Europe through the British Empire and then throughout the American colonies and the new United States. After the Revolution, a cultural emphasis on expanded education gave rise to a new genre of instructional books and manuals, which further distributed these formal epistolary practices and rules to new generations, reinforcing these cultural connections between status and language use.[13]

Extending the maxims of respectability further, guidebooks included written communication as another realm where one's identity and status ought to be properly displayed. Letter-writing manuals offered detailed instructions for writing a range of personal and business letters, codifying proper form, grammar, and "phraseology" through detailed rules and sample letters.[14] Above all, letter-writing manuals stressed that the tone of the letter was meant to transparently convey both the relationship of the correspondents and the character of the writer. As "indices of taste," letters were thought to provide windows to the soul: The writer demonstrated his or her own education, refinement, culture, and "inborn nobility" through his or her personal correspondence.[15] These doctrines were even more important for merchants and entrepreneurs conducting business and engaging in trade through correspondence. Through letters, merchants negotiated their tenuous identities, promoted themselves, built relationships, and maintained their reputations.[16] Acknowledging the epistolary conventions of the educated elite helped to reinforce and preserve one's reputation as a learned businessman and as a member of the middle class. Likewise, poor writing or bad manners could damage one's reputation and, by association, one's livelihood.[17]

Character and Race

It is important to emphasize, however, the ways in which cultural understandings of language use, as a deployment of class identities, worked to reinforce social hierarchies even as intellectuals and tastemakers championed the egalitarian spirit of the new United States. To put it simply, the standard of "good character" was also exclusionary. Around the time of the American Revolution, epistolary etiquette and manners grew to be seen as an individual's assertion of "personal agency, access, and participation" in the public sphere, divorced from the nation's emerging economic and social structures. Mainstream white society universalized language etiquette, ultimately obscuring the power dynamics associated with the culture of character and contributing to the myth of America as a classless society.[18] But, importantly, economic and racial barriers prevented many individuals from accessing the education that would enable them to use proper language and epistolary etiquette in their written communication. Slave-owning communities in the American South policed the boundaries of their class privilege by restricting literacy to white people. In the North, gradual emancipation laws had facilitated the growth of urban communities of free blacks, many of whom began to accumulate wealth and political power by 1815. But institutional racism still prevented many African Americans from attending schools, even as segregated secondary schools began appearing in the north by the 1830s. Efforts to further exclude blacks from political and social participation in all areas of the country followed: Pennsylvania, for example, barred blacks from voting in 1838, joining several other states that had already restricted the franchise to white men.[19] Just as the culture of character promised access to the middle class for socially mobile whites, it offered a benchmark to exclude non-whites for their inability or presumed unwillingness to perform according to the culture's dictates, or their poor taste in attempting to do so.[20]

In the economy, these percolating racial tensions resulted in an increasingly segregated market, as the culture of character presented structural barriers for non-whites' economic participation as both producers and consumers. Commercial print culture marginalized and ridiculed free black participation in American society, crafting a popular culture that weaponized racial stereotypes to reinforce social hierarchies in both the North and the South. Images of commercial streetscapes and retail stores in city directories represented the ideal consumer as white and middle class, wholly excluding African Americans from conceptualizations of the emerging consumer market in the United States. Such representations reinforced the identification of middle-class codes of conduct with whiteness, presenting this linkage as a universal truth and reminding African Americans of their marginalization.[21] Yet, even though the rubric of character could be exclusionary, free black elites in the antebellum period attempted to use respectability politics to elevate the social and political status of blacks, especially in the North. They focused on outward displays of African American respectability, intellectual acumen, and economic success to leverage the same codes of propriety that defined the white middle classes. In newspapers, literature, ephemera, and photography, free blacks displayed their middle-class identities, making forceful arguments about their contributions to American society and their eligibility for full citizenship rights.[22]

These efforts to display respectability and propriety became increasingly important as northern free-black communities often drew the ire of working-class whites.[23] In Philadelphia, especially, rising incomes ought to have qualified free blacks for entry into the middle class; instead, race relations grew exceedingly tense after 1820. The economic successes of free blacks in the city seemed to defy "the racial order that underwrote the American economy" and contradicted the stereotype that African Americans were "irresponsible, dependent, and even irrational individuals."[24] Several public outcries resulted, including the highly popularized caricatures of Edward Williams Clay, whose "Life in Philadelphia" series (1828) ridiculed free blacks for their attempts to display middle-class status, sharply criticizing their language, dress, and behaviors as foolishly aspirational. Clay's images spawned a host of copycat prints from artists in New York and London, who further capitalized upon the supposedly poor manners and gaudy fashions of Philadelphia's rising black elite.[25]

In one such print, "The New Shoes" (1833), the exclusionary aspects of white middle-class culture become clear (figure 1.1). Set in Sambo Paley's Boot & Shoe shop, the central interaction in the print takes place between a male shop clerk and a female consumer, as she inquires about the varieties of shoes available. The woman wears an elaborate dress outfitted with feathers, greenery, flowers, ribbons, and a lace veil. Rather than the demure, restrained fashion choices depicted in *Godey's Lady's Book*, this woman's clothing is mismatched, gaudy, and loud, prompting the viewer's judgment at best, and, at worst, our revulsion. The artist has exaggerated her facial features, emphasizing a bulbous nose, thick lips, and a wide grin (which reveals a missing tooth or two)—features that are echoed in the other black figures in the image. The woman's squat figure, knobby ankles, and oversized feet make her appear mannish—more akin to the bearded clerk beside her than to the petite and feminine women heralded by *Godey's*. Finally, the artist renders the verbal exchange between customer and clerk in a broken dialect, poking fun at the figures' flawed language skills.[26] Asking for white or pink shoes, the woman expresses disdain for black as a "dirty" color, while the clerk attempts to reassure her of its functionality, despite its poor aesthetics.

Yet, the exchange and the woman's preference for white and pink over black, presents a double entendre in this case. The artist satirizes the woman's aversion to her own color—her dislike of the black shoes suggests that she similarly dislikes her own skin color (or perhaps her own community). "Dirty" suggests that black is earthly, impure, and perhaps even sexually improper. Not only has she expressed preference for white or pink shoes, but the artist implies that she would prefer to be white herself—she is aspiring beyond her station, emulating the white middle class in her appearance and fashion preferences. But the clerk's subtle reassurance serves as a corrective to such aspiration: Acknowledging black's ugliness, the clerk reminds her that she would still find it "a Good Color to Wear." Here, the clerk's voice stands in for the artist's; he attempts to push back against the woman's (and, by extension, free blacks') aspirations, reminding her (and them) of the supposed natural order of things and of black's subordination to white. Black remains functional, even though it is "not . . . so Handsome to look at."[27] This image reinscribes a racial order configured around the equivocation of middle-class gentility and whiteness, using satire to invalidate black claims to respectability and, by extension, to citizenship.[28]

Caricatures like this one illuminate both the structural boundaries of citizenship and the limitations of economic wealth and character in conferring status. While our black consumer has the money to buy the right clothes and

Figure 1.1. William Summers and Charles Hunt, "Life in Philadelphia: The New Shoes" (London, c. 1833). Digital Repository, The Library Company of Philadelphia. Online at https://digital.librarycompany.org/islandora/object/Islandora%3A60231.

accessories, she still somehow fails in her attempt to perform middle-class status. Further, the image reveals white anxieties about the potential disruption of social hierarchies, and/or the expansion of the middle class itself. Here, racial arguments about white supremacy masquerade through cultural ideals associated with class-based identities, language, and consumption. The caricature serves both to render African Americans ineligible for middle-class membership and to reassert the superiority of whites for their apparent ability to perform those classed identities better.

Commercial Morality

Anxieties about social mobility and class status—whether in regard to oneself or in fearing the potential rise of Others—extended to the commercial sphere as well, as economic transactions held the power to make or break one's financial stability. Just as consumers might be concerned about the reputability of the merchants they encountered on the street, merchants, dealers, and manufacturers worried about the relative trustworthiness of distant trading partners and customers, particularly the unfamiliar ones. In response to such anxieties, intellectuals used the same codes of character and virtue to outline appropriate and ethical commercial behaviors, scorning the deceitful activities of confidence men and condemning capitalistic greed. One early argument came from Reverend Joshua Bates in 1818, who linked republican understandings of civic virtue with commercial honesty and asserted that willful deception deprived trading partners of their property rights, and rightful income.[29] Condemning such dishonesty and theft, Bates extended the concepts of Christian morality into the realm of commercial practice.[30] He argued that individual responsibility and virtue should prevent widespread fraud, in much the same way that the Articles of Confederation had foregrounded virtue as central to the success of the American Republic.[31] By this logic, individual responsibility, guided by high moral standards and virtue, would absolve the need for federal regulation of economic activity.

As arguments about commercial morality developed after 1820, "ethics" took the place of "virtue" in this discourse, but moralists continued to worry that commercial dishonesty and fraud ultimately threatened the stability of the American economy itself. As one merchant complained, "Fraud and deception in our business concerns have too often taken the place of honor and honesty. . . . The astounding and overwhelming frauds which have been committed . . . have served to create universal alarm in every quarter."[32] Falsehoods made a mockery of those who adhered rigidly to the standards of virtue, he continued, rendering "all our hard and diligent strivings for a name and character vain and futile."[33] The American capitalist system rested very tenuously on public confidence, and fraud shook those already unstable foundations to their core. The more newspapers reported on fraud, the less confidence the public would have in the goods they bought and in the merchants they patronized.

An emerging literature on business etiquette promised to alleviate this problem, teaching aspiring entrepreneurs and clerks about ethical business practice, building a positive reputation, and, most important, evaluating the trustworthiness of others. As they had in etiquette guidebooks for a general middle-class readership, the authors of these business manuals argued that cultivating good character would help one establish successful business relationships. This meant portraying oneself honestly, demonstrating respect for others, and acting responsibly with integrity, which included standing behind one's claims, refunding customers when necessary, and upholding the letter of the law.[34] These dictates became the hallmarks of good business practice, while also defining those that failed to follow these rules as illegitimate.

In an 1857 primer for businessmen, Samuel Wells underscored the same standards of morality prescribed by clergymen and other intellectuals decades earlier. As a practical manual, the book provided detailed advice on how to keep accounts, collect payments, repay debts, correspond with customers and trading partners, and place advertisements. But each topic also reminded readers that appropriate behavior in these areas required continued adherence to the principles of character because one built his reputation gradually through each daily interaction with others. Highlighting the importance of character, honesty, and honor to commercial practice, Wells linked these moral principles to economic success, while noting that dishonesty was sure to lead to economic ruin.[35] Customers' experiences ought to match a businessman's promises for quality goods and services, Wells noted, reminding his readers that pleased customers would be more likely to recommend said business to others.[36] Through advice like this, business literature socialized entrepreneurs to the moral standards upheld by the antebellum middle class, linking commercial honesty and morality with the path to material wealth. As entrepreneurs, merchants, and clerks interacted in the commercial sphere, they helped perpetuate the cultural acceptance of these middle-class ideals. Together, they built an expansive business culture that stemmed from middle-class codes of conduct, helping to maintain and spread the vocabulary of genteel expression.[37]

Gentility and character, as defining elements of American culture in this period, further shaped commercial developments in the built environment, as new urban shopping districts emerged by the 1840s. These shopping districts were "cleaner, brighter, and more elegant than ever before," featuring buildings with new architectural forms and interior designs that projected an air of respectability.[38] The artisanal workspaces that had been so visible in colonial shops moved to "back rooms," making way for new merchandise showrooms that separated manual work from nonmanual work, production from consumption. Such changes were necessary to draw middle-class consumers, such as Lydia Maria Child, back to downtown spaces, where rapid industrialization in the first decades of the century had precipitated vice and crime.

In lithographs that captured these new retail environments, merchants demonstrated the respectability of their commercial spaces by depicting elaborately decorated showrooms modeled after the middle-class parlor.[39] Glass display cases, gas lighting, and enlarged showrooms dramatically shifted the experience of shopping, while window displays became more elaborate and entertaining as shopkeepers competed for patronage. *Hunt's Merchants' Magazine* told subscribers to furnish their retail spaces using the same taste and visual aesthetics that governed the parlor. Fine carpets, ample lighting, and ornately carved furnishings would thus replace the rather plain retail interiors of the colonial and early national periods. Through directives like these, the magazine emphasized visual presentation and merchandising, suggesting that merchants imagined their customers as individuals who needed to be visually impressed in order to patronize the store.[40]

An 1856 engraving of Daniel Appleton's New York City bookstore offers an illustrative example of these merchandising strategies (figure 1.2).[41] The store's well-lit interior featured Grecian columns; marble busts; and tall, elegant bookcases rendered in the popular neoclassical style of the day. Well-dressed white men and women browse through the shop; their middle-class status clearly visible in their clean, fashionable appearances. The store's architectural and iconographic references to Greco-Roman society and literature help saturate the space in intellectualism, refinement, and culture, while the patrons inside the store cement its identity as a respectable space for middle-class enjoyment. Fashioning his store as a "public parlor," Appleton borrowed a "material vocabulary of gentility"—as instructed by *Hunt's Merchants' Magazine* and other trade publications—to craft a respectable haven from the hustle and bustle of the city street.[42] The symbols of education and refinement, as well as the store's well-lit interior, demonstrated its safety and trustworthiness for patrons who might be concerned about the dangers of the city. Furthermore, including unaccompanied women and children in the space helped domesticate it and pacify fears of moral transgression (such as deception and fraud): If the space was safe for families and children, then by association it must be a respectable, morally sound space for all. Such merchandising would have helped retailers like Appleton frame consumption as a proper middle-class activity, while visual representations of his shop interior would encourage aspiring middle-class viewers to identify with the established middle- and upper-class individuals in the print.[43] *Hunt's* advice and Appleton's décor suggest that patrons came to expect these material elements of respectability in the shops they visited. In these ways, retailers and others used visual modes of communication, couched in class-based symbolism, to build rapport with selected members of the public. Material culture and the visual realm thus became important venues for commercial appeals.

Yet, merchants and retailers also fashioned their commercial spaces, in part, to perform their own identities.[44] Just as members of the middle class expressed their character and propriety through manners, dress, and the material comforts of the parlor, merchants established their reputations through the physical appearance of their stores, through their communications with the outside world (through clerks and in advertising), and through their customers' experiences. Visual representations of Appleton's store, demonstrating the pleasant experiences of upper- and middle-class families, reflected just as positively on Appleton and

Figure 1.2. Jocelyn Whitney, "Interior View of Appleton's Book Store, 346 & 348 Broadway, New York," in The Historical Picture Gallery, or, Scenes and Incidents in American History (Boston: Bigelow, 1856). Digital Collections, The New York Public Library. Online at https://digitalcollections.nypl.org/items/510d47e1-05db -a3d9-e040-e00a18064a99.

his firm as they did on the experience of shopping itself. Like print advertisements, lithographs of the store's interior helped to advertise Appleton's services, as well as the propriety of his shop, to potential customers. Therefore, while *Hunt's Merchants' Magazine* helped to coalesce a class of middling merchants with shared cultural values, the publication also told readers how to appeal to an emergent, middling class of consumers by demonstrating those same values. Adopting appropriate fashions and furnishings for one's retail space and mirroring propriety in written communication would demonstrate a merchant's character in much the same way that other individuals did in dress and speech. Such demonstrations became a central component of developing advertising strategies in the antebellum period. These, in turn, provided a foundation for advertisers' later attempts to both understand their audiences and appeal to those audiences in print.

In these ways, the business community relied upon middle-class codes of conduct to evaluate trustworthiness in the antebellum United States, using the rubric of character to assess acceptable commercial behavior, credit risks, financial stability, and investment opportunities.[45] In their written interactions with each other and with the public, merchants adopted many familiar strategies to demonstrate propriety and trustworthiness. They used language codes to show their manners and education; they modeled humility and transparency to build reputation; and they evidenced character by showcasing their faith in individual virtue, by avoiding vice, and by repaying debts promptly. Such strategies eventually became habits that would persist in the advertising industry as it developed through the nineteenth century, with a continued emphasis on gaining consumers' trust.

Testaments to Character

Just as Appleton and other merchants constructed their retail spaces to demonstrate propriety, they communicated their respectability in print ads to the public, using language cues and testimonials to gain credit with potential consumers. Broadly defined, testimonial advertisements used endorsements from satisfied customers in order to convince future clientele that the product or service was worthy of patronage. Endorsements from public figures had been a common advertising tactic among eighteenth-century firms, such as Josiah Wedgwood's pottery studio. Wedgwood famously distributed plateware samples to various royals across Europe in the 1770s, with the hope of gaining their endorsements. When the elites acquiesced, Wedgwood then coaxed aspiring middling folk to emulate the tastes and fashions of high society, naming the goods after their royal users (e.g., "Queensware") and offering the same patterns and designs for sale in his urban showrooms.[46] Introducing these techniques through British imperial channels, Wedgwood helped to prime the American market for the sort of emulative consumption that would make testimonials and endorsements from public figures meaningful by the 1820s. His success likely inspired subsequent entrepreneurs to solicit similar endorsements from well-known personalities or former business associates, which could be used in advertisements to generate public interest and lend credence to advertisers' claims.[47] Throughout the nineteenth century, these testimonials typically came from ordinary individuals, local or regional officials, and public figures; they provided evidence of personal experience with a tone of gratitude and praise, issued in a familiar epistolary format. Paradoxically, testimonial advertisements promised to be successful because they drew from familiar cultural idioms related to personal interaction and communication, as well as then-common cultural tendencies to grant authority to even anonymous printed materials.[48]

Importantly, testimonial advertisements grew out of two distinct yet related cultural practices: a tradition of writing letters of recommendation in the business sector and the popular revivalist practice of religious testimony, or "witnessing."[49] Letters of reference had been common commercial tools since the early modern period and typically could be used to gain access to credit or employment. Viewed as a cornerstone to cultivating and maintaining good business relationships, reference letters provided insight into the character of both the bearer and the writer. A letter of reference generally attested to the individual's merits and responsibility, vouching for the individual so that person might experience economic success. Recommenders were almost always previous or current business associates of the bearer, though respected and notable members of the community (such as lawyers and bankers) might also be called on to write such letters. Reference letters had become critical components in initiating economic transactions by the late colonial period, and, for this reason, nearly any merchant might be asked to write such a letter for a trading partner, an employee, or a peer. This informal system of reference letters would later inform the first credit-reporting system in the United States.[50]

After 1820, the American business community reworked and formalized older guidelines for business correspondence, recognizing the economic importance that references and letters could have. Whereas the language of friendship and devotion appeared frequently in personal letters, business correspondence was to remain devoid of such flowery language—instead maintaining a tone of unemotional respectfulness in its straightforward, transparent prose.[51] Guidebooks stressed that plain speech was the best way to cultivate confidence among trading partners and potential customers, and they offered models for straightforward phrases that emphasized the writer's indebtedness to the recipient, including closings such as, "I remain, yours respectfully," "We are, yours obediently," or "Yours Faithfully."[52] Such language choices helped correspondents avoid unintended disrespect, which could offend others and damage the economic relationship.[53] For reference letters, guidebooks instructed recommenders to assess an individual honestly, commenting on his or her character with a clear, level head. Writing a letter of recommendation was a responsibility to be taken with great care and respect, for the consequences of a poorly written letter might mean the difference between economic stability and bankruptcy for the bearer.[54] This bestowed a great deal of power on the recommender, whose own integrity was on the line if he abused such power. The reciprocal nature of exchanging and preparing letters of reference contributed to a general understanding, among the business community, that an individual's virtue and concern for the common good would override any impulses to wield this power unfairly.[55]

Testimonial advertising in the nineteenth century also mirrored a practice of religious witnessing from the revivalist and evangelical traditions. In Christian practice, to "bear witness" meant experiencing God's message or presence in a personal way, and individuals often "testified" to these revelations by regaling fellow parishioners of their conversion experiences. As a mode of sharing and developing faith, religious testifying became a prominent component of Protestant worship, especially in evangelical events after 1820.[56] Converted individuals typically shared stories of their lives wrecked by vice and desperation, the critical intervention performed by a preacher, and their positive transformation after recommitting to God. As a regular component of large religious gatherings, testifying individuals became walking proof for both the power of faith and the specific preacher's sermons. Preachers buttressed their own reputations among the revivalist community by presenting converted individuals whose salvation stories were particularly powerful and emotional.[57] Again, early nineteenth-century advertisers drew from these existing cultural paradigms, appropriating salvation stories to show the efficacy of their products and services for sale.

One common place to find testimonial advertisements in the antebellum years was in ads for the patent-medicine industry, which had taken shape domestically after 1800.[58] As early as the 1820s, patent-medicine manufacturers began using free almanacs to publicize their formulations, capitalizing upon a growing popular interest in seasonal cycles and light reading material. Families kept these ready-reference booklets handy for regular consultation throughout the year, making repeat exposure to the advertising material unavoidable. Retailers typically distributed the cheaply printed books free to the public; their pages featured testimonials alongside astronomical data, household tips, cartoons and jokes, and advertising material from the sponsor.[59] Visually, patent-medicine testimonials appeared as formal letters with standard salutations and closings, as blurb-like snippets with short bylines, and as full-page expositions featuring the writer's engraved portrait and/or other illustrations. Describing the symptoms and problems associated with particular ailments, testimonials for patent medicines offered textual evidence of the products' usefulness, alongside the manufacturer's usage instructions and other reference information.

In Philadelphia, mid-century consumers could pick up an almanac for Dr. David Jayne's medicines at the druggist's counter or by mail and peruse testimonials. Jayne's almanacs followed a format that would become typical for patent-medicine almanacs published for the rest of the century in the United States. Published annually, the booklets were printed on cheap paper with a slightly sturdier cover. Inside, readers found information about each of Jayne's medical preparations (which included an expectorant, a hair tonic, and ague pills), a glossary of diseases and common ailments, testimonials supporting his products, and other standard almanac material (such as lunar cycles, calendars, and weights and measures).[60] In 1851, after only six years in business, Jayne had become so successful that he was able to move into a new eight-story granite building in Philadelphia.[61] The new structure, which reportedly housed manufacturing facilities and offices for Jayne and his sons, featured a modern architectural design and was pictured on the cover of his almanacs. Business must have continued to expand, for, by 1858, Jayne's almanacs boasted an annual circulation of more than 2.5 million.[62] While the cover image and statistics might be overlooked by some, to discerning members of the middle class the picture of the modern office building would offer visual evidence of Jayne's commercial success, his financial worth, and his shared company among other widely successful firms in Philadelphia (figure 1.3). Like Appleton in New York, Jayne leveraged the impressive appearance of his company's physical space to create a positive image for his products by association. Moreover, the vast circulation figures he included on the cover provided numerical evidence of his strong reputation and success as a manufacturer whose product was in high demand. Jayne likely intended to use this information as an indication of the widespread public affirmation of his products' popularity and value.[63]

Jayne often included testimonials from noteworthy public figures and other entities in his almanacs, leveraging their cultural capital to boost sales. In his 1846 almanac, for example, Dr. Jayne included testimonials from J. S. Maginnis, Professor of Biblical Theology at the Hamilton Literature and Theological Seminary (Hamilton, New York), and Reverend J. M. Peck of Rock Spring, Illinois, a Baptist minister. Each testifier offered praise for Jayne's medical preparations, encouraging friends and the public to patronize the physician for medicinal relief.[64] Jayne also published testimonials from doctors, congressmen, and newspaper editors, sometimes including notarized statements from county clerks, magistrates, and even Philadelphia Mayor John Swift.[65] Calling attention to the product and its virtues, one editorial "unhesitatingly" pronounced Jayne's products to be "the best article[s], without any exception."[66] Including letters from such well-known public figures enabled Jayne to exploit the reputations of local academics, clergymen, and others, appropriating their cultural authority for himself. These supportive words from prominent public figures encouraged everyday readers to emulate their behavior and trust Jayne's products. Moreover, the appearance of widespread support, offered in print, drew from then-common cultural tendencies to grant authority to even anonymous printed materials.[67]

In many ways, the testimonials that appeared in patent-medicine almanacs followed the same conventions that structured commercial letters of reference and religious witnessing. First, testimonials established an existing relationship between the writer and the product, typically based on prior satisfactory experience.

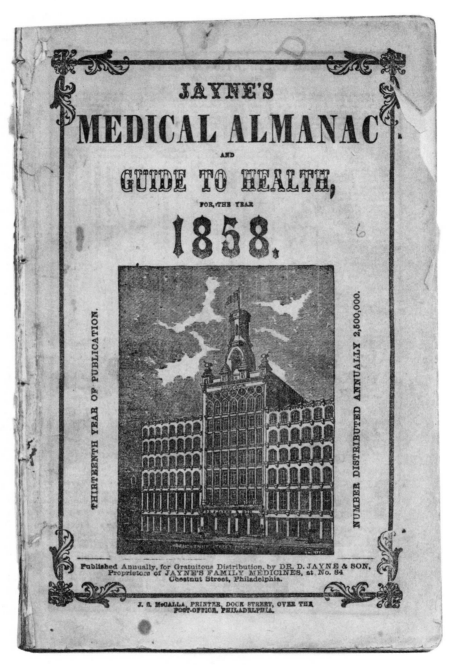

Figure 1.3. Cover, *Jayne's Medical Almanac and Guide to Health, for the year 1858* (Philadelphia: Dr. D. Jayne & Sons, and J. S. McCalla, 1857). Rare Books Collection, The Library Company of Philadelphia.

A letter typically documented the writer's medical problem, the failure of other remedies, and the writer's desperation to find a cure. Testifying to the value of Jayne's hair tonic in 1848, Henry Scrantom of Rochester, New York, recounted his dismay at having lost his hair prematurely. Having used Jayne's other remedies in his family "for years, and always with the desired results," he decided to try the tonic (though he admitted he had very "feeble faith" that his hair would grow back).[68] The dire straits described in patent-medicine testimonials thus paralleled religious witnessing closely, as "saved" testifiers often referenced the vice and desperation they faced before hearing a stirring sermon that brought religious awakening. Next, the testimonial writers chronicled the benefits of the medicine, occasionally giving specific details about dosages applied and the duration of treatment. Of course, for Henry Scrantom, the result was "remarkable"—a full head of soft, black hair—and thus Scrantom was convinced of the "invaluable" worth of Jayne's tonic.[69] Scrantom's testimony argued that Jayne's tonic had the power to transform skeptics into believers. Again, this rhetorical tactic closely paralleled religious witnessing as, like a medicine, the preacher served as a conduit for salvation. Expressing satisfaction with the results, most testimonial letters typically concluded with hearty praise, encouraging others to patronize the company.[70]

Sprinkled throughout the letters were references to the reputation of the manufacturer, the respected character of the medicine, and the writers' own indebtedness for being returned to a state of full health and emotional capacity. The formal tone that framed such testimonials helped situate them within the genre of commercial references, while their content paralleled religious transformation stories. In 1848, W. A. Hayles, a retailer in Louisville, Georgia, wrote to tell Jayne that his medicines were becoming "very popular," and Hayles was selling out of his stock. He reported interacting with many satisfied customers, promising to forward "several certificates [i.e., endorsements], from the first class" of people.[71] In stressing the gentility of the endorsers, Hayles's letter emphasized the trustworthiness of their statements. Moreover, women often numbered among Jayne's supporters in print, leveraging cultural assumptions about the inherent honesty of middle-class women to improve the believability of the testimonials.[72] As such, testimonial ads painted a picture of down-and-out members of the middle class restored to their former vigor and character by the medicines at hand. The ads suggested that patent medicines could offer a form of physical salvation for desperate, but otherwise virtuous, individuals.

In these ways, advertisers like Jayne repurposed the business reference letter, something that typically only circulated in private encounters between business associates, and turned it into an outward-facing, public communication to advertise commercial goods. Vouching for the character and abilities of another person meant putting one's own reputation and character on the line: The letter became a symbol of the trust between the correspondents, especially in the expectation that the bearer of the recommendation would perform at the standard attested to by the recommender. This assumption of trust was important to the efficacy of reference letters, as objects that ensured the employability and credit-worthiness of individuals and the continued positive reputations of firms. When manufacturers adapted the format of reference letters for advertising, they arguably appropriated the same assumptions of virtue and trust onto the testimonial letters they printed. The cultural understandings that had invested reference letters with virtue and honesty mapped similar symbolic meanings onto testimonial letters used in advertising.

Occasionally, writers indicated that they could also attest to the character of the manufacturer, knowing him personally beyond a commercial relationship. In lending his endorsement, for example, Professor J. S. Maginnis added that he had had "the gratification of a personal acquaintance with Dr. Jayne," finding him to be "an exemplary member of society, [who] sustains a high reputation in Philadelphia as a regular and skilful [sic] physician."[73] Likewise, other testifiers referred to Jayne as a "gentleman" who was worthy of the public's "confidence," referencing Jayne's respectability as a member of Philadelphian society to elevate the status of his products.[74] Such written verifications of Jayne's personal character purposefully used a vocabulary that would have been familiar not only to socially mobile middle classes but also to aspiring working-class populations as well. Jayne was not some faceless figure out to make a quick buck; rather, he was (reportedly) a well-respected contributor to society, known among his contemporaries and other notable Philadelphians for his status and character. With his integrity established through these multiple testaments and the success of his operation visualized through the engraving featured on the cover, the almanacs presented a collective message that Dr. David Jayne was worthy of the public's patronage and trust.

A Language for Advertising

Like Jayne, owners or managers of other firms turned to print culture to communicate their classed positions to potential customers, and here the vocabulary of respect and character remained prevalent. Most advertisers composed their own newspaper ads in the first half of the nineteenth century, as custom held that nobody could know a business better than its owner-manager.[75] Like other members of their class, merchants learned how to use appropriate linguistic cues to signal respectability by studying other forms of writing, including business correspondence and newspaper advertisements placed by others in their trades. In crafting newspaper ads, they followed the requirements for genteel performance for the same reasons that other members of the middle class did: to let strangers and peers know that they were respectable. In some ways, it was even more important for merchants and businessmen to follow the class-based prescriptions for proper behavior. Their livelihoods depended on credit, and their ability to get credit depended on maintaining an air of virtuous respectability, which would translate into a positive reputation.

In New York City, for example, advertisers used the words "respectfully" and "humble" when framing their addresses to the public, and they modeled their newspaper ads after the cultural conventions governing written correspondence. They signed their names beneath closings designed to convey gratitude and respect, in formulations that imitated formal business correspondence. In both the mainstream (i.e., white-owned) and African American presses, the word "respectfully" appeared frequently throughout newspaper advertisements in the 1840s.[76] Advertisers "respectfully" solicited the patronage of New Yorkers, inviting potential customers to call as if they were visiting a friend's parlor. In 1841, for example, Victor Magne, a French tailor, addressed his ad with an epistolary salutation, "respectfully" announcing "to gentlemen of taste and fashion" that he made "fashionable," ready-to-wear clothing "in the French style." He thanked customers for past favors and asked for continued patronage from the public.[77] Likewise, the July 1840 issue of the *Colored American* (published in New York City), included several notices "respectfully" informing "friends and the public" of services available, including those for Mrs. Peggy Williams's boarding house in Troy, New York; Richard Carrol's bath house on Church Street; and the King Street Garden and restaurant operated by Lyman Lyon.[78]

Other advertisers modeled their ads more closely to epistolary styles. The printing firm of Ackerman & Miller, for example, placed an advertisement in the *New York Tribune* in January 1845 that replicated the visual format of letters:

TO MERCHANTS IN WANT OF SIGNS FOR NEW FIRMS, &c.— The undersigned having been in business for a number of years in the SIGNS and ORNAMENTAL PAINTING BUSINESS, . . . during which time we have gained the reputation of executing our work as well, if not superior, to any other establishment, beg leave to submit the following. . . . You are respectfully requested to call and ascertain our charges, before leaving your orders elsewhere.

Yours, respectfully,   ACKERMAN & MILLER.[79]

Copying the format of a handwritten letter, this epistolary advertisement used a salutation and closing appropriate for business correspondence. The proprietors invited potential customers to visit their Nassau Street firm politely, with an overt emphasis on the respect motiving this communication. In this way, the advertisement mimicked the physical object (a letter), suggesting that the printers may have considered both media to be appropriate methods for reaching the public.

As advertisers self-consciously attempted to convey their respectability in print, epistolary closings such as "I am, your humble servant" also punctuated newspaper advertisements through the second quarter of the nineteenth century. For example, from July to November 1841, Dr. George Rogers placed several ads in the *New York Tribune*, advertising his Vegetable Pulmonic Detergent, which he marketed as a cure for cough, cold, and consumption.[80] Rogers often placed his ads under the headline "Important to the Public," and they regularly appeared alongside ads for other proprietary medicines and retail merchants. In one instance, ads selling cures for rheumatism, sperm oils, lathes and woodworking tools, and feather beds flank the page, sandwiching Rogers's ad between hawkers from all walks of life. At first glance, Rogers's ad appears no different than the rest: The small classified ad adheres to the format of the page, using a bold headline to demarcate Rogers's text from that immediately preceding and following in the column. His name appears in truncated form at the bottom right, like most of the ads on the page. He invited the public "to call" at his office, promising "gratuitous advice" and "testimonials from our most worthy citizens."[81] Reminding readers that he was their "humble servant," Rogers closed with an epistolary convention drawn from middle-class etiquette. From the earliest days of the new Republic, printed solicitations had been vying for individuals' attention throughout the urban public sphere, in handbills, broadsides, newspapers, shop signs, and other written exclamations that cluttered the visual landscape of the city street.[82] While these impersonal exclamations increasingly affronted the public eye, advertisers such as Rogers sought to stave off the clamoring visual noise by tempering their solicitations with genteel language and gestures of status. His advertisement, while starting with a phrase that paralleled public notices and handbills, closed with a phrase more closely aligned with intimate correspondence.

These businesses used language as symbolic cues to embellish their advertisements. The words "respectfully" and "humble" conveyed a sense of deference, following the common prescriptions for business correspondence as laid out in contemporary letter-writing manuals. Like a carefully chosen hat, the word "respectfully" signaled one's membership in the middle class and could speak to other, like-minded readers on terms they would find familiar. The firms mobilized the language of character in order to self-identify as respectable and, in turn, to entice prospective customers to feel comfortable patronizing their shops. Doing so emphasized the firms' status in print, in much the same way that shop interiors resembling middle-class parlors helped to visually cement propriety into the commercial space. While the shared public experience of reading advertisements in newspapers (and on the street, through broadsides and other media) helped to constitute an urban consumer identity, I would argue that a primary factor in the constitution of such identities was the familiar taxonomy of genteel language.[83]

Yet Rogers's overtly formal closing provides a somewhat startling juxtaposition to the visual format of his ad. His use of a bold headline and the declaration that his announcement was "important to the public" signals a more informal, anonymous style of address emerging in the antebellum commercial sphere. The mixture of forms used by Rogers suggests that modes of commercial communication were in flux in the 1840s. The phrase "Your humble servant" had been a common closing in advertisements at least from the colonial period; in 1765, an ad published in the *Pennsylvania Gazette* for Samuel and Robert Purviance and Co., of Baltimore, used the same closing in requesting patronage.[84] Rogers's use of the phrase harkened back to the epistolary forms utilized by eighteenth-century artisans and firms, and demonstrated the continued currency of these forms into the second quarter of the nineteenth century. As late as 1849, etiquette manuals would continue to stress the importance of humility in letter writing, using the closing phrase "Your Humble Servant" or a variant thereof in nearly all model business letters offered to readers.[85] Yet, by the early 1850s, several letter-writing manuals had replaced this phrase with the closing "Respectfully Yours." Commenting on the change, one manual suggested that the older emphases on service and humility had become outdated, and professions of respect and sincerity were now preferred.[86] At the same time, the epistolary phrases so popular in early newspaper ads had fallen out of favor among white business owners by the 1850s. While the word "respectfully" had been a common convention among advertisers in the mainstream press before 1850, the trope experienced the height of its popularity in the 1840s. It saw reduced use in those papers by 1860 and had almost completely disappeared from mainstream newspapers by 1880. "Your humble servant" followed a similar trajectory, declining even more sharply in the mainstream press by 1855.[87] These shifting guidelines at mid-century, coupled with the changing usage patterns for these language conventions, suggests that there was a shift in the culturally accepted forms of business communication in this period, at least among advertisers in the mainstream press. As fashions and tastes changed, so did the tropes that met the requirements for plain speech, as dictated by business guidebooks.

Yet, in African American newspapers, the word "respectfully" remained a common phrase in advertisements placed through the end of the century. In urban and semi-urban papers intended for black readers, the word "respect-fully" appeared on approximately 23 percent of advertising pages between 1870 and 1900.[88] In 1871, for example, William Powell advertised his hotel in the *National Standard* (New York City), noting:

> This House . . . is airy, neatly kept and well arranged for the promotion of health, and is designed especially for the comfort and conveniences of re-spectable families. The location is central, and in . . . a quiet and respect-able neighborhood. . . . As an example of the assiduous care to provide for the public wants, the undersigned respectfully calls the attention of per-sons visiting the city, to the POWELL HOUSE, and solicits their patronage. Wm. P. Powell, Proprietor.[89]

Drawing on the familiar conventions of epistolary rhetoric that proliferated in advertisements several decades earlier, Powell stressed the quality and propriety of his establishment. He noted that it would be especially comfortable for "re-spectable" families, as it was located in a "respectable neighborhood." Powell leaned heavily on class-based language cues here to demonstrate his own educa-tion and propriety; to transfer those qualities, by association, to his hotel; and to appeal to an equally respectable class of patrons. In 1884, R. H. Bundy "respect-fully" notified the public that he had moved his "hair dressing and shaving parlor" to a new location, fitted in the "most modern . . . elegant and comfortable" style with "first-class artists in attendance."[90] Like Powell, Bundy emphasized the up-scale nature of his business, using class-based language to elevate the character of his barber shop to a modern, sophisticated "parlor" that employed "artists" rather than common barbers. Bundy rooted his appeal in the assumption that potential clients would be drawn to such gestures of opulence and grandeur. He signaled class and status through references to material culture and décor, just as Appleton had done several decades earlier. But African Americans' use of the phrase "respectfully soliciting" wasn't limited to New York City. Similar exam-ples appeared in black newspapers published in Philadelphia; Washington, DC; Savannah, Georgia; Richmond, Virginia; New Orleans; and San Francisco, among other places, through the 1890s.[91]

Why did this advertising language persist in African American–owned news-papers throughout the postwar decades, when it had fallen so quickly out of favor in the mainstream press by 1870? Perhaps a certain level of self-consciousness persisted among African American entrepreneurs and newspaper editors (who often helped customize ads before printing), pushing them to demonstrate high levels of respectability in order to earn whites' respect. Just as it had in the pre-war years, the black press continued to play a leading role in advocating for

African American equality, while modeling respectability in the public sphere remained an important mode of demonstrating black eligibility for equal rights in the era of Jim Crow.[92] While it is difficult to know for sure, the lingering use of this formal language also suggests that African American audiences may have continued to appreciate (or even expect) such formalities long after such references were considered old-fashioned by advertisers in the mainstream press.

For black and white audiences then, language and etiquette remained incredibly important, not only to support one's claims to class status and belonging but also to ensure the continued favor of business partners. Some manufacturers used the same language and tone in corresponding with potential clients and other business partners that they used in their advertisements, illustrating the elision between advertising and correspondence that must have occurred for some readers. In response to inquiries and orders made in the 1850s, clerks at J. C. Ayer & Co., manufacturers of Ayer's Sarsaparilla and Ayer's Cherry Pectoral, often signed notes to clients using one of the following closings: "Very truly, your faithful servant," "Your faithful friends," or "Your friend and servant, James C. Ayer."[93] J. C. Ayer's annual address to customers in the 1850s, printed in his advertising almanacs, adopted a similar tone of friendliness in using this latter epistolary closing to frame the letter.[94] Ayer's attention to etiquette is significant not simply because it was what was required of him as a well-mannered, middle-class businessman, but because he addressed potential consumers with the same respect accorded to business associates.

Yet Ayer also deviated from the rules prescribed by business-etiquette manuals, blurring the distinction between personal and commercial correspondence. His insertion of the word "friend" into his closing reframes his relationship to the reader, gesturing toward an imagined intimate connection they might have. His correspondence and advertising became mutually reinforcing communicative devices that personalized his statements through carefully chosen epistolary forms and language. With this, Ayer placed his readers within a sphere of familiar, intimate address: His readers were not just potential customers but potential friends and, therefore, peers.

Genteel language thus worked on two levels to augment and validate the commercial appeal within the advertiser's message. The words themselves seemed to equate class with trustworthiness, and thus were likely intended to cultivate trust by self-consciously emphasizing the class status of the signatory. Merchants "respectfully" invited customers to call, as if they were inviting friends to step into their personal parlors for conversation. They reminded customers that they were humble servants with altruistic intentions, as George Rogers did. Through words such as "humble" and "respectfully," antebellum advertisers solicited patronage in the most transparent terms available to them. But the epistolary forms—the phrases of respect and humility that framed their signatures in print—also provided a textual cue that the signatory was an educated member of the genteel middle class. The words helped to signal the merchant's standing in society, in much the same way that testimonials did for Dr. Jayne in Philadelphia. Just as members of the middle classes self-consciously displayed their status through fashion and manners on the city street, advertisers paraded their education and worth through the language they chose to represent themselves in print.

Yet genteel advertising language also appears to be a very self-conscious disavowal of illegitimate enterprises, particularly when used by patent-medicine men like Rogers and Jayne, whose trade was already under attack by social critics and reformers. In some ways, their overt claims to respectability (and, therefore, legitimacy) could be a signal of their own anxieties or even a discreet admittance of their precarious position on the sliding scale of legitimate commerce. In other ways, Rogers and Jayne might have intended to separate their own enterprises from the myriad unsavory aspects of commercial life in the antebellum city. The boundaries between legitimate and illegitimate commercial practice and goods remained tenuous at best during the antebellum years, and patent-medicine manufacturers were often subject to accusations of quackery and fraud.[95] But patent-medicine dealers weren't the only ones using these language codes. As the examples of Victor Magne (a tailor), Ackerman & Miller (a printing firm), and William Powell (a hotel proprietor) show, firms in varied industries liberally deployed the language cues of the middle class. The ubiquity of these phrases on the antebellum newspaper page gestures to the very self-conscious and yet habitual modes of building rapport with strangers in this period. With so much uncertainty in the marketplace, antebellum advertisers who adopted the epistolary codes of middle-class society tried to demarcate themselves—with varying degrees of success—from smooth-talking con men looking for an easy mark. They negotiated the perils of the market using language, thereby claiming a place for themselves within the boundaries of the respectable middle class and speaking to like-minded consumers who would recognize those same language cues. This specialized advertising "language" of character offered a means of reconfiguring the relationship between producers and consumers, as one disrupted by distance and increasingly mediated through print. In short, this advertising language used familiar words and ideas to build rapport and, ultimately, to win consumers' trust.

Importantly, these strategies were not so different from those used by advertising agents. Volney B. Palmer, one of America's first advertising agents, couched his newspaper appeals in middle-class rhetoric while leveraging both cultural capital and credit relationships to build his business. In the years immediately following the Panic of 1837, Palmer positioned himself as a trustworthy agent and demonstrated savvy in addressing the economic and cultural anxieties of middle-class merchants hit hard by the depression of the 1840s. Promising minimized risk, expanded markets, and economies of scale, Palmer couched advertising as a safe commercial investment that would grow profits and ensure future financial stability.

Palmer's early life followed a fairly typical trajectory for young entrepreneurs at the time, as he tried his hand at multiple professions and trades before settling on advertising relatively late in life. Born in Wilkes-Barre, Pennsylvania, around 1799, Palmer spent his childhood and teens assisting his father with the family newspaper business. In his thirties, he worked as an independent proprietor in the coal industry, and he served as a treasurer for a canal company that connected Schuylkill County (which lies northwest of Philadelphia) with Baltimore. This role allowed Palmer to become intimately familiar with the commercial distribution systems then expanding across the Eastern Seaboard, as well as with the high demand for the coal being shipped from Pennsylvania mines into urban manufacturing centers.[96] By 1842, Palmer had married and relocated to Philadelphia, where he ran a real estate and coal office, serving as an urban representative and sales agent for out-of-town sellers. Then in his early forties, he began placing notices in local newspapers offering to help urban wholesalers and distributors reach rural merchants through the "country newspapers" that he counted as clients.[97] His years working in the family newspaper trade had cultivated a respect for the value of newspaper advertising, and Palmer's connections with the canal companies in and around the Lehigh Valley likely prompted him to try to increase the flow of goods out of the cities and into the Pennsylvania countryside.[98] Increasing the demand for manufactured goods in the countryside would accomplish this task, and Palmer probably recognized that he could raise demand by advertising such wares in the country newspapers. Cleverly, Palmer exploited an economic opportunity to promote trade between the urban centers and the developing rural areas along the Eastern Seaboard, contributing to the expansion of trade and distribution networks between 1840 and 1860. The move earned him the reputation of America's first adman.[99]

Palmer's business was simple: He served as a middleman to both country newspapers and urban merchants, wholesalers, manufacturers, and others, buying and selling advertising space between the two groups. Palmer procured advertising space in bulk from country newspapers, most likely on consignment. At his Philadelphia office, he hawked the advertising space in those newspapers to urban wholesalers and distributors looking to expand their markets—but he did so at a premium price. Once he'd taken his cut, he forwarded the payments and advertising notices back to the country newspapers, and likely offered to purchase additional advertising space for future issues, but always at a discounted rate. In many ways, it was a win-win situation—urban wholesalers reached new markets, country newspapers gained valuable advertising revenue, and consumers in rural areas grew more aware of the industrial goods increasingly available to them.[100] To sweeten the deal, Palmer offered to write notices for his urban clients at no extra charge, and provide feedback to those clients who submitted prewritten notices.[101] In this way, Palmer acted as more than just a broker of space; he provided copywriting and editing services too, making his firm a precursor to the full-service agencies that would dominate the advertising industry by the 1890s. After just four years, Palmer's advertising business was thriving and he had opened additional offices in Boston, Baltimore, and New York. He remained a successful advertising agent through the next decade, bringing in partners to help manage his branch offices in 1858, before retiring in 1861.[102]

Like the other business owners discussed in this chapter, Palmer often referenced class distinctions when appealing to potential clients in his newspaper advertisements.[103] He consistently presented himself as a respectable businessman who dealt with only the "best" country newspapers and who could dramatically expand his clients' trade. Equating the newspapers he represented with the highest caliber of people, Palmer emphasized class distinctions designed to appeal to his urban audience of middle-class merchants, manufacturers, and wholesalers. Like other firms at the time, he couched his appeals with formalized language— "respectfully" inviting potential clients to visit his office and peruse his files, illustrating his transparency—while attempting to quantify his success by referencing the well-known businessmen he counted as clients. Finally, Palmer demonstrated his integrity and virtuous character by framing his efforts to help others as a public service.[104] In these ways, Palmer's advertising techniques paralleled the same invocations of status that newspaper readers would find from tailors, printers, or even patent-medicine dealers at the time. Though his audience was different—Palmer spoke to other business owners, while many other merchants addressed the general public—the language and forms Palmer used remained the same. His advertising conventions, like those of his clients, used rhetorical cues that would signal his status and character to his peers.

Further incorporating conceptions of class, Palmer frequently appealed to the vanity of his potential clientele by using a syntax of progress, entrepreneurship, and industriousness. In 1846, Palmer noted that savvy merchants with "superior facilities for doing business" knew that no expense could be spared on advertising.[105] By associating his trade with the most knowledgeable of businessmen, Palmer pointed to the popular values of diligence and enterprise then fomenting in American culture, situating his trade within a paradigm of middle-class inventiveness and industry.[106] He leveraged the cultural importance of these values when presenting himself to the public, just as Gilded Age manufacturers would later present images of their factories on advertisements to showcase their contributions to economic progress.[107] Palmer continued to connect entrepreneurship with advertising over the next decade, noting in one ad that "shrewd men of small capital long ago discovered the secret of making fortunes by extensive advertising in the country newspapers."[108] With this, Palmer enticed his readership to consider themselves such "shrewd" men who could also make exponential profits through smart business decisions. Moreover, Palmer appealed to the middle-class values of frugality and restraint when he promised fair rates and economies of scale: His services could bring efficiency to business operations, he noted, as he could place a single notice in any number of papers, without any additional effort from the client. He promised to send the notices to the "most widely circulated" and "desirable" newspapers in the country, which in turn reached approximately 50,000 subscribers (according to Palmer's estimate).[109] Palmer's system thus pledged to save his clients time and money, eliminating their need to research reputable rural papers, correspond with editors, and follow up with the same in order to settle payments.[110]

Calling to those who had been shaken by the recent financial crises, Palmer presented his system as a "safe" advertising investment by assuming the risks of corresponding with rural newspapers himself.[111] The booms and busts of the 1840s and 1850s meant a nearly constant revolving door of business ventures in this period. Banks, retail firms, and newspapers frequently failed, only to be replaced quickly by new enterprises in the same locales.[112] This sort of frequent turnover necessitated an agent who could verify the trustworthiness and reputations of one's potential business partners at a distance.[113] Palmer proposed to eliminate the guesswork in this rapidly changing economy by acting as a face-to-face representative for both his urban and rural clients. Rural editors needed someone in the city to negotiate advertising deals, and find legitimate firms who would not palm off nefarious goods on unsuspecting rural populations (thus threatening the reputation of the newspaper). Likewise, urban wholesalers and manufacturers needed someone who could broker advertising deals with honest rural newspaper men, making sure their advertising investments were not wasted on fraudulent or defunct papers. Palmer served both sides of this equation, offering a verification service—like a rudimentary credit report—that would put legitimate firms in touch with legitimate editors. To further promote his services as secure transactions, Palmer offered to act as a currency exchange, accepting payments from urban clients in local currencies and exchanging them for rural currencies before forwarding payments to country newspapers.[114] In short, he promised to maximize his clients' profits while minimizing risks.

Finally, potential customers could feel safe with Palmer because he was backed by myriad testimonials from country newspapers. As the commercial moralists had argued, portraying good character in print wasn't enough to ensure success;

it was also important to model strong character in practice. Testimonials helped substantiate Palmer's claims of quality service and success.[115] Editorials often appeared in his clients' newspapers and elsewhere, testifying to the value of Palmer's business. Entreating Philadelphia businessmen to advertise in the country papers in 1845, the editors of the *Jeffersonian Republican* (Stroudsburg, Pennsylvania) emphasized the "great advantage" that could be had by making one's "name and business known" to the country populations. They noted that country merchants regularly traveled to the city to purchase goods at wholesale but only patronized "a few . . . stands in the city" because they were unaware of or unfamiliar with others. Noting that "thousands" of dollars in trade came to Philadelphia through this process, the editors argued that the "rapidly increasing" populations of Monroe and Pike Counties (in eastern Pennsylvania) created a tremendous opportunity.[116] Newspapers, they argued, could help minimize the anxieties of country merchants when visiting the anonymous city by familiarizing such merchants with a wider array of urban firms. Palmer was the agent who could accomplish this task, bringing increased publicity, new sales, and potentially exponential profits by helping Philadelphia merchants tap expanding markets north of the city.

Such editorials and testimonials used the cultural capital of the press to garner attention for Palmer's services. Shifting political paradigms had helped democratize authority in the antebellum years, and during this time the impersonal reportage of antebellum newspapers took on heightened public authority in the urban cityscape.[117] Palmer's newspaper clients helped to bolster his reputation by testifying to his industriousness and his business acumen in print, in ways that mimicked an older practice of soliciting letters of introduction from respected business partners to establish new credit relationships. In a similar show of support, other newspapers working with Palmer often printed short notices identifying him as their advertising agent in the city. They entreated merchants and manufacturers to "expand" their businesses by authorizing Palmer to receive subscriptions, place advertisements, and issue receipts on their behalf.[118] Thus leveraging his existing credit relationships with the country papers in order to create new relationships with urban clients, Palmer simultaneously used the reputations of these editors and the cultural authority given to the press to build his own commercial reputation.

*   *   *

In the decades that followed the Revolution, the culture of character reverberated throughout American society, impacting the built environment, race relations, language use, and business practice. By the 1830s, the cultural codes of gentility—including transparent, honest expression and respectable behavior—served as a shorthand reference for legitimate business enterprises. Merchants, manufacturers, and early advertising men utilized this vocabulary of gentility to generate rapport with existing and potential clientele in advertisements that amounted to self-conscious, calculated demonstrations of class. Using strategies modeled after existing correspondence practices, advertisers created an epistolary style of advertising that spoke to the public as consumers. Testimonials and epistolary phrases signaled advertisers' knowledge of middle-class etiquette to peers who would appreciate the same. At the same time, admen such as Volney Palmer crafted appeals that spoke to merchants' classed identities and economic concerns. Responding to contemporary economic fears brought by the boom-and-bust nature of the period, Palmer promoted advertising as a kind of insurance policy that would grow sales while protecting his clients from the uncertainties of long-distance trade. Mobilizing the cultural capital enjoyed by newspaper editors and publishers, Palmer presented himself as a respectable businessman and appealed to his audience's vanity by arguing that "shrewd men" knew the value of advertising in the country papers. While Palmer's rhetoric was calculated to anticipate the concerns that ruled the day, his arguments about the value of advertising had much longer reaching effects. Palmer's tactics provided a model for later advertising agents, including George Rowell, N. W. Ayer & Son, and J. Walter Thompson, who would also seek to convince potential clients of the value of advertising. Half a century later, these admen would make similar arguments about advertising's ability to ensure returns on investment, about smart business decisions made by shrewd entrepreneurs, and about their own professional skills and acumen. In these ways, Palmer's efforts forever transformed the shape of American commerce.

In each of these antebellum-era strategies—through testimonials, language, and arguments rooted in cultural values—advertisers and admen demonstrated an intense preoccupation with pleasing consumers, while they simultaneously concentrated on representing themselves as respectable. But newspapers offered only one avenue for reaching the public. Other media—such as handbills, posters, and, especially, labels—were becoming increasingly important communicative devices for conveying status and distinction. Advertisers and admen fixated on tackling the growing problems of anonymity and fraud by emphasizing virtue and character as qualities that could be readily discerned in the media circulating through the public sphere. In emphasizing the importance of commercial morality and virtue, they sought to impose order on a commercial system whose structures had not yet solidified. Rooting out frauds—in public discourse, trade publications, and the courts—became an intense preoccupation for both advertisers and admen as the century progressed. Their focus on building and maintaining reputation in print and distinction in the market was an important step in codifying strategies that would become the brand-building tactics heralded by admen later in the century. In these ways, antebellum advertisers adopted the language and symbols of gentility emphasized by the white middle class and cemented those ideas into the foundations of advertising practice so that, by the end of the century, the concepts appeared commonplace and obvious. In advertising and, later, in trademark law, the codes of gentility held up by the white middle class would come to influence legal understandings of ethical and unethical business competition, as well as appropriate self-representation in the marketplace. As economic uncertainty continued to rattle the American economy, manufacturers took steps to protect the hard-earned reputations they had built by targeting the dishonest crooks who threatened their economic livelihoods. The courts became a primary arena where these fluctuating definitions of legitimate trade and illicit commercial activity prompted wider conflict, particularly surrounding the functions, meanings, and property rights associated with trademarks.

CHAPTER 2

Policing Fakes

Trademark Regulation from Jackson to Reconstruction

He who filches from me my good name, Robs me most villainously.

—*G. W. Peine, 1839*

In July 1837, Joseph Gillott used the *New York Morning Herald* to announce the new availability of his celebrated steel-tip pens in the United States. Gillott, a British metalworker, had first patented his pens in 1831 and began selling them at home and abroad shortly afterward.[1] Two weeks after launching his US sales, Gillott placed a longer ad, warning potential customers to be wary of counterfeit pens sold falsely under his name. The ad referenced the reputation of Gillott's pens, their superior quality, the inferiority of the imitation goods on the market, and the immorality of the producers of such imitation goods. Gillott described his own products as having "well merited and universal celebrity" among merchants and others in Europe, resulting in their "unparalleled" demand. In contrast, Gillott constructed an image of the "unprincipled" makers imposing their "spurious," "unfinished," and "utterly worthless" imitations upon "unwary" and unsuspecting consumers (figure 2.1).[2] Through moralizing and judgmental language, Gillott crafted an oppositional relationship between his pens and his competitors' "imitation" goods. He cautioned the public and instructed them to seek out particular marks and packaging to distinguish his genuine goods at the point of purchase. These dichotomies between authentic and inauthentic, high quality and worthlessness, and moral versus immoral producers would become important themes that structured the efforts of advertisers in

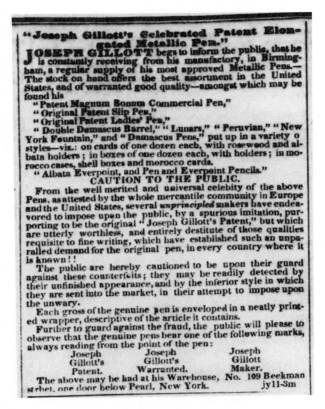

Figure 2.1. Advertisement for Joseph Gillott's steel-tip pens, *New York Morning Herald*, July 24, 1837. Library of Congress, Chronicling America: Historic American Newspapers. Online at https://chroniclingamerica.loc.gov/lccn/sn83030312/1837-07-24/ed-1/seq-4/.

the early nineteenth century, particularly as they began to invest more time and effort into protecting their commercial reputations in the American market.

Like Gillott, several firms and manufacturers made similar complaints in the city papers, connecting the idea of genuineness to a product's worth in the 1830s and adding confusion to the already blurred lines between authenticity and fraud at the time. Through repeated warnings in print, many advertisers warned the public to scrutinize products in the marketplace, searching for signatures, trademarks, or other indicators of authenticity. Casting doubt on competitors, these firms leveraged public fears about fraud as a tactic to establish their own validity. At the same time, manufacturers pursued legal action against trademark infringers, helping create important precedents for how and why trademarks would be protected in the United States. Merchants and manufacturers thus responded to the problem of counterfeit goods by seeking redress in the courts, framing their arguments for redress through the lenses of virtue and moral behavior. The courts, in turn, articulated similar principles in decisions that would become common law. In the common-law and advertising practices that matured after 1830, judges and advertisers constructed the specter of counterfeits in opposition to genuine goods, applying the same moral principles that had defined creditworthiness, insurability, and professionalism in the pre–Civil War years.[3] The boundaries between legitimate and illegitimate commerce, as defined in the courts, thus developed out of and in parallel with cultural standards of respectability championed by the white middle class. By 1870, federal law codified these cultural standards as benchmarks for lawful business practice.

Jurists' arguments in trademark cases both maintained and expanded middle-class prescriptions for proper behavior. Before the passage of the first federal trademark statute in 1870, manufacturers, judges, and legislators justified trademark regulation to prevent harm to the public, on the one hand, and harm to the manufacturers of the genuine goods, on the other.[4] Counterfeit goods amplified uncertainty in the market, disguised a product's origin, and prevented the individual consumer from seeking redress in the event of product malfunctions or defects. Judges sustained that trademark protections were thus necessary to maintain the common good, creating an exception to prevailing understandings of *caveat emptor* (the legal notion of buyer beware).[5] Moreover, jurists and others argued that counterfeiters harmed legitimate manufacturers by diverting trade and damaging reputations.[6] Developing, manufacturing, and introducing a new product to the market required a significant financial investment. Counterfeiters leveraged such efforts to make a quick profit—shortcutting their own time and capital by "stealing" the investments of others and diverting consumers toward the fakes instead. These thieves borrowed the reputations of their competitors in order to make a sale, but, in so doing, the counterfeiters also threatened to damage those reputations by offering an often inferior, but always fraudulent, product in place of the genuine. Because of this, protecting the hard-earned reputations of certain enterprises—their goodwill—became a primary concern of American courts.[7]

Cautionary Ads

Some of the earliest developments in this story came in the immediate aftermath of the Panic of 1837, when several firms began using the specter of counterfeit goods to draw support for their products, including the manufacturers of proprietary medicines, pens, threads, and other household goods. In newspaper advertisements throughout American cities, manufacturers combined warnings of the dangers associated with counterfeit products with derogatory remarks about deceitful merchants who misrepresented the spurious products as genuine. Some firms likened counterfeit goods to the passing of counterfeit bank notes, as did the Philadelphia-based patent-medicine manufacturer, Benjamin Brandreth.[8] Like Gillott, Brandreth's ads referenced the widespread public acclaim that his products had won, for a product never earned the flattery of counterfeiters until it had cultivated a reputation worth stealing. Brandreth also decried the harm that imitation goods brought to the public—another common tactic among patent-medicine manufacturers at the time. Brandreth and others adopted language saturated in moral dichotomies of good/true versus bad/false, and, in so doing, they created an important and lasting advertising tactic around policing fakes.

Joseph Gillott's advertising campaigns help illustrate how this tactic continued to influence advertisers' strategies over the next several decades. Following Gillott's entry into the US market in 1837, Gillott's ads maintained his emphasis on the status and fame attained by his pens, the poor quality of the imitations produced by (immoral) counterfeiters, and the importance of correctly identifying (and selecting) packages bearing his signature. Gillott deployed the same tactics on both sides of the Atlantic, both in *The Times* of London and in newspapers in New York City. Tailoring his advertising copy to the audiences and specifications of these different locales, Gillott demonstrated a consumer-oriented focus in framing his advertising messages.[9] In New York papers in 1838 and 1839, he referred to his "Special Appointment [as] Pen Manufacturer to the Queen" and reminded potential customers that each product carried his personal guarantee. Continuing, he noted, "The public may therefore confidently depend upon the maintenance of those qualities which have obtained for [the pens] so great a reputation."[10] In publicizing his status as appointed by Her Majesty the Queen, Gillott deployed a strategy popularized by Josiah Wedgwood in the eighteenth century, which had leveraged the celebrity of the aristocracy to elevate the status of Wedgwood's pottery and encourage the public to emulate such royals.[11]

Gillott also continued to warn the public about frauds circulating on the market and urged them to look for his facsimile signature, which he often reprinted with his ads (figure 2.2).[12] The signature on a product label was a common trope in antebellum print culture. From the early modern period, signatures had been emblems that symbolized authenticity and authority, connecting the object or document bearing the signature to the individual represented in script (as well as his or her reputation). In this way, signatures became "registers of personal absence and accountability" by linking the signed object with an official owner, distributor, or otherwise responsible party.[13] Like bankers' signatures on paper money, a signature on a product label communicated to the public through a

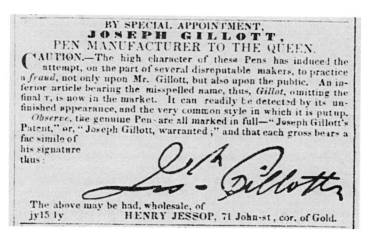

Figure 2.2. Advertisement for Gillott's pens, *New York Tribune*, July 16, 1841. Library of Congress, Chronicling America: Historic American Newspapers. Online at https://chroniclingamerica.loc.gov/lccn/sn83030212/1841-07-16/ed-1/seq-4/.

shared vocabulary of visual symbolism. Gillott used his newspaper advertisements to train the public to navigate the increasingly confusing retail marketplace, instructing potential customers to look for his signature on product packaging and providing, where possible, a facsimile of that signature to prompt memory recall at the shop counter. Signatures could work as proto-trademarks in this way: As a ready reference gesturing to the manufacturer's guarantee of product quality, the signature on product packages drew from cultural and historical understandings of honor, integrity, and legally binding agreements associated with an individual's handwritten signature on official documents.

Finally, Gillott deployed descriptive terms that were saturated in the middle-class culture of character and morality to position his "genuine" products in contrast to inauthentic, spurious, and inferior imitation goods. He continued to use oppositional words and phrases, such as "high character" and "disreputable," to separate his products from rogue competitors. This tactic elided the character of his goods with that of his person, suggesting that his identity as a British entrepreneur was still profoundly shaped by artisanal mindsets tied to craft production and the fruits of one's labor.[14] Likewise, Gillott suggested that the inferior quality of the imitation goods similarly reflected the immoral character of their producers. He disparaged retailers who would carry the imitations, noting that his genuine article could only be found at "respectable stationers and fancy goods dealers"—a statement that was likely meant to shame retailers who carried the imitations and perhaps even to stave off competitors by coercing retailers to refuse to carry them.[15] Proclaiming such retailers guilty by association, Gillott narrowed the boundaries of legitimate commerce to exclude those who deviated from the standards of respectability by selling imitation goods.

The cautionary ads placed by Gillott, Brandreth, and others yield several important conclusions about newspaper advertising in the second quarter of the nineteenth century. First, competition among firms had pushed some to distinguish themselves as authentic, in opposition to supposedly inauthentic competitors, particularly through the moralized language of the white middle class. Though historians have established the use of fear as a common advertising tactic among members of the proprietary medicine trade (such as Brandreth), the efforts of Gillott and others show that a wide range of industries leveraged public anxieties about the commercial marketplace in order to amplify sales.[16] Anti-fraud discourse has indeed been part of American capitalism since the beginning, and the stories presented here outline the ongoing conflicts over cultural authority in the marketplace—particularly around the questions of authenticity, reputation, and fraud.[17] Second, the timing of these developments was important. America's consumer culture had expanded in the 1820s and 1830s, and consumers now encountered a wider range of product choices on the market from both new and established firms. Increased competition made success more difficult, while economic downturns could motivate struggling firms to engage in morally questionable commercial activity.[18] Anecdotally, Gillott and others pointed to their widespread appeal and massive sales as evidence of what might now be called their "brand value," which also made them vulnerable to counterfeiters. While the specter of counterfeits may have been a rhetorical strategy to attract attention in print ads, some firms, including Gillott's, faced documented infringement and had legitimate causes for concern.[19] Through advertisements, these manufacturers constructed signatures, trademarks, and other labeling conventions as marks of authenticity. Their efforts laid the foundation for the cultural and legal importance of trademarks as proprietary symbols that designated ownership and responsibility in the marketplace, and that linked moral behavior with authentic and/or legitimate businesses.

Yet, legal protections for trademarks remained unsecured in 1840. Gillott's status as an importer in the US market would have made him especially vulnerable to counterfeit products and trademark infringement: No state or federal laws prohibited selling such imitations in the United States, and his physical distance, as a resident of the UK, complicated his ability to identify and respond to imitations. Furthermore, common-law doctrine had yet to address the specific rights of foreign or domestic manufacturers vis-à-vis trademark protections in US courts. Thus, Gillott's stern cautions to the public in 1838 and 1839 really represented an impassioned plea to the integrity of potential competitors and the skepticism of informed consumers—he had no real footing for legal protections in the US courts. But, over time, things changed. As trademark lawsuits began to filter through the US courts, judges echoed the same moralized protests against counterfeiting and unfair competition that had characterized the complaints of Gillott and others.

Protecting Marks and Building Brands

Trademarks were not new to antebellum Americans; rather, the practice of using identifying marks to establish ownership, manufacture, or association had a long and varied tradition in Western history. From artisans' initials stamped on their wares in antiquity, to personal crests worn by medieval knights into battle, to "brands" burned onto property, individuals throughout history have used marks to distinguish their wares from other like objects.[20] In the early modern world, artisanal guilds regulated the use of particular marks in order to locate responsibility for inferior materials or workmanship. Used in this way, "trademarks" established a liability for the product, backed by the guilds, which ensured "honest and efficient workmanship."[21] Through repeated social and commercial use over time, trademarks gained cultural meaning. By the mid-eighteenth century, the "trade-mark" became an assurance of quality, fashion, and/or status among British merchants. American colonists grew familiar with trademarks and trade names, first through imported British goods in the colonies and, later, when domestic manufacturers began adopting such marks to distinguish their goods.[22] The scale of global trade that persisted from the early modern period necessitated using such marks to communicate through distribution channels and with the public. As the pace of consumption increased in the eighteenth century, individuals began to seek out the goods of particular tradesmen—such as Josiah Wedgwood's pottery, or Samuel Lane's shoes—for their quality and status. Wedgwood, for example, knew and understood the value of advertising his mark in order to cultivate a particular identity and value for his products—in other words, to build his "brand."[23] Therefore, by the 1830s, trademarks had centuries of social conventions behind them, the most common of which was to provide shorthand for the manufacturer's workmanship, reputation, and relationship with the public.

While the Founders saw the value in protecting one's intellectual property through copyrights, they did not include protections for trademarks in the Constitution. One primary reason for this was that the Framers saw federal intellectual property protections as granting the owner a particular monopoly in the market, which conflicted with free-trade ideologies at the time. For this reason, the first copyright and patent protections (passed in 1790), provided only limited monopoly over one's inventions, aiming to strike a balance between protecting inventions and incentivizing further innovation.[24] Though petitions for trademark protections came to Congress as early as 1791, legislators remained hesitant to grow the power of the federal government to regulate industry in this way.[25] Instead, they preferred to encourage virtuous behavior in the market, arguing that manufacturers would be motivated to produce high-quality goods (and exceed government standards) if their reputations depended on it. Over the next several decades, legislators continued to underscore the importance of virtuous market behavior, suggesting that they trusted that the reciprocal relationship between virtue and reputation would serve as an informal (and preferable) regulatory force in the American market. In this system, consumers would police reputation through their purchase choices and by word of mouth, while an entrepreneur's motive to maintain a positive reputation (and profits) would push him or her to behave morally.[26]

Though no federal statute protecting trademarks would be passed until after the Civil War, two ad hoc measures soon evolved to protect trademarks at the federal level: copyright registrations and design patents. Under the 1831 amendments to the copyright law, prints and labels used in commerce could be registered for protection with a variety of federal agencies, including the Library of Congress, federal district courts, and the Smithsonian (after 1846). By 1850, copyright registration for commercial labels was an established practice.[27] In many ways, simply printing the word "copyright" on a label could help deter unauthorized imitation and copying, by giving the impression of legitimacy through the simple association with federal regulation. Copyright registrations were typically filed by printers seeking to protect their own work, but, as time progressed, admen and manufacturers likely encouraged this practice for its mutual benefits to themselves.[28] In 1842, Congress authorized the Patent Office to accept "design patents"—a measure originally conceived to protect textile designs but which was broad enough to include designs for prints, labels, and trademarks. Again filed mostly by printers, registrations under this provision accelerated after 1855, protecting trademark designs from a range of industries, including consumable goods, foodstuffs, clothing, patent medicines, tobacco, alcohol, and industrial implements.[29] Elaborate, original artwork was necessary for both label copyright and design-patent registrations, and it had the added benefit of making it more difficult to imitate a product's appearance, particularly before the patent office began making descriptions of patents publicly available in 1861.[30] Yet, while effective, design patents were rather difficult, expensive, and time-consuming to procure— hurdles that likely prevented many producers from securing them.[31] In these ways, changes in copyright and patent protections expanded the available avenues for de facto protections of trademarks before a federal trademark law existed.

Still, because there was no clear enforcement mechanism at the federal level, counterfeit products persisted in the American marketplace. By the early 1840s, cases of trademark infringement began making their way through the state and federal courts, first in the manufacturing centers of the East Coast, such as New York and Boston. The judges hearing these cases attempted to define the distinctions between legitimate and illegitimate commerce, which were still very much in flux during this period. Applying codes of conduct then popular with the white middle class, judges often scolded infringers for their immoral behavior, characterizing the commercial harm resulting from infringement as a moral issue. These judges navigated the murky boundaries of capitalism to forge common-law precedents—developed from moral arguments about proper behavior—for trademark protections in the United States. Brought by British thread manufacturers, the first trademark lawsuits in the United States would open a genuine discourse on the nature of American commercial competition, while the judges in these cases mapped the cultural values of honesty, integrity, and responsibility onto legal standards for ethical commercial behavior and trademark use.

Defining Unlawful Behavior in the First Lawsuits

In March 1843, John and William Taylor of Leicester, England, filed a bill of complaint in the New York Chancery Court against Daniels Carpenter of Foxborough, Massachusetts. For more than a year, Carpenter had allegedly imitated the labels and packaging of their "Taylor's Persian Thread," a popular brand of cotton sewing thread.[32] Noting that the spurious article was "well calculated to deceive," the plaintiffs added that their local agent, Benjamin Warburton, had discovered it for sale in at least three distribution houses in New York City. They complained about their lost profits and the other damages Carpenter caused, noting that "the inferior quality and false measure of the said spurious Persian thread, is greatly *prejudicing the reputation* of . . . [our] Persian thread in the market; and, unless the said imitation is discontinued or prevented, [it] will ultimately *destroy the character and standing of the genuine article*."[33]

The Taylors had good reason to be concerned, for this was not the first time someone had attempted to supplant them in their trade. Entering the market in 1828, the Taylors had quickly risen to prominence in the textile trades, developing a reputation for high-quality goods and leveraging Britain's imperial network to distribute their products across North America and the West Indies. Imitations had also emerged fairly quickly; in 1834, the Taylors won their first infringement lawsuit in British Chancery court, and they spent the next two decades fighting legal battles against imitators.[34] The transatlantic flow of goods in the late colonial and Early National period had brought new consumer markets and new opportunities for expansion, but it also brought new and distant competitors (like Carpenter) who understood the value of the Taylor name and tried to use it to sell spurious goods. Having successfully defended their commercial reputation at home in British courts, the Taylors had the benefit of legal precedent on their side when they approached the American courts for relief in 1843.[35]

Pointing to the potential damage done to their market share, the Taylors' bill of complaint used the words "reputation," "character," and "standing" to refer to the popularity of their product and its potential for future profits (i.e., goodwill). While the first and last terms might be applied to an inanimate object, the word "character" signified a deeper, metaphysical being that was supposed to be separate from outward appearances; in the language of the middle class, "character" referred to the soul. While the Taylors might have applied "reputation" and "standing" to their threads, their use of the word "character" suggested a reference to the identities *behind* the product—that of the Taylors themselves. The Taylors' bill of complaint thus elided the reputation of the product with their own commercial reputations, acknowledging the clear economic connections between a product's success on the market and the owner-proprietor's wealth and status. Reputation remained a key component of middle-class understandings of identity in the 1840s—both in the United States and in Europe—and provided a yardstick by which one measured his or her status.[36] Should this infringement be allowed to continue, the Taylor name would become further associated with subpar goods, the bill asserted, and, by association, the Taylors' reputation (as a firm and as individuals) would surely suffer. The Taylors requested an injunction from the court and damages, arguing that Carpenter's "inequitable and wanton piracy" should not go unpunished.[37] Here, the Taylors emphasized the immorality of Carpenter's alleged actions, which deviated from middle-class standards of honesty and integrity. In so doing, they used cultural standards of respectability to define commercial standards of ethical behavior and suggested that Carpenter's actions should be considered criminal.

While Daniels Carpenter was not a common criminal, his personal history and actions can help us better understand why someone would choose to produce or sell counterfeit goods at this time. Carpenter had served his country in the War of 1812 and, afterward, he became one of the largest landowners in Foxborough, Massachusetts. But Carpenter probably suffered major losses during one of the period's many financial panics and, by 1842, he had turned to counterfeiting to supplement his income.[38] Counterfeits work best when borrowing the reputation of highly valued goods and products, which carry the largest potential for profits. Carpenter's victims—two of the most prominent English thread manufacturers at the time—were an ocean away and thus unlikely to ascertain the extent of the fraud quickly. From his job in the local thread factory, Carpenter had both access and opportunity to package and sell counterfeit threads: He would have been aware of the key aspects of the thread business, including packaging and shipping practices, primary avenues of distribution, and the potential profits that could be had in selling one of his competitors' highly demanded wares.[39] He may have even skimmed products from his employers for fraudulent distribution and sale. His was an organized operation, calculated to cover his tracks: He had commissioned fraudulent labels from a Boston lithographer and retained agents in both Boston and New York to sell his fakes to wholesalers, who would then distribute the goods to retail merchants. Opportunity may have been the primary mitigating factor in precipitating Carpenter's frauds, but his insider knowledge certainly helped him execute and sell his forgeries more easily.

Carpenter answered the Taylor complaint in February 1844, admitting that he had willfully imitated the plaintiffs' goods but, incredibly, denying any wrongdoing. To the Taylors' assertion of inferior quality, Carpenter claimed that his threads were just as good. He further asserted that he had the "full right and lawful authority" to imitate the plaintiffs' goods because he was a citizen of the United States (in actuality, he misunderstood these privileges), while arguing that the complainants had no rights to protection in the United States as foreigners (actually, they did). Besides, Carpenter concluded, he told his jobbers and wholesalers that he had produced these threads; in his view, it was not his fault that they failed to inform the public.[40] Importantly, Carpenter's refusal to accept responsibility and his flat denial of wrongdoing points to the still tentative legal status of trademarks in the 1840s in the United States, as well as the cultural salience of *caveat emptor* among entrepreneurs like Carpenter.[41] Moreover, his assertion of primacy over the Taylors suggests that a certain nationalism or protectionism (or both) pervaded popular understandings of economic competition in the United States.

Anxiously awaiting a decision by the New York Chancery court, J. and W. Taylor also filed suit in the US Circuit Court, District of Massachusetts, in December 1843. Carpenter had continued to vend the counterfeit goods in Boston despite the ongoing suit and a temporary injunction issued by the New York judge.[42] Defending himself before the federal judges, Carpenter recycled much of the same defense, maintaining that foreigners had no rights to trademark protection in the United States, whereas his rights as a US citizen ought to allow him to imitate the goods of foreigners.[43] Hedging his bets, Carpenter also filed multiple motions for dismissal and postponement over the next year, stalling court actions in both cases. In the meantime, he took steps to unload his stock of fraudulent threads. In July 1844, Daniels Carpenter placed an order with a Boston lithographer for 168,000 thread labels bearing the name of another thread manufacturer, the Scottish firm J. & P. Coats. Carpenter likely intended to re-brand his spurious Taylor threads with the Coats label instead, but something spooked him and he didn't follow through: The printers later reported that Carpenter failed to pay for or accept delivery of the false Coats labels.[44] Perhaps Carpenter caught wind of the impending guilty verdicts against him and decided to cut his losses in the counterfeit thread game.

Both the New York Chancery and the Federal Circuit Court decisions came in late 1844. In New York, the court noted that the quality of the spurious good was immaterial, as was the plaintiffs' status as foreigners. Finding for the plaintiffs, the court disdained the defendant's brazen admittance of wrongdoing and agreed that Carpenter had clearly meant to defraud the public "with the intention of supplanting [the Taylors] in the goodwill of their trade and business."[45] Drawing from legal precedents related to fraud in the UK and the United States, the court condemned Carpenter's attempt to steal the Taylors' future profits, the damage he'd done to their reputation (by masquerading a false product as the Taylors' threads), and the public harm Carpenter caused through the fraud itself. Connecting trademark infringement to property rights, reputation, and the common good, the court aggregated these faults as immoral and unfair commercial practice.[46]

In the federal decision, Judge Joseph Story agreed, and he reiterated the importance of protecting the property rights and reputations of "honest" manufacturers to preserve the common good.[47] He asserted that Carpenter's defense added insult to injury in attempting to deflect responsibility, calling Carpenter's actions an "unmitigated and designed infringement of the rights of the plaintiffs, for the purpose of defrauding the public and taking from the plaintiffs the fair earnings of their skill, labor, and enterprise."[48] Among these earnings, Story included future expected profits based on the Taylors' positive reputation. Perhaps unluckily for Carpenter, Story had become a bit of an expert in commercial law, having recently published a legal treatise on the common-law protections for a form of reputation he called "goodwill." He issued a perpetual injunction against Carpenter, noting the obviousness of Carpenter's dishonesty and the universal, commonsense definitions of right and wrong that guided his decision.[49] Importantly, Story's decision linked the legal protection of trademarks and trade names with exclusive property rights in goodwill and reputation. Story argued that trademarks both signified reputation and, simultaneously, served as a vehicle for building reputation, and thus the trademark warranted protection under the law. Living up to his reputation as a champion of morality in the market, Story drew upon the principles of middle-class virtue when upholding property rights in trademarks as both morally and commercially sound.[50]

Though he lost both suits, in New York and Massachusetts, Carpenter did not relent. He appealed, but the appellate courts upheld the Taylors' rights, taking pains to emphasize the egregiousness of Carpenter's frauds. In federal court, Judge Levi Woodbury called Carpenter's actions and defense "abhorrent" and noted the court's responsibility to ensure that fair competition also included protecting the public's typical avenues for redress in an open market. When Carpenter masqueraded his goods under the Taylor label, "the public [would] not have . . . the guarantee of goodness, which they expected . . . Nor would they have the remedy against the plaintiffs, which they otherwise might have if the article proved inferior."[51] With this, Woodbury identified an important matter at the heart of infringement cases. In a typical transaction, purchasers would be entitled to redress from a seller when goods or services failed to perform as expected. Carpenter took away this opportunity when he sold imitation goods: He deflected responsibility for any defects in his own wares—by disguising them under the Taylor label—and pushed responsibility, unfairly, to the Taylors instead. Like Story, Woodbury drew from middle-class standards of behavior in defining ethical commercial practice in opposition to Carpenter's actions. Finally, Woodbury emphasized that such behavior had larger implications for American trade; prosecuting commercial deception and fraud would only serve, in his view, to further "elevate our own character as a nation, and the purity of our judicial tribunals."[52] For Woodbury, protecting trademarks was a matter of national integrity.

The precedents set by the *Taylor* cases privileged the commercial importance of reputation and established a role for the government to regulate morality in the market. Upholding the rights of "alien friends," the courts identified an exclusive right to commercial goodwill—the value gained from one's reputation in the marketplace—which remained irrespective of the owner's citizenship. This was a step toward protecting trademarks as property, but it also underscored the cultural value placed on reputation in the antebellum period. In the eyes of Story, Woodbury, and others, securing these rights was the moral and just thing to do, but importantly, it also ensured that the manufacturer would be protected from unfair competition—that is, an unfair advantage given to a competitor in the marketplace. The principles of free trade insisted that unfair advantages be prevented at all costs, and thus the courts ironically upheld a mode of protectionism (monopoly rights in trademarks) in order to ensure free trade. Trademark protections also ensured that the public would be safeguarded against imposition and fraud, giving consumers due process in addressing any grievances about product quality with the rightful supplier. Drawing on the lessons of the Revolution, these courts stressed the importance of commercial transparency and accountability by upholding the public's right to address grievances in the marketplace, and by preventing mislabeled goods from infringing upon that right.

Moreover, the courts emphasized the immorality of Carpenter's actions because he had threatened a key element of social and cultural identity in this period. The antebellum middle classes had relied upon reputation to define their classed positions in society. Carpenter's infringement was, in essence, an attempt to leverage the Taylors' reputation for his own profit, thus endangering their good name. Any effort to damage a person's reputation would have been met with disgust and outrage by the educated classes in these years because a person's reputation was key to his or her livelihood. Therefore, Carpenter's actions would have been considered an egregious assault on reputation, particularly among members of the white middle class—a group that, no doubt, included many of the judges determining the cases discussed here. The effects of the *Taylor* case later rippled through the American commercial sector, as lawyers, proprietors, and other judges took note of the new legal precedents it established.[53]

Following the *Taylor* decision, subsequent cases expanded the sphere of responsibility for infringement beyond manufacturers to include jobbers and printers, policing additional steps in the supply chain to punish and reduce trademark infringement. A series of cases revolved around the Scottish thread manufacturer J. & P. Coats. In 1844, Coats's New York agent had responded to complaints of imitation Coats threads being sold in the city and tracked the spurious articles to Holbrook, Nelson, & Co., a distribution firm. Acting as a deputized police force, Coats's agent completed the detective work necessary to trace the fraud and filed the legal paperwork needed to initiate the lawsuit for his employer. The plaintiffs asserted that the poor quality and cheaper price of the counterfeit thread caused "serious injury" to their livelihood and reputation; they requested a perpetual injunction plus damages.[54] In their defense, Holbrook et al. deflected responsibility for manufacturing the thread and offered up Malcolm McGregor of Newark, New Jersey, as the culprit. Reportedly, McGregor had approached the distributor in May 1844 to sell his threads, labeled with imitation designs printed by a Boston firm, B. W. Thayer & Co. (McGregor had purchased the labels from Thayer & Co. in March and April of that year).[55] The goods arrived at Holbrook's warehouse bearing the imitation marks, wrappers, and labels in the Coats style. The defendants then sold the cases to a retail merchant in New York City. Holbrook et al. insisted that they had not misrepresented McGregor's thread, nor intentionally drawn customers away from Coats. As middlemen, Holbrook et al. stressed their innocence, referencing *caveat emptor* by noting that shoppers freely acknowledged and accepted the risks inherent in the marketplace. Besides, Holbrook concluded, the plaintiffs had been unable to produce an actual customer harmed by the imitation, and the firm's profits had been so minimal that it was hardly worth taking the court's time in recovering such a small sum.[56]

Judge Lewis Sandford disagreed, issuing an opinion that established important precedents for trademark protections in common law. First, he rejected Holbrook et al.'s claims of innocence and ignorance. For while the defendants said they had "acted in perfect good faith . . . [they] knew that the article they were selling was spurious; that it was going out to the public under false and deceptive colors, and was designed and well calculated to take in purchasers who were in pursuit of the genuine thread."[57] Moreover, Sandford argued that it made no difference if the imitation product was of similar quality or whether the maker had informed the purchaser that it was, in fact, an imitation. With this, Sandford cast aside questions about the role of the consumer in determining cases of trademark infringement. While proponents of *caveat emptor* had generally presumed consumer skepticism at the point of purchase (thus preferring to apply a very narrow definition of infringement in such lawsuits), proponents of consumer protection (and what later jurists would call the "unwary purchaser" doctrine) favored wider and more expansive definitions of infringement.[58] Sandford's 1845 opinion foregrounded consumer protection arguments half a century before Progressives took up the cause: It did not matter if the fraudulent good caused any documented injury to the public; the fraud still had the potential to harm the manufacturer's reputation. Importantly, Sandford's stipulation that several components of the case were irrelevant (namely, the quality of the imitation, the profits made from its sale, the plaintiff's citizenship, and the public's relative understanding of its true origins) helped to establish the importance of protecting trademarks in their own right. He limited the consumer's personal responsibility in such cases—rejecting *caveat emptor*—to protect the property interests of commercial firms.[59] Finally, Sandford further expanded the sphere of responsibility in cases of trademark infringement by suggesting that distributors and merchants could be held liable for impositions upon the public, even when they had no hand in the manufacture of the imitation itself.

A subsequent case, also involving J. & P. Coats, demonstrated that printers could also be held responsible in trademark-infringement cases. In early August 1844, just after filing suit against Holbrook et al. in New York, Coats filed suit in the US Circuit Court of Massachusetts against B. W. Thayer & Co., the lithographer used by McGregor in the *Holbrook* case. The named co-defendants, Benjamin W. Thayer and John H. Bufford, had been printing counterfeit labels for Coats's six-cord threads for months. The spurious goods wearing these false labels had apparently been sold in "great quantities" in both New York and Boston, often by dealers who also sold the genuine article, and the likeness between the genuine and false labels was so close that even those "who are most skilled in such matters are deceived and imposed upon" (figures 2.3 and 2.4).[60] Again, Coats asked for an injunction, claiming damage to its profits as well as its reputation in

Figure 2.3. Round labels for J. & P. Coats threads, provided by the plaintiffs, in *Coats v. Thayer* 1844 (unreported). US Circuit Court for the District of Massachusetts; Case Files, 1790–1911; Record Group 21: Records of District Courts of the United States, 1685–2009; National Archives at Boston.

Figure 2.4. Fraudulent labels produced by B. W. Thayer & Co., in *Coats v. Thayer* 1844 (unreported). US Circuit Court for the District of Massachusetts; Case Files, 1790–1911; Record Group 21: Records of District Courts of the United States, 1685–2009; National Archives at Boston.

these cities. Like the Taylors, Coats depended on a positive reputation with American consumers to maintain the profitability of its brand, and it used moral language to condemn the printers who threatened that reputation by creating imitation labels.

The *Thayer* case demonstrates the somewhat haphazard attempts at counterfeit prevention in the antebellum years. While *Taylor v. Carpenter* had shown the liability of manufacturers in selling counterfeit wares, *Coats v. Holbrook* showed the liability of distributors (also known as jobbers) for the same. In suing Thayer & Co., the Coats firm asserted that printers were just as culpable in perpetrating the sale of counterfeit goods because they provided the conduits for false representation (i.e., falsified labels).[61] Judge Story agreed, issuing a preliminary injunction when he first heard the case in August 1844.

The printers, Thayer and Bufford, complied with the court, likely hoping to avoid any negative publicity. In answering the bill of complaint, they provided a full accounting of their orders and profits (though they complained that they had only been paid for about half the orders). Over the previous year, Thayer & Co. had been approached by several individuals to produce the labels in question, typically with the solicitor providing a paper sample of the genuine label for Thayer & Co. to copy.[62] By their own accounting, Thayer & Co. had produced more than 850,000 prints in five distinct designs, each closely resembling the packaging and label designs for genuine Coats products. These prints were then sold to twelve unique customers (mostly manufacturers and distributors) in quantities ranging from 1,000 to 200,000 prints, with most customers placing subsequent orders. Thayer & Co. stood to make about $325 from all of this work, which was about 70 percent of a year's pay for printers at the time.[63]

Remarkably, the client list for B. W. Thayer & Co. included Daniels Carpenter, the defendant in the *Taylor* case. In July 1844, a month before Coats brought suit against Thayer & Co., Carpenter had placed an order with Thayer for 168,000 labels in the Coats style, while he'd been actively stalling the court's activities in the *Taylor* lawsuits. His luck running out, Carpenter could not have known that the *Thayer* suit would fall on the desk of the same judge hearing the *Taylor* case in Massachusetts—Joseph Story—who would surely recognize Carpenter's name once the printers divulged their client list. Interestingly, Carpenter's lawyer, Silas Plimpton, later agreed to defend Thayer in the federal case brought by Coats.[64] Carpenter probably received a tip from his lawyer about the added heat from the federal court, which prompted his disappearance when the printers attempted to deliver and collect on his order in the summer of 1844. But Thayer probably also got a tip: A month before Coats filed its lawsuit, Thayer suspiciously sold the printing plates in question *despite* receiving additional orders for the profitable fake labels.

Defending their actions before the court, Thayer and Bufford deflected responsibility as middlemen, just as Holbrook et al. had done. Despite printing the falsified labels for almost a year, Thayer & Co. denied that it had intended to infringe on the plaintiffs' business, and argued that it should not be held liable for the illegal actions of its clients.[65] Ultimately, the printers settled out of court:

They agreed to a perpetual injunction and dissolved their firm. But the damage to their reputation had already been done. His name sullied by the accusations of fraud, Benjamin Thayer left the printing business and experimented rather unsuccessfully with a variety of side ventures for the next few decades. Thayer's partner, John Bufford, was lucky in that his name remained hidden away in the unpublished legal records for *Coats v. Thayer*. Bufford would later establish himself as a premier lithographer in the United States, developing a well-recognized reputation as an industry leader first in art prints and, later, in small advertisements known as trade cards.[66]

These cases illustrate the ways in which definitions of lawful versus unlawful competition remained unclear in this period, and they highlight the shifting economic circumstances that might push a person to adopt more flexible moral standards. The Panics of 1837 and 1839, and the depression that lasted until the mid-1840s, likely would have pushed small business owners to seek out additional revenue streams to avoid bankruptcy. Counterfeiting someone else's goods would be an easy way to do so, as Daniels Carpenter had demonstrated. Easy entry into the market meant more competitors, pushing merchants and manufacturers to try to extend their trade into proven markets with established demand and solid consumer bases.[67] The appeal of counterfeiting something as abundant and easily faked as sewing thread is thus not hard to understand. Consumers would have a hard time recognizing that the fake was made of only three and not six cords (as the label professed) or that it didn't come from the reputable firm in Paisley, Scotland.

Moreover, it was not unusual for printers to engage in such questionable activity. Establishing a print shop was an expensive endeavor that required a significant amount of startup capital, making profit margins slim during the first few years in business, even in a good economic climate.[68] As competition grew in the 1820s, printers faced an increasingly challenging market and could be motivated to take on marginal or even illegal work in order to stay afloat. By the 1840s, the production of counterfeit currency had increased in the nation's East Coast cities, with ringleaders farming out jobs piecemeal to a variety of printers and engravers in order to deter authorities.[69] Perhaps Thayer & Co. saw the production of counterfeit thread labels as a lesser, more palatable offense than engaging in the production of counterfeit currency—a necessary evil to supplement their income and stave off bankruptcy. Unfortunately, their gamble did not pay off. When their case landed before Judge Story on the federal bench, Thayer & Co. may have helped to expose a ring of counterfeiters working to produce fraudulent threads for the American market.

Profitable counterfeiting rings in this period depended on a network of players who each worked to ensure the success of the fraud. Like other business ventures, counterfeiting required logistical coordination among manufacturers, distributors, and other middlemen to thrive. In many ways, clandestine practices, such as counterfeiting and smuggling, existed alongside legitimate commercial practices out of necessity.[70] McGregor and Carpenter manufactured and/or procured generic threads that could be relabeled under the Coats mark. Thayer & Co. printed the labels using designs copied from the original Coats packaging. The printers' skills played an important role, as the success of the venture depended on the exactitude of the fake label and its ability to pass for the original. McGregor consigned his forgeries to a jobber (Holbrook et al.) in New York City, like Carpenter had done in Boston, and these agents helped distribute the now fraudulently labeled products to retail merchants in their respective locales.[71]

Simply adding the middlemen helped to lend an air of legitimacy both to the products and to the transactions. Legitimate commercial firms, like the Taylors or Coats, would not have sent an owner or factory manager directly to the retail merchant with a shipment of goods; those goods would have been funneled through local agents, wholesalers, and jobbers. Creating a supply-and-distribution chain for counterfeit threads, McGregor and Carpenter mimicked the practices of legitimate firms to further disguise their goods, drawing upon the expertise and reputations of printers, commission merchants, and sales agents to complete their con. In this way, legitimate firms like Thayer and Holbrook often cooperated with marginal enterprises (such as McGregor's) or with individuals whose previous successes had given way to more tentative economic status (Carpenter). Such cooperation epitomized the shades of gray that characterized commerce in the antebellum United States, and which caused so much anxiety among the middle classes.

While opportunity, access, and insider knowledge helped make a con successful, money was always a motivating factor. Though both Holbrook et al. and Thayer & Co. claimed to have made only meager profits, counterfeiting these threads had the potential to reap large rewards, particularly for the suppliers (in these cases, Carpenter and McGregor). Holbrook sold his cache of McGregor's counterfeit threads to a merchant in New York City, at a substantial discount—about $0.12–$0.18 cheaper per dozen than genuine Coats threads. The discount incentivized merchants to purchase the cheaper goods from Holbrook— instead of ordering from Coats's local agent in the city—because of the wider profit margins that were possible. This meant a loss of profits not only for Coats but also for its agent, who took commission on the threads he sold to retail merchants.[72] If McGregor had succeeded in selling his entire cache of counterfeit threads (more than 180,000 units), even at the discounted rate, he could have earned close to $5,000 (minus his costs for supplies). For comparison, this amounts to more than *ten times* the average printer's annual salary at the time (and printing itself was a skilled profession, with tradesmen already earning more than the average laborer).[73] Counterfeiting a product as simple as threads could thus be quite profitable, as long as one did not get caught. As Judges Story and Sandford had noted, all links in the distribution chain played a part in ensuring the success of the fraud, all links stood to profit, and thus all links were guilty when it came to pawning off fraudulent goods to the public.

While the *Thayer* and *Holbrook* cases were still making their way through the courts, J. & P. Coats undertook a new advertising campaign to warn the American public about the counterfeit threads. In April and May 1845, the firm placed newspaper ads that highlighted the qualities of their genuine article, chastised the spurious frauds who attempted to swindle the unsuspecting public, and called out imitators directly. The firm proclaimed its desire to "protect its customers, the public, and its own interests" against the fraudulent traffic in imitation goods, and it denounced the attempts of "I & B Coats, J. P. Coats, [and] J & P Goats" to "deceive the public and escape the penalty due to deception and fraud." Finally, the ad noted the injunctions that Coats had won against these multiple frauds and solicited information from the public that would further "lead to the detection of forgeries on their stamp."[74] J. & P. Coats continued this coordinated newspaper campaign over the next five years. In one unfortunate coincidence (or fortunate, for the modern historian), Coats's ad denouncing spurious goods made by "Coates & Co." appeared directly beneath an ad for those goods, put up for sale by Beals, Bush & Co. in New York (figure 2.5).[75] For the unwary purchaser, such ads would surely add to the confusion of the marketplace.

Figure 2.5. Advertisements for Coats's and Coates & Co.'s threads, *New York Herald*, July 12, 1847. Library of Congress, Chronicling America: Historic American Newspapers. Online at https://chroniclingamerica.loc.gov/lccn/sn83030313/1847-07-12/ed-1/seq-3/.

This effort to publicly shame counterfeiters was a mode of asserting authority in the marketplace and, in particular, of defining legitimate modes of trade in the fluctuating commercial sphere of the time. Coats used its status as a victim of trademark infringement in order to exclude certain competitors as immoral and illegitimate. Like Gillott, Coats suggested that merchants who sold the spurious counterfeits were also guilty, by association. With this, J. & P. Coats contributed to a public discourse—initiated by Gillott and others a decade earlier in the 1830s—about the value of authenticity in American culture and the dangers of frauds masquerading as genuine goods in the marketplace. This discourse on commercial honesty and frauds would evolve through ads such as these, through legal complaints filed against trademark infringers, and through judiciary opinions on the same. It defined commercial standards of ethical conduct, setting up an oppositional relationship between legitimate and illegitimate, lawful and unfair, which was rooted in white middle-class definitions of fraud and transparency.

The timing of the Coats ad campaign is also significant in that it demonstrates how the problem of counterfeits could motivate a firm to undertake a more territorial and assertive approach to protecting its brand reputation with the public. Before 1845, few advertisements for Coats thread had appeared in regional or national newspapers in the United States.[76] It was only after the problem of counterfeit goods presented itself that the firm undertook a coordinated, nationwide advertising campaign to set itself apart from both legitimate and illegitimate competitors. Moreover, these infringement cases help demonstrate the appeal of counterfeiting for someone like Daniels Carpenter, who recognized the profit potential behind the Taylor and Coats brands. Like the Taylors, Coats must have experienced some form of brand loyalty in this period, for if consumers cared nothing for the brand name, then Carpenter could have placed his own goods with retail merchants under his own mark and might have reasonably expected to sell large quantities with his cheaper price. If there was no brand loyalty in this period, why would Carpenter go through the trouble of falsifying the Coats and Taylor labels, and risk getting caught? Even if he truly believed that his actions were lawful, his drive to counterfeit still suggests that the Taylor and Coats brands had some value, as Carpenter clearly expected to turn a profit by borrowing their trademarks and names. Carpenter's efforts to cash in on the reputations of the Taylors and J. & P. Coats—in other words, their goodwill—demonstrates both the presence and awareness of brand loyalty in this period.

It is also important to consider why Coats and Taylor—both English thread manufacturers—faced trademark infringement in the early 1840s and were motivated to police their brands more stringently. The constriction of credit in England in the 1830s, as well as the increased competition within the US market—especially following the establishment of textile mills in Lowell, Massachusetts, in the late 1820s—would have meant tighter finances and tougher competition for thread manufacturers importing into the American market.[77] Anxious to retain their respective market shares, both Coats and Taylor had received reports of imitation goods and deployed their local agents to investigate.[78] They likely did so out of a strict sense of fair competition and ownership over one's wares, which had pervaded English commercial culture since the guild system of the early modern period, and was reaffirmed through recent cases in the British courts.[79] Such a tradition underpinned Coats's and Taylor's actions, which demonstrate increased sensitivity to the value of their brands and calculated efforts to maintain their reputations abroad. While Taylor sought further litigation against known counterfeiters, Coats took up an advertising strategy to warn the public about imitation products.[80] Both manufacturers faced an uphill battle, however, as they depended on their local agents in the United States to carry out the crucial maneuvers that would eliminate unfair competition and restore demand for their genuine products.

Legislating Against Deception

This flurry of judicial activity around trademarks in the mid-1840s caught the eye of local lawmakers who proposed a series of legislative protections against fraudulent marks and labels. In 1845, the state of New York criminalized "knowingly and wilfully [*sic*]" forging and counterfeiting goods, stamps, or labels, as well as procuring or selling such items, with the "intent to defraud the purchasers, or manufacturers."[81] The law stitched together harm against the public with harm toward the manufacturer (and, implicitly, his goodwill), discreetly sidestepping *caveat emptor* by maintaining that no documented harm to the public was necessary for prosecution—one only had to show the defendant's intent to defraud either the public or manufacturers. In many ways, the New York statute emerged in response to the changing economic climate of the 1840s, which had ushered in both increased competition and fraud in a variety of industries.[82]

Importantly, however, the New York law also took a cue from the case of *Taylor v. Carpenter*, which had condemned Carpenter's fraudulent intent and flagrant mockery of the principles of honest and fair competition. In fact, while Carpenter's case was before the New York Appellate Court, several state senators weighed in on the issues at stake. Criticizing Carpenter's calculated deception, Senator John A. Lott connected transparent communication with legitimate competition, and, in contrast, he linked infringement with unfair competition.

He stressed that "honest competition relies only on the intrinsic merits of the article brought into market, and does not require a resort to a false or fraudulent device."[83] Through this logic, the simple act of procuring and employing fraudulent labels rendered Carpenter a dishonest man. Lott further criticized Carpenter's attempt to benefit from another man's hard-earned reputation, a shortcut that, according to Lott, should have no place in American commerce. Lott's critiques—like those of Judges Story and Woodbury—are characteristic of a broader move among businessmen to infuse American commerce with morality in the 1840s. Responding to widespread business failures after 1839, many intellectuals and "commercial moralists" had proposed to correct economic troubles by restoring high moral and ethical standards to the market, particularly in lending and credit relationships.[84] Pushing back against rampant fraud (however unsuccessfully), these men attempted to raise up the values of honesty and transparency as part and parcel of American commercial practice, cementing the white middle-class culture of character into American common law.

Continuing, another senator explicitly defined the state's responsibility to protect commercial morality and reputation through trademark regulation. To Lott's arguments, Senator Joshua A. Spencer added that fair competition required merchants to depend on their own character and merits—not those of others— to earn goodwill from the public. Legislative protections for trademarks would ensure this, he noted, as "it is of no small importance to a manufacturer . . . that his brand should inspire confidence in the public mind, and thereby secure a ready sale; . . . the assurance that he can securely enjoy its exclusive benefit, is always found to be among the highest incentives to ingenuity, laborious exertion, and honorable and faithful conduct."[85] Linking confidence in the trademark with confidence in honest business dealings, Spencer argued that the principles of fair competition—on which the American economic system rested—required the protection of trademarks from unfair competitors. With this, Spencer articulated the legal importance of trademarks as intangible assets that embodied the goodwill value of the brands they accompanied. He blurred the distinction between the trademark (or "brand," to use his word) and the reputation and goodwill of the manufacturer. In so doing, Spencer pointed to the symbolic ways in which the mark could be a repository of goodwill and a sign that inspired confidence. Spencer's arguments prefigured advertising practitioners' enunciation of "branding" as a specific practice by nearly fifty years, while he presupposed federal protections of goodwill by a century.[86]

New York's was the first criminal statute to protect manufacturers against unfair competition from goods bearing counterfeit marks, labels, and stamps, but other states soon followed suit. These included New Jersey in 1846, Connecticut and Pennsylvania in 1847, and Massachusetts in 1850, with a total of nine states enacting trademark protections by 1860.[87] Echoing Lott, Spencer, and existing common-law protections, subsequent legislators framed the new state laws as protections against unfair competition, as safeguards for consumers, and as capitalistic incentives to invention. Some states even instituted labeling and trademark requirements in key industries, such as cotton and alcohol.[88]

While the states worked to police trademark infringement, manufacturers continued to warn consumers about fakes, pointing, like Gillott had done, to visual evidence that would distinguish genuine from spurious goods on the market. In 1857, newspaper ads for the British-made Lea & Perrins' Worcestershire Sauce suggested that the "numerous imitations on both sides of the Atlantic speak loudly of our merits." The company denounced the "unprincipled parties" who would create these "spurious" variations to swindle and harm the public[89] (figure 2.6). The ad pointed to the bewildering volume of transatlantic exchange as both the culprit for infringement and a badge of merit: Lea & Perrins' used the global circulation of its goods both to gesture to widespread acclaim and to implicate distant counterfeiters in a plot to defraud the public. Including a facsimile label, these ads functioned like counterfeit detectors—the published reference books used to help individuals distinguish fake from genuine currency circulating throughout the United States. Building from the public's familiarity with this existing media, the ads instructed the public to examine product bottles for the name Lea & Perrins' stamped in the glass, on the stopper, and on the label. With this, the firm attempted to educate consumers about its commercial identity, explicitly linking that identity to its labels and trademark.[90]

Over the next few decades, judges continued to apply moral standards in trademark-infringement cases, sometimes finding that the plaintiffs were in the wrong. In nearly eighty cases of trademark infringement heard in US courts by 1870, the plaintiffs only won about 60 percent of the time.[91] Occasionally, judges determined that the plaintiffs had abandoned their trade names or marks, or that a product's name had become, in essence, a generic term (such as Worcestershire sauce).[92] Judges also rejected suits in which the plaintiffs had misrepresented the product somehow, finding that such dishonesty invalidated the plaintiff's claims to exclusive property in the mark or trade name. For example, in the New York case of *Fetridge v. Wells* (1857), the judge acknowledged that Wells had infringed upon Fetridge's reputation, but the judge also found that the plaintiff's trade name had deceived the public through "false representations." Thus, Fetridge was ineligible for trademark protections because he himself lacked "pure hands and a pure conscience."[93] Here, the judge indicated that the moral standards of the middle class were absolute: He defined ethical standards for commercial behavior by emphasizing the immorality of misrepresentation and deception, no matter who the actor.

Figure 2.6. Advertisement for Lea & Perrins' Worcestershire Sauce, *Daily Nashville Patriot* (TN), July 3, 1857. Library of Congress, Chronicling America: Historic American Newspapers. Online at https://chroniclingamerica.loc.gov/lccn /sn96091000/1857-07-03/ed-1/seq-2/.

Amid the sectional crisis of the 1850s, Congress debated the obligations of the federal government to its foreign allies on the issue of trademark protections. By mid-century, several European countries had passed trademark-protection laws, which drew considerable attention in the US press.[94] Manufacturers across the Northeast and Midwest pressured Congress to formalize common-law protections into a comprehensive federal statute. Following the piecemeal regulations of each state could prove cumbersome, especially as interstate trade increasingly stitched the national market together.[95] The first federal bill to protect trademarks was proposed by Representative James K. Moorhead from Pittsburgh, Pennsylvania, in March 1860—several months before the election of Abraham Lincoln. Petitions soon followed in support of the bill, from citizens in Pittsburgh; Lowell, Massachusetts; and St. Louis, Missouri. Though the bill made it through committee without revisions, the members of the House refused to vote on it in the spring of 1861. The congressional record chronicled the heated debates over the bill's constitutionality, reflecting the sectional divisions that would carry the nation to Civil War. While representatives and senators from manufacturing areas likely favored federal intervention, many others resisted, claiming that common-law protections were sufficient, that the states ought to decide, and/or that Congress lacked the authority to regulate commercial marks.[96] But Moorhead was not deterred: He introduced a similar measure to the following Congress, and nearly every year thereafter for the next seven years, though the chaos of the ongoing Civil War likely minimized the priority of the measure. Pressure to act finally came when the United States signed treaties for trademark protections with Russia (1868), Belgium (1868), and France (1869). Still, Congress (and experts in the trade press) remained divided as to whether trademark protections posed too great a limitation on free trade.[97] While members of Congress debated their power to regulate trademarks, the Patent Office began accepting foreign registrations under the terms of these treaties.[98]

Congress could have taken a cue from the common law related to trademarks, however, as treaty obligations to "alien friends" had been recognized in the American courts since *Taylor v. Carpenter*. The importance of ethical obligations to foreign nations—especially those considered close trading partners with the United States—figured heavily in the earliest trademark lawsuits and took particular shape around the concepts of duty and honor toward others. As Judge Woodbury had noted in 1846, extending protections to "alien friends" was an important move to ensure the integrity of the United States with its allies. When the first dedicated treaty provision to trademark protection was finally signed with Russia in 1868, the federal government was formally recognizing a provision that had already been tested and proven in the courts for more than two decades.

While Congress debated its authority to regulate trademarks in the 1860s, trademark-infringement cases continued to make their way through the courts, with litigants often leveraging the power of the press to sway public and industry opinions in favor of expanded trademark protections. While awaiting a decision in his infringement lawsuit, Joseph Burnett, a manufacturer of hair tonic, published an open letter in the *New York Times* warning retailers to avoid imitations created by "certain mean and unscrupulous persons [who] have pirated [my] name, and are attempting to rob us of our property and reputation."[99] Burnett likened his competitor (and the defendant in his suit), Phalon & Sons, to pirates and criminals, using words such as "mean," "deceive," and "dishonest" to sharply criticize Phalon's business practices as unethical and immoral (figure 2.7). Repeatedly, Burnett stressed the potential damage to his reputation, emphasizing its importance to his livelihood through language that was central to white middle-class understandings of honest self-representation. Like J. & P. Coats and Gillott before him, Burnett used the press as an open forum to denounce the

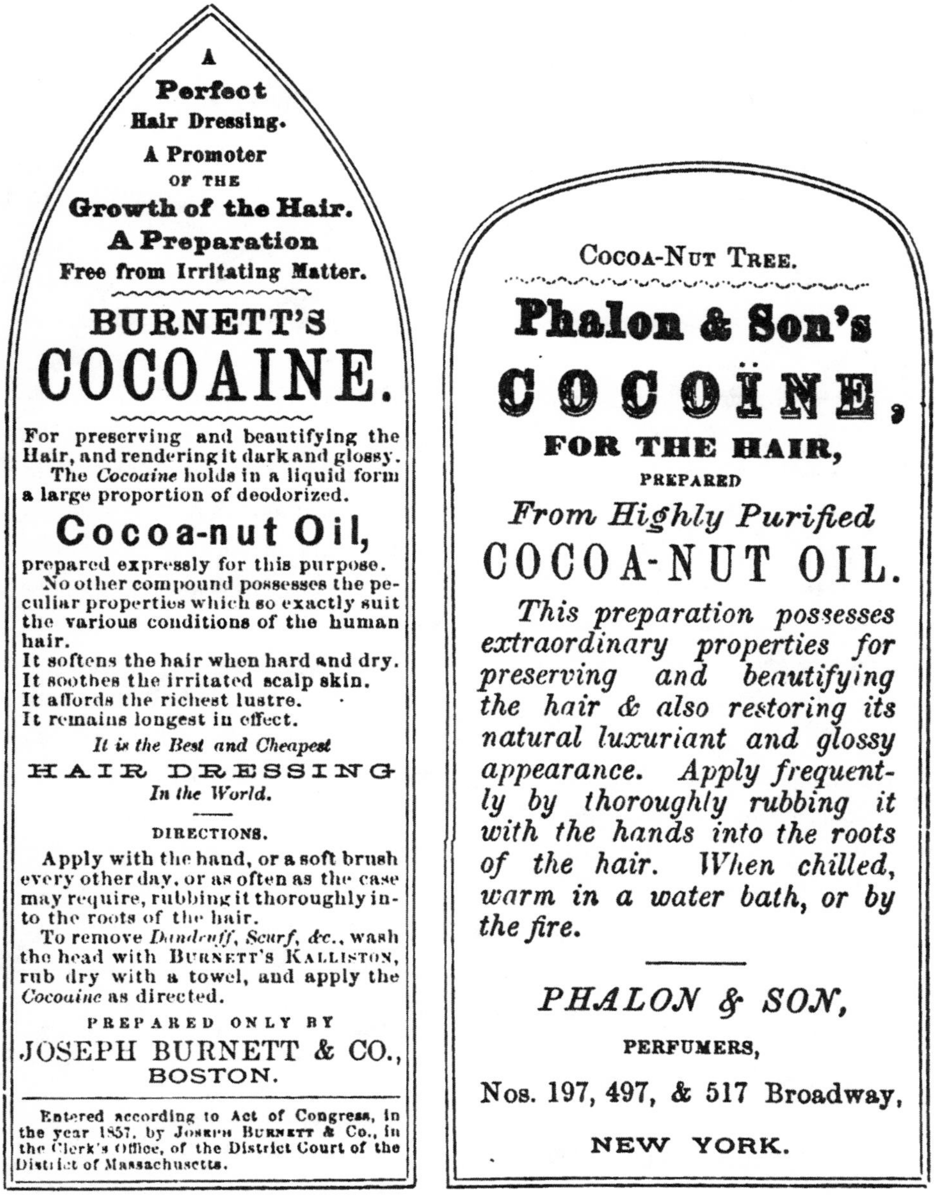

Figure 2.7. Labels for Burnett's Cocoaine (left) and Phalon's Cocoïne (right). Reprinted from Rowland Cox, *American Trade Mark Cases* (Cincinnati, OH: Robert Clarke & Co., 1871), 378.

fraudulent activity of counterfeiters who infringed upon trademark rights and to warn the public about the dangers of purchasing imitation goods. Burnett eventually won his case, and the appellate court's ruling established the rule of first use (or seniority) in awarding trademark protections.[100]

Burnett's letter to the press illustrates how many firms understood the public nature of trademarks and participated in a broader public discourse about the connections among trademarks, commercial reputation, and economic solvency. While the courts could provide some legal relief from infringement, Burnett and others also had to navigate the court of public opinion and thus sought redress in the press to recuperate goodwill for their brands.[101] Trademarks had long been used as public devices for commercial communication, functioning as short-hand marks symbolizing the manufacturer, his reputation, and the quality of the product. For Burnett, Coats, and Gillott, the press provided a venue both to build and maintain that reputation through advertising, while the courts provided a mechanism to protect the time, money, and energy spent on cultivating the public support that would constitute the goodwill value of the brand.

In all, trademark-infringement cases heard in US courts before 1870 established several important precedents that would impact the writing of the first federal trademark protections. These precedents included the government's responsibility to protect both foreign and domestic manufacturers' property rights (*Taylor, Coats*), the timing of products' entry into the market as a factor in determining trademark ownership (*Burnett*), extending the sphere of responsibility to include printers and wholesale jobbers (such as Thayer, and Holbrook), and assessing the moral foundations of each actor's behavior in the transaction, even when that meant that the plaintiff would be held accountable for deceptive activity (*Taylor, Fetridge*). Nearly forty years of commercial practice had helped to shape the legal precedents that provided the foundations for trademark protections in the United States.

It is important to note that, in the case of trademarks, the law did not predict business practice; rather, it lagged behind practitioners' understandings of fair competition.[102] These legal precedents drew from the cultural principles of integrity, exclusivity, and fair competition, which derived, in part, from the white middle-class emphasis on transparency. This culture of character had persisted in business culture through the 1860s and saturated judiciary decisions regarding trademarks. Now these standards of character would become law as congressmen took steps to draft and pass a federal trademark statute.

In the spring of 1869, federal senators introduced two bills that proposed protections for domestic and foreign trademarks. When the Senate referred its finalized bill to the House, the House elected to fold the provisions into a separate bill that provided expanded protections for patents and copyrights, reasoning that all three matters could be grouped under the rubric of intellectual property. The legislative package was passed in 1870, with stricter criminal punishments for trademark infringement appended in 1876.[103] Still working as a Reconstruction Congress, Republicans had taken advantage of their majority to push through a cache of new laws that expanded the regulatory power of the federal government, including civil rights laws and other measures. The new trademark protections became possible in this moment of revised perspective toward the government as a guarantor of (rather than a threat to) individual liberties.[104] Establishing the right to trademark protections for domestic and foreign persons, firms, and corporations trading in the United States, the new trademark law created a system for registering trademarks in the US Patent Office, which also had some enforcement powers. The law guaranteed exclusive trading rights for those registrants who could swear, under oath, to ownership over said mark and could attest to its duration of use in commerce.

Importantly, the law denied protections for marks that contradicted prevailing notions of fair competition and honest business practices. Specifically, it excluded marks that misrepresented the products or manufacturer, marks used in "unlawful business," marks for "injurious" products, marks obtained fraudulently, and imitation or counterfeit marks.[105] In short, the law policed the production and distribution of particular commodities, as well as their packaging and advertising, by prohibiting dishonesty. It followed a subjective definition of dishonesty that relied upon the Christian moral standards, as developed and publicized by the white middle class. While retaining common-law protections for trademarks and establishing consequences for infringement, the law formalized the boundaries between legitimate and illegitimate competition and products.[106] The 1870 federal law thus built upon the previous thirty years of case law, which had cemented the importance of transparent communication through advertising and commercial labels. Since *Taylor v. Carpenter* (1844), state and federal judges had framed trademark infringement as immoral and, in many of the cases discussed here, judges took pains to emphasize their disdain for defendants' willingness to defraud the public and destroy the goodwill of the plaintiffs.[107] In so doing, they implied that such deceitful actions resulted from the defendant's poor character traits. Those judges had applied moral language, drawn from the cultural idioms popular among the antebellum middle class, to commercial practice. Commercial codes of ethics developed out of these cultural standards after 1840. Now, the moralized association between trademark infringement and deception was codified in federal law.

The business and legal communities received the 1870 law with gratitude. The trade press had been following relevant trademark-infringement lawsuits for several decades, frequently printing summaries and guidelines based on current jurisprudence. Moreover, petitions from firms in Pennsylvania, New York, and Massachusetts had arrived in Congress supporting the proposed bill, which, they argued, would be easier to navigate than the patchwork system of state laws (now in twenty-two states) that existed.[108] Once the bill became law in 1870, firms scrambled to take advantage of the new protections. In the first six months, the US Patent Office registered trademarks from a variety of industries and, by 1879, approximately 8,000 trademarks had been registered by the Patent Office and more than 160 cases of infringement heard in US courts.[109] Finally, members of the legal profession commemorated the development with publications that re-capitulated 75 years' worth of trademark case law in the United States. Antici-pating a dramatic rise in prosecutions and lawsuits surrounding trademark infringement, Rowland Cox, a prominent Manhattan lawyer and well-known trademark specialist, published one such reference manual in 1871. Cox's book claimed to offer a complete accounting of every infringement case in the United States, as well as an index of common-law precedents on the subject and the cases that established them.[110] Intended as a primary reference for Cox's profession, the book reiterated the 1870 law's emphasis on honest representation by offering de-tailed evidence from decades of case law where judges had stressed the same. Cox himself added commentary in the front matter and footnotes, connecting these moral standards of honesty with fair competition and heralding the trademark statute as an important step in securing consistent protections across the United States. The book won so much acclaim among lawyers and scholars that a revised edition was published in 1892, in an indication of the important role that lawyers had come to occupy in the developing field of commercial intellectual property litigation and trademark design.[111]

An Enduring Challenge

While the 1870 law may have seemed to finalize the doctrine of trademark pro-tections, legal debates raged on in the courts. Into the 1870s, state and federal judges moved to expand existing common-law precedents, while others balked at the encroaching power of the state. This persistent tension between pro-regulatory and anti-government (or libertarian-esque) perspectives vis-à-vis the economy can be seen in the case of *Colman v. Crump* (1871, 1877), where a broad interpretation of infringement was applied by the courts. Colman, a British mus-tard manufacturer, had sued the American merchant Samuel Crump for adopt-ing the firm's "bull head" trademark on his own mustard. The court found for the plaintiffs, granting exclusive rights to the mark. Whereas previous case law stipulated that defendants' labels and trademarks had to bear a nearly exact fac-

simile to the plaintiff's marks, in this case, Judge J. Allen of the New York appellate court held that merely close resemblance was sufficient, where a purchaser
of "ordinary caution" might be deceived.[112] Like Judge Sandford in the case of
Coats v. Holbrook (1845), Allen showed flexibility in his willingness to set aside
the notion of *caveat emptor,* considering the ease with which a consumer might
be deceived. Allen departed from previous case law, however, when he argued
that the intent of the defendant mattered little; rather, it was sufficient to establish the property rights of the plaintiff and show the potential for damage. Finally, Allen held that even in cases where many manufacturers used similar
trademarks—such as the bull's head used in this case—the plaintiff was not prevented from claiming an exclusive right to its use.[113] The ramifications of this decision were vast: Several varieties of mustard sold in the United States had
adopted a version of the bull's head mark, and this ruling could effectively render all of them illegal in their infringement upon the Colman trademark. Allen's
decision had the potential to upend nearly an entire segment of the condiment
industry. His broad ruling suggests that he believed the 1870 law should have created more expansive rights in trademarks than it actually did, by including
broader definitions of plausible deception.

Yet, despite these new federal and common-law protections for trademarks,
several American merchants fought back. Following the initial lawsuit against
Samuel Crump, a coalition of grocers and other merchants in New York City
met in February 1872 to discuss the invasive power of a foreign firm (Colman),
which threatened a potential $50–100 million in damages to American mer-
chants if successful. The coalition formed the oddly named Colman Mustard
Protection Association (CMPA), to protect domestic merchants against the
"blackmailing" lawsuits brought by the London firm, J. & J. Colman. According to
newspaper accounts, the CMPA feared that Colman intended to bring additional
suits against domestic grocers, dealers, and others for selling non-Colman
mustards bearing the bull's head logo. While these merchants bore no responsibility for manufacturing and packaging the fraudulent products, *Coats v.
Holbrook* had shown that merchants could be held liable for selling counterfeit
and imitation goods. The CMPA organized a fund to assist domestic defendants, identifying some 800 lawsuits already underway in New York City
alone. Echoing the protectionist claims of Daniels Carpenter nearly thirty
years earlier, the CMPA asserted the privilege of domestic producers over foreign ones, and accused Colman of coercing would-be defendants into submis-
sion, concluding that "no dealer who has sold any mustard . . . can feel safe."[114]
In rallying to protect grocers and dealers from the expansive threat of foreign
legal action, the CMPA pushed back against federal regulation and protection of
trademarks.

The organization and actions of the CMPA point to the ways in which understandings of trademark rights remained contested in the public sphere as late as the 1870s. Despite a federal statute and decades of common-law protections against infringement, the CMPA fought against what it believed was an unlawful monopoly given to Colman, a foreign trader. Privileging the rights of domestic merchants instead, the CMPA suggested that the property rights in trademarks were not absolute—or at least they weren't in the eyes of some members of the American business community. The enduring challenge from these Gilded Age merchants paradoxically drew upon the tenets of both protectionism and free trade, in rhetoric that paralleled the arguments made by an out-of-luck man from Foxborough, Massachusetts, in the years following the Panic of 1837.

*   *   *

In these and other ways, the specter of counterfeits remained a shadowy figure throughout the nineteenth century. Many manufacturers used advertisements as a public forum to chastise imitation and counterfeit goods, cautioning the public to scrutinize labels and trademarks. While some firms' diatribes may have been only rhetorical, others, such as Gillott, Coats, and Burnett, faced documented cases of infringement that threatened their profits and reputations. Such manufacturers took to the press and to the courts to defend their commercial rights, linking the intangible concept of goodwill to the concrete capital investments made in growing one's business, and quantifying the economic consequences of a damaged reputation in terms of lost profits. Cautionary warnings about fraud in newspaper advertisements carried these legal and industry-related arguments about commercial reputation into the public sphere, socializing the public to the new, trademark-centered commercial culture that was taking shape. As Coats and others sought legal redress for trademark infringement, they learned to articulate and protect the symbolic meanings and cultural capital embedded in those marks. As such, the arguments that surrounded trademark litigation in the nineteenth century offered an important platform for conceptualizing what would later be known as brand identity.

And yet the problem of counterfeit goods persisted, pushing firms and the courts to develop more concrete definitions of legitimate versus illegitimate commerce. Importantly, these definitions remained contested. Some infringers, such as Daniels Carpenter and Samuel Crump, fought back intensely. They questioned manufacturers' claims to exclusivity, crafting a litany of defensive arguments that hinged upon questions of citizenship, property, language, and use. In response, jurists honed in on questions of individual virtue (or lack thereof) when determining guilt in cases of infringement. In trademark-infringement

cases heard before 1870, judges applied standards of conduct that had proliferated through white middle-class advice literature, including the prescriptions for
honesty and high moral character that epitomized the antebellum culture of
character. These judges took pains to chastise defendants for their immorality,
professing a desire to raise American commerce above such wanton fraud.
Showing their willingness to marginalize and even suspend notions of *caveat
emptor* from the mid-1840s, the judges hearing trademark-infringement cases
developed a rubric for defining fraud that centered on morality and the property
value of commercial reputations. Their moralizing statements became the rhetorical framework underpinning common-law trademark protections in the
United States, which in turn influenced the drafting of the first federal trademark statute in 1870.[115]

Trademark law developed in fraught and uneven ways over the nineteenth
century, but these precedents gradually coalesced around the financial necessity
of protecting one's commercial goodwill. While legal scholars have long acknowledged the influence of common-law doctrine on federal statutes, it is important
to note the ways in which business practice, legal rhetoric surrounding trademark
use, and the law participated in a mutually reinforcing discourse in the nineteenth-
century United States. That discourse grew out of white middle-class doctrines
of proper moral behavior, as codified through the antebellum culture of character. Judges and advertising practitioners preached and upheld these concepts to
ensure honesty in the marketplace, to protect the "unwary" public from fraud,
and to save "legitimate" manufacturers from infringement.

Still, trademarks remained *visual* symbols dependent on appearance, style, and
iconography to convey their messages of trust and goodwill. As newspaper advertising developed over time, advertisers learned that their consumer-oriented
appeals ought to also consider the visual realm. Whereas language and texts
could be useful to establish rapport with potential customers—especially when
drawing from epistolary conventions—one first had to gain the reader's attention. Newspaper readers after 1830 encountered an ever-expanding advertising section, which challenged advertisers to find new and innovative ways to
format their ads. Importantly, just as advertisers had developed rhetorical strategies of building rapport—especially drawing from white middle-class idioms—
they used visual tactics to cultivate attractive appeals in print. These visual
strategies continued to build upon the cultural lessons of the antebellum years,
prompting advertisers to seek the expertise of printers and newspapermen who
knew how to manipulate print media to gain public attention. As the century
progressed, these new visual strategies would become commonplace, but they
were no less innovative in driving advertisers' efforts to communicate effectively
with the public and gain their trust.

CHAPTER 3

Visual Texts

Design and Novelty Across America's Newspapers

In 1894, Lewis Saxby, a New York City lithographer, sang the praises of a well-orchestrated visual appeal in advertising. He argued that the "genius" of pictorial advertising lay in its power to communicate to the public, yet Saxby cautioned his readers not to wield such power lightly. Emphasizing the value of original artwork over copied images, Saxby noted that distinct pictures created an association with the product and thus facilitated success in far greater ways than mere texts. Saxby's audience—advertising professionals, printers, and others—had been ensconced in a multiyear debate over the supremacy of images versus texts in advertising campaigns. The debate raged on through the pages of the trade journal *Printers' Ink* at a moment when the advertising industry underwent intense professionalization and agencies expanded to offer more specialized services. Saxby's comments steered readers to commission new images for their ads, in a move that appeared to shift advertising practice away from text-heavy campaigns and toward the visual.[1]

Yet, Saxby's comments are perhaps better phrased as the capstone to a development that took place much earlier in the century. From 1830 to 1900, printed advertisements became increasingly oriented toward visual appeals that used eye-catching designs to capture and arrest the reader's focus. Printers adapted a range of strategies, old and new, to accomplish this task in newspapers and other media. To attract the consumer's eye, they utilized new fonts, white space, bold and italic lettering, and words grouped creatively to form larger pictures on the newspaper page. Printers reimagined the text as an artistic element that could convey information in a visually appealing way; in short, the texts themselves became visual. The widespread popularity of cost-efficient newspaper layouts at mid-century threatened to eliminate visually attractive advertising designs, but advertisers and printers did not relent. Taking a cue from the famed show-man P. T. Barnum, they continued to create novel, eye-catching displays that incorporated entertainment aesthetics into advertising. By the end of the century, Saxby and others debated the relative superiority of images over texts, codifying, in professionalized jargon, the strategic visual appeals and en-tertainment aesthetics that had developed over the previous six decades. Through continuous experimentation in newspapers, printers and advertisers laid the groundwork for the fusing of advertising and entertainment at the end of the century.

Importantly, this concern with novelty and visuality reveals a decidedly con-sumerist (rather than producerist) focus in advertising from the earliest years, even in the absence of formal market researchers and professional associations.[2] The task of gaining consumers' trust required a multipronged approach, includ-ing both rhetorical and visual modes of appeal, on the one hand, and eliminat-ing deception and fraud in the market, on the other. Just as Volney Palmer and others sought to reach consumers through the language and codes of middle-class propriety, newspaper advertisers betrayed their concerns with captivating the public through entertaining images and designs. The changing visual appearance of newspaper advertising over the course of the nineteenth century thus demon-strates advertisers' continued efforts to understand their audiences and to mobi-lize that knowledge to better speak to those audiences *as consumers*. Long before the birth of the modern advertising agency, printers helped advertisers find visual routes that would entreat consumers to trust the firm and its mark.

Printers' Early Innovations

From the colonial period, newspapers had played an important role in driving a burgeoning consumer culture in what would later become the United States. Mer-chants understood how and why individuals displayed their taste, cosmopoli-tanism, and status through the goods they acquired, and eighteenth-century newspaper ads point to a keen awareness of status in driving consumption. Ap-pealing to individuals as consumers even at this early stage, advertisers contrib-uted to a commercial discourse that broadened markets in the colonial period and offered consumers access to the goods that would help form their national and imperial identities. These shared experiences informed Revolutionary and post-Revolutionary politics, laying the foundation for a consumer-oriented soci-ety in the United States.[3] At the center of these developments, advertisements kept information about the goods circulating and the people buying. Newspapers and other printed materials carried word of the latest fashions and tastes to the people in the colonies, while advertisements reinforced the desirability of luxury goods and communicated their availability to the public.

Printers played an integral role in crafting advertisements in the eighteenth century, and the pace and style of British printing had a heavy influence on American craftsmen's work. At the time, typefoundries catered largely to the book-publishing trade—which used movable type and manual presses in a style called "letterpress" printing—and thus there was a limited range of typefaces and other characters available to "job" printers servicing newspapers and the rest of the population.[4] As a result of these technological limitations, eighteenth-century advertisements often consisted of simple inventories of goods for sale, formatted in dense paragraphs that were no different from the other justified columns of text on the newspaper page. Merchants supplied their handwritten notices to the newspaper printer's office, and decisions about the appearance and formatting of the notice typically fell to the compositor—the craftsman who compiled the elements of moveable type that would make up the printed ad.[5]

Early American job printers (or "jobbers") made liberal use of capital letters, italics, and other decorative elements, such as asterisks and flowers, in order to provide contrast in the printed materials they produced. As early as the 1730s, Benjamin Franklin had implemented basic design elements to increase the visual attractiveness of his newspaper, the *Pennsylvania Gazette*, including italic and capital characters to set off certain texts, and small woodcut images in the advertising section.[6] Simple woodblock prints and engravings added visual interest to printed advertisements and stationery and, often, the images used on these printed materials mirrored the shop signs that consumers might view on the street. If a client wanted more sophisticated images, custom woodblocks or copperplate engravings could be made, but commissioning engravings was expensive and was a luxury that few could afford.[7] To compensate, perhaps, some merchants regularly requested decorative borders, centered text, or enlarged headings to distinguish their advertisements from the rest of the newspaper page. Others paid extra to have their inventories arranged in smaller columns (rather than paragraphs) to make the advertisements easier to skim.[8] By the time of the Revolution, newspaper notices had already grown more elaborate: To plain text ads, merchants and others added small woodcut images, testimonials, and engraved designs. Though eighteenth-century advertisements were limited in the range of visual elements they could include, the use of ornaments such as these suggests that printers (and some merchants) were very much aware of the importance of distinction in advertising and made use of whatever means they had to achieve it. In short, eighteenth-century American printers recognized that the success of any given advertisement rested on its ability to *visually* attract a wide audience, whose consumption drew them into a growing global market.

This understanding pushed innovations that would enable a greater range of visual elements and designs in the new century. Around 1800, new decorative typefaces became available from European typefoundries, including fonts that used dramatic lines, generous spacing, and oversized letters. The 1810s and 1820s saw the introduction of shadowed letters, sans-serif fonts, and "fat face" letters with bulbous shapes; many of these were also available in extremely large typefaces created specifically for outdoor advertising. While some American printers took advantage of these imported typefaces, others began creating their own unique typefaces using carved wooden blocks. Though wooden type was not as durable as metal type, it was cheaper; the softer medium also allowed engravers to create more subtle and intricate designs, which led to its wider use in the United States by the late 1830s. Rather than delicate letters, viewers encountered "bold shapes trapped within heavy black contours."[9] These new display types changed the visual experience of print, as the characters became more image-like.

Such innovations were necessary in the competitive market for newspaper publishing in the Early Republic, which depended heavily on advertising revenues for solvency. By the late 1820s, job printing had expanded rapidly, and printers competed for clients by showcasing their eye-catching designs for advertisements, posters, and other ephemera. American typefoundries responded by adding more variety to their products, catering to the needs of the jobber by organizing product catalogs by display types, ornaments, borders, and pictorial and decorative elements that would enhance the visual spectacles created by printers. In fact, distinctive typefaces were so desirable that some merchants paid extra for exclusive access to certain fonts.[10] In this way, typefaces could take on a branded feature, offering a unique appearance that would distinguish one's ad from the crowd of others on the page.

Jobbing printers exercised a great deal of control over the size, shape, scope, and style of the materials they printed, particularly through the composition stage of the printing process. Generally, customers were responsible for furnishing their own texts (known as "copy"), and printers often refused to accept responsibility for any content-related mistakes.[11] When it came to layout, however, printers consulted with customers, offering advice and guidelines about what might be done in print and what design elements could be effective. Often, the compositor had full autonomy to make creative decisions for the client; as the decades progressed, compositors grew increasingly skilled at innovating new and interesting visual designs in print.[12] A compositor in the Early Republic and antebellum years might gather his ideas by looking at the work of other local printing firms—including handbills, posters, and newspapers—or perhaps he perused the pages of the local typefoundry's latest catalog of new fonts and decorative elements. As they had in the late colonial period, compositors continued to capitalize the initial letter (also known as a "drop cap") and used reinforced borders between ads to signal the start of a new announcement.[13] If the customer desired images in his or her ad, printing houses and newspaper publishers typically kept a cache of generic stock woodcuts on hand, such as small "manicules" (pointing hands), ships, hats, or houses.

These efforts at distinction gradually became commonplace through the 1820s and 1830s, and newspapers grew into their now-standardized format by about 1840.[14] As figure 3.1 shows, regularly spaced vertical bars (also known as "rules") divided the page into seven columns, containing rows and rows of miniscule text separated only by the occasional bold header, drop cap, or small thumbnail image. Even these elements begin to take on a standardized sense about them, falling into the clean, orderly columns with only minimal disruption of the flow of text. The texts are still long and formal, and they blend together with these rudimentary visual elements fairly seamlessly, threatening to melt into one indistinguishable block of text. Perhaps it is no surprise then that Frank Presbrey, reflecting on these predecessors from the vantage point of 1929, could see nothing but unsophisticated, provincial notices that begged for something bolder and more exciting.[15]

While compositors and printers had a hand in crafting the look of advertisements, the appearance of newspaper advertising also owed a lot to economics in the early nineteenth century. Periodic paper shortages had plagued the United States since its founding, resulting in contracted print runs, smaller newspapers, and fewer images in an effort to conserve paper. Fluctuating subscriptions necessitated that newspapers subsidize their publishing costs by selling advertising space, which they could do more efficiently with smaller type and fewer images. British newspapers faced similar economic constraints, imposed by heavy taxes early in the century and editorial restrictions later. As a result, both American and British newspapers increasingly adhered to the so-called Agate Rule after 1825.[16] Printing advertisements in agate type (5½ point) and enforcing column divisions upon the page allowed editors to maximize advertising space (and thus revenues) in each issue. In an effort to further economize space, several major American newspapers instituted a ten-line limit on daily advertisements following a paper shortage in the mid-1830s.[17] These moves imposed a visual order on the newspaper page, giving a highly uniformed appearance that was only infrequently challenged by bold lettering, italics, and small woodcuts.

Moreover, technological limitations also shaped the look of early nineteenth-century printed works. Changing lines of movable type was a labor-intensive process, and thus editors typically offered discounts for advertisers who purchased ad space for months on end, as an incentive to reduce the amount of time spent changing the movable type in each page's frame before going to press.[18]

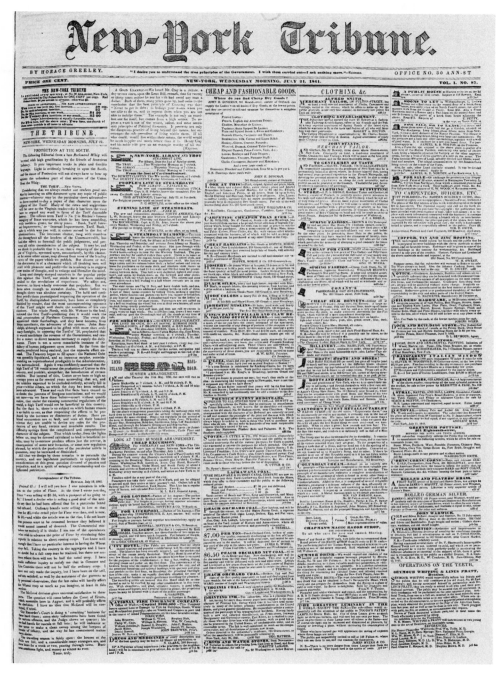

Figure 3.1. Front page, *New York Tribune*, July 21, 1841. Library of Congress, Chronicling America: Historic American Newspapers. Online at https://chroniclingamerica.loc.gov /lccn/sn83030212/1841-07-21/ed-1/seq-1/.

Woodcut images were an imperfect solution to including pictures in print. Wooden blocks lacked the durability of metal type, yielded only limited print runs, and had to conform to precise size measurements to fit into the column molds used in newspapers.[19] The added labor costs associated with commissioning images, or even using stock cuts from the printer's inventory, made widespread image use difficult for many advertisers. The integration of stereotyping after 1820 provided some efficiency, but including larger or more custom images in newspapers remained a rather costly endeavor.[20] For these reasons, it was difficult and expensive to have a visually dynamic newspaper advertising campaign in the antebellum period.

Advertisements appearing in the New York papers in the 1830s and 1840s reflect these limitations, but they are not entirely devoid of innovation.[21] For example, ads that appeared in the *New York Herald* from 1837 through 1840 largely adhere to a single-column format, using small type and very formalized language to address the reader. Bold fonts and drop caps commonly set off one ad from the next. But a few innovations are present. Though infrequently, some advertisers purchased double-column ads, inserted larger images, and made creative use of white space to draw visual attention to their messages. Double-column notices, like other design innovations, required more technical work on the part of the printer, who would have to see the metal rules dividing each column sawed in half to accommodate the larger notices.[22] For these reasons, only some newspapers accepted such designs: While the *New York Herald* largely held firm to the Agate Rule in the 1830s and 1840s, the *New York Tribune* and others allowed some deviation, including a few small custom images.[23] Yet, the added cost for a double-column ad could really pay off. When viewed against the rest of the page, for example, the 1838 ad for Wilson's Patent Manifold Writers draws the eye through its large font and center justification of the text, which in turn creates white space around the primary message to set it apart from the ordinary rows of type surrounding it (figure 3.2). The ad immediately below Wilson's uses repetitive text and a larger font, creating a headline effect to attract the reader, promising "Vinegar!! Vinegar!!! Vinegar!!!!" Likewise, the ad for Cullen's Prophylactic Pills uses two images to frame its text, which makes use of varied font styles and white space to further draw the eye.[24] Placed in the center of the page, the wider format of these ads prompts the reader to successfully land on their information when skimming the page.

Innovations in woodblock type also allowed advertisers to create relief texts that would disrupt the visual organization of the newspaper page. In an 1838 ad for Hay's Liniment, the placement of italic white letters on a black background makes the word "cured" pop, contrasting with the black-on-white color scheme of the rest of the page (figure 3.3).[25] It calls to readers desperate for relief from

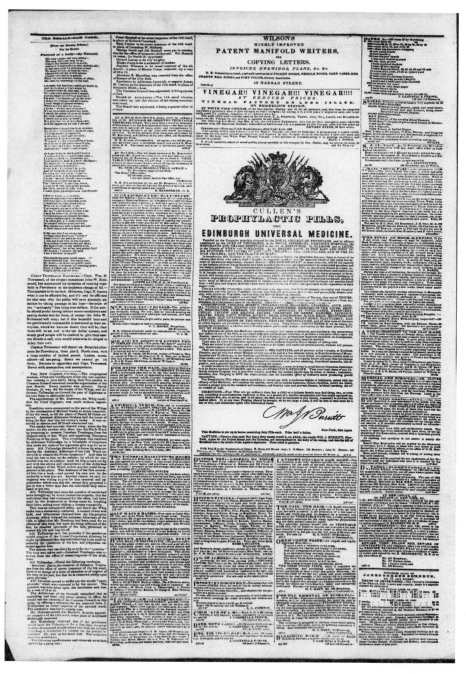

Figure 3.2. Advertisement for Wilson's Patent Manifold Writers (at center), *New York Morning Herald*, June 9, 1838. Library of Congress, Chronicling America: Historic American Newspapers. Online at https://chroniclingamerica.loc.gov/lccn/sn83030312/1838-06-09/ed-1/seq-4/.

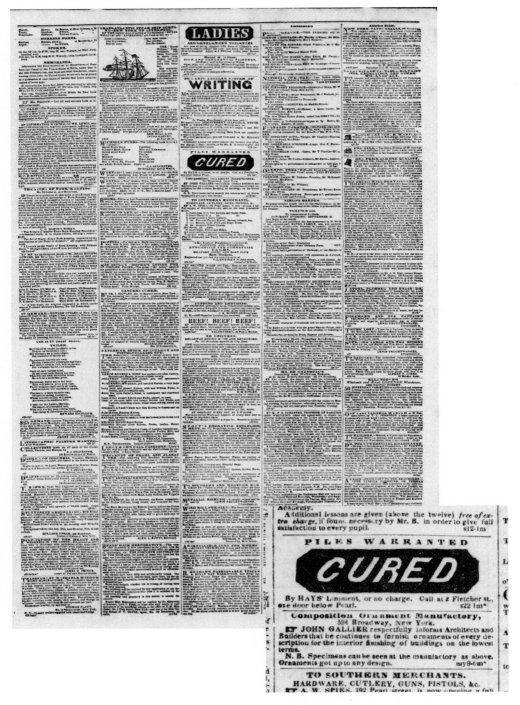

Figure 3.3. Advertisement for Hay's Liniment (at upper center), *New York Morning Herald*, September 29, 1838, with detail. Library of Congress, Chronicling America: Historic American Newspapers. Online at https://chroniclingamerica.loc.gov/lccn/sn83030312/1838-09-29/ed-1/seq-3/.

"piles" (i.e., hemorrhoids), guaranteeing a cure. Known as a "streamer," this style of relief text was an American invention of the mid-1830s. Printers hollowed out the type in wooden blocks and added "extensions" above and below the letters, joining them together with soft wax to hide the joints between blocks.[26] Cheaper than commissioning a custom image from an engraver, the streamer provided an effective mode of generating novelty without a major financial investment.

Indeed, the streamer for Hay's Liniment draws the eye so successfully that it obscures other visual strategies on the same page. Looking closely at the page, we can observe a few miniature woodblock prints adorning the ads to the far right, notably a hat, a ship, and a house. To the left of Hay's streamer, a larger image of a ship appears. Another streamer appears in the same column above Hay's ad, for ladies' toiletries. Tiny manicules also appear throughout the page, attempting to draw the reader's attention through their familiar pointing hands.[27] But these images are not as successful as Hay's streamer; with its bold outline and central placement on the page, Hay's streamer presents a louder call for the reader's attention. Though innovative when Franklin had used them a century earlier, the miniature images had now become commonplace in newspapers, pushing advertisers like Hay to seek out different strategies to attract the viewer.

In addition to new fonts, larger ads, and graphic texts, some advertisers began incorporating white space as a formal design element that would distinguish one's ad from the rest of the page. This might include enlarged margins, aligning texts to the center, or progressively increasing one margin to create a diagonal design with the text. In an 1841 ad for Gilley's Dry Goods, the text forms a diamond shape that adds more white space around the otherwise banal list of goods available (figure 3.4).[28] This ad departed from earlier ads placed by the firm, which had largely adhered to the typical classified style. The diagonal design used here allows the Gilley ad to stand out as unique from the others on the page, promising to draw the reader's attention through the simple addition of negative space. Opting for a change in format, Gilley's ad put a new twist on the laundry lists of goods that had filled eighteenth-century retailers' advertisements, showing that even a small innovation—such as adding white space—might succeed in attracting readers and new customers.

White space had long been regarded with importance in the printing trades. In book publishing, printers knew the necessity of the margins both for function and aesthetics: Leaving white space around the text made binding book pages easier, but the space also provided a "comfort to the eye" in framing and delimiting the text.[29] Margins provide a visual boundary to the text, alerting literate viewers (who are familiar with such conventions) to the starting and stopping points on the page. Benjamin Franklin understood that basic rule in the 1730s when he began inserting extra blank space in various ways: between advertisements,

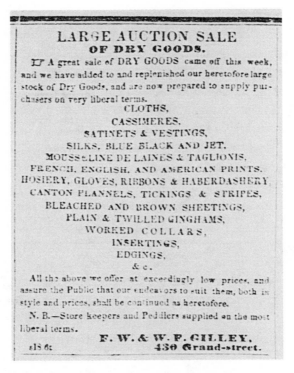

Figure 3.4. Advertisement for F. W. & W. F. Gilley Dry Goods, *New York Tribune*, September 21, 1841. Library of Congress, Chronicling America: Historic American Newspapers. Online at https://chroniclingamerica.loc.gov/lccn/sn83030212/1841-09-21/ed-1/seq-3/.

around headings and headlines, and to set off illustrations.[30] Printers in the 1840s carried this principle into their compositional work for advertisements, knowing that additional white space would highlight important information and would draw the eye through basic literacy conventions.

Finally, antebellum advertisers utilized custom images to embellish their ads. For example, the owner of Hovey's Trunk Repository inserted a custom woodcut of his storefront in an 1841 issue of the *New York Tribune*, while the manufacturers of Lee's Blacking included a circular, logo-like image in the paper.[31] While both images fit within the standard boundaries of a single newspaper column, they break the monotony of the dense columns of text by presenting something novel (figures 3.5 and 3.6). Hovey's storefront image recalls the street-view maps commonly offered in city directories of the time, providing a visual reference for readers just as the directories did. It reminds readers of the physical experience of shopping, inviting them into the virtual space of the storefront image and encouraging them to seek out the actual shopfront on Pearl Street. Once commissioned,

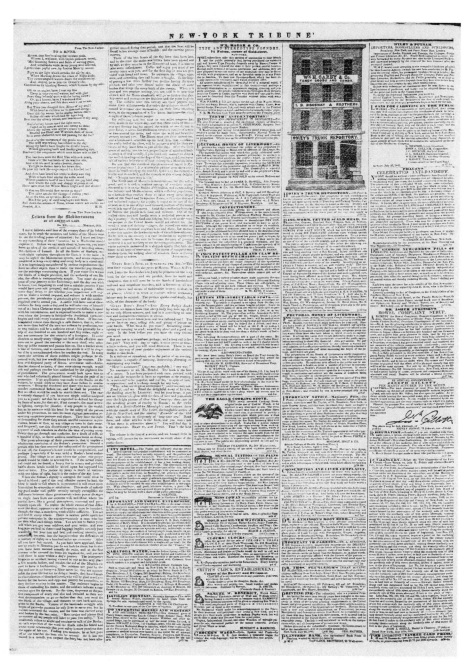

Figure 3.5. Advertisement for Hovey's Trunk Repository (at top right), *New York Tribune*, August 10, 1841. Library of Congress, Chronicling America: Historic American Newspapers. Online at https://chroniclingamerica.loc.gov/lccn /sn83030212/1841-08-10/ed-1/seq-4/.

Figure 3.6. Advertisement for Lee's Blacking, *New York Tribune*, July 1, 1841. Library of Congress, Chronicling America: Historic American Newspapers. Online at https://chroniclingamerica.loc.gov/lccn/sn83030212/1841-07-01/ed-1/seq-4/.

expensive custom images like Hovey's shopfront and Lee's logo could also be reused in other advertising media, such as trade cards, handbills, and company stationery.[32] Such reuse provided an efficient return on investment, but the practice also established visual continuity in representing the firm in the public sphere, allowing advertisers to build public recognition through the repetition of particular visual elements in print. Such self-reinforcing advertising ecologies comprised an early effort at cultivating symmetry across media to build one's commercial (or "brand") identity.

Outside New York, advertisers used similar tactics to set their commercial messages apart from the rest of the newspaper page, but rural editors throughout the eastern United States showed flexibility in accommodating more diverse advertising formats. Variable font selections, bold lettering, italics, and diagonal margins are all common in these issues, as they were in the New York papers. Yet a wider selection of fonts can be seen in the rural papers, suggesting that rural printers made more frequent use of the newly available woodblock typefaces either because they were cheaper or because they offered more decorative options. For example, in 1837, C. B. Fisher (Bloomsburg, Pennsylvania) used a range of tools in an attempt to create visual interest and to draw the reader's attention to the ad for his dry goods store, including a small woodcut print, a bold headline, and seven unique fonts (figure 3.7).[33] Despite this variety, Fisher's tactics weren't much different from those of his peers on the page; several woodcut prints are visible in other columns, as are other uses of varied fonts, bold and italic type, and drop caps. In other rural papers, merchants used larger woodcuts to draw the reader's eye, such as the manicule or other stock prints. Still others used custom images specially designed for their products or services.[34] Importantly, these examples suggest that novelty defined early newspaper advertising strategies, pushing printers to continually innovate new fonts and designs to attract the public. While it is difficult to assess the relative success of one tactic over another, the increasing variation across different ads and different newspapers provides a visual record of the ways that advertisers clamored for the reader's attention in these years.

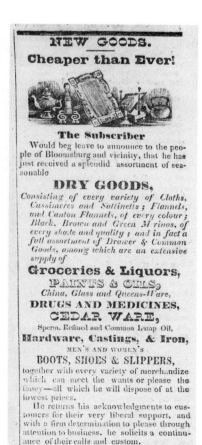

Figure 3.7. Advertisement for C. B. Fisher, Dry Goods, *Columbia Democrat* (Bloomsburg, PA), December 23, 1837. Library of Congress, Chronicling America: Historic American Newspapers. Online at https://chroniclingamerica.loc.gov/lccn/sn85025180/1837-12-23/ed-1/seq-3/.

Competing for distinction on the page, some merchants played with the orientation of their ads, shifting text or rotating the ad to create visual interest. Occasionally, merchants' advertisements appear to be rotated 90 degrees in the newspaper column so that the text or image reads sideways.[35] Some such instances may have occurred out of necessity rather than design, as when a merchant gave the editor a woodblock cut that would not fit in a standard newspaper column without altering its orientation. Regardless, the end result certainly serves to draw the reader's attention to the oddity. Even on a page with a fair amount of visual variety, ads turned sideways successfully stand out from the rest, as in an 1845 ad for John Sillban's shoe shop in Fayetteville, North Carolina (figure 3.8). Incorporating a small woodcut print and an alternative font, Sillban's ad appears in the center of the page, and reminds viewers to find him at the "Sign of the Big Shoe."[36] In other cases, woodcut designs could be used to create curved headings. In 1836, C. C. Alvord collaborated with his local printer to craft the words "Furniture Warehouse" in a half-moon shape above his advertisement in the *Rutland Herald* (Vermont).[37] There, the text acted like a doorway, arching across the column and inviting the reader to enter. Early design elements like these used existing technologies to make advertisements more visual, thereby demonstrating advertisers' concern with attracting consumers through entertaining and quirky images.

The images used in antebellum newspapers also offer clues that help explain early attempts at coordinated advertising campaigns, as well as the roles of local editors and sales agents in such campaigns. For example, from at least 1845 through 1847, similar ads for the patent medicine Wistar's Balsam of Wild Cherry appeared in newspapers in Ohio, Pennsylvania, Michigan, Wisconsin, Mississippi, Missouri, and Vermont. Two principal images were used in these ads: one featuring an angel offering a plant to a kneeling Native American man (possibly a stock image) and another custom picture of a cherry tree with a banner carrying the product name in relief (figure 3.9).[38] Though small and discreet, these images offered a measure of visual distinction, setting the Wistar's ads apart from the orderly columns of text on the page. The manufacturer likely provided his team of sales agents with woodcuts and copy to use in placing the ads in local papers: The texts vary only slightly from paper to paper, while some of the ads make use of manicules to highlight certain portions of the text (though placement of these also varies). These small deviations suggest that the local agents had some autonomy in determining the emphasis in the ad—that is, which phrases might be highlighted with manicules, bold lettering, or exclamation points—and the agents likely collaborated with local editors and/or printers to determine the best sales strategy for particular locales.[39] While the ads appeared simultaneously in newspapers throughout the eastern and midwestern states, there was only

Figure 3.8. Advertisement for John Sillban's shoe store (at center, rotated), *North-Carolinian* (Fayetteville, NC), May 3, 1845, with detail. Library of Congress, Chronicling America: Historic American Newspapers. Online at https://chroniclingamerica.loc.gov/lccn/sn84020750/1845-05-03/ed-1/seq-1/.

Figure 3.9. *Left*: Advertisement for Wistar's Balsam of Cherry, *Cadiz Sentinel* (Cadiz, OH), December 3, 1845. Library of Congress, Chronicling America: Historic American Newspapers. Online at https://chroniclingamerica.loc.gov/lccn /sn84028793/1845-12-03/ed-1/seq-4/.
Right: Advertisement for Wistar's Balsam of Cherry, *Somerset Herald* (Somerset, PA), August 3, 1847. Library of Congress, Chronicling America: Historic American Newspapers. Online at https://chroniclingamerica.loc.gov/lccn/sn83025917/1847-08 -03/ed-1/seq-4/.

moderate coordination of their designs on a national scale. Still, the geographic reach of Wistar's ads suggests that advertisers had the ability to execute marketing strategies across the growing United States well before the railroads expanded in the 1870s. Employing the network of roads, turnpikes, and canals in place by the 1840s, Wistar's and others peddled their products using a team of local agents, many of whom worked directly with local newspaper editors—or, perhaps, through one of the emerging advertising professionals like Volney Palmer—to place advertising notices for their employers.[40]

As the 1840s progressed, the built environment became increasingly saturated with ads in a variety of formats, the most visible of which were the expansive posters that papered city walls and buildings. The introduction of lithography in the 1820s had ushered in an explosion of visual culture, particularly in the cities. Printers opened storefronts and marketed their images to middle-class patrons, who responded by collecting framed lithographs to decorate their parlors. Magazine wrappers, city directories, and trade cards provided additional venues for advertising in the city. These shared a reciprocal relationship with poster and newspaper design, where printers applied similar techniques across different media. Poster advertisements featured bolder, more fluid designs and decorative elements that showcased retail stores, factories, and merchandise.[41] Advancements in the mass production of wooden type facilitated the creation of monumental advertising posters for circuses, theatrical announcements, and retail stores, which crowded onto fences, omnibuses, and other flat surfaces in the antebellum city.[42] Large-scale posters could stretch from approximately 3 x 4 feet to heights of up to 9 feet and widths that took up entire buildings. By the 1840s, a few specialized printing houses in New York and Philadelphia serviced the majority of theatrical and circus companies in the United States, working year-round to satisfy demand. Printers successfully introduced color posters in the large-scale formats, creating multicolored letterpress styles that would remain a staple in the industry for several decades.[43] These posters created a visual spectacle on the city streets, and they pushed newspaper printers to craft more attractive advertisements that would better compete for the public's attention.

By the 1850s, the printing industry had been primed for exponential growth. Transportation improvements and industrialization had ushered in the rapid flow of knowledge between the cities and growing rural communities, while the increasingly literate public craved information in larger quantities. Steam-powered printing presses and new papermaking techniques, especially the development of wood-pulp paper in 1843, economized the publishing industry and gave printers a ready supply of materials. In addition, the expansion of electrotyping, which facilitated larger print runs by making printing plates more durable, in turn enabled greater use of images in print.[44] As the printing industry grew, publishers began offering new literary magazines, a greater variety of ephemera, expanded newspaper editions, and collectible chromolithograph prints. The established and aspiring middle classes devoured these printed materials.[45] Chromolithographic firms supplied cheap, novelty images to a public yearning for colorful images, while newspaper publishers and job printers rapidly papered American cities and hamlets with black-and-white dailies, handbills, magazines, and other media.[46]

The "Tyranny" of the Agate Rule

In light of these developments, advertising seemed poised to take off in the 1850s, but economic constraints and the Agate Rule continued to structure newspaper advertising, especially in major American cities. The adoption of cylindrical press methods in the 1840s made newspaper printing more efficient with its higher print runs, but it also made deviating from the regular columns of agate text more costly. In 1847, James Bennett, editor of the *New York Herald*, formalized the Agate Rule when he banned all display advertising, two-column layouts, and images from his paper. According to one former employee, tensions had arisen between advertisers who paid for stock cuts and those who did not, leading some to suggest that the latter had an unfair disadvantage.[47] When viewed through the lens of Jacksonian politics, Bennett's ban on display ads could be seen as a democratizing effort to level the playing field against unfair competition, particularly when he broke with the tradition of selling advertising space on a long-term basis and insisted that advertisers renew their copy every two weeks. But Bennett's insistence on form over content also represented an attempt to craft a more "businesslike" aesthetic for his newspaper, which might set it apart from the sensationalism that had otherwise characterized the penny press at the time.[48] Bennett thus sought to elevate the public reputation (and perceived integrity) of his newspaper by altering its physical appearance: He eliminated display and flourish (at least visually) in the paper, in an attempt to demonstrate decorum, restraint, and professionalism.[49] Bennett achieved this by leveraging the same cultural values that had driven other advertisers' assertions of middle-class status and education at the time, including Volney Palmer and Joseph Gillott.

Bennett's rule had a domino effect on other urban newspapers: While US newspapers had been trending toward a larger quantity and variety of visual elements in advertising after 1830, many major papers reversed course in the 1850s. Unlike the papers of the 1840s, which allowed some variable fonts and custom images, the New York papers of the 1850s were remarkably uninteresting in their visual presentation of advertising material.[50] This design rigidity paralleled what was happening in London as well; when comparing the pages of the London *Times* to the *New York Times* at mid-century, one notices an even stricter adherence to the straight and narrow columns of agate type in the British publication.[51]

Still, some advertisers showed ingenuity in attempting to set their messages apart despite the newly imposed limitations within newspaper publishing: They used all caps, they used bold or larger fonts, and they made strategic use of white space by centering text, adding space between lines, and adjusting margins. The diamond shape used by Gilley's Dry Goods Store in 1841 became more commonplace, though printers and advertisers found ways to shift margins further to create cascading designs down the column.[52] Other advertisers repeated the same lines of text down an entire column in a style that was later called "iteration copy." Robert Bonner, publisher of the *New York Ledger*, was famous for advertising his paper using this tactic. In one 1857 example, he publicized a new story written by Emma Southworth, "The Bride of an Evening." Purchasing a whole column in the *New York Times*, Bonner repeated the phrases "Mrs. Southworth's New

Story—The Bride of an Evening—Now Ready In—The New York Ledger" over and over in sections that filled the column from top to bottom.[53]

Manipulating texts in these ways, printers and advertisers engineered designs that turned the texts themselves into images. A clear example of this strategy can be seen through the ads of famed New York photographer Mathew Brady, whose gallery at 359 Broadway became a popular spot for shoppers and tourists. In 1856, Brady placed ads in the *New York Times* and *New York Tribune* that arranged the text into larger shapes that spelled out his name and address vertically on the page (figure 3.10).[54] The text within each ad describes his photographic prints, their quality and beauty, and their widespread popularity. Visually, the ads work on multiple levels to speak to the viewer, drawing the eye first to the innovative use of white space and second, to the actual content that fills up each vertical letter. Other advertisers adopted similar tactics, but not always as successfully as Brady.[55] Importantly, Brady's strategy demonstrates an effort to subvert the rigidity of the Agate Rule and other limitations imposed by New York papers. Turning their texts into images, Brady and others demonstrated their concern with reaching consumers on visual terms.

Novelties such as these also helped to incorporate an element of entertainment into the newspaper, itself an important medium for communication in American society. Throughout the antebellum years, city readers turned to the newspapers for political commentary, for social gossip, for market and economic information, and to read about events around town.[56] By reading the newspapers, they learned about important cultural, economic, and political events, including the murder of Helen Jewett, the election of Andrew Jackson, the war in Texas, and the performances of the Swedish Nightingale, Jenny Lind. Newspapers thus stitched together local and national publics in these years, providing a shared experience that constituted readers—especially urban readers—into collective bodies.[57] Just as they learned through experience to turn to newspapers to get the latest on local and national politics and economics, readers would also learn to turn to newspapers for entertainment.

Advertisers exploited this newspaper habit, incorporating novelty to dazzle, to prompt curiosity, and to entertain. As P. T. Barnum wrote in 1855, unusual and distinct advertisements were necessary to cultivate public attention. Crediting his success as a showman to his advertising acumen, Barnum asserted that "a constant succession of novel advertisements and unique notices in the newspapers . . . serves to sharpen the curiosity of the people."[58] Barnum suggested that "novel" and "unique" ads would prompt individuals to find pleasure, humor, shock, and surprise in the advertising sections of the newspaper, and thus encourage readers' subsequent return and perusal of the page. Barnum acknowledged how advertisements could function as a mode of entertainment—as

Figure 3.10. Advertisement for Brady's Gallery (third row from left, at top), *New York Times*, August 21, 1856. Courtesy of the *New York Times*.

events-in-print that might be consumed, discussed, and remembered collectively. Moreover, he stressed the importance of repetition—one innovative advertisement might conjure a few sales, but a constant stream of interesting ads kept the product in the consumer's eye and, over time, would build consumers' product awareness. In these ways, the shared experience of witnessing visually interesting and entertaining advertisements week after week on the newspaper page helped contribute to the development of America's consumer society in the mid-nineteenth century. Addressing individuals as consumers, advertisements encouraged and developed a nascent consumer consciousness first established in the Revolutionary period.[59] But newspaper ads also laid the foundations for the overt emphases on entertainment that would structure advertising into the twentieth century.

While New York City newspapers remained limited by the Agate Rule at mid-century, newspapers outside the city displayed a gradual and continual expansion of visual tactics to appeal to readers. Many of the rural papers surveyed here showed greater ingenuity and flexibility in accommodating a variety of advertising tactics, including a wider range of fonts, larger and more intricate images, and larger ads overall. Typefoundries continually released new fonts, which rural editors and printers readily implemented. Diagonal margins and other textual designs became more common, while small woodcuts and custom images multiplied. Toward the end of the 1850s, double-column ads increasingly appeared in newspapers outside New York. Rural newspaper pages encapsulated the expanding variety of design techniques and immersed the reader into a cacophony of visual elements that continued to grow louder and more arresting each year.[60]

Changing editorships frequently played a role in the appearance of advertisements in local papers. Just as Bennett did with his *New York Herald*, the owners or editors of local newspapers exercised a great deal of control over the notices they printed. A change of hands at the helm of any given paper could mean that a wave of new products might be advertised to local consumers or, at the very least, the appearance of those ads might shift based on the editor's flexibility and/or willingness to allow novelty and innovation. For example, a clear shift is apparent in the approach to advertising taken in the *Mountain Sentinel* (Edensburg, Pennsylvania) between 1852 and 1857. While earlier examples show little variation in the advertising page, the latter years show a wider range of fonts, styles, and images used. How might we explain such visible changes? No new technological developments emerged in the intervening five years. Rather, the changes appear to result from a shifting willingness, on the part of the editor, to allow such elements to be printed. The paper thus likely changed hands at some point in the interim, given the slightly altered title for the latter years (*The Democrat and Sentinel*) and the new variation in fonts and approaches to advertising in the same.[61]

Aside from newspapers, antebellum Americans also encountered advertisements in a variety of other media, as posters for circus shows, theatrical productions, and other traveling entertainments papered the countryside and city streets. Roadside fences, barns, cliffs, and other natural locations bore the names of patent-medicine advertisers, clothing bazaars, and other consumable goods, while the tyranny of the Agate Rule pushed many urban advertisers to use sandwich boards, building murals, and posters more regularly. The "mania" for outdoor advertising reached epic proportions after 1840, fueled by the expansion of leisure entertainments (such as the circus). By the 1860s, approximately 275 professional billposting and painting firms across the United States employed thousands of artists to stencil sidewalks, paint rocks and large billboards near railway lines, create advertising murals in the cities, and plaster walls with broadsides and posters.[62] Without a doubt, American advertising had grown tremendously in scale and in style since 1800.

Writing in the early 1860s, William Smith, a London theater manager, synthesized these changes in print advertising over the previous half century. Smith especially praised innovations in the United States, such as using diagonal margins in a "zig-zag style" and incorporating product shapes into cards and ads. Pointing to the expansion of visual elements in newspaper advertising, Smith offered advice to his readers on how they might use advertising successfully. His treatise acted as a trade manual, prescribing rules that were tailored to a range of industries. Above all, Smith stressed the importance of novelty: "Shakspeare [sic] was perfectly correct when he said 'the eye must be fed.'"[63] Images and unique visual designs were necessary, in Smith's view, to attract the reader's eye and build publicity. He reasoned that one reader's interest could generate additional public attention as the information spread through word-of-mouth across town, ultimately resulting in multiple sales. As he noted, "Anything that strikes the eye as being *odd* or *strange* attracts attention, and gets talked about. What more can any advertiser wish for?"[64] Linking visual elements and entertainment, Smith pointed to the usefulness of design in creating a buzz among the public: "The more you can get persons to talk of any novelty, the greater will be the demand for it."[65] Honing in on the purpose of advertising—to cultivate demand for a product or service—Smith advised businessmen to favor visually interesting layouts over deceptive headlines, noting that the former would be more advantageous in avoiding the potential damage to one's reputation caused by the latter. In short, Smith privileged savvy visual design as a key mode of achieving advertising success. With this, Smith summarized a generation of advertising innovations built upon appealing to the public through visually interesting, attention-grabbing, and buzz-stirring designs that capitalized upon the aesthetics of entertainment.

Experimentation and Coordination at Mid-Century

The Civil War had a tremendous impact on the American economy and consumption, which, in turn, affected the ways in which individuals experienced advertising. Wartime production resulted in the greater availability of ready-made goods and led to increased marketing in print media. These goods benefited from expanded distribution and communication networks, another side effect of wartime mobilization.[66] Technological developments that enabled more efficient printing practices also facilitated the expansion of newspapers and printing houses dedicated to producing images for public consumption.[67] Finally, the growth of the illustrated press during the war years facilitated the exponential spread of images in newspaper advertising as the century came to a close.

Illustrated newspapers built upon the technological innovations of the 1840s and 1850s, including improvements in the printing process, cheaply available wood-pulp paper, and the expansion of telegraph service. These developments enabled the rise of British publications such as the *Illustrated London News* and *Punch* in the 1840s and, a decade later, *Frank Leslie's Illustrated Newspaper* and *Harper's Weekly* in the United States. These illustrated newspapers adopted mass-production methods to provide "eye-witness" accounts of the intensifying sectional crisis to readers across the United States, communicating information through engravings.[68] The public responded with an almost insatiable appetite for printed pictures. As a result, commercial lithographers expanded in the early 1860s, the market for job printing boomed, and the illustrated press saw almost immediate success. A new age of visual culture had arrived in the United States.

Yet, despite these developments, advertisements in New York newspapers in the early 1860s showed little progress in expanding the types of visual appeals used. As in previous decades, bold fonts and centered text remained common. Taking a cue from Mathew Brady and others, a few advertisers formatted their agate-typed ads into shapes or used shifting margins to create visual interest. For example, an 1860 ad for Ward's Shirts promised a "perfect fitting shirt, made to measure, six for nine dollars," using the text-into-shapes strategy to spell out the word "S-H-I-R-T" vertically down the page.[69] Unfortunately for the firms represented in neighboring columns, Ward's tactic visually overpowers other, less innovative strategies. Two columns to the right, an ad for *American Agriculturalist* might have been more successful if it had been placed elsewhere in the paper, for its shifting margin creates a diagonal line, adding white space to frame its text.

Other neighboring ads also utilize added spacing to set their messages apart on the page. Again, were it not for Ward's presence on this page, these other advertisers might have been more successful in their strategies to attract the reader's attention.

But the text-into-shapes strategy wasn't always successful. When Frederick Lewis, one of Ward's competitors, used the tactic to advertise a sale in 1863, the strategy faltered (figure 3.11).[70] Unluckily for Lewis, his ad appeared immediately adjacent to a large stylized design for Pearl Mottled Soap, which visually overpowered his rather vague ad, spelling out "6 for 15." Lewis's choice to spell out the price, rather than his firm name (as Brady had done) or product category (as Ward had done) meant that readers would not get as clear and direct a reference to his product as was achieved by Brady and Ward. While Lewis's ad achieved novelty, it needed to create a direct reference to the product in order to associate the visual novelty with his business (and thus create a memorable experience for the viewer, which might encourage a purchase). Lewis's ad failed to do this, but the large logo for Pearl's Soap successfully meets both goals. Unique on the page, it creates visual novelty to inspire memorability and, by embedding the brand name into the image, it provokes an association between that memorable visual experience and the product for sale. These examples remind us that a particular advertisement's success still remained somewhat unpredictable at mid-century, as placement could be as important as design.

Figure 3.11. "6 for 15," Advertisement for Frederick Lewis (third row from left, at center), *New York Times*, March 26, 1863. Courtesy of the *New York Times*.

The mid-1860s marked a shift for the *New York Times*, as larger woodcut images began appearing regularly in the paper. Still, the paper limited the images to a single column, rarely allowing display ads to take up more space. For example, ads for Mrs. S. A. Allen's Hair Restorer regularly featured woodcut designs and intricate fonts. In the February 17, 1863, issue of the *Times*, the ad appears in a column that also includes woodcut images for Smith & Brother's Pale Ale, and Isaac Smith's Umbrellas (figure 3.12).[71] Building upon strategies pioneered earlier in the century, the ad for Allen's Hair Restorer used at least four distinct fonts, decorative borders, large bold print, and a small image of a crown to attract the viewer. The ads below it also use design elements, placing a portion of the texts in relief, as was seen in the 1838 streamer ad for Hay's Liniment (see figure 3.3), and employing referential shapes as William Smith suggested. The white texts stand out in relief against the black background of the images, which serve a double role in highlighting the texts and illustrating the products for sale (a beer keg and an umbrella). Though each of these advertisers used woodcut prints and other design elements in their ads, they represent outliers in the *New York Times*, as most of its pages still conformed to the Agate Rule during the Civil War years.

Newspapers outside New York also continued to employ many of the tactics pioneered in previous decades, but they did so on a larger scale and more frequently. In short, rural editors showed more flexibility in allowing greater variety on a single page. Ads that used the text-into-shapes tactic appeared regularly, as did bold fonts, catchy headlines, and texts and images rotated sideways. Advertisers and printers added generous amounts of white space around certain ads and created cascading designs with diagonal margins flowing down the newspaper page, intermingling these tactics with iteration copy, large and small woodcuts, and even larger fonts (figure 3.13).[72] Images also began appearing more regularly in larger, two-column sizes, and in greater variety. For example, an 1860 issue of the *Holmes County Republican* (Millersburg, Ohio), demonstrates a variety of stock and custom images, varied font styles and sizes, manicules, bold headlines, shifting margins, reinforced borders, and other design elements to set ads apart from each other (figure 3.14).[73] One ad for B. Cohn's Clothing Store bisects the column into an X shape, using bold lettering placed on the diagonal to crisscross through the ad's text. Fighting for the viewer's attention here, Cohn's ad competes with one for Koch's Corner Store in the upper-right corner of the page, which features a crude drawing of a woman riding a strange dragon-like bird with a long, squiggly tail. On the same page, another ad for Koch's store replicates an image of a man holding a sandwich board, using a design that oddly resembles the advertising trade cards that would flood the American market a decade later.[74] In all, the visual paradigm represented on this page typifies the range of strategies at play in mid-century newspaper

Figure 3.12. Advertisements for Mrs. S. A. Allen's Hair Restorer, Smith & Brother's Pale Ale, and Isaac Smith's Umbrellas (at far right), *New York Times*, February 17, 1863. Courtesy of the *New York Times*.

Figure 3.13. *Wyoming Democrat* (Tunkhannock, PA), December 18, 1867, p. 4. Library of Congress, Chronicling America: Historic American Newspapers. Online at https://chroniclingamerica.loc.gov/lccn/sn84026601/1867-12-18/ed-1/seq-4/.

Figure 3.14. *Holmes County Republican* (Millersburg, OH), May 17, 1860, p. 3. Library of Congress, Chronicling America: Historic American Newspapers. Online at https://chroniclingamerica.loc.gov/lccn/sn84028820/1860-05-17/ed-1/seq-3/.

advertising—especially in rural communities—and the innovative tactics used to cultivate entertaining, visual modes of attracting the viewer.

On the eve of the Civil War, the United States also witnessed the first successful attempts to coordinate national advertising campaigns in the mainstream press. While previous decades had seen simultaneous ads placed in a variety of locales but varying in form and content—such as those placed for Wistar's Balsam of Wild Cherry—the coordinated campaigns that emerged in the late 1850s marked a departure in placing identical ads across the United States. From 1857 through 1863, coordinated ads for Lea & Perrins' Worcestershire Sauce (L&P) appeared in newspapers in Tennessee; Vermont; Washington, DC; New York City; and elsewhere (see figure 2.6). Prominently featuring an image of the labeled bottle, the ad claimed that the imported product had been "pronounced by connoisseurs to be the only good sauce," reprinting an excerpt of praise from a "medical gentleman at Madras."[75] Likely placed by Lea & Perrins' local agent in the United States, John Duncan & Sons, the ads mobilized the expanding periodical press to publicize the quality and desirability of this imported good and, hopefully, to promote higher sales.

In the latter half of the 1860s, the standard L&P ad got bigger and used bolder headlines, though the text remained almost identical to the earlier version.[76] This slight shift points to a greater awareness, on the part of L&P and its agent, for the need to promote images that would capture the audience's attention. At home in London, restrictions similar to the Agate Rule prevented the firm from using images in its advertisements, though the copy remained consistent with its American ads. The flexibility of the American press, especially rural newspapers, thus enabled L&P to craft a campaign that would make the bottle and label a focal point in print ads.[77] Through 1894, the Lea & Perrins' bottle continued to be a central feature of the firm's US advertising campaigns, promising to familiarize consumers with the label's appearance and prevent confusion at the point of purchase.[78] Making use of the kind of simultaneous publicity promised by Volney Palmer, L&P leveraged existing infrastructure networks consisting of printers, agents, and newspaper editors to create a coordinated national advertising campaign well before the emergence of the "modern" advertising agencies of the 1890s.[79]

Yet, while the infrastructure and desire to create coordinated national campaigns can be evidenced in the mainstream press at mid-century, many brand-name goods are conspicuously absent from the African American press in those years. Instead, most advertisers appearing in black-owned newspapers seem to have been local retailers, wholesalers, and other service providers, such as boarding houses, undertakers, tailors, and others. Notably, several of the most prominent products that were advertised on a regional and national scale in the mainstream press do not appear in the black-owned press, including Joseph

Gillott's Steel-Tipped Pens, Orris Tooth Paste, Benjamin Brandreth's Vegetable Pills, and Lea & Perrins' Worcestershire Sauce. At the height of their popularity, these products were heavily advertised—but only in mainstream newspapers owned by whites. For example, in a twenty-year span, the manufacturers of Orris Tooth Paste and Brandreth's Vegetable Pills ran between 400 and 800 advertisements in New York City papers alone—but none of those appeared in African American–owned papers. Similarly, in the latter half of the century, advertisements for Mrs. S. A. Allen's Hair Restorer appeared more than 1,400 times in newspapers across the United States, but, again, not in any African American–owned papers.[80] Though not exhaustive, this data suggests that the color line extended to advertising in the black press.

There are several plausible explanations for these omissions, but it is hard not to fault persistent racism as a potential mitigating factor. Given the collaborative nature of advertising practices at the time, derogatory sentiments harbored by any link in the chain—such as advertising professionals, local agents, company management, or even other business partners—could push a firm to deliberately discount the African American consumer market out of racial prejudice. Fluctuating advertising budgets, ignorance of black-owned publications and their reach, and/or access issues also likely contributed. In fact, the African American press emerged largely because of such exclusionary policies among the owners, editors, and printers of mainstream newspapers. In the antebellum years, African American businessowners were often turned away from advertising in white-owned papers or saw their notices significantly changed. For example, one man recalled a frustrating refusal from the editors of the *New York Sun* in 1845, noting that the editor had informed him that "the Sun shines for all white men, and not for colored men."[81]

Yet, while racial barriers restricted black access to advertising in white-run newspapers, the flow of information from white advertisers to black newspapers was not always as limited. Some white business owners placed their advertisements in both black and white papers, recognizing the benefits of engaging both markets. One prominent example is Volney Palmer, whose advertising business thrived on his ability to offer access to ever-widening consumer markets. In 1850 and 1851, the *National Era*, an African American newspaper in Washington, DC, listed Palmer as its official newspaper agent, authorized to take and place newspaper advertisements at the same rates required by the paper. (S. M. Pettengill, Palmer's successor, later appeared in the same paper using a similar notice.) The notices are simple and free from the flowery endorsements that typically characterized Palmer's advertisements; nevertheless, the notices are telling. First, they suggest that Palmer (and quite possibly others) recognized the business opportunity in generating advertising revenue for African American newspapers, which means that he likely also recognized the market potential of targeting African American consumers as a key demographic. Moreover, if Palmer had contracted with these papers to serve as their advertising agent (as he did with other publications), he would have likely also maintained a client list of African American newspapers that could be made available to merchants, manufacturers, or agents wishing to target these markets (if they had desired to do so).

Other agents also recognized the potential of targeting the black consumer market. As early as 1850, several local sales agents placed advertisements in the black press for their employers' wares, particularly in transitional regions bridging North and South with large free black populations. In 1850, the local Washington, DC, agent for Wistar's Balsam of Wild Cherry, R. S. Patterson, placed advertisements for his client's products in both the *Republic*, a mainstream paper, and the *National Era*, an African American paper.[82] Patterson's advertisements appear nearly identical, using the same design strategy and similar copy to appeal to readers. A decade later, agents for Wheeler & Wilson sewing machines and Aetna Insurance in Cincinnati followed similar tactics, advertising their clients' products in the *Colored Citizen* and in other white-run newspapers.[83]

Interestingly, the manufacturers of these companies seem to have used a relatively decentralized approach to advertising, which differed from that of some of their competitors. Whereas Lea & Perrins' had a single US agent managing publicity, sales, and distribution across the country, other firms employed multiple agents assigned to manage similar tasks by county or by region. Empowered to choose appropriate advertising channels for their clients' wares, the agents for Wistar's, Wheeler & Wilson, and Aetna, mentioned above, selected African American newspapers in addition to mainstream papers, thereby enlarging their potential sales markets. While it is difficult to know whether the agents' personal identities, politics, or other affiliations may have influenced their decisions to do so, the rarity of these examples suggests that such cross-racial publicization may have been frowned upon or considered futile by other agents and firms. Importantly, ingenuity in advertising included not only adapting designs and developing new techniques but also recognizing the potential of additional markets—such as African American consumers—in growing the popularity and recognition of one's product and brand.

Images Triumphant

By 1870, visual elements, design, and entertainment aesthetics had dramatically transformed the look of newspaper advertising in the United States. The Gilded Age saw a dramatic relaxation of the Agate Rule as editors competed to give the public what they wanted: images. New technological advancements helped make this possible. First, the monotype and linotype processes streamlined newspaper publishing by mechanizing the typesetting process and eliminating associated labor costs. Improvements to electrotyping, chromolithography, and other printing processes also facilitated wider use of images in print, while the invention of the halftone process in the 1880s enabled the printing of photographs alongside type. All of these changes made printing more efficient and economical, but images especially became cheaper to reproduce. As a result, daily newspapers began to feature news illustrations regularly by the mid-1880s.[84] It wasn't just the advertising sections that changed after the Civil War; newspapers overall became more visual in the Gilded Age.

Despite these developments, however, New York newspapers continued to show slow progress in advancing more expansive and visually interesting advertisements. Some papers held fast to the Agate Rule, frustrating advertisers' attempts to include images when publicizing their wares. For example, though the Smith brothers had advertised their pale ale in the *New York Times* using a custom woodcut in the 1860s (see figure 3.12), the editors of the *New York Herald* continued to restrict display advertising in their paper a decade later. Undeterred, the Smiths purchased enough space to occupy three-quarters of the front page to advertise a one-day promotional sale in 1876. Readers of that morning's paper encountered a full five columns that filled the page with repeated content, detailing the firm's name, address, and the terms of the sale (figure 3.15).[85] Combining strategies developed nearly twenty years earlier, the full-page advertisement uses modified iteration copy and the texts-into-shapes tactics to subvert the *Herald*'s rigid restrictions on display advertising. Like a modern-day flash sale, the Smiths' promotion likely caused quite a stir within the city, prompting interested patrons (and perhaps even spectators) to flock to the Smiths' brewery to take advantage of the sale and/or to witness the spectacle. Regardless of its outcome, the promotional sale certainly had the potential to bring in massive profits for the 18th Street firm—a promise that likely justified the added expense of placing such a large front-page ad in the *Herald*.

By this time, newspapers increasingly competed with magazines for advertising revenues. In response, publishers touted the quality of their presses, the accuracy of their typesetting, their affordable rates, and their widespread circulations. They often referenced their "modern" practices that took advantage of the latest technological developments in order to entice additional clients to patronize their services. The multiplication of advertising agencies further added pressure to the increasingly tight publishing market, as the agents' negotiating power and expanding client lists depressed advertising rates.[86] These market and cultural pressures pushed design changes in the advertising sections of the *New York*

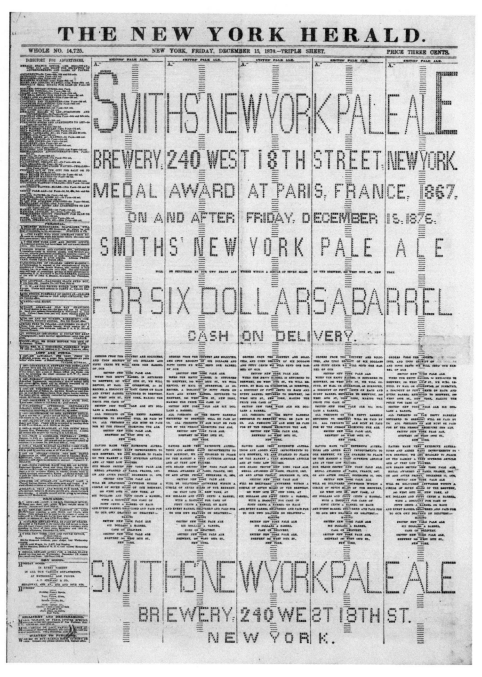

Figure 3.15. Front-page advertisement for Smith's Pale Ale, *New York Herald*, December 15, 1876. Library of Congress, Chronicling America: Historic American Newspapers. Online at https://chroniclingamerica.loc.gov/lccn/sn83030313/1876-12 -15/ed-1/seq-1/.

Times and other large urban papers, which eventually relaxed their adherence to the Agate Rule.

But one's effectiveness in newspaper advertising was still relative, as placement and neighbors on the newspaper page could make or break an ad's success. A double-column display ad might visually overpower drop caps on the page but fail to outshine a diamond-shaped ad in an adjacent column.[87] Elsewhere, however, diamond-shaped texts might pale in comparison to large graphic headlines or extremely wide margins. Yet headlines might also be foiled by a clever advertiser who bought multiple spaces on a single page to build familiarity through repetition, as Koch's corner store did in 1860 (see figure 3.14).[88] What's more, custom images still threatened to derail all of these strategies. As new techniques emerged and strategies clashed, one might not know which competitors would appear on the page or how (and whether one's chosen strategy would work) until the ink had dried. Though printers had observed and calculated supposedly proven techniques for decades, advertising still remained a somewhat hit-or-miss business. Competing strategies and techniques vied for attention on the page in an often haphazard approach, the success of which, ironically, depended on one's consistent irregularity and novelty in comparison to others.

By the mid-1880s, images appeared regularly in the New York papers, which had finally caught up to the strategies employed in areas outside the city for decades.[89] A wide selection of fonts, centered headlines, strategic white space, and a range of medium-sized images decorated the page. Some of the century's earlier advertising strategies—such as iteration copy and texts-into-shapes designs—faded into obscurity, replaced by a wider variety of images, ranging from cheap woodcut images to increasingly sophisticated custom designs.[90] As New York's newspapers expanded the range of display advertisements they accepted, several firms began to place the same custom logo or design across multiple publications, just as L&P had done in the 1850s. Firms such as Royal Baking Powder and Castoria brand castor oil used this visual repetition of the logo to build readers' familiarity with their brands toward the end of the century.[91] Moreover, the new flexibility in display ads paved the way for the rapid inclusion of larger, custom images in the 1890s, especially as quarter-page ads became common among New York newspapers.[92] In 1896, the *New York Times* fully embraced the visual turn prompted by developments earlier in the century when it launched its illustrated magazine supplement, printing the first photographs in the paper using halftone technology.[93]

By the end of the century, newspaper advertisements both within and outside New York City had slowly aligned according to the principles of visual attraction and entertainment aesthetics. Readers of both the mainstream press and the black press, in rural hamlets and in urban centers, could witness a similarly expanding scope of custom images, with quarter-page and half-page advertisements deploying large fonts and interesting designs. Yet, while urban papers displayed more and more custom designs, many of the older tactics of visual attraction remained common in the rural papers, including streamers; cascading margins and diagonal texts; a wide variety of fonts within the same ad; and clever, pictorial borders that framed the advertising message.[94] Three-quarter and full-page advertisements began appearing simultaneously in various newspapers in the 1890s, first placed by large department stores such as John Wanamaker's in Philadelphia and New York City, and Neuburger's in Freeland, Pennsylvania. One full-page advertisement for Dr. Warner's Coraline Corsets even combined an editorial-like advice column with a more straightforward catalog of the firm's various product lines, in a strategy that prefigured the infomercials that would dominate TV airwaves in the latter part of the twentieth century.[95] By the end of the nineteenth century, the newspaper page had been all but taken over by advertising.

Advertising professionals observed all of this and took to the trade journals in the 1890s to comment on the importance of knowing one's audience, while taking credit for many of the strategies that had been pioneered earlier in the century.[96] Taken together, admen's advice to trade readers was threefold: First, stressing the importance of the consumer's perspective, Jed Scarboro told his readers that a good copywriter studied and understood his audience: "If he is to forge a link to bond the advertiser to the consumer, he must study the public needs as well as the advertiser's, in order to fit the link without friction."[97] Scarboro's advice underscored the consumerist focus that Palmer and others had adopted earlier in the century, a tactic that had been honed and refined by printers through newspaper advertising as the decades progressed.

Second, various experts argued that visually attractive ads were vital to a company's success: They stressed using eye-catching fonts, borders, diagonal margins, and white space to add distinction even to the simplest classified ads. Channeling William Smith a generation earlier, trade journals in the 1890s reminded admen and others that novelty was key to successful advertising. "To catch the eye and retain the attention is the object of a good advertisement," George P. Rowell's agency suggested.[98] Bold, attractive, and tasteful ads were sure to draw attention, chimed George Batten, and there was general agreement among industry leaders that larger ads were worth the investment.[99] Novel and entertaining advertisements betrayed an effort to leverage cultural aesthetics to speak to customers. Such ads contributed to the task of gaining consumers' trust by creating memorable and pleasurable experiences for the viewer, which, admen hoped, would translate into positive feelings toward the product in the viewer's mind.

Finally, advertising professionals pointed to the important role that images played in ensuring the success of an advertising campaign. Articles in *Printers' Ink* reminded readers that purchasing images for use in advertising was a sound investment, guaranteed to give many returns. Admen made recommendations on the types of images to use, they explained the various processes for reproducing images in print (and associated costs), and they gave readers tips on how to procure attractive images for ads. Editorials underscored the affective influence of images on consumer desires, proclaiming that "the power of hypnotism lies in a cleverly displayed ad."[100] As one expert noted, images brought the "desired conspicuousness" that advertisers needed in order to gain public attention and procure sales.[101] Consistency across media was also important: Charles Austin Bates advocated coordinating posters with trade cards and newspaper ads in order to keep the campaign familiar in the public eye. But Bates cautioned readers not to try to achieve this cheaply: Poster work was best done by a skilled artist, draftsman, or designer, in Bates's view.[102] Agreeing with Bates, lithographer Lewis Saxby proclaimed that the "genius" of pictorial advertising was its ability to associate exclusive qualities with a particular product. He argued that employing a skilled artist to create original, symbolic designs would enable manufacturers to win over a larger segment of the market.[103] Saxby and Bates were responding to a growing trend toward using cheap, copied artwork or stock cuts in advertising. In voicing his preference for original artwork, Saxby contributed to an ongoing debate in *Printers' Ink* about the value of images over texts in advertising, and about which kinds of images worked best.

The terms of this debate echoed broader industry concerns in the 1890s, particularly regarding the role of printers in creating advertisements. As the advertising industry professionalized, admen increasingly displaced printers in the creative process, preferring to mediate interactions between the clients (those advertising their wares) and the printers, who had traditionally consulted with the client directly to design the ad. Agencies also began producing their own artwork, hiring art directors and artists educated in newly established professional art schools to work alongside copywriters in developing campaigns. These "creatives" further jeopardized the role of the artistic printer in crafting and curating interesting advertising matter—a role he had enjoyed since the colonial period. The printers' role became one of taking direction, rather than giving it. As the agencies expanded their authority, some trade journals even recommended giving detailed layout and design instructions to compositors, further emphasizing their declining importance in the creative process.[104] Many advertising professionals praised these developments, noting with pride the ways in which admen had drummed up important business for local newspapers and increased the scale of commerce in the United States. Echoing other intellectual currents at the time, these writers emphasized the "progress" made by their industry, pointing to the agents' leadership roles in cultivating expertise and instituting scientific principles to improve advertising practice.[105]

Tensions between the printing industry and the expanded advertising agencies pitted these professionals against each other, despite their long history of working together to meet customer demand. The growth of periodical advertising by 1900 had marginalized the ephemeral advertisements produced by job printers—including trade cards, the subject of the next chapter—while consolidations in the printing industry in the 1890s left many printers out of work and/or seeking ways to expand their clientele.[106] Skilled printers, who had managed advertising design and imagery for more than a century, worried that the growth of the agencies would devalue their labor by minimizing their intellectual contributions to advertising practice. Their fears were not without good reason; the mechanization of typesetting, through machines such as the linotype and the monotype, had already displaced many professional typesetters and compositors. Pushing back in the 1890s, printing-industry leaders wrote passionate editorials underscoring the important role printers played in the advertising industry and urging readers to see the value in working directly with local newspaper publishers. They pointed to the specialized local knowledge that a small-town newspaperman could offer, noting that his trusted role in the community would be an asset in crafting the right advertisement.[107] Reminding advertisers of the value of the printer's expertise—a role that had traditionally been an asset in advertising practice—these editorials pushed unsuccessfully against industry trends that marginalized the intellectual and artistic contributions of printers.

By the early twentieth century, sympathetic editorials began advising printers to develop their own writing skills, or hire writing specialists, in order to provide expanded advertising services to customers and remain competitive. Printing houses such as R. R. Donnelley in Chicago advertised the quality of their services and the creative potential of their compositors.[108] Full-service printing facilities competed in this way because the advertising agencies were edging them out—but the writing was already on the wall. A decade later, the agencies employed entire departments of layout artists and others, catering to the clients' whims and desires with a newfound theatrical flair. The new art directors rejected the eclectic styles of the nineteenth century, preferring simple, streamlined, and even minimalist designs that reflected a new, "modern" aesthetic. Their recommendations shunned the advertising techniques developed by skilled printers over the previous seventy-five years, couching the typographic work of printers as old fashioned, and even visually repellent. Instead, the agencies held up the modernist aesthetics of college-educated layout artists who knew the latest trends and technologies, applied through new scientific methods. By the

1920s, the skilled, artistic printer had been completely supplanted—in function and in prestige—by the new profession of graphic design.[109] Printers, who had interacted directly with the public and knew their tastes, were now sidelined in favor of market-research techniques that promised to better understand consumer preferences.[110] Consequently, advertisers and admen lost an important connection point to the public.

*   *   *

American newspaper advertisements changed dramatically over the course of the nineteenth century. As printed materials papered American cities and the countryside in the antebellum years, advertisers and sales agents worked with printers to identify and implement visual strategies that would attract the eye and set certain ads apart from the cacophony of voices competing for public attention. Newspapers across the United States increasingly printed ads from local merchants alongside those of nationally marketed retailers and manufacturers, showing the national and international character of the American market from the antebellum years. Between 1830 and 1900, printers' experimentations to gain readers' attention had resulted in more varied advertising styles, including graphically designed names, logos, and other images. Long narratives grew minimal, images became more elaborate, and the advertisements got bigger overall. Even the texts themselves grew more visual over the course of the century, using fanciful and stylized fonts, custom headlines, rotated orientations, and large shapes to catch the eye. Importantly, a great number of these emerged in the 1840s and 1850s, growing out of the collaborative work of printers and advertisers. Together, these changes shifted advertising's visual landscape, establishing the principles that would guide advertising into the twentieth century.

Surprisingly, New York was not the epicenter of innovation in the realm of nineteenth-century newspaper advertising. Though the large metropole might have been considered the center of the advertising industry by 1900, restrictions and traditions among the city's newspaper publishers limited advertising innovation in that medium before 1880. Outside New York, however, newspaper advertising evolved at a steady pace. While adherence to the Agate Rule actively discouraged the expansion of display advertising in the large urban newspapers, rural editors showed much more flexibility and ingenuity in developing ads with visual appeal. When the *New York Times* finally lifted its formerly rigid rules, its pages seemed to suddenly burst with advertising images and graphically designed displays. Thus, the rapid expansion of images in print that seemed to characterize the post-Civil War years can rather be described as a gradual and incremental progression from the late 1820s forward, which was only interrupted by the

Civil War and rigid adherence to the Agate Rule at mid-century. These waves of innovation moved from the American countryside to the metropole, and eventually from New York to London: In the last decade of the nineteenth century, images finally began accompanying advertising more regularly in the London *Times*.[111]

Concurrent with this expanding visual landscape was a shift toward entertainment aesthetics in advertising. Antebellum-era merchants and printers learned that interesting, entertaining designs and images would grab consumers' attention, and they gradually learned to do this more efficiently. Printers and advertisers incorporated flair and novelty into print advertising to generate buzz, implementing the advertising principles prescribed by P. T. Barnum and others. While today Americans flock to the televised Super Bowl game to be dazzled and entertained by memorable, humorous, and novel advertisements, in the nineteenth century, they flocked to the newspaper page.

This expanding use of visual elements in advertising, including the innovative designs and images discussed here, demonstrates advertisers' interest in creating memorable and compelling ads for consumers. In short, advertisers cared very much about how the public would receive their ads, as their focus was decidedly consumer-based from the early nineteenth century forward. This overt emphasis on tailoring advertisements to meet consumer preferences structured both rhetorical and visual strategies for grabbing the reader's attention, building rapport, and ultimately gaining the reader's trust. Through their collaborations with printers, advertisers learned that text, image, format, and design could all be important tools to win over consumers. Building trust was a multipronged, collaborative process that evolved slowly over time, with multiple actors contributing innovations from various nodes within the industry.

Advertisers and printers did not waste the lessons learned in newspaper advertising. By the time of the Philadelphia Centennial Exhibition, printers had widely introduced a new medium for advertising—the handheld trade card. Adapting the trade card from mass-produced chromolithographed prints, printers must have anticipated the popularity of these objects. Trade cards could be cheaply produced and easily distributed, and they offered advertisers a host of new opportunities to engage the public with colorful, meaningful images. Capitalizing upon a public fad for collecting images, printers helped develop compound advertising appeals rooted in both middle-class cultural values and entertainment aesthetics. After the Civil War, the strategies of visual advertising that had framed the previous four decades would come together through the advertising trade card and the popular practice of creating scrapbooks.

CHAPTER 4

Leveraging Scraps

Trade Cards and Entertainment Aesthetics

In the summer of 1876, Elizabeth Wills Vernon of Brooklyn, New York, attended the Centennial Exposition in Philadelphia. Walking by the dazzling displays, she would have encountered a dizzying variety of colorful programs, trade cards, and other ephemera from the fair's many exhibitors. Vernon collected these as she moved through the exposition, using them to record the spectacles she saw in her scrapbook. She took great care to document the sights, sounds, and faces she witnessed at the exposition that summer: Her scrapbook provides a visual map of the fair's many halls, events, and displays. Intermingled with drawings of the Corliss engine and other technologies, she pasted advertising trade cards, large engravings clipped from *Frank Leslie's Illustrated Newspaper*, signatures of family members and dignitaries—including famed American poet Henry Wadsworth Longfellow—and hand-colored fashion plates.[1] On the title page, she created a chromolithographed signature, pasting the initials "EWV" out of die-cut scraps and decorating the page with flowers and birds (figure 4.1). The act of creating the scrapbook, of cutting and pasting the found materials on the page, offered Vernon a pastime that was both creative and entertaining, allowing her to engage with the story both passively as a viewer and actively as its creator. Collecting printed ephemera like a tourist taking photographs, Elizabeth Vernon memorialized the fair in her album, curating a mini-exposition that she could return to again and again. The book offered a slide show in print that could be shared with family and friends, highlighting Vernon's skill in the craft of album-making as she used the book to entertain herself and others.

These three elements—chromolithography, entertainment, and personal expression through albums—came together in the 1870s as printers experimented with a new advertising medium: the chromolithographed trade card. These

Figure 4.1. Title page, Elizabeth Wills Vernon's "Centennial Scrapbook" (1876). Jay T. Last Collection of Fairs and Expositions Prints and Ephemera, Huntington Library, San Marino, CA (priJLC_Fair).

handheld, colorful objects communicated information about products and services, and circulated like calling cards had in the antebellum years. Creating an immediate sensation, trade cards won the favor of a wide range of consumers by appropriating the format, iconography, and usage patterns of other forms of exchange media. Above all, trade cards were entertaining: They were cute, pretty, and funny, and they facilitated the scrapbook hobby for many Americans. The visual evidence left behind by album makers shows how users prized the cards for their entertainment functions, adapting this inherently commercial medium for noncommercial practices. Printers and advertisers facilitated such adaptation by infusing trade cards with the codes of personal expression developed by the antebellum middle class. In particular, printers incorporated images of children and flowers, as well as texts that framed the ads as gifts, drawing on sentimental themes to cultivate public interest. They recognized the American public's collecting habit and exploited it as a new advertising medium. Albums show that individual consumers appropriated commercial objects for sentimental purposes in these years, precisely at the same time that market culture was appropriating sentimental images for commercial ends. In effect, trade cards helped commod-ify sentiment by packaging it for consumption by the American middle class.[2]

Many historians recognize the trade card craze of the late nineteenth century as a precursor to "modern" twentieth-century advertising.[3] Some scholars sug-gest that trade cards reflected the manufacturers' desires, aspirations, and un-derstandings of their place in the world, and/or that the cards betray the Gilded Age's preoccupation with abundance and opulence. Others argue that the cards served to socialize individuals—especially women and children—to the gendered, racial, and classed roles prescribed by American society and to the consumerist ethos that would prevail in the twentieth century.[4] Yet, in addition to these func-tions, trade cards made advertising entertaining, and thus shifted the ways that American consumers would engage with the market. As objects that people col-lected, treasured, modified, displayed, and gifted to others, trade cards' materi-ality remained vital to their popularity. To better understand the reception of trade cards as advertisements, we can look at their collection in albums and scrap-books, which hold important clues about the cards' role in building commercial reputations, cultivating sales, and expressing classed and racial identities. As a medium with such proven popularity, trade cards allowed advertisers to experi-ment with new consumer-focused visual appeals that blended entertainment and commerce to create memorable advertising experiences. This tactic would prove invaluable to later branding efforts.

The Chromo Craze

America's fascination with colorful pictures began in the 1820s, when dry goods merchants and stationers began importing lithographed prints from Europe and offering them for sale in their shops. The American middle class then forming in the cities was quickly hooked. A decade later, printing houses in New York, Phil-adelphia, and Boston began offering lithographed sheet music covers, book illus-trations, and hand-tinted collectible prints. Demand continued to rise, and lithographers along the East Coast found ways to integrate color into the print-ing process, while the introduction of steam power and wood-pulp paper allowed for more efficient and higher volume outputs by the 1850s.[5] At mid-century, Americans had fully entered a "craze" for chromolithographed (i.e., color litho-graphic) pictures, goaded on by the editorials of tastemakers such as Harriet Beecher Stowe.[6] Printing firms became the primary suppliers of these novelty im-ages, which they made available at a variety of price points to a public yearning for a colorful oasis from the newspapers and other black-and-white media circu-lating in American culture.[7]

During the Civil War, the market for chromolithographs expanded, and the number of lithograph firms in the United States grew to meet consumer demand. Boston lithographer Louis Prang had found success making reproductions of famous art works in the 1850s and 1860s and expanded his operation to include prints by local artists during the Civil War. Some of Prang's most popular prints depicted sentimental themes in figurative and iconographic form (figure 4.2). In one 1867 print adapted from a painting by J. G. Brown, Prang depicts a girl framed by leaves and foliage, gazing politely at the viewer through friendly brown eyes. Her plump, rosy cheeks and clean, pretty clothes reveal her station in the middle class. This is a portrait of natural beauty and childhood innocence: The girl's demure expression gestures to her inner character and purity, while the serene autumn landscape reinforces and highlights her pleasant physical features and appearance. The print typifies the types of chromos that Stowe recommended to her readers, suggesting that such aesthetically pleasing pictures would help cultivate character among those aspiring to middle-class status in the United States.[8]

Figure 4.2. J. G. Brown, J. Howard Collier, and Louis Prang Co., "The Flowers in Her Hair" (1867), chromolithograph. Prints and Photographs Division, Library of Congress (LC-DIG-pga-07891).

In nineteenth-century popular culture, outward appearances were often visually linked to a person's inner character and value.[9] In short, virtue and morality seemed to be visible on the body. Nathaniel Currier's temperance prints offer some of the clearest depictions of this widespread cultural belief among Americans (figure 4.3). In "The Drunkards Progress" (1846), the viewer watches helplessly as the young middle-class man falls to temptation. Along the way, he transitions from an upright, fashionable gentleman to a sloppy drunk, descending into poverty, crime, and death. Along his downward spiral, his body appears more crooked and emaciated, while his clothing is exceedingly wrinkled and torn, and lesions freckle his gaunt face.[10] Intended to dissuade viewers from alcohol use, Currier's print draws from then-common visual tropes to illustrate the man's fall from grace. His degenerative progression toward drunkenness—depicted as a moral and personal failure—manifests in highly visible ways. With this, Currier marks the corrosive effects of inadequate self-discipline and poor character on the man's body, crafting a cautionary argument in favor of temperance. Currier would continue to make such visual arguments against alcoholism well into the 1870s. Placed alongside Currier's visual diatribe against immoral vices, Prang's 1867 print offers a clear contrast: It symbolically references the virtue and purity of character prescribed by middle-class tastemakers.

Figure 4.3. Nathaniel Currier, "The Drunkards Progress; From the First Glass to the Grave" (1846), hand-colored lithograph. Prints and Photographs Division, Library of Congress (LC-DIG-ppmsca-32719).

In the same years, Prang experimented with small-scale chromolithographs he called "album cards." These 2 x 4 inch prints contained full-color images of flowers, birds, leaves, and other plants on a plain white background, and were commonly sold in sets of twelve. Introducing the cards in 1864, Prang intended these for collection in his patented *American Album*, a leather-bound scrapbook with precut slits to hold the cards.[11] The cards were immediately popular; in just a few years, Prang had sold several hundred thousand cards across the United States and the UK.[12] With the album card, Prang capitalized upon the popularity of collecting chromos while appealing to an older culture of exchange and album-keeping that included friendship albums, commonplace books, and scrapbooks.[13]

The developments of the Civil War years, including the popularity of chromos and the illustrated press, cultivated a deep public fascination with printed imagery, while Prang's album cards primed the American market for the emergence of advertising trade cards in the 1870s. In 1876, Prang began using his album cards as calling cards for his business: He printed commercial information about his firm on the cards, copyrighted the designs, and distributed them widely (figure 4.4). Other firms did the same, and the fad for advertising trade cards soon exploded.[14] Measuring approximately 3 x 5 inches, the colorful cards typically featured an image and a manufacturer's or retailer's name and location on

Figure 4.4. Louis Prang & Co., trade card (1875). Courtesy, the Winterthur Library: Joseph Downs Collection of Manuscripts and Printed Ephemera.

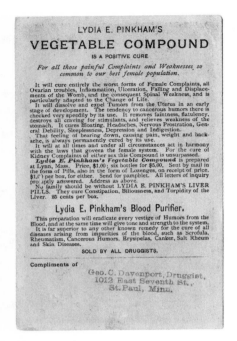

Figure 4.5. Knapp & Co., "Lydia E. Pinkham's Grandchildren," trade card for Lydia Pinkham's Vegetable Compound (1889), with reverse view. Warshaw Collection of Business Americana, Archives Center, National Museum of American History, Smithsonian Institution.

the front side, with product information, testimonials, awards won, and other solicitations appearing on the reverse. Trade cards were available from printing firms in various East Coast and Midwest cities, in both custom designs and blank "stock" (or generic) varieties that could be customized later through letterpress overprinting or ink-stamp (as George Davenport did in figure 4.5).[15] While expensive custom cards utilized an idiosyncratic range of images to advertise the product, stock cards generally relied on a common set of images that included children, flowers, birds, and other small animals. Lithographers typically produced these stock cards in series—that is, an array of similar designs, themes, and narratives that could be purchased individually or as a set. Because of this, and due to their more affordable nature, stock cards overwhelmingly dominated the supply of trade cards circulating on the market.[16]

American consumers encountered trade cards through a variety of venues, as retailers and manufacturers distributed the cards freely. The cards appeared on retail counters and as product package inserts, salesmen distributed cards with samples and catalogs along their routes, and consumers could even collect and mail in coupons or premiums for additional cards. Though nearly ubiquitous, the cards remained highly desirable objects: gifts from the world of commerce that patrons sought out and collected. Many merchants even incorporated the terminology of the gift directly onto the cards, offering them to the public with their "compliments."[17] Such language helped obscure the commercial function of the trade card, and instead framed it within a culture of gift-giving. Though altruistic and personal on the surface, a statement like this was likely intended to cultivate a measure of guilt in the consumer, who might feel obliged to repay the gift in some way.[18] It is important then, to remember that the fundamental objective of advertising—even advertising trade cards—was to increase sales. If the desirable cards were available only by collecting and sending in coupons or premiums, the consumer could be motivated to purchase increased quantities of the appropriate goods in order to obtain the coupons or premiums required to procure more trade cards. If the cards were available for free at the shop counter, a patron would still have to visit the store to satisfy his or her desire to possess more cards. In this way, trade cards deliberately appropriated and manipulated the cultural ideas associated with gift-giving for commercial gain.

Why were trade cards so popular? Part of their acclaim rested on the material similarities linking trade cards with other portable cards that circulated among individuals throughout the nineteenth century. Trade cards formed a subset within a larger genre of ephemera that I have called "exchange cards," a group that also included greeting cards, calling cards, and other small prints. As I have argued elsewhere, twentieth-century collectors and archivists separated exchange cards into smaller categories based on the objects' presumed functions (cards used at holidays became "greeting cards," while those used for advertising became "trade cards," and so on). But for nineteenth-century individuals, these were all simply "cards"—interchangeable objects that could be reused and repurposed for a variety of occasions, and which all circulated in a culture of exchange that supported individual efforts to build and maintain relationships.[19] Men, women, and children in the Gilded Age exchanged trade cards with letters between friends, as prized awards, and as tokens of sentiment— just as calling cards were enclosed in letters, reward-of-merit cards were offered to schoolchildren for achievement, and greeting cards supplemented holiday well-wishes.[20] Moreover, printers contributed to the flexibility of this medium: Marketed by printing houses and stationers to both the public and other retailers, the exchange cards that circulated as advertisements could also be purchased and used by individuals for a variety of other purposes.[21] Louis Prang's designs illustrate this multipurpose nature of chromo cards: As figure 4.6 shows, an individual might receive the same card from a small retailer inviting her to patronize his store or a relative wishing her a happy New Year.[22] Such adaptation of chromolithographed exchange cards provided the objects with a sort of

Figure 4.6. Louis Prang & Co., stock trade cards (1878). Jay T. Last Collection of Printing and Publishing: Louis Prang Archive, The Huntington Library, San Marino, CA (priJLC_PRG_bin 11).

blank-slate quality, making them suitable for both personal and commercial purposes.

Second, chromolithographed trade cards circulated as corporate calling cards, paralleling the older social traditions of exchanging personal calling cards. As exchange cards that initially passed from manufacturers and retailers to consumers, trade cards communicated economic information and acted as commercial representatives, just as calling cards had aided interpersonal communication between visiting friends for over a century. Middle-class etiquette dictated that one should present his or her card when calling upon another person at home. As a formal announcement of the visitor's presence, calling cards had evolved into highly symbolic objects by the mid-nineteenth century. In the persistent culture of sentimentalism and middle-class sociability, one's calling card served as a material demonstration of one's character.[23] Etiquette expert Abby Longstreet thus counseled her readers to choose one's card carefully, emphasizing that "Its fashioning . . . [is] an explanation of much of its owner's individuality."[24] Calling cards provided a mode of publicly displaying oneself to others, making the cards a form of cultural currency that referenced and reinforced social networks.

Adapting trade cards as similar surrogates for face-to-face interactions, printers and advertisers grafted this new medium onto the older cultural practice of exchanging calling cards. Trade cards could act as material signifiers for the manufacturer in much the same way that calling cards did for individuals, and thus trade cards offered a new mode of conveying commercial reputation and character in the 1870s. Praising the advertisements, experts optimistically remarked that the cards could even have as much impact on consumers as face-to-face interactions with traveling salesmen.[25]

A wealth of cultural conventions governed the leaving and exchanging of calling cards in the nineteenth century, and here trade cards also functioned in parallel ways.[26] Yet, while it became a courtesy to leave a card when calling on a friend or family member—an act that positioned the card as a remembrance of the visit itself—when visiting a retail store the visitor would instead receive a trade card, transforming it into a souvenir and reminder of the visit.[27] Instead of referencing an interpersonal visit, the card referenced the world of commerce and the individual's experience and interactions with that world. Advertisers reinforced these overlapping uses of exchange cards in the language they chose for the cards themselves. For example, department store mogul John Wanamaker in Philadelphia spoke to potential customers on trade cards in language that echoed formal dinner invitations: He "cordially" invited individuals to "call upon" his store.[28] According to one store biographer, Wanamaker frequently stood at the entrance to his store personally welcoming individuals into his space, much like the host of a dinner party would upon receiving important guests.[29] His written invitation to the public invoked a culture of social calling that reframed his commercial space as an extension of the domestic parlor, while his formal language echoed the class-based appeals that had characterized newspaper advertising several decades earlier.[30] The card's friendly invitation and intimate design helped to reposition Wanamaker's relation to his customers within the realm of sociability, instead of one centered on economic exchange and commerce.

Sentimental Icons, Commercial Images

Third, chromolithographed trade cards were popular because they depicted entertaining, appealing themes and subject matter. Printers knew and understood this: As Bufford's lithographic firm noted in 1885, "A handsome picture will be kept, talked over, asked for, and bring customers."[31] Just as they had in newspaper advertising and chromo prints at mid-century, printers drew from their own professional knowledge in experimenting with images that would be most popular and appealing on trade cards. They developed designs and themes that borrowed from the top-selling collectible prints that had been popular during and after the war (see, for example, figure 4.2), reworking these themes to make the new advertising media successful. Offering some advice on the subject, one prominent lithographer suggested that the most "pleasing" subjects included children, "pretty women," and small animals; advertisers were thus sure to find success if they selected images comprised of these supposedly universally appealing topics.[32] In fact, one of the most popular themes to appear on both stock and custom cards was children—at play, creating mischief, and in portrait with flowers.[33]

In adopting images of children for trade cards, printers exploited changing cultural understandings of childhood to transform the symbolic potential of the new advertising medium. Since the early nineteenth century, the middle class had romanticized childhood as a stage of life that ought to be sheltered from the harsh realities of modern urban society. Children signified those ideal virtuous qualities that adults prized most, including innocence and purity, and trade cards overwhelmingly depicted white children dressed and posed according to the behavioral standards of the middle class.[34] During the Gilded Age, childhood became an even more important haven as industry drew more and more working-class families into the factories. Play became a luxury and a marker of middle-class status, and representations of children in popular print culture tended to concentrate on both nostalgia and playfulness. Such a romanticization of childhood also found currency in the budding reform movements that would carry Progressives into the next century.[35] When crafting romantic and pastoral images of young children, lithographers took their cue from the sentimental pictures popular at mid-century, and thus transferred middle-class nostalgia for childhood innocence onto the handheld chromo cards.

For a culture that presented disease, poverty, and vice as semiotic characteristics that transformed and disfigured the body, plump cheeks and even a flushed complexion demonstrated health and youthful vigor. In one such example, the cherubic faces of "Pinkham's Grandchildren" (see figure 4.5) match the rosy cheeks and smiling faces of the girls depicted by Prang in the 1860s, thus creating a visual association between the older antecedents and the newer, smaller chromos (see figure 4.2). In contrast to Currier's emaciated "drunkard" (see figure 4.3), the chubby frames and lacy, white dresses of the Pinkham children suggest that they belong to doting parents, who feed and provide for the girls. These details gesture to the girls' middle-class status, as do their straw hats embellished with large satin ribbons and the fresh shine on their boots. Sheltered from the harsh factory labor that consumed many working-class children at the time, the girls gaze pleasantly at the viewer, as if posing for a family portrait. The older girl embraces the toddler as a sister would, while the younger girl tilts her head downward somewhat bashfully, fidgeting with her fingers. Their endearing depiction offers a momentary escape from the bitter realities of postwar industrialization, diverting our attention instead toward domesticity and family values.[36] If, as Katherine Grier has argued, images of children in public spaces served to domesticate and render the space suitable for genteel audiences, then, in advertisements, images of childhood innocence could divert attention away from the initial commercial function of the trade card, adding a similar air of domestic gentility.[37]

Yet, in addition to offering a glimpse of sentimental escapism and nostalgia, children on advertising cards could also serve to bolster advertisers' strategies for building rapport with potential consumers. Returning to the Pinkham card (see figure 4.5), the youthful glow of the girls' plump cheeks symbolizes health and happiness, adding a visual layer that reinforced the Pinkham Company's discursive claims about its products on the reverse of the card: "a positive cure" that "no family should be without."[38] Lydia Pinkham's Vegetable Compound was a popular patent medicine from the 1870s through the 1920s; the firm often relied on marketing that specifically targeted women and revolved around the grandmotherly company figurehead, Lydia E. Pinkham.[39] Gazing upon the sweet and snuggly children in the trade card, the viewer might imagine Lydia Pinkham as a nurturing, family-oriented woman. The card provokes an identification between white middle-class viewers and Pinkham, positioning her as a familiar face and a potential friend, whose positive influence in her family is reflected in the children's rosy cheeks. Moreover, the trade card establishes a visual association between Pinkham's medicines and the angelic white faces on the card, offering a symbolic, yet reassuring message of product purity to receptive viewers. Whether printers intended images of children to be symbolic distractions or whether they were simply drawing from the most popular images of the day, in adopting pictures of children for trade cards, printers demonstrated their aptitude in identifying and successfully exploiting public tastes. Doing so allowed printers (and, by association, the advertisers represented) to establish rapport with potential customers through a shared set of cultural values established by the white middle class—just as Volney Palmer had done a generation earlier.

Flowers, clasped hands, and other icons of sentimentality also adorned trade cards, further cementing the cards' entertaining appeal and maintaining viewers' familiarity with sentimental iconographies. In fact, after children, flowers were the next-most popular image included on advertising trade cards.[40] As they are today, flowers were a popular commodity in the nineteenth century and held a central place in the culture of emotional expression. From the 1820s through 1900, an entire genre of literary works developed to catalog the symbolic nature of flowers, outlining a "language" of cultural meanings associated with specific blossoms. The popularity of this literature, especially among members of the white middle class, points both to the savviness of printers in adapting floral

Figure 4.7. Unknown printer, trade card for Fleischmann's Yeast (c. 1880), with reverse view. Courtesy, the Winterthur Library: Joseph Downs Collection of Manuscripts and Printed Ephemera.

imagery for exchange cards and to the likelihood that many consumers would recognize this "language of flowers" when it appeared in popular culture.[41]

On trade cards, floral iconography paralleled images of children by invoking cultural understandings of emotional connection and human relationships. In one advertisement used by Fleischmann's Yeast (figure 4.7), a white woman's bejeweled hand delicately holds a single red rose. The card's reverse warns the reader against imitation products, pointing the consumer to the Fleischmann signature appearing on all packaging, without which "none other is genuine."[42] Knowledgeable consumers who encountered this card likely would have recognized the language of flowers here, especially the common association linking rosebuds with purity and confidence in others. Symbolically, the rosebud on the front of the card reinforces the messages about product purity on the card's reverse, providing a subtle reassurance of Fleischmann's integrity and altruism.[43] Moreover, the delicate hand offering the single blossom references gift-giving. Just as the card itself could be considered a gift from the world of commerce— and from Fleischmann to the viewer—the hand becomes a surrogate for the giver (Fleischmann), offering us the rose and its metaphorical meanings (confidence) as a gift. In these ways, the card distills cultural ideas about authenticity and trust, deploying carefully chosen iconography to visually communicate with the viewer. Commodifying sentimental themes, advertising trade cards thus entertained audiences while simultaneously promoting consumption.

Whiteness in Advertising

In a small but significant subset of advertising trade cards, printers incorporated satire and caricature, drawing from common racial tropes that both presumed and helped construct a white, middle-class audience as the ideal consumer demographic.[44] Many trade cards presumed a white audience, either directly or indirectly. Racial caricatures functioned to directly exclude nonwhites from the potential audiences for such images, using humor as a means of white social integration by establishing group identity and a sense of racial solidarity. Those who understood and laughed at a particular joke would become a group of insiders, in opposition to the outsiders who either missed the punchline or who were targeted by the joke itself.[45] Like a joke given at the beginning of a speech, humor in advertising served two goals: It warmed up an intended audience of insiders to the message presented, but, importantly, it also made the message itself more memorable. Caricatures of immigrants and nonwhites used belittling satire to reinforce existing social hierarchies in American culture in the post-Reconstruction years, a period that witnessed the rapid expansion of Jim Crow laws, immigration restrictions, and other exclusionary cultural forces. Advertising images featuring white subjects helped normalize public assumptions that the typical American consumer was white. For example, the white children in figure 4.5, the white hand in figure 4.7, and other visual evidence of white subjectivities provided a less abrasive, but no less harmful, mode of normalizing the hegemonic position of whiteness in American culture, thereby further marginalizing nonwhites. Assuming a white audience also meant that the printers and designers of these cards assumed such audiences would be entertained (rather than offended or hurt) by the satire. In creating such in-groups, these trade cards appealed to white consumers along racial lines, bolstering and securing whites' own identities through ridiculing representations of immigrants and African Americans. As such, trade cards offered subtle and not-so-subtle messages that extended the color line through America's consumer culture.

Many of these cards drew from themes in popular culture, such as Gilbert and Sullivan musicals.[46] In a card picturing a rotund Buttercup from *HMS Pinafore* (1878), the printer depicts a squat, bow-legged woman, instead of the petite and rosy-cheeked beauty described in the score (figure 4.8).[47] The woman displays a broad upper lip, red hair, and a plump figure supported by a large, unfeminine frame. Her hair color and caricatured features represent common stereotypes associated with Irish women in the nineteenth century. From the 1850s through 1900, mainstream American culture racialized the Irish alongside other minority groups as a separate (and inferior) race from native-born whites. In the most common representations, Irish men took on ape-like characteristics not unlike caricatures of African Americans, while Irish women appeared brutish and haggard (figure 4.9).[48] While our red-haired woman is anything but dainty, the caption "They call me Buttercup with Magnola [*sic*] Hams" suggests that her possession of the hams could transform her in the eyes of potential suitors. Calling to mind the life-enhancing properties of consumption that would be touted by advertisers several decades later, this card nevertheless parodies such claims to curative metamorphosis by rendering the change unfathomable and absurd in this case.[49] The portly Buttercup—whose size mimics the thick and meaty hams she holds—couldn't possibly embody the petite and feminine Buttercup from *Pinafore*, and thus the trade card satirizes ethnic Otherness in order to appeal to a presumed audience of non-Irish white insiders.[50]

Ethnic caricatures such as this were common in the 1880s, especially as nativism rose against Irish and other immigrant populations in the Northeast and against Asian immigrants in the American West.[51] In another card for Magnolia Hams, a well-dressed Ulysses S. Grant travels to China, where he is greeted by locals offering their plumpest rats for his lunch. Declining, Grant gestures to his black servant wielding a large cured ham on his shoulder, noting his preference for Magnolia Hams (figure 4.10). Here, Grant becomes a metonym for white

Figure 4.8. Krebs Lithographing Co., "They Call Me Little Buttercup," trade card for Magnolia Hams (c. 1880). Ephemera Collections, The Huntington Library, San Marino, CA (ephBTM).

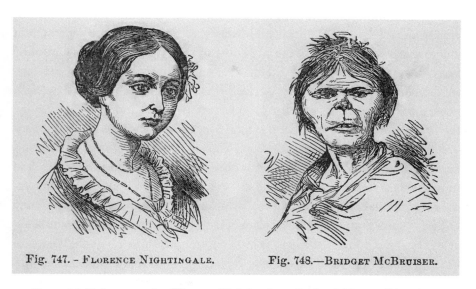

Figure 4.9. Unknown artist, "Florence Nightingale vs. Bridget McBruiser" (1866). Reprinted from Samuel R. Wells, *New Physiognomy: Or Signs of Character, as Manifested Through Temperament and External Forms, and Especially in "the Human Face Divine"* (New York: Fowler & Wells, 1875 [1866]), 537.

Figure 4.10. Krebs Lithographing Co., "That Is a Plump Rat Chang Whang," trade card for Magnolia Hams (c. 1878). Ephemera Collections, The Huntington Library, San Marino, CA (ephBTM).

American culture: The assumed white viewer is invited to identify with Grant and to share in his disgust at the possibility of eating rats. He is surrounded by nonwhite Others, some quietly threatening—as in the foreign host—some dutifully subordinate, as in the black servant. The racial hierarchy created between white and nonwhite in the image is replicated, in visual and satirical form, by the implied superiority of American food over Chinese cuisine. Satirizing non-Western diets by depicting rats as haute cuisine helped to reinforce the Otherness of Chinese culture, while implicitly justifying discriminatory policies toward immigrants at home.[52] Furthermore, the cards' culinary critique seems to foreshadow imperial arguments that the "white man's burden" included civilizing Others at home and abroad, thereby connecting American capitalism to missionary efforts in China at the time. Grant's introduction of Magnolia Hams to China promises to reform the Chinese, replacing their inappropriate cuisine with an American product, while opening an overseas market for American goods. Aside from chuckling at the joke on this card, white middle-class viewers are invited to feel a sense of pride in having supported such a noble, civilizing effort through their consumption of Magnolia Hams.[53]

As the servant in this card suggests, African Americans became common subjects in caricatured trade cards circulating in the post-Reconstruction years. Popular culture critiqued African American life, dress, behavior, and suitability for inclusion in mainstream (white) society, often dismissing African Americans' attempts at social mobility (just as it had done in the age of abolition). In advertising, servile and demeaning images of African Americans—such as the iconic Aunt Jemima—became popular as visions of a romanticized antebellum past emerged under the Lost Cause ideology after 1870.[54] In these ways, black caricatures in this period signaled white anxieties over the social position of blacks in post-emancipation society and a corresponding desire, among whites, to discipline African Americans into prewar roles.[55]

One popular advertising trope depicted blacks using soaps, cleansers, and various shoe and stove polishes in a frank linkage between their skin color and the application (or removal) of blackening.[56] Between 1880 and 1888, for example, New York varnish manufacturer Clarence Brooks & Co. used more than thirty different trade card designs featuring satirized and caricatured African Americans to advertise its products. In the "Darktown Fire Brigade" (figure 4.11), for example, a team of bumbling volunteer firemen scramble to get the blaze under control. Drawing from familiar visual stereotypes, the card presents figures with swollen lips, frizzy hair, and overly muscular physiques.[57] Like Bridget McBruiser and the *Pinafore* card (see figures 4.8 and 4.9), the Darktown card stresses the figures' supposed deviation from white society's definitions of beauty in order to ridicule the group as ugly, not to mention unprepared and inept in fighting the fire.[58] The bumbling firemen hold a ladder against the burning building, while a young woman clings precariously to the ladder's top and a frightened cat leaps from a window. At the center of the image, one fireman threatens to impale the young woman with a hook as she slips from the ladder. The viewer's only reprieve from this potentially gruesome sight is the rubber stamp added by Brooks's local agent at the center of the image. The men's comical failure to stop the flames from engulfing the building underscores their ineptitude, both figuratively and literally, at living independently in American society. Other cards in the Darktown series (and other caricatures like it), replicated these racialized tropes and narrative satires to diminish African American life and civic potential. Through such slapstick representations, white spectators would have been encouraged to assume a privileged and safe position away from the danger, which allowed them the racial and physical distance necessary to take pleasure in the obviously painful failures of African Americans.[59]

Importantly, the effects of caricatures like these extended beyond marking the inferiority of blacks and reinforcing the solidarity of whites. Just as Edward Williams Clay's prints had done in the 1820s, caricatures of African Americans continued to serve as a social corrective, chastising behaviors deemed improper or uncouth by white society in order to render blacks ineligible for inclusion in the citizenry. Such images could thus alleviate white anxieties about the

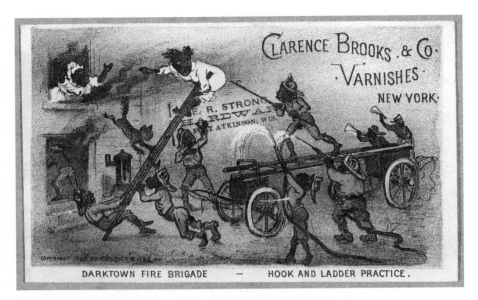

Figure 4.11. Thomas Dallow and Currier & Ives, "Darktown Fire Brigade—Hook and Ladder Practice," trade card for Clarence Brooks and Co. Varnishes, New York (1888). Ephemera Collections, The Huntington Library, San Marino, CA (ephBTM).

potential for African American political power in the years following emancipation.[60] One final example further demonstrates this point. As it had done with both Irish and Chinese immigrants, the manufacturers of Magnolia Hams took direct aim at African Americans' place in American society. In figure 4.12, a group of African American men crowd around a larger-than-life ham, clamoring for a bite. At the left, one man struggles to wrap his mouth around a torso-sized chunk of meat, his large teeth barely piercing the ham as he gazes hungrily, and somewhat fiercely, toward the viewer. In the center, a red-shirted man slices through the gigantic ham with a sword-like carving knife, while his impatient friend to the right reaches toward the blade. The scale of these figures in relation to the overwhelming ham renders them childlike and elfish, while their exaggerated and animal-like facial features dehumanize them. These visual elements, like the tagline with its broken dialect ("What's de use talking 'bout dem 'mendments when Magnolias is about?"), belittles African Americans' capacity for political participation. The men relinquish a discussion about citizenship and the franchise—specifically, in the reference to the Reconstruction Amendments—in favor of an instant gratification of bodily desires (hunger).[61]

But the scene also conjures white anxieties about the inherent danger of African American power: The extremely large knife, wielded menacingly by these animal-like figures, slices effortlessly into the flesh-toned (almost white) ham. The ham becomes a stand-in for white flesh—an object that the insatiable figures

Figure 4.12. Krebs Lithographing Co., "Dem 'Mendments," trade card for Magnolia Hams (c. 1878). Ephemera Collections, The Huntington Library, San Marino, CA (ephBTM).

cannot wait to consume—and thus the card gestures to the potential danger in allowing blacks into the American citizenry (because they would devour it whole). Yet, the card also attempts to reassure white viewers, implying that as long as these men remain content with their ham, they would not wield that knife elsewhere (or toward other white targets). Proposing the potential danger of blacks to justify their ineligibility for citizenship, images such as these helped to bolster white supremacy precisely at the same moment that racial categories replaced class as a primary determinant of one's fitness for inclusion in the American polity.[62] Rendered as objects rather than subjects both here and elsewhere in advertising, African Americans are wholly excluded from the ideal audience for American advertising. In this way, many printers and manufacturers implicitly denied blacks the opportunity to participate in the kind of middle-class consumption undertaken by the white viewers of these cards.[63]

Serialized Entertainment

In addition to sentimental icons and ethnic caricatures, printers used serialized narratives and themes to boost trade cards' desirability as visual entertainment.

Serial trade cards allowed printers to maximize their trade card output without the added cost of designing new plates to print cards individually: Serials came in sets of six to eight cards that used similar designs, layouts, colors, fonts, and images. Some of these were strictly visual, containing no texts, while others included anecdotes, bits of conversation, jokes, and commentary. In fact, many printing houses issued all of their stock cards and even some custom cards in serial form. Printers encouraged retailers and advertisers to purchase cards in series by offering discounts and free customization with large orders.[64]

Serialized trade cards borrowed their form from the serialized narratives found in contemporary literary magazines. Fiction published in serial form first emerged in the United States in the 1840s and grew to dominate many of the "family" weeklies and monthlies after 1865.[65] Subscription costs had also declined after 1865, making serials increasingly available to an expanding middle-class audience with the leisure time and money available to spend on such pleasurable reading. In this way, serialized trade cards, as a new media form, built upon individuals' familiarity with existing media. Readers accustomed to following a segmented literary narrative through installments in magazines could easily transfer this skill to trade cards. Thus, serial trade cards reinforced existing cultural literacies related to social reading and appealed to consumers' impulse to seek out and collect media that would allow them to complete the story.[66]

In one set of cards advertising Diamond Package Dyes, the printer incorporated both visual and literary elements to craft a humorous narrative (figure 4.13). In the first card (upper left), the viewer enters a scene where two women fight over one man's love. In subsequent cards in the story, the women both entreat him with promises of devotion, but while one woman pretends to kill herself by jumping into the ocean in order to win the man's sympathy, the other threatens to kill herself (or him) in the absence of his love. The penultimate scene sees the red-haired woman pointing two guns, one at herself and one at the man. He's holding the weakened other woman in the moment after she's been pulled from the sea, though she's still forlorn and holds a bottle of poison to her lips. While the reader might expect a depressing and dramatic conclusion to such a Shakespearean setup, the final card shows the three deciding to move to Utah (presumably as polygamists), and "live and dye happy."[67] In its depiction of romance, attempted suicide, and attempted murder, this narrative draws on themes popularized by Shakespeare's *Romeo and Juliet* and Leoncavallo's opera *Pagliacci*.[68] Yet, the cards invert and parody the melodrama of Shakespeare and Leoncavallo by adapting contemporary debates surrounding polygamy and its practice in the West. The satiric twist at the conclusion of this short tale lies in the threesome's decision to move to Utah (as an alternative to suicide and murder), thus resulting in a humorous conclusion to what otherwise appeared to be a very dire

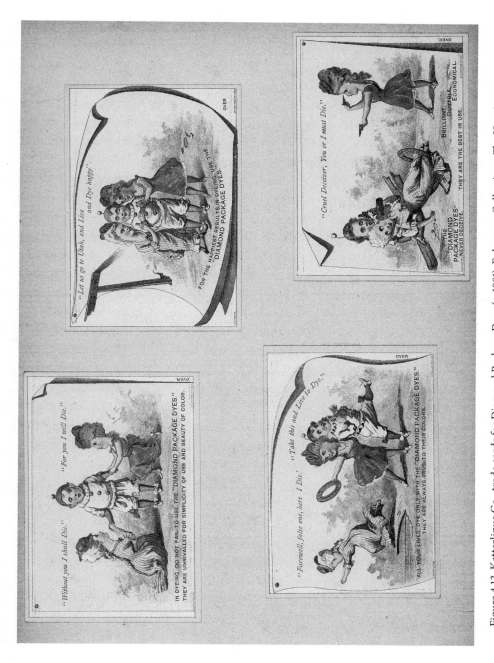

Figure 4.13. Ketterlinus Co., trade cards for Diamond Package Dyes (c. 1881). Ephemera Collections, The Huntington Library, San Marino, CA (ephBTM).

situation.[69] Cultural familiarity with these contemporary themes and debates would ensure that certain individuals would understand the transgressive humor of this narrative.

Throughout this series, the viewer is reminded of the product for sale—Diamond Package Dyes—as the text continually uses misspellings and puns to include the product (clothing dyes) in the text itself (often substituting "dye" for the word "die"). The weird little characters and their interesting costumes contribute to the humor of these cards (however dark), poking fun at the treatments of love and devotion that filled sentimental greeting cards and theatrical melodrama at the time. Humor and narrative thus work together in the cards, inviting the viewer to enter the story in progress and enjoy the cards as something other than advertisements. At the same time, the intentional and repeated references to the product (dye) throughout the narrative demonstrate a linguistic attempt at building consumer awareness of the product. This set of trade cards condenses several layers of the viewer's experience—enjoyment of the humorous serial form, entertainment in scrapbooking, and economic education of the product's qualities—into a singular encounter tied to Diamond Package Dyes. In so doing, this particular set of serial trade cards represents one possible method of integrating entertainment and advertising messages into a memorable experience associated with the trademarked product, one that might prompt the consumer to recall the experience upon subsequent encounters with the product in public space. This sort of blending of commercial message with memorable entertainment, encoded into a material object that could prompt memory recall, prefigured the branding techniques that would later emerge after 1920.

Design Innovations

As these examples suggest, chromolithography, print and design innovations, and entertainment aesthetics came together in important ways in advertisements during the last quarter of the nineteenth century. Printers' work on outdoor advertising would also lend important lessons for nascent visual branding strategies. Chromolithographed posters could be spied across the United States, both in and outside retail spaces. In the countryside, large rocks and other natural elements became home to painted advertising murals that promised to catch the eye of passengers riding on one of the recently expanded railway lines.[70] Cities boasted an expanding cacophony of advertising signs, posters, and billboards that engulfed urban architecture. Individuals might feel dwarfed by the towering circus displays that stretched up the walls of the highest buildings or bewildered by the fluid, artistic designs of contemporary theatrical posters. The exponential growth of outdoor advertising after 1865 even pushed some states to enact limitations and restrictions on the size, frequency, and placement of out-door advertisements in an effort to discourage the public "nuisance" they cre-ated.[71] Not to be outdone, urban department stores created dazzling window displays and immersive streetscapes that enticed pedestrians to enter, where they found lavish, theatrical "dream worlds" that touted the abundance and opulence of the Gilded Age.[72] These spectacular visual experiences transformed American culture and society.

As outdoor advertising seemed to explode in volume, attracting and keep-ing the public's attention became even more challenging. Poster artists created new graphic typefaces and image-heavy designs, while printers devised ways to print colorful posters with increasing precision and efficiency.[73] A key design innovation came when French poster artists, such as Jules Chéret, created graphically interesting and minimalist designs that were "novel and striking" in order to capture public attention in the unpredictable urban environment.[74] Texts became more graphic, melting the rigidity of existing line justifications and flowing organically with the dancing silhouettes showcasing the new mu-sical revues at the nightclubs of Paris. Such integrative designs joined word and image into a "single visual utterance" that reconfigured the sights and expe-riences of the nineteenth-century city.[75] These posters would pave the way for twentieth-century developments in graphic design, particularly in the way post-ers reduced advertising messages to a truncated form of visual and symbolic communication.

Chromolithographed trade cards also forced American advertisers to learn how they might abbreviate their commercial messages in distinct, visually interest-ing designs, as the cards had to communicate commercial information to suc-ceed as advertisements. Just as they had with newspapers, printers gradually devised ways to maintain and improve visual interest in trade cards without sac-rificing the success of the commercial message. This meant reminding readers of the commercial purposes of these objects by integrating trademarks and other identifying symbols onto custom trade cards. Thread manufacturers in the 1880s, for example, used their trade cards as mini-posters that consistently reminded viewers of the logo and the product.[76] In trade cards for J. & P. Coats and Clark's brand threads, the product labels and logos became central elements of the cards' designs, to varying degrees of success. In some cards, the logo appears as an afterthought: Printers might have added it to stock cards at random or incor-porated spools of threat that float awkwardly in the pictorial scene (figure 4.14).[77] These somewhat clumsy additions—which often overlapped with or distorted other visual elements of the design—draw attention to the logo, but they betray rather unsophisticated attempts at cultivating a visual awareness of the trademark among potential audiences.

Figure 4.14. Unknown printer, trade card for Clark's Mile-End Thread (c. 1880). Warshaw Collection of Business Americana, Archives Center, National Museum of American History, Smithsonian Institution.

In contrast, a series created by Louis Prang in 1878 demonstrates a more elegant approach to balancing the narrative elements of the trade card's imagery with logo awareness.[78] One card shows a child sitting on top of a large spool of thread, waving his hands wildly in the air while other children attempt to wrangle a kite that has gotten loose. The action of the scene creates a sense of urgency and excitement, while the brilliant red background highlights the gold, white, and blue design of the Clark's trademark (figure 4.15). Tucked into the barrel shape beneath the sitting child, the logo appears slightly to the right of center and draws the viewer's eye through its successful use of contrasting colors. The round Clark's logo overtakes the barrel, transforming the object upon which the child sits into a large spool of thread. This is the very thread providing the kite string for the yellow flyer caught in the strong gust of wind, and the rescue line to which the four boys cling and pull. Integrating the logo into the narrative in this way centralizes it as a primary visual element in the scene, while the narrative also reinforces the

Figure 4.15. L. Prang & Co., custom trade cards for Clark's O.N.T. thread (1878). Jay T. Last Collection of Printing and Publishing: Louis Prang Archive, The Huntington Library, San Marino, CA (priJLC_PRG_bin 11).

manufacturer's claims about the inordinate strength of their six-cord threads. Moreover, Prang designed the scale of the scene to occupy the card's entire frame, using diagonal lines in the composition (created by the figures' angled postures and the kite string) to subtly redirect the viewer's gaze toward the Clark's logo. This would likely frustrate album makers' attempts at cropping or trimming certain details from the card's narrative.

Other cards in this series mirrored the color scheme and design elements of this card to highlight the round trademark for Clark's O.N.T. threads, creating visual symmetry and cohesion among the cards in this series. Incorporated into the cards' narratives, the Clark's logo thus becomes an organic element of the cards, not an intrusive and clumsy addition, as in figure 4.14. Both commercial and entertaining, these cards provided a subtle reminder of the product to reinforce the consumer's familiarity with the trademark logo, fusing the individual's experience of the market with his or her experience of the material object. Like outdoor posters, custom advertising trade cards such as these condensed word and image into "visual utterances" that would cultivate memorability and build brand awareness.[79]

By the early 1880s—less than ten years after the introduction of chromolithographed trade cards—writers in the *New York Times* and trade journals were already commenting on the "card mania" that had overtaken the American public.[80] Despite the fact that many cards were designed specifically for white audiences, the fad for collecting chromo cards attracted children, businessmen, young women, and the elderly of all classes and races in the United States and reached from places as remote as the Adirondacks to the bustling avenues of Chicago and the growing urban community in San Francisco.[81] Late in her life, Emma Osgood Carnes spent entire days scouring New York City for the desirable chromos to include in her scrapbook. Diary entries between 1882 and 1885 record her excitement at finding interesting pictures and her deep disappointment when her searches turned up nothing. Carnes's diary illustrates the coveted nature of these cards and their seemingly short supply.[82] Hunted and consumed in large quantities, chromo cards had become essential objects in a parallel cultural practice: album-making and scrapbooking. The intense popularity of album-making in the last decades of the nineteenth century had helped to trigger the "chromo craze," prompting individuals such as Carnes to go to great lengths to search out and acquire suitable cards to include in their albums.

Collecting and Consuming Through Albums

As Emma Carnes's story suggests, most of the trade cards circulating in American society at the end of the nineteenth century would end up in albums, as users collected, exchanged, gifted, manipulated, clipped, pasted, and saved these objects. Since the early nineteenth century, albums had been treasured and entertaining objects for middle-class Americans. Some individuals gave and received blank books as holiday presents, while others bequeathed their albums to family and friends upon their death. Users collaborated on and compiled albums over months, years, and even decades, and they grieved when special albums had been lost or accidentally destroyed.[83] For these individuals, the scraps contained in their albums—the chromolithographed bits of paper, engravings, newspaper clippings, exchange cards, and other tokens they saved—helped them record, remember, and celebrate life, materializing emotion through the objects on the page. Though other ephemera would also be included, many scrapbooks and albums were composed entirely of trade cards; in fact, many of the cards remaining in archival collections today show marks of former album use, including adhesive residue on the text side of the card and cropped edges showing the user's manipulation.[84]

Surviving albums from the Gilded Age point to the myriad ways that individuals used trade cards to create stories, memorialize experiences, and entertain. Scrapbook-keepers might choose to organize their album pages thematically, with attention to pattern and symmetry, or in a narrative form. Blank, pre-bound albums could be purchased at dry goods and stationery stores, though some individuals adapted old ledgers or configured handmade tomes to collect ephemera.[85] Idiosyncratic and deeply personal, scrapbooks (and especially the arrangements on the scrapbook page) can, therefore, be significant tools for understanding American culture as they demonstrate their makers' attitudes toward consumerism, reading, fantasy, and historical events.[86] Yet these albums can also provide clues as to how people responded to advertising and how they incorporated advertising objects into their lives. Appropriating trade cards for personal albums, users showed their willingness to transform this commercial medium for alternative modes of expression. They prioritized the entertainment potential of the trade card, and in the process, they subverted its original intended purpose (advertising).

For example, in certain collage and "paper doll house" albums, individuals regularly appropriated found commercial imagery in order to form coherent narrative scenes.[87] One user constructed a parlor scene from trade cards, wallpaper samples, and engravings (likely taken from ladies' magazines, sales catalogs, or pattern books) (figure 4.16).[88] The oversized baby distorts the scale of the page, having been pasted behind a chair but on top of a velvet couch that has been hand-painted red. Though the album maker's scissor cuts are fairly meticulous, bits of white space peek around the edges of the furnishings in the room, thereby exposing the constructed nature of the page. Clipping the found images from their original contexts, the user has obscured and concealed these sources. We might never know the initial context for the image of the baby, were it not for the appearance of the same baby on a stock card produced by Major and Knapp (c. 1880) in another album (figure 4.17).[89] In the paper dollhouse album, the trade card provided the user with the raw material needed to construct a narrative that likely aided fantasy play, imaginative artistry, and even aesthetic or domestic education.[90]

While the maker of this collage album did not reflect on the book's meaning here, other individuals did include such reactions for posterity. For example, when Elsie Sargeant Abbot collected advertising trade cards and other printed souvenirs from the 1893 Columbian Exposition, she pasted them into her album, and scribbled that the display for Van Houten's Cocoa was "very attractive" (figure 4.18).[91] This rare self-reflection in an album allows historians to glimpse Abbot's interactions with the world of commerce, providing clues as to other

Figure 4.16. Page from paper dollhouse album (c. 1885). Courtesy, the Winterthur Library: Joseph Downs Collection of Manuscripts and Printed Ephemera.

Figure 4.17. Pages from "Art Scraps Book" (1880). Courtesy, the Winterthur Library: Joseph Downs Collection of Manuscripts and Printed Ephemera.

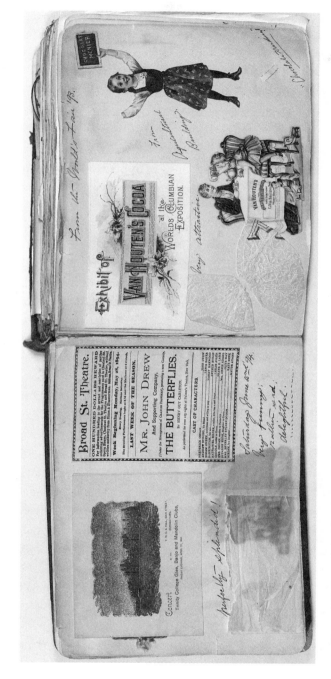

Figure 4.18. Pages from Elsie Sargeant Abbot's scrapbook (1893–1899). Courtesy, the Winterthur Library: Joseph Downs Collection of Manuscripts and Printed Ephemera.

contemporary viewers might have responded. While the album initially offered a repository for her memories of the fair, Abbot continued to use the book to record her daily life long after the exposition had ended. Theater programs and photographs intermingle with pressed flowers, handwritten notes, and other ephemera in the album, chronicling the experiences she had as a young middle-class woman traveling about the Eastern Seaboard. Next to a program from a concert, Abbot wrote that the performance was "perfectly splendid!"[92]

For Abbot, the advertisers' cards she collected from the fair became material signifiers that memorialized her interactions with the world of commerce, just as pressed flowers and letters would concretize her private relationships with family and friends. She curated her album to blend these spheres in imitation of her own daily life, like a visual diary preserving her memories and emotions. The chromolithographed images on trade cards provided visual mementos of Abbot's experiences in much the same way that snapshots might capture everyday life for the generation that followed. Interlacing her experiences as a consumer with her private thoughts and emotions, Abbot's album facilitated the projection of sentimental emotions onto advertising trade cards, commercial goods that had become surrogate objects for emotional and personal expression through the cultural practice of album-making.

In developing and distributing trade cards, printers were integrating advertising into an existing culture of exchange and fundamentally transforming consumers' relation to the market. If most users manipulated trade cards for album-making, we might be tempted to see trade cards as altogether unsuccessful advertisements. But chromolithographed trade cards actually succeeded all too well: They helped precipitate a cultural fad for collecting chromos and creating albums, which must have had an indirect effect of boosting product sales and consumption (even if individuals only purchased more products to obtain more cards). Grafted into an older practice of album-making, the cards—and especially the sentiments and experiences the cards referenced—became a treasured component of interpersonal exchange in this period. With trade cards, printers found a way to create memorable and meaningful advertisements for public consumption. In fact, the cards were so meaningful that, when actual cards were not available, individuals improvised.

For example, in the 1890s Stella Morris Osgood kept an album that acted as both diary and scrapbook, sequentially recording events from her daily life and materializing these experiences through paper goods. In late February 1894, she received three hand-painted cards from Fanny Wright.[93] Crafted on plain white cards measuring about 3 x 5 inches, the watercolors are vertically oriented and feature simple designs: one card shows a diagonal sprig of red holly berries, another features a similar sprig of wild blue violets, and the third shows several purple and yellow pansies. These cards seem to intentionally mimic Prang's wildflower album cards from the 1860s and the trade cards that Prang would produce a decade later (see figure 4.4). Perhaps Wright had seen Prang's album cards pasted in a tome by a friend or relative; it is difficult to imagine that she created them without any prior knowledge of Prang's chromos. Knowing that individuals gifted chromo cards as expressive tokens, it seems possible that Wright's handmade reproductions may have been intended to serve as surrogate chromos, however augmented and improved because of their handmade status. Her impulse to produce the handmade gifts for her friend makes the gesture all the more important: a true token from Fanny's heart for Stella. Yet it is important to remember that Stella Osgood consumed Fanny Wright's handmade cards alongside other printed ephemera that symbolized aspects of Osgood's public and private life, suggesting that, for her, the handmade cards not only bore resemblance to the other printed objects she saved, but they were equally as important.[94]

Yet, as striking as Osgood's album cards are, hand-drawn images like this were not unusual inclusions for scrapbooks. Several women sketched cascading blocks and rectangular grids onto their scrapbook pages, collecting signatures on the blanks to create an illusion of a pile of calling cards spilling across the page.[95] Other albums included drawings of stock trade cards delicately rendered in pencil, offering an artistic study of the physical object. In Lizzie Cadmus's album, for example, Albert Whitman crafted a skillful flower around his signature, penned to celebrate Valentine's Day in 1880. Here, a beautiful pink blossom outlines and frames a text box enclosing his signature, mimicking the appearance of a decorated calling card (compare figures 4.19 and 4.4).[96] Memorializing his relationship with Lizzie through this image, Albert's drawing becomes a surrogate for the material token he perhaps wished he could give: the chromo card. His drawing points to the emotional significance of giving such a card as a present. It suggests that the material object could be an expressive and meaningful token that symbolized interpersonal relationships, and one that would continue to evoke emotion and memory when saved in an album.

Moreover, Whitman's drawing demonstrates the reciprocal nature of American consumer culture as it evolved in the 1880s and 1890s. Whitman appropriated an object of commercial culture—rather, he copied the object and appropriated its cultural meanings—into what was otherwise a semiprivate display of friendship (the autograph album).[97] Just as commercial culture might borrow from the codes of sentiment—printing flowers and children on chromo cards that sold banal objects like shoes—so too might these ubiquitous objects of commerce be borrowed for sentimental purposes.

Yet here, it is not just the commercial object that gets borrowed but its simulacra—its immaterial trace; its aura—that has been borrowed to communicate

Figure 4.19. Page from Lizzie Cadmus's album (1877–1882), showing Albert
Whitman signature, February 14, 1880. Courtesy, the Winterthur Library: Joseph
Downs Collection of Manuscripts and Printed Ephemera.

emotional connection, to maintain social networks, and, above all, to entertain.
Purposeful and deliberate, drawings like Whitman's enable us to see the ways
that Cadmus's album generated multiple layers of entertainment, both for the
signatories and for the owner herself. Penning a thoughtful verse and adding a
pretty picture to Cadmus' album, the signatories might take pleasure in crafting
a personal gift for their friend, Lizzie, who would likely reflect fondly upon such
drawings each time she reopened her album. Trade cards and albums prompted
these interactions as they circulated through American society. With each exchange, each pasted scrap, and each glimpse, trade cards had the potential to
generate pleasure for users, and individuals gradually learned to find (and even
to expect) entertaining pictures and narratives in advertising. Printing and advertising innovations facilitated all of this. Trade cards had become integral
components of daily life and personal experience in the Gilded Age, helping to
mediate relationships while reconfiguring individuals' interactions with the market and the world of commerce.

Trade Cards' Decline

Many factors contributed to the decline of trade-card production and distribution around 1900, including changes in advertising agencies and technologies. Seeking more control over advertising designs, advertising agents began

promoting magazine advertising as a more efficient medium, especially given rising subscription rates, wider distribution areas, and the new photographic reproduction techniques available. They did this as debates over the value of advertising imagery raged on in the trade press. While Lewis Saxby praised the design skills of printers, many other admen were quick to hold up chromolithographed trade cards as the sort of quaint, old-fashioned, and unscientific advertising tactics that ought to be shed in the new century. They grouped the work of printers with such old-fashioned techniques, encouraging potential clients to seek out the modern perspectives and state-of-the-art training of professional admen instead. Moreover, as collectible objects, chromo cards were eclipsed by two other rising media, both of which provided new modes of entertainment: postcards and snapshot photographs. The consolidation of the lithographic industry after the depression of the 1890s and the growing popularity of illustrated postcards meant fewer producers of handheld exchange cards and a shifting demand toward the mailing variety.[98] These developments coincided with a rise in personal photography and the compilation of photograph albums, especially following the introduction of the famous Kodak "Brownie" camera in 1900. Instead of projecting domestic fantasies onto found imagery, more and more album makers could use their own snapshots to create personalized friendship galleries.[99] With fewer printers making them, and few firms or consumers demanding them, the trade card fad fizzled around 1900, almost as quickly as it had ignited.

*   *   *

Recognizing an opportunity to capitalize on two popular cultural practices after the Civil War—collecting chromolithographs and making albums—printers and lithographers had experimented with consumer-focused appeals to create a memorable new advertising medium. From the 1870s through the 1890s, printers used trade cards to elicit an emotional response to advertising and thus departed from the "reason why" strategies that had commonly framed earlier advertising modalities.[100] Chromolithographed trade cards helped advertisers establish rapport with consumers by drawing from familiar iconographic tropes, deploying heartwarming images of children and flowers, humorous serial narratives, and crude representations of ethnic Others in order to advertise goods and services. Printers knew and understood that such images would heighten the cards' popularity with the public. They purposefully designed trade cards to work within existing cultures of collecting and exchange, reconfiguring older media—like calling cards, album cards, and collectible chromo prints—for commercial purposes. As a form of cultural currency, advertising trade cards facilitated the expression of classed and racialized identities for both producers

and consumers. In so doing, trade cards established lines of communication between these groups, reframing their interactions within a realm of sociability
rather than commerce. Importantly, trade cards did not inevitably foreshadow
the success of magazine ads later; they were an advertising experiment intended
to capitalize on an existing cultural fad: the chromo craze. But this fad holds the
clues to understanding the chromolithographed trade card's impact as an advertising innovation that transformed advertising practice moving forward. Examining the practice of album-making points us toward the reception of
advertising trade cards, illuminating their functions as entertaining and meaningful objects in the nineteenth-century culture of exchange.

But to fully understand their rise as advertising media and popularity as
album collectibles, we must situate trade cards on a timeline that also traces the
changing visuality of newspaper advertising and the growing necessity of establishing, maintaining, and protecting commercial reputations. To function
as advertisements, trade cards leveraged existing cultural ideas about communicating identity and character. As a result, they helped advance expert understandings of the visual work of advertising imagery and provided new modes
of communicating one's character to the public. Printers and advertisers
would not have engaged in this experiment if they had not already recognized
the utility of sentimental icons in referencing character and authenticity, on the
one hand, and the entertainment potential of mass-produced chromo cards, on
the other. Printers had learned those lessons through their newspaper work
over the previous four decades and applied them when designing advertising
trade cards.

A breakthrough came when printers such as Louis Prang successfully integrated the trademark logo onto entertaining trade cards (see figure 4.15). His cards
for Clark's O.N.T. threads fused two important consumer experiences into a
singular event: an encounter with entertaining material objects and a visual
encounter with the trademark logo. Through their material appearance and format, all trade cards had invited consumers to appropriate the objects as raw
materials for their scrapbooks; the medium itself had emerged already embedded into an existing culture of album-making that depended on such goods for
personal expression. As such, these complimentary souvenirs from the world of
commerce held the potential to earn goodwill for advertisers through simple
references to reciprocity and gift-giving. But Prang's Clark's O.N.T. cards, along
with other custom cards with integrated product labels and trademarks, expanded that potential by creating a direct association with the trademark. The
Clark's cards offered visual utterances that layered all of these meanings
together—sentiment, gift-giving, commercial experiences, memorable narratives, collectability, and personal expression—condensing them into the logo

itself. In the evolution of branding practices, trade cards provided a brief yet highly influential step toward investing the trademark logo with emotion, reputation, and personal experience—qualities that today's practitioners assert as essential to successful branding campaigns.[101] This evolution was collaborative and experimental, and it would not have been possible without the creative and intellectual contributions of printers, their clients (advertisers), their industry partners (admen), and their audiences (the public).

From the standpoint of admen, trade cards might have been considered a failed experiment. Users' willingness to reorient, trim, cut, and otherwise manipulate trade cards in albums demonstrated consumers' outright disregard for the commercial message as they privileged the image over text. Though trade cards' collectability provided a positive benefit, in the end this entertainment function led to their discontinued use as advertisements. This ought to remind historians that, at least in advertising, processes and practices are never predetermined, and success is never guaranteed. Yet, even as the cards became prized objects that consumers gifted, regifted, and preserved in albums, the cards' commercial messages and origins could never be completely erased from viewers' memories. Integrating colorful and amusing images onto media that circulated in an existing culture of reciprocal exchange, Louis Prang and others shifted the terms of advertising and consumption toward an emphasis on visual images. This experiment was just one step in the ongoing development of advertising practice, helping to facilitate a transition from textual variations on the black-and-white newspaper page to the loud, visually arresting posters and billboards that papered the city streets by 1900. As an early form of "advertainment," trade cards offered a glimpse at the profit potential of using entertainment media in advertising campaigns.[102]

While the memory of trade cards faded after the turn of the century, their lessons remained—colorful, entertaining advertisements had become a necessity in America's commercial culture. Vision and visuality ruled the day, as newspapers, posters, and trade cards had shown the profitability of using images to augment advertising appeals. In the 1880s, advertisers continued to experiment with tactics that would cultivate rapport with consumers. At the same time, they found new visual ways to demonstrate character and class. They continued to emphasize character through carefully chosen rhetoric, utilizing the middle-class language of respectability to speak to like-minded consumers. Testimonials and endorsements also continued to provide valuable strategies for earning consumers' trust, and advertisers found new ways to curate these letters of recommendation to maximize their relatability for audiences. Keeping in mind the old paradigms of earning a positive reputation, advertisers thus adapted to the changing industrial environment of the Gilded Age and Progressive Era.

In considering new visual strategies, advertisers combined these lessons about reputation and character with the push toward entertainment aesthetics. Advertisers continued to work with printers, but they also took advantage of the new services offered by expanding advertising agencies. Through the last quarter of the century, the industry unveiled fictional trade characters and advertising personalities that further developed the narrative potential of entertaining advertisements, while preserving the same goal of earning goodwill. Maintaining their focus on consumers' preferences and tastes, advertisers and admen adjusted their strategies to reference contemporary public concerns about food safety, while drawing from older, familiar images that symbolized purity and health. Their acute understandings of American culture provided the intellectual and iconographic framework that allowed advertisers and admen to tailor their messages to the white middle class. Again, they combined text and image in ways that cemented together the dual approaches of building rapport and crafting memorable visual experiences through entertaining and novel images. But most important, advertisers continued to take steps to build their brands, layering each of these important discourses together to conceptualize corporate identity as something intrinsically connected to visual symbols and advertising, which in turn helped to organize, symbolize, and quantify consumers' trust.

CHAPTER 5

Visualizing Character

Earning Goodwill Through Word and Image

In the first decade of the twentieth century, the Franco-American Food Co. unveiled a new advertising personality called the "Little Chef." The fresh-faced white boy held a steaming pot, and wore a clumsily buttoned coat and a white chef's hat atop his plump, curly haired head. Ads featuring the youngster often touted the pure ingredients used in Franco-American foods and invited readers to visit their "kitchens." "My standard is high," began one 1909 ad, positioning the child as the company's master chef. In the ad, the Little Chef speaks directly to the viewer, inviting us to see the production process ourselves. "I select all food materials before they enter the Franco-American kitchens, and test all our products before they go out," he continues. His eyes gleaming, he brings his finger to his smiling lips to get a taste of the dish he's prepared. "In this way," he explains, "the Franco-American reputation for Quality [*sic*] never diminishes" (figure 5.1).[1] The boy leans over, somewhat precariously perched on two tiny black-booted feet, holding the pot in front of him as if beckoning to the reader. His smile invites the reader into his space, while the first-person perspective of the copy reinforces the intimate interaction we have with him as Franco-American's humble representative. The child becomes a visual metaphor for a range of quality controls implemented by Franco-American and, through his speech, he personifies corporate responsibility. With the Little Chef, Franco-American created a stand-in for the corporation—a fictional personality through which it could project its altruistic intentions toward the public. The Little Chef acted as a public relations figurehead, a being that might intercept the public's questions and anxieties and preemptively calm any fears of adulteration in the packaged product. All of this was communicated through print. Word and image work together in this ad to construct a humble and virtuous public persona

Figure 5.1. N. W. Ayer & Son Advertising Agency, "My Standard is High," eighth-page print advertisement for Franco-American Foods (1909). N. W. Ayer & Son Advertising Agency Records, Archives Center, National Museum of American History, Smithsonian Institution.

for Franco-American, thereby helping to build and maintain the company's reputation and goodwill.

While the chromo craze was still underway in the Gilded Age, merchants and advertisers continued to develop the entertainment aesthetics that had evolved through print ads and trade cards. Yet, they also continued to rely on established modes of demonstrating character in print, for "character" remained an important framework for risk assessment in American business and finance.[2] The strategies for building reputation had, by this point, become second nature in the American commercial sector, disbursed through success manuals and institutionalized in trade journals such as the *Layman Printer* and *Printers' Ink*. These strategies included printing testimonials and endorsements, inviting customers to visit the factory, and creating visual representations of company sincerity. By 1900, entertainment aesthetics and the culture of character came together, literally, through fictional trade characters. Drawing from established rhetorics and iconographies of virtue, these spokes-characters offered the potential to build both real and imagined connections between producers and consumers. Trade characters depended on vision and symbolism for their success; they commodified the field of vision in order to cultivate desire among consumers. Like the other visual media discussed in this book, trade characters became the conduits through which corporations built, maintained, and quantified their reputations, or what today's practitioners would call "brand value."

In the world of American business in the 1880s and 1890s, open demonstrations of good character—whether of an individual or a firm—remained central to cultivating successful commercial relationships. Even as credit transactions became more formalized, trade continued to be highly negotiated through a personalized language that drew from older notions of honor and trust. Moreover, the criteria for measuring creditworthiness had not changed much since the earlier part of the century. In addition to capital holdings, a person's reliability in paying debts, his or her tendency to engage in (or avoid) vice, and his or her reputation in the local community remained important factors in determining creditworthiness (which was, by definition, a measure of a person's trustworthiness and integrity).[3] Yet, it is worth noting that social and cultural biases also structured creditworthiness: Prevailing gendered and racial stereotypes limited the professional and investment opportunities for both women and blacks, which could prevent them from demonstrating their reliability in ways that might earn additional lines of credit. Barred from serving on juries and relegated to second-class status, African Americans faced discrimination and predatory lending practices under America's hardening Jim Crow policies.[4] Thus, antebellum-era definitions of virtue and respectability—however flawed these were—continued to structure economic relationships in many ways at the end of the nineteenth century.

Cultural discourse mirrored this institutional apparatus in emphasizing the importance of virtue and character for the market. In the Gilded Age and Progressive years, wealthy industrialists such as Andrew Carnegie began promoting older notions of virtue and character as essential ingredients for social mobility and economic success in America's rapidly industrializing society.[5] In autobiographies, speeches, and business primers, Carnegie and others articulated a moralized vision of the world that blended Protestant ethics with then-prevalent conversations about rugged masculinity and struggle—conversations that were ensconced in racialized arguments about degeneracy and Social Darwinism. In this self-help literature, the older concepts of "honesty, frugality, industry, reliability, and loyalty" were reframed as "the force of character" and "true manhood," phrases that stood as euphemisms for a particular strand of white, Christian, and middle-class masculinity that was virtuous, yet tough, and able to endure the challenges of modern industrial life.[6] Carnegie and his peers argued that one's character helped configure drive and inventiveness, fashioning entrepreneurship in ways that paralleled the moralized rhetoric of their antebellum counterparts. In short, strong character could translate into strong capital—at least for some—and thus cultivating character was important to both personal and financial success.

Epistolary Advertising in the Gilded Age

For these and other reasons, demonstrating character remained an important goal for advertisers, just as it had been earlier in the century. Gilded Age advertisers continued to rely on language and epistolary conventions to display their character and transparency to others. Many of these displays still took place in letters, where individuals articulated personal and commercial relationships, negotiated status, and maintained social and commercial networks. As they had earlier in the century, manufacturers in the Gilded Age used letters to accept, fill, and invoice orders from customers; informally advertise new products and services; maintain relations with existing customers; and solicit new customers, particularly in business-to-business oriented industries such as printing.[7] Efforts to economize this form of general communication even led some business owners to develop newsletters and mass mailings that would accompany product catalogs, in an early form of direct-mail advertising.

A look at some examples of these otherwise mundane letters illustrates how manufacturers attempted to interweave novelty and character into informal communications, thereby blending correspondence with advertising. Epistolary conventions still structured some advertising practices, and, in general, the symmetry between business correspondence and advertising suggests that some firms saw both media as equally important avenues for directly communicating with clients. In many ways, circulars acted as both private correspondence *and* advertisements—they arrived in personally addressed envelopes with formal salutations and signatures, but their content was entirely commercial in character.

Boston lithographer Louis Prang frequently used epistolary forms to appeal to the retail stationery trade in the 1870s and 1880s, through both scheduled and ad hoc distribution schemes. For special notices and seasonal announcements, Prang created reproducible form letters printed in a script-like font, sometimes even including a facsimile of Prang's signature at the close (figure 5.2).[8] The scripted font diverged from the common serif style fonts used in formal printed notices and newspapers (such as Agate or Times New Roman) and gave the appearance of handwritten correspondence. As a skilled printer, Prang could have chosen any number of fonts to communicate his message. This font choice was deliberate, selected perhaps in an effort to mask the mass-produced nature of the letter or to show off his firm's skill and technological acumen. The letter's form gestures to the presence of human hands, creating the fiction that Prang himself had taken the time to compose the missive. By adjusting the form and appearance of his advertisements, Prang connected the mailing to genres of correspondence, which were, in turn, linked to literacy, education, and character.[9] In his efforts to incorporate these visual forms into otherwise textual product announcements, Prang appropriated the symbolism of this culture of letter-writing for his commercial ventures.

In the mid-1880s, Prang began issuing a newsletter to clients under the title "Weekly Letter." The circulars described new designs and products for each season and included editorial commentary on issues relevant to the printing industry. These newsletters grew to be a more efficient and regular mode of communicating the information previously contained in his form letters, and thus show the evolution of Prang's direct-mail techniques over time. Again, Prang took steps to emphasize the epistolary form in these circulars. Whereas Prang often signed his official business correspondence with closings such as "Truly Yours," "Yours Respectfully," and "Sincerely Yours," each "Weekly Letter" ended with the closing "Your Friends, L. Prang & Co."[10] Inserting the word "friend" into the closing changed the nature of Prang's constructed relationship with his clients—from a relationship defined strictly by business to one that implied a more personal connection between the correspondents. As J. C. Ayer had done in the 1850s, Prang placed his readers (comprised of current and potential customers) within a sphere of familiar, intimate address. Moreover, the weekly distribution of these circulars, in letter form, helped construct the fiction of a personal relationship with his clients maintained by regular, friendly correspondence.[11]

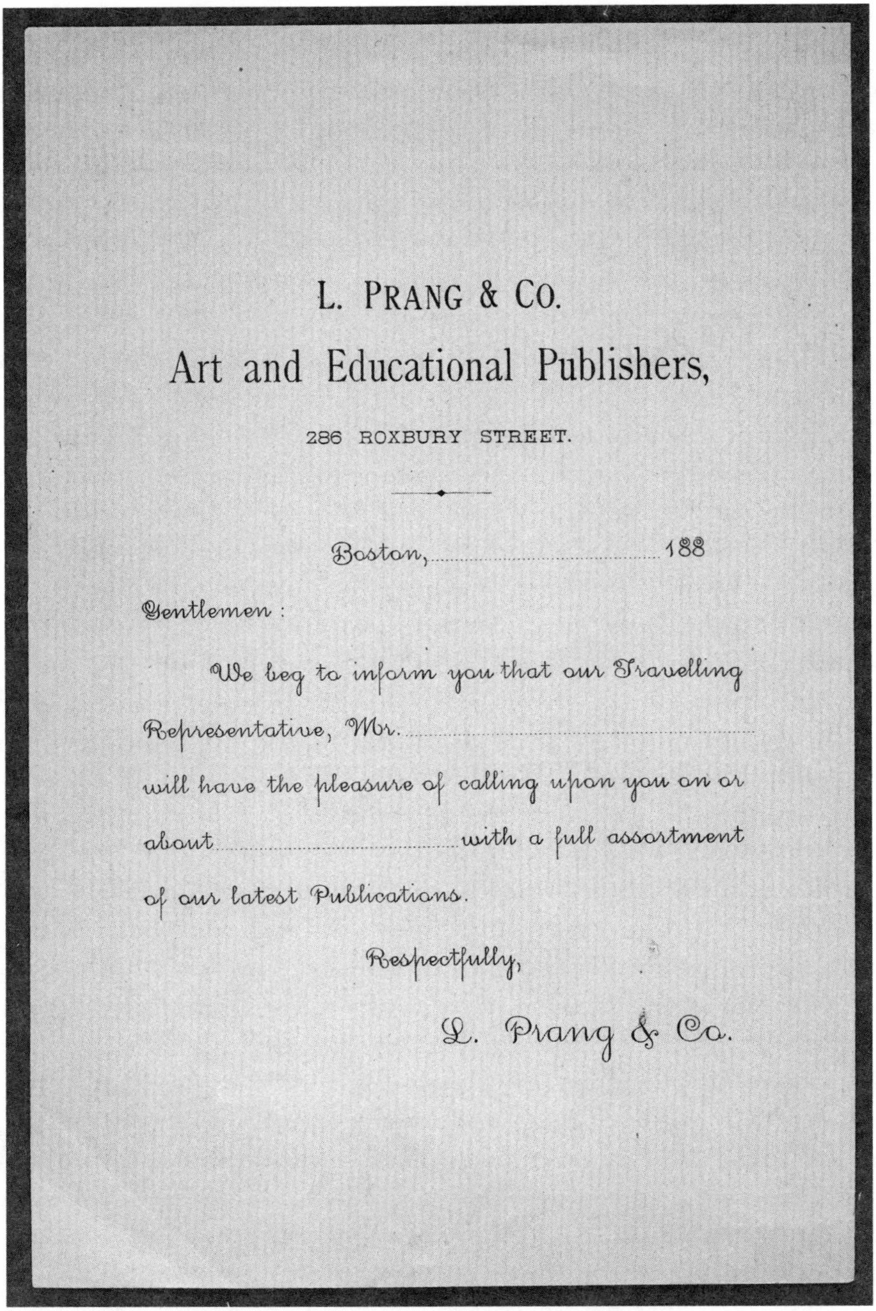

L. PRANG & CO.

Art and Educational Publishers,

286 ROXBURY STREET.

———◆———

Boston,..188

Gentlemen :

We beg to inform you that our Travelling

Representative, Mr...

will have the pleasure of calling upon you on or

about..with a full assortment

of our latest Publications.

Respectfully,

L. Prang & Co.

Figure 5.2. Louis Prang & Co., "Notices to the Press" (1880–1889). Jay T. Last Collection of Printing and Publishing: Louis Prang Archive, The Huntington Library, San Marino, CA (priJLC_PRG_bin 6).

Prang's example suggests that formal indices of character continued to structure business-to-business correspondence in the Gilded Age, just as they had in Volney Palmer's time; this was especially true for the advertising industry. For example, advertising agent J. Walter Thompson (New York) regularly sent rate guides and advertising primers to current and potential clients between 1880 and 1920.[12] Each book included an introductory letter to the reader, signed by Thompson, that framed the solicitation within familiar epistolary conventions. The letters laid out Thompson's business philosophy, but they also attempted to substantiate his (and his firm's) character. First, the letters emphasized the personal attention the client could expect with customized service tailored to his or her particular needs. This promise of personal attention became a key selling point in business-to-business appeals well into the twentieth century.[13] To demonstrate his integrity, Thompson established high ethical standards for his clients and industry. In one 1887 guidebook, Thompson publicly refused to work with merchants and others whose moral character could not be verified, adding that he only accepted clients from "the solid, mercantile class, who use advertising as a means to increase their already established business, or to introduce some meritorious new article to the public."[14] To earn the patronage of the "better class" of American consumers, Thompson urged his readers to set similarly high moral standards for their trade partners. Like Volney Palmer, Thompson drew upon then-salient cultural and class-based ideals to appeal to potential clients, suggesting that the most intelligent and enterprising modern men understood the importance and value of advertising. He deployed language cues to position himself and his desired clients firmly within the middle class, while promising to deliver "comfortably" situated patrons of the same class.[15]

Decades later, Thompson explained his tactics for personally addressing the reader in this fashion. First and foremost, Thompson suggested that it was necessary to keep in constant contact with customers so that communications became habitual and familiar. If communications came too infrequently, he cautioned, customers might get into the habit of "thinking of you as someone they 'used to know'" rather than as a trusted friend and business partner.[16] To reinforce his professions of altruism, Thompson signed the letters. One letter from 1887 closed with the words "Yours Very Truly, J. Walter Thompson" scrawled at the bottom of the page in handwritten script.[17] Subsequent publications replicated this form of intimate address, including alternate epistolary closings, such as "Very Truly Yours," "I remain, at your command," and "I remain, at your service."[18] Addressing clients in this familiar way helped Thompson maintain a reputation for personal care, attentiveness, and integrity that added to the air of legitimacy and respectability he constructed about his business.

As an industry that traded in trust and reputation, advertising agents first had to convince potential clients of their own trustworthiness, and then convince the public of the trustworthiness of their clients. In other words, admen had to manage their own goodwill in order to successfully manage the goodwill of others. Emphasizing the importance of regular communication again in 1911, Thompson formalized a general principle that had framed Prang's advertising in the 1880s, and scores of other advertising tactics since the 1840s. Thompson's vocal position as an industry leader after 1900 helped further institutionalize these principles, drawn from an earlier epistolary culture, into generally accepted advertising practice.

Authentication Through Testimonials

In a further effort to demonstrate his firm's worth to potential customers, Thompson's rate guides often included sample advertisements and client lists.[19] As a portfolio of successful advertising campaigns, the firm's lists of satisfied customers provided prospective clients with qualified references and examples of the firm's work. This strategy had been common among advertising firms for decades: Volney Palmer built his advertising business using the names and reputations of current clients to win the favor of new clients. In the 1870s, the advertising firm of N. W. Ayer & Son (Philadelphia) used endorsements from its clients on handbills to publicize the firm's services to local businesses. Indeed, many of the firms researched for this study continued to publish client lists into the 1920s.[20] Such lists worked as informal endorsements of the agencies, much like formal reference lists had done earlier in the century. Like a strong credit report, recommendations and endorsements carried cultural capital that translated into material wealth for the bearer. They provided written guarantees of the bearer's talents and worth, and cultural conventions stressed the importance of providing only honest recommendations when asked.[21]

Given this enduring value of endorsements and recommendations, it is perhaps not surprising that, after the Civil War, advertisers throughout the American Northeast and Midwest broadly relied on testimonials—especially expert testimonials—in ads for products as diverse as household foodstuffs, farm implements and supplies, cosmetics, and services.[22] Celebrity, expertise, and integrity typically contributed to the making of a reliable commercial witness—in fact, the individual's public persona, including perceptions of his or her moral character, often determined the believability of the endorsements he or she provided.[23] In the line of infant foods, for example, manufacturers frequently boasted the endorsements of well-known doctors who could verify the nutritional benefits of the products.[24] In other industries, lawyers, local magistrates, authors, and even politicians might lend their endorsements to the product. In the 1860s, one proprietary medicine merchant published testimonial letters that had been notarized or witnessed by local officials.[25] Louis Prang frequently used endorsements from prominent authors—including Henry Wadsworth Longfellow and Harriet Beecher Stowe—in promoting his chromolithographs, while several other manufacturers claimed the patronage of persons of "high social position" or nobility.[26] Even bankers could serve as useful references: In the 1890s, Sears catalogs included reference letters from regional bankers attesting to the character of the company's proprietors, Sears-Roebuck's local reputation, and the extensive lines of credit it held in Chicago and other major cities.[27] In these ways, witness certifications, professional references, and celebrity endorsements lent additional support to manufacturers' claims in print, drawing from an older culture of writing recommendation letters.

Choosing the right experts to endorse one's product was as important as what the endorser said in any given advertisement. Expert testimonials allowed manufacturers to appropriate the cachet of the expert and his or her title or office, and attach such cultural capital, by association, to the product or service endorsed. Cultural understandings of honor and character had long prescribed honesty in penning such recommendations, for one set his or her own reputation on the line in doing so.[28] The success of testimonials thus hinged upon these cultural assumptions about individual integrity, which were, in turn, connected to enduring class-based assumptions about a person's status and character. A doctor, lawyer, or local magistrate was expected to be honest and operate with integrity because of his educated position and professional status. For Sears, the bankers' endorsements worked in a similar way: They materialized the firm's character, providing evidence of the Sears's economic capital in order to grow its cultural capital (i.e., its reputation) with the public. Yet, while some celebrities and experts willingly lent their names for promotional purposes, others likely did not. Firms that printed endorsements without permission could still leverage the reputation and goodwill of such public figures with few consequences, as readers would have little opportunity to verify the endorsements and celebrities were unlikely to discover the misuse of their names.

Yet, patent-medicine advertisers also used the testaments of presumed "average" men and women. These manufacturers built large quantities of endorsements from plebeian customers that capitalized upon the anonymous authority of print to convincingly recommend the goods at hand. Printing the words of ordinary men and women alongside those of doctors and druggists placed average consumers on equal footing with experts, homogenizing the speakers' status while reinforcing their shared experiences with illness and salvation. This discursive

exchange created in proprietary-medicine almanacs implied a leveling of authority where any user's personal experience could be as important for validating the
product as the professional recommendation of doctors or other experts. As one
New Orleans newspaper editor remarked of testimonials in 1901, "Personal statements of that kind have a tremendous influence in small communities, and
those signed by plain, everyday working people are at present regarded as more
valuable than the indorsement [sic] of celebrities."[29] While celebrities might be
compensated for their testaments, it was generally assumed that average men
and women were not. Yet regardless of the speaker, testimonials would only be
successful if they managed to convince the reader that they spoke nothing but
the truth.

As advertising tactics became more refined over the course of the nineteenth
century, firms developed rhetorical strategies to enhance the believability of the
testimonials they printed. First, advertisers asserted that testimonials came from
individuals who only wanted to share their good fortunes with the public. By
stressing the unsolicited nature of these testimonies, advertisers painted each testifier as an upstanding individual whose honesty and virtue provided the only
motivation for his or her statements. Illustrating character—both of the manufacturers and of the testifiers they quoted—was key: Manufacturers stressed
their own sense of duty in wanting to help the general public just as they underscored the selfless intentions of testifiers. As they had done in the antebellum
period, testimonial writers also displayed their character in the language they
used, in their adherence to proper epistolary forms, and in their outspoken altruism. For example, the *Ayer's American Almanac* for 1854 suggested that the
"sincere convictions of men who testify without interest and without bias" alone
demonstrated the virtues of the Ayer formula. To emphasize this point, Dr. J. C.
Ayer noted that "many [writers] give as their motive in writing, the humane
wish that others in distress may be benefited like themselves."[30] Stressing the
honesty and do-gooder attitude of the writers who vouched for his product, Ayer
aligned his own good intentions in spreading the virtues of his formula with the
good intentions of the thousands of testifiers supporting him.

Moreover, several manufacturers conjured images of praise-filled letters flood-
ing their mailboxes on a weekly basis, indicating that the sheer quantity of positive testimonials could be evidence enough of product worth. The 1878 edition
of *Green's Pictorial Almanac* for the August Flower and German Syrup published
only a few testimonial excerpts but offered to provide one thousand letters from
"prominent men . . . anxious to tell us of the wonderful cures and great merits of
German syrup and August flower" in a separate pamphlet available on request.[31]
The firm thus suggested that there were simply too many letters to print. But by
offering to send additional testimonials in a supplement, the manufacturer received

many of the benefits of displaying the letters without actually having to print them. Prospective customers might feel reassured of their purchases and gain new faith in the product simply by knowing that those testimonials existed. When especially powerful testimonial letters appeared on their desks, manufacturers did not hesitate to reprint them in multiple almanacs, brochures, and other advertisements. For example, the publishers of *Bristol's Illustrated Almanac* reused testimonial letters from Henry P. Marshall, Andrew O. Smith, Charles R. La Porte, and James P. Rodgers in the 1866, 1869, and 1875 editions.[32] Reprints like these further increased the appearance of large quantities of letters continuously arriving by post.

Since the writer's integrity remained a contributing factor in a testimonial's believability, manufacturers often emphasized the unbiased nature of the testaments they received. G. G. Green's 1878 *Almanac* excerpted a letter from a newspaper editor, who noted that "notwithstanding our inability to agree upon a plan for advertising, I will do your medicine justice. . . . Our druggist persuaded me to try a bottle of your German syrup in which I found immediate relief. I am fully convinced it is the best medicine."[33] Here, the begrudging tone actually improves the letter's impact: Noting his business disagreement with the manufacturer bolstered the validity of this editor's testament. His implicit disavowal of the potential for personal gain acted as a rhetorical mechanism for strengthening the impact of his written support of the product. To put it simply, even a man who had a business quarrel with the manufacturer could endorse the product because the product itself was indeed that worthy of praise. Using this testimonial, Green augmented his corporate reputation by emphasizing the virtue of his product as told through a demonstrably impartial third party.

In perhaps a further gesture toward integrity, manufacturers provided readers with the opportunity to personally verify the testaments appearing in print. Several manufacturers published the writer's full name and location alongside the testimonial so that readers could presumably contact the testifiers directly and confirm their endorsements of the product. One firm even encouraged this kind of personal verification. In a publisher's note to the 1854 edition of *Ayer's American Almanac*, J. C. Ayer suggested that even the "humblest yeomanry" and those in the "proudest stations on earth" could confirm the worth of his remedy. Moreover, he intimated that he selected which testimonials to print based on the identities and residences of the writers themselves, noting that "the statements . . . are purposefully taken from different sections of the country, in order . . . to give every man a reference somewhere within his own neighborhood. . . . How loudly they speak is seen [here], but how sincerely can only be appreciated by a personal interview with a patient."[34] Ayer suggested that unsolicited testimonials arrived so abundantly that he had the option to choose letters from the widest geographic representation possible. In so doing, he admitted to tailoring the cache of testi-monials based on demographic or regional factors in order to increase the po-tential for the testimonials' success.[35] This statement also suggested that his formula enjoyed near-universal appeal across the United States and abroad. En-couraging the reader to seek out those testifiers in his or her own town and ver-ify their statements, the manufacturer presented a bold confidence that dared readers to prove him wrong.

Placing the onus of verification on the reader became a common tactic for self-conscious patent-medicine manufacturers attempting to prove the reliabil-ity of the testimonials they printed, and several manufacturers defied the public to uncover false testaments. One prominent example included a regular challenge issued by the Lydia E. Pinkham Company, which manufactured a "Vegetable Compound" for women's ailments and reproductive issues. Boldly, the company offered a $5,000 reward in 1901 for "any person who can show that any of the tes-timonial letters in this book are not genuine or were published before obtaining each writer's special permission."[36] Anticipating public skepticism, the company appeared to denounce charges of fraud and misrepresentation with an especially flamboyant claim of transparency. Such self-conscious claims suggest that alle-gations of testimonial falsehood may have been common and may have threat-ened to undermine the reputation and financial success of the company.

Finally, advertisers attempted to authenticate the testimonials they presented by printing what appeared to be the faces and signatures of the testifiers them-selves. In the 1880s, *Ayer's American Almanac* printed illustrations of individu-als suffering from various ailments alongside testimonials that discussed these particular sicknesses. In later editions, the almanac printed illustrations of healthy, well-dressed individuals beside testimonials, with the implication that the cuts depicted the writers themselves.[37] This almanac set up a pattern of rep-resenting before and after pictures of satisfied customers, images that might add visual weight to the testifiers' personal statements. Other patent-medicine alma-nacs followed suit. Various editions of *Warner's Safe Cure Almanac* included fac-simile signatures and portraits printed alongside the statements of prominent individuals, including the president of Harvard University and the editor of *Century Magazine*.[38] Moreover, in a Pinkham booklet for 1901, one testifier's story was featured with a full-page engraved portrait. Mrs. S. J. Watson's tale chroni-cled her desperation and woe before finding a cure with Pinkham's product. Word and image reinforced the message here: Her pleasant and alert expression un-derscored her return to health, as outlined in the text.[39]

In these examples, faces and signatures provided an illusion of authenticity because they drew from existing cultural codes related to print culture. Signatures had long played an important role in demonstrating authenticity in the public sphere, as Chapter 2 pointed out. When printed with testimonials, signatures appeared to lend authority and veracity to the texts, offering a modicum of accountability to otherwise anonymous printed statements. They authenticated the words they accompanied, just as signatures on product labels demonstrated genuineness or frontispiece portraits authenticated biographies and autobiographies.[40]

On another level, testimonial portraits visually underscored the veracity of the statements by implicitly situating the speakers within the white middle class. In many cases, the reader encountered portraits depicting well-dressed individuals who conformed to Victorian representational codes of demonstrating propriety. Their middle-class dress, clean bodies, tidy hair, and restrained expressions indicate their social status. Persistent popular theories about the visibility of vice and immorality on the body would reinforce the reader's categorization of these individuals within the middle class, as the negative effects of sickness are depicted as temporary ailments that do not damage the individual's inherent character. Such coded references to class and character would implicitly counteract any potential suspicions of dishonesty or fraud.[41] Furthermore, the language used in these testaments reinforced a white, middle-class perspective. Formal epistolary forms, mannered language, and references to middle-class professions and nuclear families all contributed to the performed identities of these testifiers in print, layering additional proof of their character. In these ways, signatures and portraits gave testimonials the illusion of veracity by suggesting that the statements came from real, trustworthy customers with real problems.

Testimonials also provided individual readers, many of whom suffered from the same afflictions, a point of reference and identification—a means of relating to the speaker on the basis of shared experience. In this way, testimonials envisioned an imagined community of users based on shared ailments and symptoms.[42] When a reader identified with the testifier along demographic lines—such as class, marital status, religion, gender, occupation, or regional affiliation—the testimonial could become even more effective in persuading the reader to relate to and trust the writer's testament. In the West in particular, publishing the testaments of locals became an important tactic for appealing to potential consumers. The maker of Bristol's Sarsaparilla regularly printed almanacs for residents in California in the 1870s and highlighted writers' residential and social status in the testimonial pages for these booklets. These "Voices from California" constructed a regional community around the familiar plight of Californians—neighbors and westerners who understood each other and who could confide in one another.[43] Reprinting testaments according to region, from users across the United States, helped to reinforce the shared experience of health and wellness among various populations. In this way, Gilded Age manufacturers created a series of imagined communities that coalesced by region, by ailment, and by the product itself.[44] Addressing consumers along these various affiliations and social identities, Gilded Age manufacturers thus laid the groundwork for dividing and targeting markets according to demographics, a practice that would become more common by the mid-twentieth century.[45]

It is very difficult to know how individuals may have responded to testimonials: Did they view them with skepticism? Did anyone ever seek out the individuals noted in these pamphlets to verify their statements? The historical record largely omits the answers to these questions. Intermittent public criticism of patent medicines—by reformers, journalists, and intellectuals—likely stoked a measure of skepticism among potential consumers. This would be especially true during the Progressive years, when muckraking journalists published exposés revealing broad testimonial scams, including paid testifiers, bribed officials, and outright fabrications crafted by desperate copywriters.[46] Despite this criticism, the patent-medicine industry was quite profitable in the half-century following the Civil War. Advancements in medicine were slow to take hold in the nineteenth century; even by the early twentieth century, many individuals lacked a safe and appropriate way to manage symptoms, residual pain, or complications from sicknesses. Given these factors, it may be fair to assume that testimonials were believable enough, at least to some consumers.[47]

In these ways, language continued to be an important vehicle for advertisers to demonstrate their character to the public at the end of the century and, through such demonstrations, to build their brands.[48] Epistolary forms and formal rhetoric helped advertisers perform their respectability, drawing from familiar cultural codes established by the antebellum middle class. Testimonials, client lists, and celebrity endorsements added more layers of appeal, again drawing from culturally recognized language forms and class-based cues to ensure believability. Finally, advertisers authenticated testimonial endorsements with portraits and signatures, encouraging readers to verify testaments and challenging doubters to find evidence of falsification. Each of these efforts helped profess the producers' character to the public, in a scheme to cultivate rapport and build goodwill. Epistolary advertising, which had grown out of the antebellum culture of character, had evolved to offer new modes of validating and reinforcing advertisers' claims in print.

In the last few decades of the nineteenth century, one notices an interesting slippage between epistolary advertising and novelty. In the 1880s and 1890s, some newspaper advertisements began using script-like fonts that mimicked the appearance of a handwritten note. As Chapter 3 demonstrated, advertisers consistently looked for new ways to disrupt the straight and narrow columns of text that ordered the newspaper page. Woodcut images and other visual idiosyncrasies could help attract the reader's eye, but the delicate appearance of a handwritten note offered something different. Especially when placed in newspaper columns, advertisements like the one for Wanamaker's Grand Depot department store, which ran from 1878 through 1880 (figure 5.3), would have stood out against the straight, uniform columns of text on the newspaper page. The scrawling words are instantly striking, highlighted by the white space framing the little note. This is an irregular script font: Unlike Prang's attempts to use standardized scripted fonts in form letters, Wanamaker's advertisement is instead printed as an image—a facsimile of the original handwritten note. Seemingly crafted from human hands, the visual symbolism of the facsimile ad contradicts the note's mechanical reproduction in newsprint.

This advertisement uses several layers of cultural symbolism to reimagine the reader's relationship to Wanamaker and his stores. First, it serves as a referent to Wanamaker's physical presence. Like a pocket missive unfolded and pasted onto the newspaper page, the words seemed to come directly from the pen of Wanamaker himself. His signature at the bottom reinforces the construction of the advertisement as a personal note and authenticates the ad's text by endorsing the printed message. Just as letters might serve to materialize friendships across vast distances, the ad offers a simulacrum for personal interaction with Wanamaker; it is a stand-in that is almost, but not quite, as good as the original. Moreover, the ad uses the culture of letter writing to recategorize the reader-consumer's relationship to Wanamaker within a more familiar social sphere. As in Prang's form letters, the epistolary style of this ad masked its commercial motives. With this, Wanamaker built upon his reputation for personalized service, as typified in his identity as the man who "cordially invited" customers to call and who would stand at the store's entryway greeting them like guests to a dinner party. Saturated in cultural references to character, manners, and sentiment, the ad presupposes that readers' familiarity with middle-class culture would enable them to recognize such symbolism and transfer those meanings to the ad. Finally, the ad's promise to fulfill each request to the dollar, yard, and satisfaction of the customer reminded readers of the personalized service available in Wanamaker's stores.[49] Form and content work together to reinforce this fiction of personal communication. The visual form disrupts the orderliness of the newspaper page, while the ad's gesture to Wanamaker's hand and its explicit promise of personal attention simultaneously disrupt the impersonality of the other ads on the page. The novelty of the scripted ad shows Wanamaker's efforts to incorporate the entertainment aesthetics then emerging in advertising, but the content and underlying meanings of the ad are still intensely focused on demonstrating his altruism and character.[50]

Such efforts to combine demonstrations of character with novelty and visually distinct designs suggest that these two goals were beginning to collapse

Figure 5.3. Advertisement for Wanamaker's Department Store (at lower center), *Christian Recorder*, January 1, 1880.

together in the last quarter of the nineteenth century. As they had since Palmer's time, admen and business owners used language and cultural capital to gain the public's trust. But the mode of appeal became just as important as the content of the ad, as advertisers and printers began to prioritize entertainment aesthetics.[51] The economic forces of competition largely drove these innovations in print and design, and advertisers doubled down in professing their alignment with the rubric of character. These two concepts—novelty and character—fused together in fictional advertising personalities (also known as "trade characters") at the end of the nineteenth century.

Visualizing Corporate Personality

As trademarks became a more important means of signaling product differentiation in an increasingly competitive market, advertising professionals clamored to create marks that would be memorable and meaningful for consumers. Trade characters emerged as one potential solution at the end of the century. These illustrated figures and animals were entirely fictional, but they drew from contemporary cultural symbols and value systems to develop successful communication avenues to the public. Recent specialists and scholars have noted that trade characters communicate in three ways: by creating product identification, by promoting a brand personality, and by providing promotional continuity.[52] Trade characters express meaning through myth, using their personalities as symbols to transfer meaning to the brand. In this way, trade characters visually represent the particular qualities and attributes a corporation wants identified with its brand, but they do so in such a way as to create the potential for an emotional bond to develop between the consumer and the character. Through carefully constructed cultural symbols, the trade character humanizes the product and appeals to viewers' emotion.[53] In the twentieth century, adult characters, children, and animals with humanistic qualities became the most typical personalities, commonly using humor and sentimental themes to appeal to the public. Experts note that the most successful trade characters today reference timely cultural ideals, but they also evolve and adapt as ideals change. This type of cultural integration can foment more favorable attitudes toward the brand and its products, especially for customers with less experience with a particular brand.[54] Finally, marketing theorists argue that consistency and symmetry across packaging and advertising builds consumers' familiarity with the trade characters over time, promoting product recognition and cultivating nostalgia as child consumers grow up and become consuming adults.[55]

Though trade characters seemed to emerge around 1900, their antecedents can be traced to earlier advertising strategies that used images associated with company figureheads.[56] Many of the now well-understood functions of trade characters—facilitating an emotional bond with consumers, humanizing the corporation or product, and promoting identification through timely cultural references—had all been tactics undertaken by admen and advertisers for decades prior to 1900. Lea & Perrins', for example, used images of its label and bottle in advertising (see figure 2.6), while Joseph Gillott and the Fleischmann Co. included signatures in print ads (see figures 2.2 and 4.7), and other companies used pictures of their factories to identify products.[57] It was not unusual then, when the Lydia E. Pinkham Co. began using its namesake's portrait on advertising in the 1870s. What is interesting about this case is the way the company continued to use Lydia Pinkham's portrait after her death in 1883. The Pinkham Co. shifted its advertising campaigns toward building brand identity in the 1880s, constructing a fictional Mrs. Pinkham as a public representative, trademark, and commercial personality.[58] As the company's initial figurehead and the visual emblem of the company's products and goodwill, the image of Lydia Pinkham became a prominent element in American commerce well into the twentieth century. In turn, she laid the foundations for the rise of trade characters such as the Quaker Oats man and others after 1900.

The construction of Mrs. Pinkham as the company's corporate personality stemmed from advertising campaigns that positioned Lydia Pinkham as a willing correspondent with customers. From the late 1870s, the Pinkham Company regularly invited women to correspond with Lydia Pinkham for "womanly" medical advice.[59] Ad copy frequently appeared in the voice of Lydia herself, entreating women to "Confide in me. Tell me your troubles, frankly and without reservation . . . 'A woman best understands a woman's ills.'"[60] Appealing to potential consumers on the basis of gender, such letters solicited both the trust and purchasing power of other women by leaning on the image of a wise, old woman willing to bestow her age-acquired knowledge on younger generations (figure 5.4). The personal assurances from this friendly stranger, offering to ease a woman's troubles and her mind, helped to characterize the company as one that cared about its consumers' particular feminine problems.[61]

Women who wrote to the company would likely receive a detailed response written by a member of Pinkham's all-female "research team" rather than by Pinkham herself, a fact that the company deliberately obscured for several years following Pinkham's death.[62] Opening with an informal salutation, such as "Dear Friend," such letters included homeopathic remedies for painful menstruation and other maladies, often (but not always) pointing women toward a Pinkham

Figure 5.4. Forbes Co., trade card for Lydia Pinkham's Vegetable Compound (c. 1880). Courtesy, the Winterthur Library: Joseph Downs Collection of Manuscripts and Printed Ephemera.

product. Letters were written on Pinkham letterhead, mailed from the company's home address in Lynn, Massachusetts, and were typically signed "Yours for Health, Lydia E. Pinkham" in the staff writer's hand, which provided a close parallel to Pinkham's own published signature as it appeared in advertising materials.[63] Soliciting letters from its customers and promising advice in return provided the Pinkham Co. with a reciprocal mode of staying in touch with its consumer base, but it also provided a constant stream of quotable material from which to cull testimonials and convincing advertising copy.[64] Before and after letters frequently appeared in Pinkham advertisements, demonstrating the loyalty of satisfied customers to future Pinkham buyers. One such letter said as much between exclamations of gratitude for Pinkham's humanitarianism. The writer, Mrs. I. C. Dale, complained that "I doctored with several doctors, but received no permanent help." According to her story, she happened upon a letter in a newspaper describing similar conditions as hers, and she thought, "If she could be cured, I surely could be helped. . . . I am so thankful now that I did [try your medicine]."[65]

Replicating the salvation narrative that had long characterized testimonial advertising, these letters placed the Pinkham Co. at the center of a community of users who needed and benefited from Pinkham's Vegetable Compound.

Indeed, much of Pinkham's appeal was to create a community of women—women who advised other women, who shared stories with other women, and who had particular knowledge of women's problems—in order to promote the sales of the products.[66] Pinkham's authority rested on the intimate knowledge of women's problems that only a woman could understand. The field of patent medicines and the emergent gynecological profession were both dominated by men at the time; thus, Pinkham's position as a female corporate figurehead was unique. The company wasted no time in exploiting this as an important factor in Pinkham's ability to solve problems and ailments unique to women.[67] Throughout its publications, the company derided the male-dominated world of doctors and pharmacists: Such men morally judged, misguided, and misdiagnosed female patients whose propriety and embarrassment truncated their discussion of intimate medical issues. Pinkham's ad copy thus implicated husbands, doctors, and employers in causing women's troubles and allowing them to persist. Have no fear, the company encouraged: "In addressing Mrs. Pinkham you are confiding your private ills to a woman . . . you can talk freely to a woman." Mrs. Pinkham's "standing invitation" to "women suffering from any form of female weakness" was to write with their concerns. Of these writers, Mrs. Pinkham asked nothing in return, "except their good will"—a subtle suggestion to the relieved sufferer that she should share her story with friends and add her own testament to the pile of praise in favor of Pinkham's remedies.[68]

The Pinkham Co. thus used testimonial advertising in very similar ways to the other examples in this chapter. Emphasizing its own altruistic intentions and those of its testifiers, the Pinkham Co. capitalized on the quantity and quality of feedback letters received at its headquarters in Lynn, Massachusetts. In emphasizing the shared identity and experiences of its users, it helped create a community of female consumers and targeted its marketing toward a fragmented demographic. In these ways, the company's advertising was unremarkable. But the company's positioning of Lydia Pinkham at the center of a circulatory discourse on female illness proved innovative. As a figurehead while she was alive, Lydia Pinkham was responsible for the integrity of the company and its products. After her death in 1883, her portrait remained central to the company's public-facing identity. It appeared on labels, in publications, in official correspondence, and in advertising, and it, therefore, created a consistent visual identity for the company that would help build its brand through 1900.[69] The imagined connections within the community of female users thus rested on the portrait of Lydia Pinkham and the fictional personality created for her through the company's advertising.

The company's gendered appeal to female consumers grew from the image of Lydia Pinkham as an "untitled" grandmotherly woman whose personal experience as an herbalist provided a commercial personality that other women might trust (see figure 5.4).[70] Pinkham's portrait, which resembled cartes-des-visites photographs, encouraged viewers to envision the human scale of production in Pinkham's company and provided a semblance of personal accountability that might speak to customers weary of the growing facelessness of corporate production in the United States.[71] Sitting in three-quarter pose, Mrs. Pinkham looks beyond the viewer with a pleasantly calm expression on her face. Her tightly pulled bun sits at the crest of her head, though tiny gray curls break free to frame her face. She wears a dark, buttoned dress bodice, with a high, ruffled white collar cinched around her neck. Its lacy frills gently grace her jawline and highlight her modest expression. Her clothes and appearance place her firmly within the middle class, while her grandmotherly demeanor exudes an authority that shines through her sage eyes and compassionate expression. Ancillary ads reinforced Pinkham's grandmotherly personality (see figure 4.5), framing her medicinal work within the sphere of domesticity rather than commerce or entrepreneurship. Taken together, these two trade cards (figures 4.5 and 5.4) invite the consumer to reunite Pinkham with her grandchildren in the scrapbook, much like a user would keep a photograph album of his or her own family members. In these ways, Pinkham's advertising used visual and rhetorical cues to demonstrate her character for viewers and to build public goodwill. The portrait became the keystone that held the company's advertising and visual identities together.

Through repetition and consistent placement, the Pinkham Co. successfully transformed this portrait into a logo for the Pinkham brand. With each testament printed in advertising pamphlets and each response letter mailed, the company helped to build the larger-than-life personality of Mrs. Pinkham. Her constructed expertise surpassed the reach of the original woman as the community grew on a national scale. By 1891, sales had increased by 12 percent, in a testament to the success of the letter-writing campaign encouraged by Pinkham Co. advertising and to the power of Lydia's portrait in personifying both the corporation and the product.[72] As her personality grew to celebrity proportions, the phrase "Many thanks to Mrs. Pinkham," became a ubiquitous closing in testimonial letters written to the company.[73] The visual continuity of Pinkham's portrait across advertising media, combined with the company's reciprocal correspondence with consumers, thus crafted a producer-consumer relationship based on habitual and familiar communication in much the same way that Prang had attempted through his form letters and circulars. Pinkham's innovation was to put a face on that epistolary exchange, framing Lydia as a trusted friend, and prefiguring J. Walter Thompson's advice to do so in 1911.[74]

Yet Lydia Pinkham's wasn't the only face trademarked in service of the consumable product. A host of other companies adopted portraits of their proprietors on packaging and in advertisements, including the Mennen Company—makers of various men's hygiene products—and Smith Bros. Cough Drops, both of which utilized portraits of company owners as logos before 1890.[75] In humanizing their corporations, these faces seemed to vouch for the integrity of the product and the implied accountability of the manufacturer. But the Pinkham Co.'s innovation was in the discourse it created around the product, which constructed a network of users enjoined to Mrs. Pinkham. Representing the proprietor provided a literal face to which consumers could relate when thinking about the product—particularly in the case of Lydia Pinkham, whose personality not only saturated print advertising and product labels, but whose "advice" emanated throughout domestic female culture in letters and word-of-mouth campaigns.[76] More than simply introducing a personal element to advertising, Pinkham's portrait helped build public goodwill by providing an icon—a face and a personality—that would symbolize the virtue of the product and corporation. In this way, her portrait-as-logo offered a glimpse of the kind of identity awareness and loyalty that could be built successfully around a brand.

By 1900, such public relations efforts seemed to be more important than ever. The corporate mergers of the 1890s had prompted public fears of soulless corporate giants swallowing American society in a flood of greed and anti-labor sentiment. When public opinion for the corporation dropped as scientific management theories threatened to make all workers mere cogs in the factory machine, public relations efforts centered on personalizing the corporation, owners, and even the factory to boost goodwill.[77] De-corporatizing household consumables in the age of incorporation meant creating likeable personalities that could appeal to a wide range of consumers through an "everyman" construction, which was not unlike the emphasis on the words of presumed average individuals in patent-medicine testimonials. Idealized and entirely fictional, trade characters provided manufacturers with an opportunity to create seemingly perfect corporate personalities—perfect in virtue, reputation, and appearance—to represent their companies in advertising and other public media. A host of manufacturers debuted new trade characters around 1900.[78] Some of these stood as fictional spokespeople, while others personified characteristics that the companies wanted associated with their goods. Cartoon or lifelike, these fictional trade characters promised to represent character, add novelty, and provide distinction.

One of the most enduring figures to emerge from this period was the Quaker Oats man. Born of several corporate mergers in the 1890s, the American Cereal Company (later renamed the Quaker Oats Company) trademarked the Quaker Oats man in 1895.[79] Like Lydia Pinkham, the mature and pleasant facial expression of the Quaker Oats man embodied his wisdom, while his name and dress appropriated nineteenth-century stereotypes of the religious sect, the American Society of Friends (figure 5.5). Throughout the nineteenth century, the Friends had been represented as modest, devout, and honest in popular culture. Donning plain black clothes, the rural Quakers of the early nineteenth century modeled the highest moral principles and an "unimpeachable" Christian faith.[80] By the late nineteenth century, the Friends had largely abandoned the plain-clothes image, but fictional representations continued to hold up these earlier manifestations, positioning the stereotypical Quaker as the epitome of virtue—particularly in business. As a referent to the Friends' reliability and honesty, the image of the Quaker Oats man enjoined these perceived characteristics with his product sponsor. Gesturing to a preindustrial past allowed the Quaker Oats Company to sug-

Figure 5.5. N. W. Ayer & Son Advertising Agency, "Children," quarter-page print advertisement for Quaker Oats (1902). N. W. Ayer Advertising Agency Records, Archives Center, National Museum of American History, Smithsonian Institution.

gest that its product conformed to those pastorally honest ideals that seemed to be diminishing rapidly as American industry grew.[81]

Early print ads for the Quaker Oats Company depicted a package of oats prominently featuring the Quaker figure. Dressed in a plain black waistcoat, the elderly man wore a ruffled shirt beneath his buttoned vest and white stockings between his black short pants and buckled shoes. His shoulder-length silvery hair flowed softly under his wide-brimmed hat, framing the smile lines on his mature face. The Quaker Oats man often held a scroll inscribed with the word "Pure" in one hand, and a box of Quaker Oats in the other—a self-referential depiction that reinforced the symbolism of the honest Quaker, who also appeared on the box's label. His plain black clothes recalled memories of devout Puritans and of iconic portraits of George Washington, where the simple black suit symbolized republican virtue in upholding the common good. The Quaker Oats man appropriates a similar set of symbols, claiming virtue for the corporation through a simple visual association with the eighteenth-century Society of Friends and the father of the United States. Such romanticism would have spoken to the popular nostalgia for the Revolutionary past that followed the 1876 Centennial celebration.[82]

In crafting the Quaker Oats man's personality to represent its emergent brand, the American Cereal Company took extra steps to cement the figure's realism for audiences. A railroad tour in the 1890s brought samples and in-person visits from an actor in costume to various small towns from Cedar Rapids, Iowa, to Portland, Oregon, while advertising in magazines, newspapers, and other media, followed with printed support.[83] Producing an actor in costume helped to materialize the constructed attributes of the product by enabling consumers to meet and converse with a fictional figurehead who reflected the Quaker Oats brand identity. Here, selling the experience was not so much an artificial construction as an artifice posing as the authentic. Consumers got an authentic experience—like a celebrity speaking tour—but with an artificial personality, a constructed character who was entirely fictional. Like the actress portrayal of Aunt Jemima at the 1893 Chicago World's Columbian Exposition, the American Cereal Company created its fictional character to better speak to audiences, while the actor could forge actual human connections with consumers. In the wake of Gilded Age social strife, these trade characters signified "simpler times" in American history, absent of industrial woes, tense labor and racial relations, and complicated production processes.[84]

The Quaker Oats man's emphasis on purity also spoke to growing public concerns about adulterated foods toward the end of the century. As industrialization mechanized food production and processing, journalists increasingly prompted concerns over food safety following the "swill milk" scandal at mid-century.[85] After spoiled meat shipped to overseas troops during the Spanish-American War (1898), *Ladies' Home Journal, Collier's,* and other magazines heightened public anxieties, prompting calls for federal regulation that would ensure the safety of packaged foods and their accurate labeling. Many reformers blamed corporate greed and dishonesty for public ill-health and suggested that producers be held to higher moral standards, which would require them to accurately represent their goods on product labels. Others noted that consumers had an economic right to be protected against fraud, for adulterating packaged foods—mixing sawdust in with wheat, for example—amounted to cheating the consumer out of the goods he or she believed to have purchased. Calls for federal regulation and consumer protection escalated over the next few years, resulting in the passage of a federal Pure Food and Drug Act in 1906 and the creation of the Food and Drug Administration.[86] These public and regulatory actions triggered a range of responses from the manufacturers of packaged foodstuffs, including self-conscious proclamations of purity, quiet changes to packaging designs and language, and loud denunciations of competitors for adulteration.[87] In selecting an icon with cultural properties that signified purity and honesty, the American Cereal Company demonstrated its attentiveness to contemporary debates about food adulteration and its willingness to use visual symbolism to gain the public's trust. The Quaker Oats man, if successful, could preemptively quash fears about the potential impurities associated with processed oats.

By the early twentieth century, ads tended to use the Quaker as not just a spokesman for oats but also as a sponsor of children's healthy growth and adults' renewed energy. He promised that his oats were free from impurities, hulls, and "black specks." In 1902 and 1903, the Quaker also told parents that Quaker Oats were more nutritious than meat. Children who consumed his oats would "play better, study better, sleep better, [and] live better" than other children, and would grow up to be "big men and fine women."[88] The claims made by the company did not end there. One ad promised to enrich not only the appetites of its consumers but their lives as well: "Here's strength for good work, light hearts for play, good bone and strong muscle, pure blood and steady nerve, growth for your children, rosy cheeks and bright eyes for your lassies, vigor and self-reliance for your sons, young hearts for your wives, strength for your brain and for your hands, good digestion . . . economy for your purse, health, wealth, and a good breakfast."[89] The company's promises of zest and self-reliance wove together aspects of contemporary social problems with advertising trends that positioned the product as a solution for such ills, encouraging readers to identify with the Quaker figure as someone who shared their concerns. According to this ad, the economical Quaker Oats not only provided the crucial breakfast for children's growth but also eased the digestion of elderly consumers and energized adults for the day. Mothers, working men, caregivers, and other adults targeted by this campaign learned that Quaker Oats stood for wholesome food and that buying Quaker Oats for their families could be considered an act of love.[90] Regardless of whether the product lived up to such boastful claims, it is important to understand the ways in which the Quaker's message may have been made more believable simply by the iconography of his appearance, which adapted cultural associations linking Quakerism with trustworthiness. By 1905, the character had gained enough currency in American culture and popular consciousness that adman Earnest Elmo Calkins, in his widely published manual for advertising executives, commented on the success of the Quaker brand as part of a new trend toward creating trademarked personalities.[91]

Like the Quaker Oats man, Franco-American's Little Chef also drew from existing cultural associations to preemptively address public concerns over food impurities (see figure 5.1). Evoking the same iconography of childhood found on trade cards two decades earlier, the company's ads appropriated the cultural ideals of innocence and purity through the child chef. In ads placed between 1906 and 1909, the fresh-faced boy grins excitedly at the viewer; his plump, rosy cheeks indicate his health and happiness. Gesturing to nineteenth-century ideas that romanticized childhood, these ads subtly encourage readers to trust the child's statements wholesale. A child is trustworthy, for his innocence seems to obscure any potential harm or dangers that might come from prepackaged goods. The iconography of childhood at work in these advertisements also underscores references to purity and wholesomeness in the texts: In several instances, the Little Chef assumed a narrative voice, explaining to the reader his role in checking all the ingredients on the way into the kettles, and the products on the way out of the factory. Popular in print ads just as they had been on trade cards, children became a common trope for trademarks in the years around 1900, appearing as trade characters for brands such as Campbell's Soups, Buster Brown shoes, Cracker Jack, Hires Root Beer, Uneeda Biscuit, Cream of Wheat, and Morton Salt, among others.[92] In an era that witnessed the massive growth of national corporations and monopolies, Franco-American adopted a smaller, nonthreatening brand identity (both figuratively and literally) that was accessible to all visitors on any day of operation throughout the year.

Part of this accessibility included encouraging the public to visit the factory, in an outward demonstration of transparency that underscored Franco-American's emphasis on cleanliness. In the first decade of the twentieth century, Franco-American's Little Chef "cordially invited" customers to visit his "kitchen" for inspections and tours of the company's New Jersey facilities.[93] Since the 1870s, manufacturers and other advertisers had illustrated the interiors of their factories and invited potential and current customers to visit for personal inspections of the manufacturing processes, just as merchants had done in the antebellum years.[94] Patent-medicine makers such as Lydia Pinkham and G. G. Green frequently published illustrations of their laboratories, showing the manufacturing process. Likewise, adman N. W. Ayer invited potential clients to visit his offices and personally witness the orderliness of his operation, taking a cue from his predecessor, Volney Palmer. One printer even invited potential clients to examine his financial records for evidence of his honest business practices and proven results, with the statement "Books open to all."[95] Illustrating the interior of the factory and inviting the public to inspect it was a way to demonstrate the cleanliness, order, and, above all, transparency of the manufacturing process and the company. Whether customers arrived to inspect offices and books hardly mattered—the public invitation itself demonstrated the advertiser's openness and it continued to be a popular tool for building goodwill into the twentieth century.

By the company's own account, hundreds of such visitors came to visit Franco-American's "kitchens" each year. Throughout much of its advertising, the texts featured superlative descriptions of Franco-American's quality ingredients and the production process: "The purest, most delicious, and nutritious of all soups, prepared with exquisite care . . . in the largest, cleanest, sunniest kitchen in existence; from the finest, most carefully selected materials obtainable."[96] With these terms, the company conjured a vision of a spotless, shiny kitchen, flooded in sunlight and filled with the freshest meats, vegetables, and seasonings one might imagine. Customer observations, allegedly reprinted from the factory guestbook, underscored this vision of a culinary utopia: "How delicious everything smells! How beautifully clean everything is! . . . I never saw anything like it." Such "unstinted praise" from visitors provided the evidence to support Franco-American's claims of quality, purity, and transparency.[97] These sensory descriptions of the factory's sights and smells attempted to replicate the visitor experience for readers of Franco-American print ads. In framing its factory as a "kitchen" one might visit, Franco-American aligned its production processes with the consumer's own private space of domestic production, inviting readers to pop by for a visit as if dropping by a neighbor's house to swap recipes. The colloquialism humbled the corporation by crafting a relatable child personality to serve as a surrogate figurehead. In these ways, text and image worked together in these ads to emphasize the wholesomeness of Franco-American foods, encouraging consumers to trust the humble corporation and to buy its product.

Franco-American emphasized the centrality of visual observation and documentary evidence to corporate discussions of character and, in turn, to efforts to build goodwill with the public. If a customer wished to visit the factory but couldn't travel to New Jersey, the company offered to provide a detailed booklet with photographs that demonstrated the company's strict adherence to the highest standards of quality and purity.[98] In offering photographs and tours of the factory, Franco-American reminded readers that seeing is believing. It built upon an operational aesthetic still at work in the early twentieth century, encouraging potential consumers to visit the factory and observe for themselves the veracity of the company's claims.[99] Visitors' post-visit remarks amounted to witness testimony that corroborated Franco-American's claims of purity and wholesome products and aligned the quality of its products with the virtue (and purity) of the company. Again, the company's self-conscious statements were likely designed to address percolating public fears about the impurity of processed foods. In other ads, the company directly addressed the work of Dr. Harvey Wiley and the Pure Food crusade, touting its membership in the Association for the Promotion of Purity in Food Products and noting that Franco-American products went beyond the minimum standard for "legal purity" to reach "absolute purity" by avoiding preservatives.[100]

In these ways, Franco-American created a cohesive advertising campaign wherein each piece helped to reinforce the company's constructed public persona (or brand). In adopting the Little Chef as its trade character, Franco-American aligned its corporate identity with cultural ideas about childhood innocence, purity, and trustworthiness. Its open invitations to customers interested in visiting the factory professed a philosophy of transparency, which further underscored the firm's iconographic construction of integrity through the child chef. Finally, the testaments of visitors helped reinforce these textual and visual messages, adding another coded layer to the company's advertising. Speaking to public concerns about food purity, Franco-American's strategies worked within contemporary discourse to tailor its advertising message to consumers' tastes (and fears).[101] In so doing, the firm presented a model for building a brand in the public consciousness, integrating visual and textual strategies through a variety of print media.

Yet, Franco-American's case did not necessarily translate into a formula for success when applied by other firms. Like Franco-American, Hires Root Beer also used a fictional child to accompany representations of its product in print, albeit perhaps not as successfully. Hires premiered its blonde-haired toddler asking for more root beer on trade cards as early as 1891 marketing the "delicious, sparkling, temperance drink" as an alternative to alcohol (figure 5.6). Hires also manufactured patent medicines and made its root beer extract available for those who wished to make root beer at home.[102] From the 1890s through the 1910s, the company used the toddler fairly regularly in advertisements, though the toddler does not appear to have ever been properly named like other trade characters. Like Franco-American, the Hires texts underscored the purity of the product, attempting to create parallel references between the iconography of childhood and the

Figure 5.6. Knapp Lithography Co., "Say Mama," trade card for Hires Root Beer (1891). Warshaw Collection of Business Americana, Archives Center, National Museum of American History, Smithsonian Institution.

Figure 5.7. N. W. Ayer & Son Advertising Agency, "Just Say Hires," sixteenth-page print advertisements for Hires Root Beer (1912). N. W. Ayer Advertising Agency Records, Archives Center, National Museum of American History, Smithsonian Institution.

text. Some ads relied on nostalgia, deliberately evoking childhood memories and reminding readers of the drink they enjoyed in their youth (figure 5.7) and the trade cards they might have collected in scrapbooks.[103]

After twenty years, however, Hires Root Beer launched a new advertising character, "Josh Slinger," in 1914. Swapping out nostalgia for fashion, the slick-haired soda-fountain clerk boasted a crisp collar, trim figure, and fashionable suit—all of which were likely intended to appeal to a different (and likely young adult) audience. Advertising copy also changed, shedding the long and lengthy discussions of product purity that had accompanied representations of the toddler, and instead focusing brief messages of youth, fashion, and fun. In one ad, an overly eager and winged Slinger offers a bottle of Hires to the viewer, hovering over the tagline "Dead for a drink?" (figure 5.8). The somewhat confusing message positions Slinger as the salvation that would cure someone literally "dying of thirst," while the text encourages the reader to "sidestep that shroud."[104] This latter statement evokes a burial shroud (or, perhaps, the Shroud of Turin— the famous burial shroud of Christ), and thus oddly encourages the reader to take off the metaphorical halo and take a drink. The odd combination of religious references and the encouragement to take pleasure in consumption mark a

Figure 5.8. N. W. Ayer & Son Advertising Agency, "Ain't it fierce?" and "Dead for a drink?" eighth-page print advertisements for Hires Root Beer (1915). N. W. Ayer Advertising Agency Records, Archives Center, National Museum of American History, Smithsonian Institution.

dramatic departure from the company's previous messages focused on temperance, childhood, and purity. This kind of inconsistency ran against admen's nascent branding advice at the time, including that of J. Walter Thompson.

Perhaps predictably, Slinger's life as a spokes-character was short lived: He was discontinued in 1918 and, in the early 1920s, Hires resurrected the toddler figure. Why didn't Slinger experience more longevity? While the concrete reasons are unclear, it can be productive to speculate as to why his tenure was so brief. First, Slinger's visual appearance may not have sat well with viewers. The bug-eyed Slinger, whose high cheekbones and thin eyebrows accentuate his lidless eyes, creepily confronts the viewer with his overenthusiastic stare. In contrast to the other trade characters profiled in this chapter, Slinger's cartoon-like appearance is almost alienating, rather than warm and inviting. Whereas Lydia Pinkham, the Quaker Oats man, and the Franco-American Little Chef all mobilized visual symbolism that signaled confidence, safety, and reassurance, Slinger's wide eyes confront and provoke the viewer, leaving an unsettling feeling. His demise may have also been related to the end of World War I and the rise of Prohibition. In some depictions, his cheeks and nose bear a slight blush, harkening to older visual tropes that showed alcohol use through a reddened nose and face. Moreover, Slinger's emphases on fun and fashion evoke a sense of spontaneity and release, which might have seemed inappropriate after the horrors of the war or the start of Prohibition, to particular viewers or admen. Built from time-sensitive references to culture and fashion, Slinger most likely lost his cultural relevance and appeal for the post–World War I generation and was discarded.

While Josh Slinger's cultural relevance faded quickly, other characters demonstrated their abilities to transform with contemporary culture, especially through serialized narratives. In 1900, the Lackawanna Railroad unveiled a new fictional personality, Phoebe Snow, in what would become one of the most successful advertising campaigns to date. Entertainment aesthetics proved key to Snow's success: Just as the manufacturers of Diamond Package Dyes had done decades earlier, the Lackawanna Railroad crafted narrative segments and story lines for Snow, the fictional New York socialite, who frequently traveled "The Road of Anthracite."[105] As a modern and fashionable New Woman, Snow was intended to rehabilitate rail travel for the new century. She wore a beautiful white floor-length gown, complete with a lacy bodice and a large, curved white hat. Her name and alabaster complexion reinforced the concept of purity symbolized in her dress—signifiers for the cleanliness and propriety of modern rail travel: Safe for a woman, traveling on this train would not sully her reputation, or her dress. In streetcar and magazine ads, Snow's clothing and demeanor signified her class status, adding an air of respectability to railroad travel simply through her presence.

Both Josh Slinger and Phoebe Snow emerged in visions of fashion and youth, yet Snow's personality held more lasting commercial and cultural appeal. As the decades progressed, Miss Snow traded in her floor-length, corseted gown for the sleek silhouettes and shorter hemlines of the 1920s and 1930s. Phoebe Snow's almost immediate popularity made her a household name by 1907, and she continued as the fictional spokeswoman for the Lackawanna Railroad into the 1950s. Her fame made her the subject of countless popular stories, songs, and even a major motion picture.[106] Witnessing the varied travels and experiences of the fictional Phoebe Snow elevated her from a mere trade character to a pseudo celebrity in American culture, as she seemed to step out of the imaginary and into reality. Like a character in a serialized novel, consumers could follow Snow's exploits as she traveled; they watched her life progress from demure single girl to mature married woman, and through ad copy they learned of her preferences for tourism, sports, and politics. Blending entertainment aesthetics with a humanized, yet highly symbolic representation of middle-class respectability (and whiteness), Snow's serialized existence demonstrated the potential of playing the long game in advertising and branding.

Cultural relevance was thus key to the success of trade characters. Like Franco-American and Quaker Oats, a host of packaged-food manufacturers debuted trade characters in the early twentieth century that attempted to speak to then-current cultural anxieties about industrialization, public health, and sanitation. In the cultural discourse crafted by such characters and their advertisements, references to "purity" take on multiple meanings. In the 1910s, for example, Fleischmann's Yeast began using a spokes-character they called "John Dough." Formed from loaves of bread, the figure wore baker's attire and claimed to be "raised" on Fleischmann's Yeast (figure 5.9).[107] Brothers Charles and Max Fleischmann had first introduced packaged yeast in the 1870s; less than a decade later the company counted well over 1,000 regional bakeries among its clients.[108] By the 1910s, the company had expanded across the United States and began to market its packaged yeast directly to consumers as a staple in the American diet. Like ads for Quaker Oats, Fleischmann's ads touted the "healthful" qualities of bread, its economic value compared to meat and potatoes, and its benefits to growing children. Holding up a loaf much larger than his body, John Dough reminds viewers that "In Bread There is Strength"—much more than appearances would suggest. The ad visually implies that diets including bread baked with Fleischmann's Yeast will result in muscular strength and overall physical vigor. In these and other print ads that positioned Fleischmann's Yeast as the "sign of good bread," the company constructed a set of attributes it wished to be associated with its product: healthfulness, quality, economy, and long-standing benefits to the community.[109] The simple bread man John Dough attempted to signify

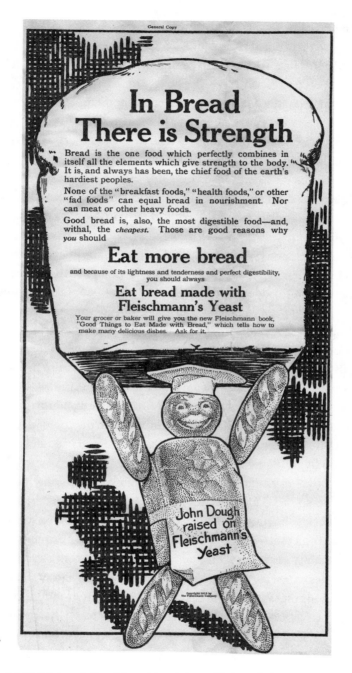

Figure 5.9. N. W. Ayer & Son Advertising Agency, "In Bread There is Strength," quarter-page print advertisement for Fleischmann's Yeast (1913). N. W. Ayer Advertising Agency Records, Archives Center, National Museum of American History, Smithsonian Institution.

these attributes through his robust form and smiling face. Though his limbs might only be constructed from loaves of bread, the character's animated humanism lent a personable quality to the product, and the company's sales multiplied over the next several years.[110]

Part of John Dough's cultural appeal hinged upon the play on words between his name and the prototypical "everyman" in American culture. Since the eighteenth century, the moniker "John Doe" had signified an "ordinary, typical citizen," especially in legal proceedings.[111] The Fleischmann Company appropriated this moniker in its own fictitious everyman, creating the implication that the bread-man espoused some connection to each and every individual in the United States. In a series of ads through the 1910s, the company crafted an origin story that asserted the importance of healthy bread as a building block of life and civilization. In one ad, titled "The Landing of the Pilgrims," the company proclaimed that "bread was their chief article of diet and the best food they could eat. . . . It helped develop that sturdy race of New Englanders, famous for its hardihood and vigor."[112] Cultivated from "old-stock American" ingredients and displaying a direct connection to the nation's first mythical founders, the Pilgrims, the character John Dough evoked a certain universalism. John Dough thus provided an opportunity to connect to American nationalism in both breadth and depth, layering rhetorical constructions of universal and long-standing benefits with visual constructions of the bread-man, and linking word and image together in a clever visual pun. Using the pseudonym John Dough, the company constructed a blank face through which (white) American consumers could envision their own childhood upbringing on healthy bread.

Yet, like other trade characters, John Dough could also be interpreted as subtly reinforcing racial hierarchies in the United States and sidestepping contemporary debates about immigration and assimilation. Growing social and class tensions had punctuated the post-Reconstruction years, as industrialization brought enormous wealth to elites and impoverished discontent to many workers. For decades, American cities, especially in the north, had swelled under the steady flow of immigrants leaving eastern and southern Europe and of African Americans leaving the South. This flow of immigrants to the United States reached its zenith just before World War I. Conservatives responded by agitating for increased immigration regulations, citing labor unrest and racial tensions in the cities.[113] Characters such as the Quaker Oats man gestured to an Anglo-centric eighteenth-century past, capitalizing upon the various cultural, racial, and food-related connotations of "purity" when evoking this concept through advertisements (particularly when the company promised that its breakfast food was free from "black specks").[114] Likewise, though the moniker "John Dough" seemed to universalize American identity, the bread-man's whiteness was ingrained—

literally, from the bleached white flour that made him—and thus Dough excluded nonwhites and immigrants from the vision of the "everyman" he created. At a time when nativists argued that ethnic and class-based tensions threatened the very sanctity of the nation, John Dough seemed to offer a reassuring vision of white harmony and unity. Assuming a white audience, John Dough reinforced the implied whiteness of the "typical" American consumer. Like the white faces appearing on trade cards, these trade characters helped universalize the trope of the white middle-class consumer, crafting a visual echo chamber that reinforced assimilationist rhetoric. Inviting consumers to identify with these trade characters, admen and commercial artists constructed the characters using a white lens, borrowing tropes of white culture and character, in order to appeal to a largely white audience. The implicit and explicit whiteness of John Dough, Phoebe Snow, and other characters therefore reinforced the marginalization of African American and other nonwhite consumers at the time.

Why did these characters have such currency in American culture in the first decades of the twentieth century? In 1929, adman Frank Presbrey credited printing technologies, especially the halftone process, with facilitating the "naturalness and greater emotiveness" of trade characters after 1900.[115] While technology may have played a part in structuring some characters' success, several of the successful characters depicted here—including Lydia Pinkham, the Hires Root Beer toddler, and early representations of the Quaker Oats man—were created without halftone technology. Another possible explanation for this influx of characters might be simple efficiency: Lifelike yet fictional trade characters could be more appealing and profitable than real-life existing endorsers in many ways, even when actors appeared as the trade characters in real life (as in the Quaker's famous train tour and in Aunt Jemima's booth at the 1893 Exposition).[116] Companies that created fictional trade characters did not have to worry about paying the added wages of celebrity spokespersons, obtaining permission for using spokespersons' names and images in print, or performing public relations cleanup when the spokesperson became involved in a scandal or died (as in the case of Lydia Pinkham). Fictionalized in personality and appearance, trade characters were born to be perfect in the public eye—conforming to whatever qualities and character the manufacturer and its admen desired for the public representative of the company.

Yet, in the archived files of advertising agencies lay the remains of a host of campaigns gone wrong, including unsuccessful trade characters and their failed slogans. Some fashionable characters who emerged in the 1910s, such as Josh Slinger, seemed to fall from the public eye as quickly as they had risen. Though John Dough's name and appearance crafted a clever pun, he was also shelved in favor of other strategies in the 1920s. Importantly, Dough didn't provide a clear visual connection between the cultural attributes expressed in his ads (purity and health) and the corporation or the product, as the Quaker Oats man did. Instead, Dough's arguments were connected to a by-product (bread)—not the actual product for sale (yeast)—and thus the reader had to do a bit of mental math to connect the campaign to the Fleischmann Company. Other companies created products or characters that, in retrospect, appear derivative and too similar to other popular brands or characters to have much staying power.[117] Unfortunately, admen could rarely predict which trade characters would actually be successful: While nearly all trade characters created between 1900 and 1930 attempted to humanize products and companies to create lasting appeal and were launched through carefully designed campaigns and media blitzes, not all of these succeeded. Trade characters had to craft the perfect blend of cultural appeal and visual symbolism, in an aesthetically pleasing form, in order to resonate with audiences. Without this proper formula, the character risked the likelihood of failure.

Thus, it must have been more than their humanistic traits that made trade characters such as the Quaker Oats man and Phoebe Snow memorable. In a word, it was their virtue—their character—that appealed to American consumers in these years. Whereas fashion trends came and went, the humble Quaker Oats man likely survived because he was more relatable in the hard times of the 1930s; his values rested less on fashion and more on traditional virtues heralded in American culture. According to adman Frank Presbrey, the Quaker Oats man (and others like him) became "as familiar as the faces of national heroes."[118] Presbrey's statement elevates these commercial personalities to the status of national legend, and gestures to the centrality of brand-name products to American consumer society. This society, which prized both character and personality— both virtue and distinction—in its commercial trademarks, would intensely rely on trade characters in national advertising campaigns through the 1960s.[119] These characters made a permanent impression on the American public because of the nature and character of the appeal itself or, rather, because of the virtues that these trade characters represented.

*   *   *

In these ways, virtue and character remained important signifiers for business success in the decades after the Civil War. Advertisers continued to demonstrate their character and class through carefully crafted rhetoric, in epistolary forms that illustrated education and through evidence such as testimonials and endorsements. But the lessons of the Gilded Age had shown the increasing importance of novelty in attracting potential customers, and advertisers continued to experiment with new strategies that would marry their goals of demonstrating character and entertaining audiences with novel appeals. Trade characters offered the possibility of meeting both of these tasks. The transitional figure of Lydia Pinkham demonstrates how a firm's initial efforts to achieve product differentiation, met through the use of the proprietor's portrait, might shift into something that had the potential to become larger than life. On the one hand, Lydia Pinkham embodied an older, antebellum notion of demonstrating one's transparency and virtue through the portrait. But the Pinkham Company's efforts to develop a community of users, through letter campaigns and targeted advertising after Lydia's death, helped to transform Lydia Pinkham into a character that lived beyond the individual. In short, the Pinkham Company turned Lydia into a brand.

In 1920, the N. W. Ayer & Son Advertising Agency proclaimed the lasting importance of character to the advertising industry and to American businesses writ large (figure 5.10). Suggesting that the "secrets of the soul are published by the face," the agency's business-to-business advertisement at once summarized Victorian theories of character and asserted the importance of these ideas to modern business. A person displayed his or her character through daily actions, the text reminded, noting:

> Character holds a mighty position in commerce. Money is lent, credits given, undertakings started; more on character than on material resources. Industries are ingrained with the characters of their founders and directors. . . . Because public information concerning the character and activities of a business increases and enlarges its success, a powerful institution devotes its vast resources to the distribution of such information. This institution is advertising. It has a great opportunity and a great responsibility . . . of carrying the character of a house and its wares to all consumers. . . . It [builds] reputation; and reputation is of greater worth than all things else—save character.[120]

With this, N. W. Ayer & Son synthesized the activities of various collaborators in the advertising industry over the previous half century. Illustrating a company's character had become a key ingredient in building a positive reputation, and advertisements had become the chief communication venue for achieving this goal. Borrowing the likenesses of prominent historical figures, Ayer's ad visualized the importance of character to intellectual, cultural, and political leaders from the past. These figures stand steadfastly before the modern businessman seated at his desk, as if to influence and guide his strategies as he makes his way in commerce. Placing the modern man in such heralded company, N. W. Ayer &

CHARACTER

THE secrets of the soul are published by the face. No one can deceive time, and no one can prevent time displaying character. Progress requires this safeguard.

The meeting of crises, the answers to adversity, the acceptance of victories, the appraisement of the present, the judgment of the past and preparation for the future, all enter into the structure of character. The habit of action based on conviction is character's strength.

Character holds a mighty position in commerce. Money is lent, credits given, undertakings started: more on character than on material resources.

Industries are ingrained with the characters of their founders and directors. Products partake of the character in kind, quality and design, of the men responsible for them. Even the personnel of organizations reflect the ambitions, ideals and methods of those who direct them.

Because public information concerning the character and activities of a business increases and enlarges its success, a powerful institution devotes its vast resources to the distribution of such information.

This institution is advertising. It has a great opportunity and a great responsibility. On it rests the sensitive task of carrying the character of a house and its wares to all consumers.

Advertising offers the vital first impression. It is the only point of contact a house may have with the great body of its consumers. It is building reputation; and reputation is of greater worth than all things else—save character.

Obviously, there can be no discussion as to the importance of advertising to industry. That is an established fact. It is important. It should be expressed and developed with a care worthy of its importance.

N. W. AYER & SON
ADVERTISING HEADQUARTERS

NEW YORK   BOSTON   PHILADELPHIA   CLEVELAND   CHICAGO

Saturday Evening Post, July 10th, 1920
Literary Digest, July 17th, 1920

Figure 5.10. N. W. Ayer & Son Advertising Agency, "Character," full-page print advertisement (1920), published in the *Saturday Evening Post* (July 10, 1920) and *Literary Digest* (July 17, 1920). N. W. Ayer Advertising Agency Records, Archives Center, National Museum of American History, Smithsonian Institution.

Son appropriated the virtue of these leaders to illustrate the strong leadership role it named for itself among the advertising community. It outlined the necessity of publicizing a firm's character to the public in order to reap success, and the central role of advertising in precipitating that success.

In nearly half a century of business, the Ayer Agency had learned the value of constructing a public personality with which potential consumers could identify. Like other advertising agents and printers that had come before, the Ayer Agency experimented with various tactics to represent character and attract the eye, finding ways to blend iconographies of trustworthiness with entertainment aesthetics. When, in 1920, it preached the importance of establishing a visible public presence through advertising, backed by sound character and reputation, the agency had proven the success of such strategies in its campaigns for Quaker Oats, Franco-American Foods, and Fleischmann's Yeast, while learning from its mistakes with failed campaigns, such as with Josh Slinger. More than just friendly faces enticing the consumer to buy the product, trade characters such as the Quaker Oats man and the Little Chef embodied the purity, quality, and reputation Ayer constructed for its clients. The characters became not only the faces of the corporations but also symbolic figures that condensed corporate narratives and reputations crafted in the public sphere—figures that symbolized goodwill.

However, these expositions on character, virtue, and reputation remained in tension with the persistent problem of counterfeit goods on the American market, indicating that definitions of fair competition remained contentious, particularly among industrialists and entrepreneurs. As the nineteenth century came to a close, the professionalization of the advertising industry collided with major disruptions in trademark law at the federal level. Following the invalidation of federal trademark protections in the 1870s, congressional representatives scrambled to pass replacement provisions, with only moderate success. In the 1890s, advertising professionals further laid out their theories of branding and goodwill in trade journals, guidebooks, and other treatises. New trade associations and formal education programs helped institutionalize older notions of commercial morality as the advertising industry established various codes of ethics for their practice. These efforts to purge fraudulent practices and practitioners from the advertising industry represented a parallel effort to those undertaken by both the judiciary, on the one hand, and legislators, on the other. While state and federal representatives debated and established trademark protections, judges in state and federal courts continued to build, through the discourse of case law, a theory of intellectual property protection in trademarks that was rooted in antebellum notions of commercial honesty. These three strategies would converge in 1905.

As advertising professionals denounced frauds, they also reflected on and re-worked common strategies to demonstrate character and build goodwill in print. This meant combining the visual and rhetorical lessons learned from news-papers, trade cards, testimonials, and epistolary advertising over the previous seventy years—wisdom that had calculated a formula for trademark-centered ad-vertising that would yield positive results. Efforts to build and symbolize reputa-tion through visual icons such as Lydia Pinkham and the Quaker Oats man represented incremental advancements in the quest to build brand awareness and identity. An important next step would include translating those strategies into more abstract, graphic symbols, as opposed to humanistic forms and characters. Character, reputation, and visuality came together in the first decades of the twen-tieth century, indicating that modern branding strategies had finally come into their own.

CHAPTER 6

Branding Trust

Law and Practice for the Twentieth Century

At the end of the nineteenth century, character and class remained important ideals for successful business practice. Since Joseph Story's decision in *Taylor v. Carpenter* (1844), jurists had sought to assert the importance of virtue and morality in cases of commercial dishonesty, especially with regard to trademark infringement. As a concept, commercial honesty had grown out of antebellum cultural maxims for appropriate behavior, as theorized by the white middle class and others. Such appropriate behavior hinged upon Christian standards of honesty and republican concepts of virtue, including the notion that one's individual virtue would compel him or her to lead an honest life.[1] Yet, maxims for commercial honesty remained in tension, for several decades, with the idea of federal regulation. Rather than expand the regulation of trademarks at the federal level, many lawmakers and industry professionals continued to deploy theories of *caveat emptor* (buyer beware), reinforcing the notion that the importance of reputation would effectively force businesses to self-regulate with honest behavior.[2] But the ever-expanding American market had created too many information asymmetries, resulting in rampant counterfeiting and deception. Legal experts bemoaned the shamefully low standards of commercial honesty within American capitalism and worried about the loss of public faith in the system itself.[3]

In response, advertising professionals took steps to ensure commercial honesty in the ads they printed. In 1887, for example, adman J. Walter Thompson issued a warning to potential clients in one of his firm's publications: "I want only legitimate advertisers of the better class," he noted, stressing that "apparently honest but really fraudulent Advertisers" would be met with disdain and their contracts severed.[4] Thompson's cautionary statement reiterated the class-based ideals of virtue that had dominated commercial conversations since the 1840s and reflected contemporary developments in American industry. Over the course of the nineteenth century, the credit and insurance industries had also institutionalized virtue, using the rubric of character to determine risk and allocate credit.[5] Admen's efforts to establish professional codes of ethics for their trade thus aligned with broader shifts in American capitalism at the time. And yet, while the lessons—the virtues—had not changed, advertising professionals developed new ways to profess honesty and virtue in commercial communication. They expanded their efforts to build brand identity, and they derided piracy and dishonesty on a broader level than the individualized diatribes offered by Brandreth, Coats, and others earlier in the century. In these ways, one can see both continuity and growth in the advertising industry from the antebellum period.

In legal cases regarding trademark infringement, the ideals of commercial honesty had also taken shape through the language of character and class. Officials and experts scrutinized appearances, behavior, and intent when judging a person's or a firm's actions, attempting to formalize prescriptions for commercial honesty and fair competition through common law and criminal statutes. The 1905 federal trademark law would bring together three distinct yet related discourses: the precedents set in trademark-infringement cases over the previous six decades; the views of advertising experts regarding the need for honesty in their industry; and a developing understanding of the monetary value (the profit potential) of goodwill. Both admen and the courts had linked a business's goodwill value to reputation and potential profits. But where jurists saw goodwill as a result of years of proper commercial activity, by the 1890s, advertising professionals began to theorize ways to create goodwill using print ads that focused on "trademark advertising." The case of National Biscuit demonstrates the ways in which the cultural ideals of integrity and character merged with visually centered advertising campaigns by 1900. Though advertising professionals and others had long understood the importance of trademarks as symbols of reputation and goodwill, National Biscuit took explicit steps to name and define this function of trademarks in its advertisements, marking a culmination of nearly seventy-five years of advertising developments. In the National Biscuit campaigns of the early twentieth century, character, reputation, and visuality came together in the trademarked logo.

Commercial Goodwill and Trademark Law

In the last two decades of the nineteenth century, the advertising industry grew dramatically. Building on the foundation established by Volney Palmer decades earlier, George P. Rowell established his advertising agency in 1865 and revolutionized the trade when he began publishing a newspaper directory four years later.[6] Other major firms also emerged during the Reconstruction years, including N. W. Ayer & Son in 1869, and, in 1871, both J. Walter Thompson Co. and Lord & Thomas. With the growth of newspaper and magazine advertising in the 1870s and 1880s, Rowell and his peers gradually expanded their services to include layout design, text (or "copy") writing, and artwork creation. As it was for many emergent industries around the turn of the century, New York would become the epicenter of these developments: The number of agencies located there grew from roughly forty in the late 1860s to nearly three hundred by 1890.[7] At the same time, courses in advertising techniques sprouted up in colleges and universities across the United States, while art schools began training "commercial artists" to serve the growing field. The new corporate agencies in New York, Boston, Philadelphia, and Chicago hired the graduates of these programs to work as writers, editors, and layout artists. Industry experts poured countless hours into researching and strategizing effective advertising techniques; some of them even turned to the nascent field of psychology to better understand the powers of suggestion and desire.[8] By the first decade of the twentieth century, the advertising industry had emerged as a respected white-collar profession. Several prominent agencies now counted multiple offices within the United States and even international branches, which included N. W. Ayer & Son; J. Walter Thompson Co.; Lord & Thomas (later Foote Cone & Belding); George Batten Co., later BBDO (est. 1891); and the Bates Agency (est. 1893).[9]

In professionalizing their trade, this new generation of admen established trade journals, founded professional associations, and began publishing a range of intellectual treatises and practical manuals on the science of advertising. Their efforts helped systematize business practices, and separate "modern" admen from their colonial roots in transient street peddlers, patent-medicine dealers, and confidence men.[10] The concept of character remained central to these professionalization efforts, helping admen justify their profession by connecting it to older notions of virtue, sincerity, and self-made manhood.[11] Fluctuations in one's reputation, triggered by dishonesty and poor business decisions, seemed to stem from poor character. In American business circles, and especially in the advertising world, character and reputation would increasingly be quantified in terms of goodwill.

Since Joseph Story's decision in *Taylor v. Carpenter* (1844), goodwill had remained an organizing principle in trademark-infringement cases in the United States. Story's 1841 treatise on the legal importance of goodwill and its principled associations with reputation and honor had been reprinted seven times by 1881, and it shaped subsequent scholars' understandings of how commerce tied trademarks to goodwill protections.[12] In 1867, for example, the editors of

Scientific American argued that trademarks remained, for the manufacturer, "a sign of his honor and a surety to the purchaser that he gets what he intends to buy," while recognition of producer's property rights in trademarks provided "not only a defense of his character for fair and honorable dealing but a protection to his patrons."[13] By 1875, legal scholars disputed the common understanding that trademarks served only to designate origin or ownership, and they began associating goodwill with marks that designated "a brand of quality," albeit one that was inseparable from the reputation of the business itself.[14] When such scholars reinforced the importance of protecting reputation and goodwill as an intangible asset, they reasserted the antebellum insistence on honesty in acquiring that goodwill. Importantly, legal scholars maintained that no protections should be granted if the plaintiff had been guilty of misrepresentation, or if the marks had been "calculated to deceive the public."[15]

Reflecting back on this period in 1929, adman Frank Presbrey noted, with approval, the industry's efforts to expunge dishonest advertising. The "gradual improvement in commercial honesty . . . became more pronounced at the close of the century," he asserted, crediting the efforts of professionals like himself who took pride in their trade.[16] From Presbrey's perspective, honesty in advertising could only productively come from self-regulation. Much like other businessmen in his era, he frowned upon state and federal regulation and downplayed the role of law in reducing commercial dishonesty. Particularly in the area of trademark protection, the federal government had been slow and, some would argue, even counterproductive in the effort to ensure commercial honesty before 1900.

Though the United States had seen trademark protections expand in common law and state laws since 1840, the US Supreme Court invalidated the 1870 federal trademark law in 1879, sending the business community and Congress scrambling. In their decision, the justices denied "intellectual property" status to trademarks and argued that protections would be better framed under the right of Congress to govern interstate and foreign commerce.[17] Newspapers reeled at the court's decision. More than two hundred trademark registrations were pending in the Patent Office, according to one report, and the patent commissioner worried publicly that American businesses would suffer if new federal protections were not in place soon.[18] In the trade papers, industry leaders shared similar anxieties: One expert noted that the decision had "put trademark owners into a panic and threw them back upon the antiquated and inefficient common-law remedies for infringement."[19] At a meeting of the recently formed US Trademark Association (USTA), experts suggested that the court's decision did not remove any inherent property rights in trademarks, as common-law protections remained in place. Still, the USTA lent its wholehearted support for renewed federal provisions. It also cited the importance of maintaining goodwill among international trading partners and suggested adopting similar regulatory structures to those already in place in France and elsewhere.[20] This concern among the American business community paralleled reactions among foreign merchants, who monitored the court's movements. Following the 1879 decision, French merchants in New York wrote to their ambassador urging him to lobby for a replacement law. Even the executive branch took action—a directive to pass new trademark protections came, almost immediately, from the president's cabinet.[21]

In Congress, a flurry of proposals to reinstate trademark protections ensued.[22] But congressional representatives argued about how to frame the new law: Should lawmakers privilege US treaty obligations, the need to protect consumers from fraud, or the idea of safeguarding property rights? Their debates often hinged upon established moral standards of ethical behavior and questions of how to reform the American market for the common good. As one congressman argued, protecting "innocent purchasers . . . from deception, fraud, and countless impositions" was of "paramount interest" to the federal government.[23] Members of the House Judiciary Committee agreed in 1880, citing prominent advertising experts and explaining the shared interest of the government and manufacturers in shielding producers and consumers from the damaging effects of counterfeit goods.[24]

Despite such support, Congress was able to pass only limited trademark protections in 1881, in order to meet the diplomatic obligations of the United States toward its trading partners. This was a welcome development for the international business community, and four new treaties were signed with foreign nations by 1883.[25] For the next twenty years, congressional representatives tried, unsuccessfully, to push through legislation that would extend protections to domestic firms. Despite this legal conundrum, businesses continued to register trademarks with the Patent Office, averaging approximately 1,500 registrations annually, while several states established their own separate registration systems.[26] In the meantime, advertising experts and industrial leaders worried publicly about the lack of suitable trademark protections at the federal level. In editorials and trade-journal reports, they urged their readers to write to their representatives and pressure Congress to act.[27] By this time, trademarks had become essential components of domestic and international trade, principally for their links to commercial reputation and goodwill.

"Trademark Advertising" and Branding

By 1890, admen began to discuss reputation and goodwill in terms of the market advantages these brought. Quoting the famed showman P. T. Barnum, one commentator reiterated the connections between reputation and commercial success: "It is necessary that I should cultivate the goodwill of each community I appeal to" since "the best advertisement is a pleased customer."[28] Considering advertisements as arbiters of reputation, admen argued that ads worked as "salesmen in print"—they positioned the printed advertisement as holding the same function as the personal relationships cultivated by salesmen.[29] Personal contact had remained an important attribute in business through the end of the century, despite (or perhaps because of) the apparent impersonality of the market. In the retail grocery trade, for example, manufacturers relied on traveling salesmen to cultivate and maintain trusting relationships with small grocers. These salesmen "brokered trust" among wholesalers, manufacturers, and retail merchants, negotiating sales and shipping terms and ensuring reliability along the supply chain.[30] Advertisements facilitated this same kind of relationship-building, admen argued, while trademarks provided an efficient shorthand for reputation and trustworthiness. Like a positive credit report, the trademark validated reputation (for what is creditworthiness, but a measure of someone's reliability and trustworthiness).

With this in mind, advertising professionals began to theorize ways to cultivate social capital through print. Writers in the trade press highlighted prominent case studies, offering readers advice on how to gain a more competitive market share. Royal Baking Powder, for example, had become so popular by the 1890s that the company was able to leverage high demand for its products in negotiating more favorable sales terms among retail grocers.[31] Apart from attracting the eye with visually arresting designs, advertising professionals suggested that one could build reputation through carefully constructed texts and symbols. This included demonstrating one's character in print, maintaining honest communication, upholding integrity in business dealings to develop a satisfied clientele, and securing one's investments by prosecuting those who sought to steal or damage one's reputation. With this, turn-of-the-century admen referenced the maxims that had come out of nineteenth-century advertising practice and promised that they could artificially create, through print, the social capital and reputation that would have taken years to accumulate in the antebellum decades.

Admen's motive here was likely twofold, with competition being the driving force in both cases. On the one hand, rapid industrialization had increased competition in the American market after 1870, resulting in a cacophony of advertising messages affronting the public eye. Admen recognized that their clients were facing tougher competition as more producers entered the market, making it even harder to stand out from the crowd. Improved strategies for winning public favor and building goodwill through print were thus necessary to remain competitive. But on the other hand, the advertising industry had also expanded dramatically in the post–Civil War years, and the increased competition in their own indus-try pushed admen to try to articulate, with varied success, the qualities and prac-tices that made their particular agencies special and worthy of patronage. Their often hurried and overzealous proselytizing would, ironically, later form the basis for some of the most important advertising theories of the twentieth century. To the established rules of the trade, turn-of-the-century admen added the necessity of creating visually attractive designs and texts that would add distinction—both to remind current customers of their satisfaction with the brand and to draw in new customers through the art of the appeal. Laying out detailed reasoning that underscored the importance of guarding one's reputation, this new generation of admen theorized such practices under the rubric of "trademark advertising" (which later became known as *branding*). Though they adopted this name in the 1890s, admen were merely formalizing elements of advertising practice that had been prevalent since the 1830s.[32]

Advertising strategists molded the principles of branding by first pointing to the importance of an attractive visual campaign. Images had become a central component in advertising strategies, as the experience with newspapers, posters, and trade cards had shown. Experts encouraged their clients to find a visual pro-gram that would speak to consumers. "Pictures make an appeal universal and irresistible," one adman noted in 1892, while another added, "The advertisement with a picture in it will get attention five times where the unillustrated ad will get it once."[33] Editorials in trade journals encouraged readers to take advantage of images to boost the selling power of their advertisements, advising readers to choose appropriate images that were connected to product attributes and tailored to particular audiences. In one instance, an expert praised the logo of the Admi-ral Cigarette company, which included the words "not made by a trust" to capi-talize upon public anti-monopoly sentiments.[34] As one expert concluded, "The advertising of the future will be illustrated. There can hardly be any question about that."[35] In the advertising of the future, illustrations should be used to grab the consumer's attention, while trademarks would help ensure that the consumer learned to associate the logo with a particular product, manufacturer, and, in turn, product quality and corporate reputation.[36]

In addition to advising clients on what to include in their ads, admen also advised them on how to do it. Admen recommended consistent and repeated use of the trademark in all advertising and across media. Such repetition, experts argued, helped facilitate the consumer's memory at the point of purchase, thereby ensuring that the advertiser's investment in branding would lead to an initial (and potentially repeat) purchase of the name-brand product. As J. Walter Thompson noted, a logo itself provided one of the most effective and efficient modes of communicating with current and prospective clients. His firm offered a "corps of artists" who could create novel and interesting trademarks and designs, and Thompson stressed that each client "MUST keep his business before the public if he would have the best success."[37] In this way, repetition and consistent use of the trademarked logo provided a key mode of building one's commercial reputation and brand.

Agency director James H. Collins agreed, and he went even further to suggest that advertisers reduce copy and instead privilege trademarks in ads. In his view, such symbols lent continuity to the advertising campaign and allowed words to be "compressed into ideas." "Readily recognized" by readers, appropriate and strategically chosen symbols could, Collins argued, cheaply communicate an entire advertising campaign by distilling the message into a singular icon.[38] Echoing efficiency models and the principles of Taylorism, which flourished in managerial circles in the 1890s, Collins argued that trademarks enabled the most economic use of advertising space and funds: The trademark could ensure the persistence of the message without the tedious repetition of a descriptive text or story.

Collins's insistence on the symbolic efficiency of trademarks coincided not just with trends toward scientific management but also with principles of modern art and design that were then gaining popularity in the United States. A broader cultural shift away from the eclecticism and ornament of the Gilded Age helped to push advertising designs toward more modern, streamlined, and pared-back aesthetics around 1900. This shift occurred in tandem with the declining role of printers and the growing influence of layout artists in the realm of advertising. In particular, many firms moved away from the ornamental symbolism of the 1870s—which had privileged children, flowers, and other icons of sentiment in communicating trustworthiness in print—and toward more abstract, semiotic designs that encoded such ideals in otherwise arbitrary symbols by 1905. Gesturing to contemporary trends in newspaper advertising, experts stressed the value of restraint in advertising design and warned their peers not to overcrowd the physical space of the advertisement. These design trends toward simplicity in the first decade of the twentieth century helped reinforce admen's arguments that trademark-centered layouts were aesthetically pleasing forms, which ought to be modeled across all advertising media.[39]

However, simple reiteration of the logo was not enough to ensure a future sale: While it helped cultivate familiarity with the brand, experts also warned that the success of the sale depended as much on the distinction of the trademark as on the "positive qualities" associated with it. As one adman mused, the trademark acted as a "commercial signature" of the manufacturer, but its value as an authenticating mark rested entirely on its singularity and the reputation it signified; for, as he put it, if "Jay Gould had a new signature for every day in the month, his checks would not pass very freely."[40] Thus, it was important to maintain a quality product for which the trademark became a referent: As a "guarantee of faith and quality on the part of the manufacturer," the trademark won the "good will and favor of the consumer" by connecting an individual's experience with the product to the mark itself.[41] Imposing a semiotic order on commercial symbols, experts noted that trademarks needed virtue as much as distinction—character as much as personality—to be successful.

In their own business-to-business advertisements, advertising agencies crafted their brand identities by modeling the symbolic importance of trademarks. From the late 1880s through the 1910s, the J. Walter Thompson Agency of New York used an image of an owl holding a lantern in its promotional publications and correspondence (figure 6.1). By his own explanation, Thompson linked the owl to Greco-Roman symbols of wisdom, explaining that the lantern signified the "true light of science."[42] This intentional symbolism sought to associate Thompson's agency with knowledge, aligning advertising practice with scientific processes. Through the visual symbolism of his logo, Thompson positioned his firm as a modern, professional entity, guided by knowledge and proven methodologies. Applying these qualities to his industry as a whole, Thompson continued: "The light of the judicious advertiser should be seen casting its radiance to the uttermost parts of the earth. . . . The true light of science in modern advertising outshines antiquated methods as much as the electric light does the old-fashioned tallow candle."[43] Using light as a symbol for the scientific rationality that he self-consciously endowed in his company, Thompson equated his position in American industry with the owl's mythical wisdom. The association with science lent credibility, making his company appear more "modern" in his view.[44] In this way, Thompson constructed a leadership role for himself in the advertising industry and suggested that his contribution included the "illumination" of the rightful path dictated by science and rationality. As Thompson developed the idea of the owl illuminating the globe in subsequent publications, light and wisdom became metaphors for the principles of honesty and integrity that were part of his mission statement.

Deploying his industry's advice for crafting memorable, meaningful trademarks, Thompson used the allegorical owl to configure a brand identity for his firm. Through repeated iterations in print, the symbol became a referent for Thompson's firm and reputation. Summarizing the communicative role of trademarks, Thompson noted that the allegorical owl could stand alone as "a whole story by itself . . . no descriptive words are necessary."[45] Thompson's strategy thus demonstrated the ways in which advertising professionals theorized how to build social capital through strategic use of the trademarked logo. Though he wasn't using the term "branding" yet, Thompson was articulating the steps to build one's brand identity in the public sphere.

Figure 6.1. J. Walter Thompson Advertising Agency, "Wisdom Lighting the Globe," in J. Walter Thompson Advertising (New York: J. Walter Thompson, 1895), p. 4. J. Walter Thompson Company Publications Collection. David M. Rubenstein Rare Book & Manuscript Library, Duke University. Online at https://repository.duke.edu /dc/eaa/Q0009.

Trademarks remained contested in the visual realm, however, as the proliferation of imitation and fraudulent goods on the market destabilized the commercial reputations that manufacturers had so carefully built in the public
sphere. As trademark cases throughout the nineteenth century had demonstrated,
the visual symmetry between the labels for genuine and counterfeit products
had the potential to cause great confusion at the point of purchase (see figures 2.3,
2.4, and 2.7). But counterfeiters not only copied labels and product packaging,
they also copied trademarks and advertising strategies. A close look at two shoe
manufacturers demonstrates this visual symmetry. When advertising his "Solar
Tip Shoes," John Mundell & Co. foregrounded his logo on trade cards and in
other advertisements for the company, which frequently featured children at
play to demonstrate the durability and strength of his product. Registering his
trademark in 1877 and 1878, Mundell's logo consisted of a sun rising over a
mountainous horizon, framed by an oval ring of text that read, "The Best Sole
Leather Tip Made" (figure 6.2).[46] In the 1880s, a local competitor named Thomas
Harris created the brand Standard Tip Shoes in direct imitation of the Solar Tip
line. Harris also used advertisements featuring children at play, and he created a
trademark that depicted a flag piercing a globe floating in water and framed by a
circle with the words "Our Sole Leather Tip Best in the World" (figure 6.3).[47] The
two trademarks are quite similar, with each consisting of a round shape with a
black frame, showing a central vignette with a light-colored sphere and water.
The parallel in the choice of texts for these marks is also clear, right down to the
placement of the words "Sole Leather Tip" at the apex of each trademark.

By copying the general design, colors, and text of the Solar Tip logo, Harris
demonstrated the ease with which certain competitors could develop and release
imitation products that would capitalize upon the reputation of genuine goods.
Each manufacturer's insistence that customers look for logos stamped on the sole
of each shoe suggests that the shoes may have appeared in a retail situation without clearly marked packaging or product labels.[48] Customers urged to look for
the Solar Tip trademark on shoe soles would likely be confused when confronted
with the Standard Tip product, especially given the similarity between the logos
and trade names. In copying the Solar Tip logo just so, Harris provided consumers with the opportunity to purchase his goods over Mundell's product—thus,
he "stole" Mundell's investment in advertising by slyly creating the possibility of
brand confusion and substitution.[49]

The most egregious offense, according to admen writing in the trade and
popular presses, was this sort of piracy from imitation products on the market.
Describing such "pirates" as villains and common thieves, admen reiterated
common-law arguments for protecting trademarks, noting that trademark infringement threatened the reputations of honest advertisers and injured the

Figure 6.2. Donaldson Bros., trade card for Solar Tip Shoes (c. 1880). Boston Public Library, Digital Commonwealth. Online at www.digitalcommonwealth.org/search /commonwealth:sq87ck79m.

Figure 6.3. Donaldson Bros., trade card for Standard Tip Shoes (1884). Boston Public Library, Digital Commonwealth. Online at https://ark.digitalcommonwealth .org/ark:/50959/sq87cm824.

public.[50] As they had for decades, trade journals in the 1890s followed infringement lawsuits with great interest and often took steps to shame the deceivers into retreat. The absence of federal regulation made this sort of self-policing in the industry even more important at the time, especially as admen strove to raise the public profile of their trade. One editorial reprinted the labels from a prominent patent-medicine manufacturer (Hood's) and its fraudulent competitor (Hodd's), denouncing the conspicuous similarities between the two labels (figure 6.4).[51] Hood's lawsuit had been filed with the US Circuit Court in St. Louis, Missouri, in July 1895, and drew attention from the printing trade for the obviousness with which Hodd's had copied the genuine product. Hinging their diatribe on the visual symmetry between the two labels, the editors censured Hodd's for its deceptive efforts to steer consumers away from Hood's preparation.

Just as judges had done earlier in the nineteenth century, the editors blamed poor character for the immoral intent behind such deceptions. Condemning Hodd's imitation as an affront to honest business practice, the editors argued, "It is because of the advertising of the genuine that pirates spring up. . . . [Hood's] fame attracts unscrupulous chemists. . . . It is the same as stealing another man's goods."[52] Again mirroring language used in the courts, the editors differentiated this type of falsity from fair competition (a constitutionally given right) by pointing to the sneaky, backhanded way that such imitators represented their goods: The "unscrupulous pirates" plundered the rightful property of the genuine producers, peddling their "cheap" and "fraudulent" imitations. Marked by dishonesty and deception, the swindlers cheated the public and "robbed" the manufacturers of the genuine products of the "fruits of their labors." Here, the editors used language that underscored the immoral, even "evil" intent that motivated the production of counterfeits.[53] Damning a counterfeiter was therefore as much a condemnation of his moral character as of his illegal actions. Business was still a gentleman's game at the end of the century—at least in the eyes of these prominent admen—making legitimacy not just a legal distinction but a class distinction as well.

Good moral character and the intent of the imitator also colored the opinions issued by state and federal judges in trademark-infringement cases at the end of the century. In the case of *National Biscuit v. Baker* (1899), for example, a federal judge scolded the infringer for his deceitful activity, noting, with sarcasm, the "curious" inability of the defendant to come up with a trade name sufficiently different from the plaintiff's.[54] Judges thus continued to enjoin the principles of "commercial honesty" and "fair competition" in establishing precedents that would later define trademark law. As one legal expert noted, ensuring fair competition meant "preventing one man from acquiring the reputation of another by fraudulent means," preventing "fraud upon the public,"

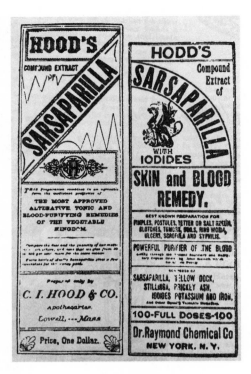

Figure 6.4. Labels for Hood's (genuine) and Hodd's (imitation) Sarsaparilla.
Reprinted from "To Punish Pirates," *Printers' Ink* 13, no. 3 (1895): 15.

and enforcing the "broad principles of equity"—in other words, it meant protecting the public as well as commercial property rights in goodwill.[55] In this way, the language of consumer protection appeared alongside language disparaging deceit and fraud, both in court decisions and in advertising trade publications.[56] Moralizing commercial exchange thus allowed the courts to police dishonest (and thus "unfair") business practices under the guise of protecting the public.

While the courts continued to hear cases of trademark infringement, counterfeiters continued to thrive, particularly in the patent-medicine trade. Imitating patent medicines could be highly lucrative because the elixirs were generally easy to prepare and demand had grown exponentially since the Civil War. As in other industries, many counterfeiters in the patent-medicine industry came from within the supply chain: druggists, clerks, and others who knew and understood medicinal preparation and who could use their professional identities to gain credible access to junk dealers (for used bottles), printers (for labels), and wholesalers (for distribution). In May 1900, Pinkerton detectives raided a rented home in Cleveland (Ohio) occupied by a counterfeiter bottling an imitation of Lydia Pinkham's Vegetable Compound. The counterfeiter, Morgan Howells, had purchased used Pinkham bottles from a junk dealer and procured a copper engraving plate for producing labels and envelopes. He then purchased his own printing press, printed counterfeit labels, filled the genuine bottles with his own prepared formula, and sold them to discount pharmacies in Pennsylvania, New York, and Ohio.[57] Posing as a sales agent, Howells gained these pharmacists' trust and sold the fraudulent medicines below cost. Like other counterfeiters, his success depended on his ability to emulate legitimate (and successful) enterprises. His luck ran out, however, when a Pennsylvania druggist alerted the Pinkham Company to the possible fraud, and the company deployed Pinkerton detectives to find the culprit. Eventually, Howells was found guilty of five counts of counterfeiting and fraud in Pennsylvania Superior Court.[58]

In many ways, this story recalls the efforts of J. & P. Coats to police its brand nearly sixty years earlier. Distanced from its consumers, the Pinkham Company depended on merchants, agents, and customers to alert the company to imitation goods. Like Daniels Carpenter before him, Howells had originally intended to engage in legitimate business by starting his own firm, but challenging market conditions intervened and pushed him to take up counterfeiting instead.[59] He recognized the popularity of the brand-name good and used his knowledge of the industry to construct a parallel manufacturing-and-distribution system that depended on a network of legitimate and illegitimate players to make the con successful. Alerted to the potential fraud by an ally on the ground, the Pinkham Company empowered local agents (the Pinkertons) to investigate, just as Coats had done with its local sales agent so many years before. When those agents uncovered the perpetrator of this fraud, the Pinkham Company sought redress in the local courts, claiming injury to its property, to its reputation, and to the public.[60] The symmetry between this case and the Carpenter cases earlier in the century suggests that, by 1900, this kind of fraudulent commercial activity had become endemic to American capitalism.

Indeed, trademark infringement had risen at the same quickening pace that marked the growth of trademark use in the nineteenth century. As firms grew in popularity and profitability, they gained larger market shares, which spawned imitation and copycat firms hoping to capitalize on that popularity. Despite the efforts of various judicial and legislative bodies to scold and punish infringers like Howells and Carpenter, the frauds kept coming, just as the popularity of brand-name goods continued to rise. Following the processes laid out by admen and previous advertisers earlier in the century, the Lydia Pinkham Company had built a recognizable brand identity through the trademarked portrait of its founder. After Lydia's death, the company morphed that portrait into a trade character and cultivated a brand story through advertisements, creating a community of users rooted in shared experience, which solidified its reputation. Finally, the company secured its market share by investigating and prosecuting imitators like Howells, and it thereby preserved the quality of its reputation through legal and extralegal means. In these ways, protecting one's brand at the end of the century mirrored the attempts of antebellum advertisers, admen, and jurists to police the boundaries of legitimate business practice. Both efforts revolved around condemning "unfair" business practices on moral, and often legal, grounds. Branding and trademark infringement seemed to go hand in hand with American capitalism.

Forging the 1905 Trademark Law

This persistent fraudulent activity pointed to the inadequacy of the 1881 trademark law in deterring counterfeits, and concerns over the law's limited scope exacerbated the pressure already building on the US Congress. Many industrialized countries had adopted internal trademark regulations throughout the nineteenth century, leaving the United States lagging embarrassingly behind. Beyond the treaty agreements with Belgium, France, and Russia that were signed in the 1860s, the United States had entered several similar agreements with other European and Latin American nations in the 1880s. A series of international conventions on intellectual property, held in Western Europe between 1880 and 1900, had applied increasing pressure on the United States to extend trademark protections beyond the limited provisions of the 1881 law. At the same time, internal pressure rose from the National Association of Manufacturers and others. In partial defiance of the 1879 Supreme Court decision, the patent commissioner, Charles Holland Duell, urged American manufacturers to register their trademarks with his office if they intended to engage in international trade. He provided tips for successful registration and underscored the importance of trademarks in facilitating America's growing exports and foreign trade, while preserving commercial property rights.[61] Some progress toward renewed trademark protections came with the 1897 Tariff Act, when lawmakers successfully included a clause to prohibit the importation of goods bearing marks that imitated or infringed upon the commercial rights of domestic manufacturers.

The tariff did a lot to extend trademark protections in the United States, and, when taken alongside the 1881 federal law, the various state laws in place, and the still-expanding common-law protections for trademarks, it might have seemed to solve the problem. But the patchwork system of state laws, common law, and diplomatic agreements meant a very uneven set of trademark protections for both US and foreign manufacturers. Registration was a cumbersome process that was prone to subjective decisions at the Patent Office, and there was no sufficient mechanism to deter future infringement. To sort out these difficulties, President

McKinley appointed a commission to review and revise the statutes relating to patents, trademarks, and commercial names in 1898. The commission included Francis Forbes, founder and first secretary of the US Trademark Association, Arthur Greeley, a former assistant commissioner of patents in the US Patent Office, and Peter Stenger Grosscup, a US District Court judge. Over the next four years, they researched model provisions, heard testimony from experts, and reviewed case law to make recommendations about what a new federal trademark law could and should do.[62]

The commissioners disagreed on exactly *how* to amend the current laws, but they were unanimous on the question of *why* federal action was warranted to protect trademarks. All three commissioners cited constitutional precedent, diplomatic obligations, and moral arguments to justify Congressional action. Primarily, the commissioners suggested that the lack of federal protections for trademarks was causing an international embarrassment for the United States, particularly among its key trading partners. The comparative advancement of America's trading partners in regulating trademarks had placed the country at a considerable economic and political disadvantage. American manufacturers could not export their goods with assurances against infringement, and thus the US economy suffered.[63] The commissioners pushed for Congressional action on domestic regulatory laws, arguing that America's international reputation was at stake. As imperialists argued vociferously for an American empire that would open new trade markets, the president's special commission reminded Congress that trademark protections carried both economic and political importance.[64]

To these arguments, Arthur Greeley added the necessity of incorporating common-law protections into any proposed bill. Framing his section of the report as an effort to privilege the public interest and preserve existing protections, Greeley noted that the thorny questions raised in the case law had left several criteria up to the subjective judgment of individual state and federal judges, including the definition of a trademark, its lawful use, and its related property rights. Congressional action was thus necessary, he argued, to provide unified prescriptions for lawful marks, to streamline registrations, and to dissuade would-be infringers from committing fraud. In his view, this would alleviate concerns among foreign traders and the manufacturing sector, and ease the burden on market entrants in researching existing marks in use.[65]

Finally, the commissioners stressed the importance of preserving the moral foundations of trademark protection, especially in the prevention of fraud and unfair competition, which was in the best interest of the American public. Borrowing the class-based rhetoric that had been common among antebellum judges and advertisers, Forbes and Grosscup argued that expanding federal trademark regulation would reform the American market by preventing "unscrupulous competitor[s] from imposing upon the public."[66] For Greeley, protecting the property rights in trademarks would ensure "honest competition . . . , which stimulates effort and leads to excellence." Trademark infringement, he argued, "injuriously affect[s] the commerce in which it is used, even to the extent of practically destroying the trade in the article . . . by destroying the confidence of the public in the article."[67] First linking property rights in trademarks with the necessity of shielding the public from fraud, Greeley joined the moral arguments against unfair competition with the legal arguments for protecting goodwill. He then asserted that preventing injury to American commerce, to specific trades, and thus to specific buyers and sellers, was an obligation that Congress had to both its citizens and its foreign trading partners. Ensuring fair competition would, in turn, preserve public confidence in the goods for sale and in commerce as a whole. Greeley's efforts helped introduce moral standards into federal trademark law and secured the constitutionality of federal trademark protections by linking them to the stability of the entire commercial system. His carefully researched arguments, grounded in the moralized rhetoric of the American judges who had established the common law relating to trademarks, became the foundation for the bill that would eventually secure trademark protections at the federal level in 1905.[68]

In many ways, then, trademark regulations grew out of America's political economy, but they were inherently rooted in moral considerations. As a regulatory regime that achieved a political goal, the 1905 law helped save face with America's international competitors and trading partners. Moral justifications, however, were necessary to ensure the success of this regulatory system. Economic decisions to regulate are not inherently valueless; rather, they are rooted in social, cultural, and, especially, moral ideals that are contingent on the actors and their subjective decisions at various points in time.[69] Advertisers, admen, judges, lawmakers, and counterfeiters all played an important role in shaping the evolution of common-law protections for trademarks. Each of them brought his or her own moral (and sometimes immoral) standards of fair competition to the conversation—some of them shaped by ancillary commentators writing in trade journals, law reviews, and the mainstream press—and all of them shaped by the cultural, social, and economic experiences of their eras. To put it another way, trademark regulation achieved both political and moral ends, thereby suggesting that, in this case, moral economy cannot be separated from political economy.

The 1905 trademark law's provisions clarified many of the subjective questions raised in Greeley's report, while preserving the moralized boundaries of fair competition that had been constructed in common law. The new law first defined trademarks as symbols that communicated the "origin and genuineness of an article with which [the trademark] has become associated."[70] The statute codified trademark use and registration, established criteria for valid designs, made registrations available under public record, assigned trademark litigation to the jurisdiction of the federal courts, and established an enforcement bureaucracy.[71] Registrations could be nullified by the trademark office when rooted in false or deliberate misrepresentations or when the new marks risked confusion with existing registered trademarks. Finally, the new law implicitly defined the protection of goodwill as a property right.[72] Clarifying the boundaries of legitimate competition, the law explicitly excluded practices that detoured from the moral standards constructed through sixty years of common-law decisions regarding trademarks: Deception, confusion, imitation, and misrepresentation remained unlawful practices outside the scope of trademark protection. After the 1905 trademark law took effect, admen praised the measure for the way it prohibited piracy and protected reputations. The law was so appealing to the business community that, in its first year, the Patent Office recorded almost 4,500 new trademarks—almost triple the annual rate of registrations from 1881 through 1904. This success continued with more than 10,000 registrations for 1906 and more than 28,000 registrations by 1909.[73]

For these reasons, the 1905 federal trademark law can be seen as the culmination of sixty years of trademark litigation and lobbying. Whereas previous laws had granted exclusive rights to use trademarks when registered, they made little effort to protect the "intangible property" (i.e., reputations and goodwill) associated with the use of such marks, despite the widespread acceptance of these associations among the business community. The law had lagged behind business practices in this regard.[74] Under the provisions of the 1905 law, two key aspects of trademark protection—securing the owners' property and guarding against consumer deception—came together. Though subsequent legal scholars would criticize the 1905 law for not extending broader protections, the law's provisions were an important first step in linking together the moral foundations for trademark protection, as defined by case law, with federal treaty obligations and congressional authority to regulate commerce. The law gestured to reputation and goodwill with the stipulation that trademarks designated the "genuineness" of goods in addition to their origins.[75] Though this was not an explicit protection, it is clear from the commissioners' report that they intended to protect goodwill. Trademarks, according to the law, symbolized reputation, while trademark protection meant safeguarding both the consumer from deception and the producer from damages to his or her reputation.

These regulatory efforts to protect consumers and property also aligned the 1905 law with contemporary currents in the Progressive movement that sought to reshape the nature of American capitalism. Progressives identified commercial fraud as a social and economic problem that required a coordinated response. In the press, business leaders described the myriad threats to consumers, investors, and business owners at the hands of unscrupulous swindlers. Muckraking journalists continued to raise public fears about impurities in packaged foods, while newspapers bemoaned the economic power of the robber-barons and the Trusts that had emerged in the 1890s. Material losses to property, health, and well-being were thus compounded by media attention to fraud and the dangers of capitalism, which in turn threatened a "loss in public faith in America's marketplaces."[76] These public anxieties resulted in substantial legislative steps that would frame the modern regulatory state, including the Sherman Anti-Trust Act (1890), the Meat Inspection Act (1906), and the Pure Food and Drug Act (1906).[77]

The 1905 trademark law ought to be reconsidered as part of these regulatory efforts to curb the social ills brought by capitalist industrialization in the United States. Progressive efforts to reassert ethical considerations into economic behaviors and structures framed many of the regulatory laws passed during this period, often under the paternalistic goal of protecting the public from physical or economic harm.[78] The commissioners' language in advocating for the 1905 law drew from many of these same arguments. Likewise, industry leaders in the medicinal and food-processing sectors paralleled such currents by calling for stricter standards of integrity and honesty from their peers, just as the admen had done in their own industry.[79] When situated within this emerging regulatory climate, the 1905 Trademark Act can be reframed as part of the Progressive reform agenda, which aimed to protect consumers and enforce honest, fair competition in American industry.[80]

Yet, we must also consider the ways in which intellectual arguments for commercial honesty paralleled other arguments for purification at the time. The 1905 law drew from long-standing cultural discourses that had come to fruition through a white middle-class perspective, developed during the height of slavery in the United States. Class-based and racialized notions of respectability and authenticity had influenced common-law decisions regarding trademarks and had become so ingrained in the American business and legal communities that the principles must have now seemed obvious and universal. But the historian cannot forget the exclusionary roots of respectability politics, which informed the moral arguments constructed by the white middle class; nor should we ignore the ways in which Progressive concerns about food purity and public sanitation dovetailed easily into arguments for racial purity and empire. It is perhaps no coincidence that the 1905 trademark law was passed as Jim Crow policies solidified, and just after America's imperial push into the Caribbean and the Philippines. Conversations about preserving authenticity and reputation in the market must have resonated loudly with reform-minded individuals who were also interested in eugenics and racial integrity. Each of these arguments revolves around an impulse toward purification, targeting a supposed unsightly and/or undesirable element that ought to be expunged from the whole. In justifying such expulsion, reformers and businessmen used moralized language to condemn the bad and raise up the good. Their moral arguments had grown out of coded language that had once referenced racial and classed identities, and it is important to recognize how that language came to influence federal law. Though seemingly devoid of such cultural references, the 1905 law was very much a product of the racial and class-based hierarchies of its time.

Despite the substantial legal changes that the 1905 trademark statute brought, public response to its passing was mild. The consumer movement had gained speed and popularity after the formation of the National Consumers League in 1899, but public attention remained focused on sanitary food production and fair labor practices rather than on regulating advertising.[81] From 1903 through 1908, however, major national newspapers such as the *New York Times* and the *Washington Post* reported on legal cases that expanded or contracted existing trademark protections, and the intensifying lobbyist efforts from businesses that would profit from a revised trademark statute. In the first few years after the passing of the 1905 act, the *Washington Post* suggested that general public interest in the statute remained low despite the 500 percent growth in registrations that demanded a larger staff commitment from the Patent Office.[82]

In comparison, admen greeted the new law as an unquestionable win, while their theorizations on trademarks and goodwill gained new force with the expanded federal protections for trademarks. From 1905 through the 1920s, admen continued to argue that goodwill could only be obtained through "tactful, prompt, *honest* dealings" that generated the public's confidence.[83] This reflected a general assumption among legal minds at the turn of the twentieth century that manufacturers had a vested economic interest in maintaining their reputations by ensuring the distribution of a consistent, high-quality product. Honesty would generate confidence, confidence brought goodwill, and the trademark became the symbol of it all. Admen's assertions that the trademark acted as a symbol of goodwill, as a guarantee of quality, or as a mark of one's (positive) reputation went hand in hand with their presumption of the ideal manufacturer's general integrity.[84] In this oppositional relationship, the honest manufacturers of superior products stood out against the dishonest, deceptive, and immoral counterfeiters, imitators, and pirates seeking to steal the honest manufacturer's goodwill and to indirectly damage his reputation. Likewise, legal experts agreed that dishonesty negated a manufacturer's trademark rights because it overturned the inherently positive relationship between the trademark and goodwill.[85]

Design, business practice, and the law thus came together in the early twentieth century, cementing visual simplicity with reputation and commercial honesty in the protection of trademarks and the goodwill they symbolized. Trends toward scientific management and efficiency in business practice coincided with design aesthetics that privileged streamlined, semiotic marks over the ornament and iconography of the Gilded Age. At the same time, advertising experts strategized ways to build social capital and reputation under the rubric of "trademark advertising," recognizing the monetary value of goodwill and the centrality of trademarks to these concepts. In response to the continuing problems of imitation, infringement, and counterfeiting, admen placed trademarks and goodwill at the center of their practice, strategizing new and better ways to communicate with the public and to understand public response to brand-name goods. Preserving brand identity (which was synonymous with reputation and goodwill) thus went hand in hand with protecting consumers from deceit and fraud. These elements of strategy, communication, and public response converged in the early branding practices of the National Biscuit Company.

National Biscuit

The National Biscuit Company (later known as Nabisco) arose out of a merger of more than one hundred regional bakeries in the northeastern and midwestern United States, at a time of intense economic instability, labor strife, and corporate growth.[86] In the decades before National Biscuit incorporated in 1898, local and regional bakeries had distributed cookies and crackers (collectively referred to as "biscuit" at the time) in bulk for purchase at neighborhood dry goods stores. Freshness and quality varied greatly, especially in areas dependent on large urban bakeries for distribution. Cookies and crackers arrived in wooden barrels at local dry goods stores, which merchants stored on the floor of the shop and shipped back to the baker when empty. In open-air containers often protected only by a cheesecloth, the products were vulnerable to changes in weather, as well as dust, dirt, and the odors of the shop; as such, they spoiled easily. National Biscuit pledged to revolutionize the market by mechanizing production and standardizing quality through innovative packaging. Its first product, Uneeda Biscuit, featured octagonal crackers wrapped in a wax-paper sleeve and packed in a cardboard box, which promised to keep the crackers clean, dry, and odor-free.[87] Like Franco-American, National Biscuit attempted to address public concerns about the quality of processed foods by suggesting that their new packages were cleaner and more sanitary.

National Biscuit launched the Uneeda brand in national media in the spring of 1899 in a campaign focused on getting as much print exposure as possible. The ad copy changed monthly and sometimes consisted of up to fifteen different advertisements in each newspaper at a time, which must have resulted in a dizzying array of Uneeda ads in any given month.[88] One early ad depicted a young boy standing in the rain holding a box of the crackers, suggesting that "wet weather won't harm" the new biscuit, which remained fresh due to its moisture-proof package.[89] The choice of the child harkened back to Gilded Age themes that treasured childhood innocence and subtly reinforced the company's rhetorical emphasis on purity. In the first year after its introduction, Uneeda Biscuit skyrocketed in popularity—with sales for 1900 topping ten million packages per month—at a time when it was estimated that all other packaged crackers combined would sell only about 500,000 annually.[90] As the company expanded with new products after 1900, the number of unique print ads it placed in various periodicals fell to approximately six to eight per year by 1905.[91] Implementing admen's mandates for consistent advertising that would build the brand, National Biscuit reduced the number of unique designs deployed so that its advertisements would become more familiar to consumers throughout the year, while streamlining copy to focus more on its brand as opposed to the products.

Early on, National Biscuit deliberately crafted its brand with a carefully chosen logo, using advertising copy to establish symbolic connections between the company's In-Er-Seal trademark and the quality of its products.[92] According to company lore, Nabisco president Adolphus Green had discovered the symbol in a book of old printers' marks in late 1898. The symbol combined a squat, horizontally oriented oval with a double-tiered cross protruding from the top; this supposedly represented the "triumph of the moral and spiritual over the evil and worldly" (figure 6.5).[93] In an interview, Green explained his attraction to the mark, surmising that it had probably come from a religious text: "The circle represents the world, and the cross symbolizes our redemption. The whole epitomizes the triumph of the spiritual over the material."[94] While the lay viewer may not have immediately recognized the religious symbolism behind the logo, Green's disclosure of his own interpretation is highly suggestive of the image he aimed to create for his nascent company. The symbol set up a dichotomy of good versus evil that implicitly aligned National Biscuit with the honorable and virtuous, in opposition to the dishonest frauds and counterfeiters that sullied the American market. Like another famously spiritual trademark, the Quaker Oats man, the National Biscuit orb and cross hinted that its mechanized production process enabled the eradication of foreign particles, smells, and impurities, making Uneeda Biscuits superior to simple handmade goods.[95] In this way, the In-Er-Seal logo was designed specifically to speak to the ideals of purity that had become so important in a culture that condemned adulterated foodstuffs. Moreover, Green's extended discussion of the In-Er-Seal logo gave National Biscuit a brand story that established its origin and provided meaning. Published in a trade journal, Green's

Figure 6.5. National Biscuit Logo, as it appeared in 1900. Reprinted from National Biscuit Company, *Trade Mark Litigation*, 5th ed. (private pub., 1915), 42. The IN ER SEAL Design is owned by Mondelēz International Group, used with permission.

interview would be read by the retail grocers who would later advise consumers at the point of sale. It established the sort of backstory that would become a central component of branding efforts later in the twentieth century.[96]

This brand story also traveled to public audiences through advertisements that connected the logo to the nation's "best bakers" and honed in on the meanings behind the logo as a representative for Nabisco and its products. After 1900, an aggressive advertising campaign promoted the In-Er-Seal logo, using careful explanations of the trademark's meaning. The company told readers that the logo stood for quality products protected from "dampness, odor, dust, and germs." It represented "the best efforts of the baker, paper maker, [and] box maker to bring the oven's best products to you in the best possible condition. . . . The contents of every package bearing this trademark design are fresh, crisp, delicate" (figure 6.6).[97] Like Franco-American, National Biscuit deliberately obscured its corporate nature—especially the reality that it operated as a massive conglomerate of regional bakeries. Doing so helped to humanize the otherwise impersonal scale

Behind the "In-er-seal Patent Package"

are the best efforts of baker, paper-maker, boxmaker to bring the oven's best products to you in the best possible condition.

The "In-er-seal Patent Package" is the only successful method of keeping fresh the baker's dainty products. It absolutely excludes all moisture, odors, dust and air. The contents of every package bearing this trademark design are fresh, crisp, delicate.

NATIONAL BISCUIT COMPANY.

The following biscuit are now to be had in the "In-er-seal Patent Package:"

Soda Biscuit
Milk Biscuit
Saratoga Flakes
Long Branch
       Biscuit
Butter Crackers
Graham Biscuit
Oatmeal Biscuit
Ginger Snaps
Handmade
       Pretzelettes
Vanilla Wafers

Figure 6.6. N. W. Ayer & Son Advertising Agency, "Behind the In-Er-Seal Patent Package," quarter-page print advertisement for National Biscuit Company (1900). N. W. Ayer Advertising Agency Records, Archives Center, National Museum of American History, Smithsonian Institution

of its massive operation, creating a subtle reference point through which consumers might identify. Similarly, other ads positioned the logo as a connecting point that bridged producers and consumers—the "link between you and the baker"— asserting an imagined personal relationship that was both mediated and symbolized by the logo.[98] In this imagined construction, the logo provided a referent on which cultural and discursive values could be mapped.

Subsequent ads began to abbreviate this discourse, reminding viewers that Uneeda was "the name that signifies the very best of baking" and telling the reader that Nabisco's logo worked as a modern "sign language" that symbolized quality, cleanliness, and freshness.[99] Importantly, these advertisements departed from earlier advertising strategies that had associated trademarks with singular products, warning customers to "beware" of substitutions or imitations. Instead, National Biscuit's advertisements scaffolded its myriad products under the larger rubric of the In-Er-Seal logo and focused on building a brand identity associated with the trademark. This tactic persisted through 1905 in ads that further connected the trademark to quality and trustworthiness. In an ad titled "Baker's Marks" (1905), the copy told readers that the trademark acted like a "turnpike guide post" pointing "the way to the food of quality," thereby guiding the consumer to buy the "most perfect of bakery products."[100] Other ads reminded readers that "when the National Biscuit Company puts this trademark in red and white on each end of a package of Biscuit, . . . it has affixed its final O.K. which absolutely guarantees the contents of the package to be the very superlative of excellence."[101] Here, the company both mystified and explained the trademark. It positioned the trademark as a guarantee of quality, like a handshake agreement from the artisan to the consumer. Such personal assurances harkened back to an earlier era of face-to-face market relations and, here, the advertisement attempts to reassure consumers that Nabisco still subscribed to the same codes of honor and character that structured such relations, even in this modern age of corporations. With this, Nabisco reinforced the notion that the advertisement—and, by extension, the trademark—could be a surrogate salesperson and reference point for consumer personal experience.

In these ads, the logo gained meaning both apart from and through the company's products. High-quality products ensured that the company's reputation for purity would be maintained, while, in turn, new products introduced by National Biscuit (or existing products introduced to new markets) gained popularity by drawing from the discursive meanings already constructed about the In-Er-Seal logo. As a sign of purity, the mark transferred its symbolic associations and goodwill to each product in the Nabisco catalog—and, later ads remarked, to grocers who decided to carry the products—thereby illustrating the transitive properties of the brand (figure 6.7).[102] Importantly, all of this work was

Building Up Store Character

Every product of the National Biscuit Company ovens suggests goodness, freshness, cleanliness—quality. N. B. C. goods as a line suggest to customers, present and prospective, the character of the store that sells them.

These products are widely and persistently advertised. People have confidence in them because they have been proved good. Consequently, for the grocer who sells them, National Biscuit Company products are good-will promoters—they bring trade and they hold trade.

The famous In-er-seal Trade Mark Packages on your shelves make selling easy.

SOCIAL TEA BISCUIT—a favorite to serve with ices or beverages. Include Social Tea Biscuit in your order.

NATIONAL BISCUIT COMPANY

Figure 6.7. N. W. Ayer & Son Advertising Agency, "Building Up Store Character," quarter-page print advertisement for National Biscuit Company (1915). N. W. Ayer Advertising Agency Records, Archives Center, National Museum of American History, Smithsonian Institution.

done by connecting word, image, and cultural meanings to the logo. This association connecting the visual symbolism of the trademark to the company's goodwill, particularly in the ways the ad positioned the trademark as a guarantee, prefigured the arguments that legal scholars would make twenty years later when making a case for expanded trademark protections at the federal level.[103]

During and immediately following the passage of the 1905 trademark law, National Biscuit continued its campaign to associate its logo with culturally constructed attributes such as purity and integrity, in an attempt to build its brand identity. New advertisements expanded upon the company's earlier assertions of its own merits, and again referenced longer cultural histories of personal assurances connected to a man's "mark" or signature. In a 1905 ad that referenced "John Doe's Mark," the company explained: "A man's Mark is his honor. It stands for him and he stands for it. It's the Old Saxon way of signifying good intentions. The government puts its mark on a bond to give it value. The National Biscuit Company puts its trade mark in red and white on each end of a package . . . to distinguish these products and to guarantee the quality, and it does."[104] The symbolism in this brief passage established a range of historical and contemporary associations that National Biscuit used to highlight its quality products and integrity. First, the company associated trademarks with a tradition of European artisanal production and personal signatures. In so doing, it connected trademarks to an older gentleman's code of honor governing the use of a man's word, IOU, or "mark," and, drawing from cultural understandings of these practices, it replaced the personal signature with the corporate trademark. Just as Joseph Gillott and Lea & Perrins' had warned customers to look for their personal signatures on product labels to ensure quality and genuineness, Nabisco pointed to its In-Er-Seal logo as a similar visual assurance. Second, the company likened trademarks on consumable goods to government stamps on paper money. Without the backing of the federal government, greenbacks held no value. It was the reputation and authority of the government that authenticated paper money, and Nabisco positioned its trademark as issuing a similar guarantee. Like an unwritten contract, the company's "mark of honor" signified its accountability to its customers. Without that mark—that symbolic signature of National Biscuit—a consumer could not be sure that she would receive the "superior" product that she most certainly wanted and needed.

Building a Brand

In these ads, National Biscuit built its brand using repeated visual iterations of its trademark logo. Through print advertising placed in magazines and newspapers,

and in posters and bills displayed throughout the urban and suburban environments, National Biscuit's trademark logo consecrated the aura of its brand identity. On one turn-of-the-century display wall in Baltimore, Maryland, the
pedestrian would have encountered multiple posters for Nabisco products, including posters showing the boy in the rain slicker (top row, center) and posters
that focused solely on the logo (middle row, far left; and top row, right) (figure 6.8).
These posters truncate the message in favor of discrete, graphic symbols. Such
posters would have been rendered in full color (with the logo appearing in a brilliant red) to tie them, visually, back to the product packaging. Though the volume of posters on the wall overwhelms the viewer, threatening to dilute each
poster's message, National Biscuit's are the only posters that focus so clearly
on the trademark logo; their design thus allows them to stand out as instantly
recognizable. Commercial advertisements like these borrowed from the design tactics of poster artists in the last decades of the nineteenth century, whose
efforts to capture the fleeting attention of passersby led them to fuse word and
image in a single visual utterance that "reconfigured the word in the context of
the image."[105]

A decade later, the words "Uneeda Biscuit" loomed high above New York
City's Seventh Avenue, beckoning to passersby as they rushed to appointments
and other engagements (figure 6.9).[106] Logo and text work together here to create
a symbolic commercial language, assisted by the size and height of the poster's
placement on the Hotel Times Square. The photograph illustrates the importance of visually distinct advertising designs, given the stark competition one
faced on the city street. Advertisements climb higher and higher up the building as they clamor for the viewer's attention, like hikers competing for prominence on a mountain. Measuring approximately 30 to 40 feet long, the Nabisco
billboard towers over the smaller posters hung in rows atop the roof of the corner building, claiming prominence with its size and location. The poster's bright
red hue, illuminated by the daytime sun, would have further amplified its voice
and thus its ability to arrest the viewer's attention (though in the evening, the
electric sign perched above would have likely distorted or obscured the Nabisco
poster). Like the smaller posters used in Baltimore, the New York billboard condensed an entire advertising campaign into a single utterance, symbolically
linked to the trademark logo.

In these ways, the trademarked logo became part of the visual landscape of
America's consumer society. Even as pedestrians hurried by the logo was there,
fading into the background of urban life yet subliminally providing a constant
and subtle reminder of Nabisco and its products. Outdoor advertising worked in
concert with other print and public displays of the logo to build collective familiarity with the Nabisco brand. Word and image came together to link constructed

Figure 6.8. Baltimore Bill Posting Co., Advertising wall showing Uneeda Biscuit posters (c. 1910–1919), photograph. ROAD Collection, Outdoor Advertising Association of America Archives. David M. Rubenstein Rare Book & Manuscript Library, Duke University. Online at https://repository.duke.edu/dc/outdooradvertising/BBB5798.

Figure 6.9. Side view of the Hotel Times Square (206 W. 43rd St., New York City), facing 7th Ave., showing Uneeda Biscuit billboard (1915), photograph. ROAD Collection, Outdoor Advertising Association of America Archives. David M. Rubenstein Rare Book & Manuscript Library, Duke University.

meanings to the trademarked logo—first in longer, discursive advertisements that included references to purity, integrity, and responsibility. Once those meanings had been established, the company deployed abbreviated messaging focused on the trademark. Each repeated iteration of the trademark—in newspapers, magazines, billboards, and shop counters—built a layer of familiarity within the viewer's mind, and, in these ways, the trademark became a visual tool for building brand identity through the consumer's experiences in commercial society. Like the fame—the aura—of a celebrated artwork created by one of the great masters, the trademark gained its brand identity through the myriad visual experiences of individual readers and viewers.[107] Of course, the company hoped that this familiarity would further extend to seeing the trademark in one's own cupboard, thereby further personalizing the bond between the consumer and the brand.

Yet, Nabisco wasn't the only company crafting a brand identity in the first decades of the twentieth century. Franco-American's ads featuring the Little Chef had helped establish an origin story that gestured to a humble French kitchen, filled with the purest ingredients, and overseen by an expert child chef. Moreover, both Smith Bros. Cough Drops and Lea & Perrins' Worcestershire Sauce deployed advertising campaigns that emphasized the companies' longevity in their communities to build brand stories. They implicated generational familiarity (and, implicitly, trust) as key characteristics of their companies' histories, using slogans such as "Your Grandpa Knows Us" (for Smith Bros.) and eighteenth-century imagery that established a colonial past (for Lea & Perrins').[108] Again, in building these brand identities, Franco-American, Smith Bros., and Lea & Perrins' applied the principles of brand development that would characterize much of the advertising of the post–World War II period. Despite the relative restrictions of the 1905 law that required logos to be attached to specific products, Nabisco and others managed to develop consistent visual identities across different print media while establishing corporate brands that would stand apart from products bearing the logo.

Importantly, however, Nabisco's brand identity could not reference a reputation built through honest business dealings and satisfied customers over several years, or even decades. Born of the merger movement, National Biscuit was a new company in 1898, without a history or an established clientele. Because of its recent creation, Nabisco had to craft a brand identity for itself in ways that differed from firms that had been engaging in the market for much longer. While Lea & Perrins' or Smith Bros.—or indeed, most of the other firms discussed in this book—had built and carefully protected their commercial reputations over many years, Nabisco's brand identity was, by necessity, entirely constructed. Instead of publicizing its existing reputation, Nabisco had to create an artificial reputation using advertisements and trade journals. In attempting to build goodwill in a very short period of time, Nabisco cleverly drew from the publicity strategies that had sustained at least two generations of advertisers before. The company's success demonstrates a turning point in American advertising: Advertising professionals had succeeded in generating goodwill and brand identity from scratch.

For these reasons, Nabisco's innovations in the early twentieth century mark a culmination of the cultural, legal, and professional developments that had defined advertising practice and trademark use since the 1830s. The trademark now signaled, in a strictly visual way, corporate responsibility and integrity—in short, its character. Though the 1905 Trademark Act required that the mark always be connected to an actual product, Nabisco defied the law in its logo-centered campaign. Its trademark came to stand as both a proprietary label for the company's products *and* a discursive symbol of the company's reputation as a legitimate enterprise by visualizing the guaranteed goodness in each box that left the factory. This was an important step in the construction of brand identity that anticipated the later efforts of firms, such as J. Walter Thompson, to establish corporate identities separate from product attributes in the 1930s.[109]

Moreover, this case study illustrates how business practice developed apart from changes in trademark law. From the moment of the 1905 law's passage, the branding strategies of National Biscuit and other companies pushed the boundaries of the law's provisions. Though the law seemed to initiate a trend toward branding, real change came from the companies and their advertising agents, who drew from the previous century's lessons and innovations to spark change after 1905.[110] These efforts to establish the corporate identity of National Biscuit through the Uneeda brand and the In-Er-Seal logo also prefigured the public relations activities of large corporations in the 1930s and 1940s, which focused on cultivating goodwill through direct expositions of corporate character and responsibility apart from product quality.[111]

National Biscuit's transformative campaign gained national recognition and the attention of industry figureheads in several trade journals. As early as 1901, advertising professionals praised the company's efforts to tell a compelling origin story, which had become a familiar tale in the trade: "everyone knows that Uneeda Biscuits are made from pure flour, by scrupulous bakers, in clean factories, and that they are packed in tight cartons. The story has been told over and over in the preparatory advertising. . . . The bare name has now become a symbol. It means something, for it represents a certain idea."[112] Using repeated phrases and attributes, National Biscuit had successfully associated the ideals of purity and careful workmanship with its products and, through those, with its logo. Adman James Collins therefore called to layout artists and art directors to adopt new strategies that followed this model, arguing that National Biscuit had changed advertising design principles forever. Having done the legwork of building its discursive associations with purity, skilled bakers, and sanitary packaging in previous print ads, National Biscuit could now reduce its advertising copy and focus simply on its logo. Collins noted that, while "the original story must be printed once in a fortnight," the bulk of the work had been done to invest the trademark with a meaningful story that would speak to familiar consumers.[113] Valued at $55 million in 1906, National Biscuit had become one of the largest national producers of household foodstuffs in only eight years—selling approximately 80 million packages annually at the time. Advertising professionals recognized and praised the way the company had transformed its trademark into an asset. The logo had become "a shorthand symbol" that conveyed the quality of Nabisco's products and aided the public in purchase decisions and memory recall.[114]

Nabisco's efforts to build goodwill also drew from decades of legal arguments that had situated trademarks as symbols of reputation, which culminated in the passage of the 1905 trademark law. The association between goodwill and trademarks had been nearly a century in the making in the American legal system, but it came of age amid Progressive calls for virtue and integrity among large corporations and for the protection of consumers. For these reasons, trademark regulation was not inevitable, but rather was contingent upon the interactions of a myriad of historical actors, each one of them a product of its time, who applied their cultural understandings of moral economic behavior in order to shape the market and the law.

Finally, like other firms in this story, Nabisco also took steps to safeguard its brand, reputation, and market share in the courts. Early on, the company brought suits against competitors whose trade names mimicked the Uneeda brand, including "Uwanta," "Iwanta," and "Ulika" biscuits. But the company didn't just protect the Uneeda name; it also policed the graphic properties associated with its logo, bringing several suits against rival bakeries whose labels copied the colors, placement, and design of the red and white In-Er-Seal logo. By 1906, National Biscuit had won approximately 250 cases, forcing competitors to abandon products, names, symbols, and labels that allegedly infringed upon its trademark, its packaging, or the Uneeda name. Though it won several injunctions to stop infringement, the company achieved many more "abandonments" through intimidation: Under threat of legal action, many would-be defendants jettisoned use of their imitation marks in order to avoid prosecution. By 1914—only sixteen years after its inception—National Biscuit had won approximately 830 cases against copyright and trademark infringement (with or without suit), with 145 of those violations involving infringement upon the In-Er-Seal logo alone.[115] Like other corporations at the time, National Biscuit leveraged the legal system to manipulate market competition, achieving, in this case, a reduction in competitors by taking a vigorous approach to safeguarding its trademark and brand.[116]

One particularly telling case ended in 1914, after five long years of litigation. The case of *National Biscuit Co. v. Pacific Biscuit Co. et al.* hinged upon the defendant's deliberate attempt to "palm off his goods as the goods of a rival and thereby cheat the purchasing public and injure the business of the rival."[117] Testimony brought into the record the history of each company, the companies' decisions to choose particular logos for their products, and the iconographic meanings associated with these logos. Recounting the brand story behind the orb-and-cross logo, Nabisco's lawyers entered the cultural and iconographic meanings associated with this sign into the legal record, almost as if this added narrative held the evidence needed to prove the company's virtue. Interestingly, both Nabisco and Pacific Biscuit chose signs with historical and spiritual connotations: the In-Er-Seal utilizing the motif of spirituality over worldliness, and the Swastika seal symbolizing "a beneficent deity, eternal life, benediction and blessing, good wishes and good augury," which purportedly came from a tradition of "prehistoric" spiritual use by both Southeast Asians and the Navajo (figure 6.10).[118] Sales figures, trademark registrations, and advertising expenditures for each company were also entered into the record, with both sides arguing that they had been the first to use their respective red and white logos.[119]

In the judges' eyes, however, the evidence failed to support the timeline constructed by Pacific Biscuit, whose branding and advertising strategy had shifted between 1905 and 1907—just after National Biscuit had gained widespread public favor. Over the course of about a decade, Pacific Biscuit had engineered at least sixteen different products that appeared to deliberately imitate various crackers and cookies in the National Biscuit line, seemingly crafted to mislead and deceive the public. The obvious similarities between these goods were, in the eyes of the court, "so conspicuous that it requires no great perspicuity to observe that the defendant's methods . . . are not attributable to any desire on its part to honestly build up a trade of its own, but rather that they are the culmination of a premeditated and single purpose of dealing under the cover of the good will of a successful rival."[120] Echoing the arguments made by Joseph Story in *Taylor v. Carpenter* in the 1840s, the court disputed Pacific Biscuit's claims of legitimacy and disdained the company's attempt to palm off spurious goods on an unsuspecting public. The judges' arguments focused on the defendant's obvious intent to deceive, which was evidenced in the close visual parallels between the Pacific Biscuit and National Biscuit lines. It was the West Coast manufacturer's devious moral character, verified through intent, on which the judges based their decision to grant the injunction.[121]

Figure 6.10. Uneeda Biscuit and Abetta Biscuit cartons, entered into evidence in *National Biscuit Co. v. Pacific Biscuit Co. et al.* 83 NJ Eq. 369 (1914). Reprinted from *National Biscuit Co., Trade Mark Litigation*, 5th ed. (private pub., 1915), 210. The IN ER SEAL Design is owned by Mondelēz International Group, used with permission.

The remarkable parallels between the opinions in the cases of *National Biscuit v. Pacific Biscuit* (1914) and *Taylor v. Carpenter* (1844), separated by almost three-quarters of a century, illuminates persistent tensions within the American capitalist system. In the antebellum period, the nascent industrial economy had facilitated a range of sketchy enterprises, shady business deals, and counterfeit products. In response, state and federal judges had applied the moral standards of the white middle class when demarcating the boundaries of fair competition. By the end of the century, Progressive reformers continued to worry about the unchecked power of capitalism to breed social ills, fraud, and destruction. Passing the 1905 trademark law promised one mode of renewing confidence and trust in the capitalist system.[122] But the dichotomies between genuine and fraudulent, virtuous and immoral, remained a problem even after the 1905 law.

Continued diligence from the courts provided a secondary mode of combating fraud and infringement, using federal regulation to bolster confidence in the system. Through litigation, producers like Nabisco not only used federal trademark law and registration as a validating force, but they also leveraged the law and courts to invalidate (and bankrupt) competitors who deviated from the ideal of honest competition. Emphasizing the damage done to the public and its own reputation, Nabisco persuaded the courts to chastise its rival and ultimately succeeded in eliminating a major competitor from its trade. Trademark law had thus proved to be both a mechanism for protecting the public and a useful tool for manufacturers seeking to gain a larger market share. Just as federal agents verified the quality of processed meats after the passage of the Meat Inspection Act in 1906, the courts and the Patent Office offered enforcement mechanisms that invalidated imitation and counterfeit marks. In this way, safeguarding one's commercial reputation—one's brand—from those who unscrupulously sought to deceive the public became an essential way to ensure public trust in the system of production and consumption. Trademark regulation offered a mechanism to ensure the integrity and perseverance of American capitalism itself.

*   *   *

In these ways, the early branding practices of National Biscuit can be considered a culmination of the advertising strategies developed throughout the nineteenth century, which had focused on protecting one's reputation, defining immoral commercial activity as fraudulent, and creating convincing textual and visual messages in print. Over time, these strategies contributed to a conceptual framework that would locate trademarks' value in their ability to link notions of reputation, honesty, and appeal. Thus, trademarks became valuable cultural, economic, and legal symbols through an evolving conversation among several important historical actors, each of whom played a part in configuring trademarks' relationship to branding. The discursive interplay between admen's evolving theories and practices related to branding, on the one hand, and jurists' attempts to define and protect goodwill, on the other, would have profound effects on the visual appearance of advertisements in the early twentieth century. Agencies like J. Walter Thompson and N. W. Ayer & Son devised ways to increase public awareness of the brand and cultivate goodwill by explaining how the trademark symbolized the manufacturer's reputation and integrity. These strategies materialized in the 1904–1906 branding campaign for National Biscuit.

Of course, the rise of multimillion-dollar corporations like Nabisco cannot be solely attributed to the success of its advertising. Economic crises in the 1890s precipitated the merger and consolidation of many industries (including large-scale bakeries). Infringement lawsuits provided another mode of decimating the competition and indirectly consolidating industries. By prohibiting fakes and knock-offs, the trademark law made illegal a large and varied sector of the market. This, in turn, facilitated the rise of multinational corporations like Nabisco, whose enlarged legal budgets helped defend the reputation of its genuine products against unlawful and immoral competitors. Moreover, the ways in which the 1905 trademark law ultimately mirrored the persistent cultural significance of intent and character highlights an important symbiotic quality to the relationship between business practice and the law. The strategies that advertisers devised for attracting consumers (using appealing images, displaying class and character, and shoring up one's reputation) informed the guidelines for ethical business practice developed in the courts and in trade literature, that in turn became the model for the 1905 US trademark law. Importantly, Nabisco's self-conscious, straightforward, and honest approach—evident in the streamlined designs and simple, transparent text of the ads—suggests that trust could be constructed and communicated visually through graphic symbols. All of this discursive activity would eventually position the trademark as a cultural and legal annotation of goodwill. By 1910, as legal experts began to see the need to expand trademark protections yet again, a prominent scholar summarized this relationship succinctly: "The good will of a business is often of greater value than all the tangible property, and a trade mark is nothing but good will symbolized."[123]

Epilogue

Trusting Brands

In 1922, the poet Vachel Lindsay wrote that American civilization was becoming more and more "hieroglyphic" in character. The proliferation of images in American culture had a universal power and appeal, in Lindsay's view. He drew particular attention to those in the commercial realm and noted that the "advertisements in the back of the magazines and on the bill-boards and in the street-cars, the acres of photographs in the Sunday newspapers, make us into a hieroglyphic civilization far nearer to Egypt than to England."[1] Advertisements distilled textual messages into value-laden symbol systems that communicated to viewers through fleeting glances. Lindsay's society was saturated with symbolic visual icons; they were everywhere he looked. But this system was not necessarily new in the early twentieth century. Since the colonial period, Americans had cherished visual symbols as markers of identity, class status, education, and sentiment. By the early nineteenth century, businessmen and others had learned to convey their status to the public through carefully chosen language and dress, in print and on the streets. Such displays tended to inform credit relationships and professional success. In each of these cases, displays of status were mediated through vision and visuality. It was no different in advertising. For advertisers seeking public patronage, printers helped devise important visual strategies for attracting public attention, entertaining readers, and communicating virtue and character. In newspapers, posters, and ephemera, they innovated new ways to join word and image, creating communicative icons that spoke to public sensibilities. Advertisers and printers had crafted ways to display their status—their reputations—through visual means, locating reputation and goodwill in the symbology of the trademark. By the first decade of the twentieth century, graphic designers had picked up this torch. The "hieroglyphic civilization" that Lindsay saw in the 1920s was thus the product of nearly a century of experimentation among advertising agents, printers, and their clients to assert the importance of the visual and to ground advertising's commercial language in trademarks.

The task of gaining consumers' trust had been multipronged, drawing from rhetorical and visual modes of appeal, on the one hand, and rejecting deception and fraud in the market, on the other. One side of the strategy involved proactively developing textual and visual tactics that would grab viewers' attention, quell their skepticism, and build rapport. But the other side of the strategy focused on improving the moral standards of market activity, as immorality and deception fanned the flames of consumer fears and disrupted advertisers' attempts to gain consumers' trust. Improving commercial honesty meant rooting out fakes and counterfeit goods, prosecuting trademark infringement, and extending the regulatory arm of the federal government to boost consumers' confidence in the American market. Both wings of this strategy—proactive appeals to consumers and eliminating fraud—were ultimately designed to generate consumers' trust, both in the market and in the products themselves. Trust was the necessary building block for the branding regime that structured American consumer culture in the twentieth century and beyond. It had evolved through middle-class cultural practices and notions of commercial honesty over time, before finding its home in federal law.

Yet, despite the relative success of the 1905 trademark law, legal theorists began to criticize the law's limitations as early as the 1920s, particularly for the ways it failed to protect the myriad understandings of goodwill already in commercial practice. According to legal expert Frank Schechter, the provision in the 1905 law that associated the trademark with a product's origins caused many judges to apply unreasonably narrow criteria to trademark-infringement cases. Few consumers, he stipulated, actually knew the "true origins" of the products they purchased, and they were "indifferent" to this information as long as the quality of the product lived up to its reputation.[2] For Schechter, the common law of the nineteenth century had demonstrated that the trademark was a direct index of the manufacturer's goodwill with the public. In Schechter's view, the trademark provided a "guaranty [sic] that the goods . . . will have the same meritorious qualities as those previously noted by him in his purchases of other goods bearing the same mark. The mark 'sells the goods.'"[3] Calling for revisions to federal law, Schechter complained that the law ought to do a better job of incorporating this broad understanding of goodwill, especially as it was associated with the brand. As business practices had evolved after 1905, legal experts continued to press legislators to accommodate the changing commercial atmosphere in the United States. Schechter's voice became one among many in an escalating call for revision that would eventually result in the passage of the 1946 Lanham Act.[4] Trademark legislation thus matured out of the 1905 law's foundation and, since 1946, it has expanded to protect these increasingly broad understandings of brand symbolism and to restrict new forms of infringement.

After World War I, the United States experienced another period of rapid economic development. As in the nineteenth century, industrialization, immigration, and the expansion of credit accompanied growth in the manufacturing sector in the United States, which precipitated an abundance of consumer goods in the 1920s. Between 1922 and 1929, the national gross domestic product and per capita incomes rose by almost 30 percent, while protective tariffs against foreign goods allowed domestic manufacturing to multiply. High employment rates, low inflation, and expanded access to credit enhanced the spending power of skilled workers and the middle class in the 1920s.[5] In the advertising industry, increased spending among manufacturers and retailers fueled innovations, and agencies continued to extend their domestic and international operations. Drawing from scientific management theories, admen incorporated new market-research techniques and applied theories of economics and psychology to craft more subtly persuasive messages to the public.[6]

With these advances, advertising professionals developed increasingly sophisticated ways to connect their clients' products to status, emotions, and cultural experience. Brands became ubiquitous in American society by the mid-twentieth century, and advertisements explicitly encouraged individuals to assert their identities through the purchase and display of particular commodities. The enduring discursive connections linking brand names, trademarks, and trust characterized many of the most memorable advertising campaigns of the twentieth century, including, for example, the 1940s slogan for Texaco Fuel: "You can trust your car to the man who wears the star."[7] By the 1970s, advertising professionals had learned to position the brand in an affective relationship with the consumer—a relationship that was built through the individual's varied experiences with the brand and characterized by memory, emotion, and personal connection—which would allow individuals to create and express their identities.[8] Building these emotional connections between the brand and the public, advertising professionals found new ways to achieve the same goals that had fueled their industry since the early nineteenth century.

In the 1980s, for example, Midas Muffler released a new ad campaign centered on the slogan, "Trust the Midas Touch." After a brief hiatus in use, the company revived the slogan in 2004, and continued to use it as of 2021.[9] In an interview that recalled the words of National Biscuit's president Adolphus Green a century earlier, Midas president and CEO Alan Feldman explained that "trust is the essence of any brand and a differentiating and enduring legacy of the Midas brand. . . . It is a way of doing business that becomes the foundation of our brand . . . [and] the campaign assures customers that they can expect professional and trustworthy service provided at great value."[10] Using the keywords "value," "professional," and "trustworthy," Feldman constructed a brand identity for his company that would, he hoped, remind consumers that they could trust and rely on his repair shops and the technicians employed there. While his buzzwords characterized the efforts of corporations to relate to their customers at the turn of the twenty-first century, his associations between the brand and customer trust paralleled Nabisco's branding efforts one hundred years earlier. This approach to building brand identity—a sense of personality associated with the corporation and its products—has become a central component of advertising strategies in contemporary business practice. To put it more simply, branding in the twenty-first century is about cultivating and building trust among consumers. Yet, as this book has shown, what advertisers today call trust has been alternatively known as goodwill, commercial honesty, and reputation in American business culture dating back to the 1830s. Though the terms have shifted, the concepts remain the same; in order to convince the public to buy, one has to gain their trust.

In some ways, though, the ideal of trust has become a vacant symbol in American advertising. Invoked as a frequent sales pitch today, the concept has become ubiquitous in contemporary advertising campaigns and carries little of the moral weight that propelled antebellum advertisers and jurists to argue so passionately about its association with reputation and virtue. It has become cliché for advertisers to incorporate the language of trust and honesty in representing their services, their products, and their corporations to the American people. It is almost as if the public expects companies to maintain this façade of virtue and honesty, even when we know that many corporations do not treat their employees well, that they may take shortcuts when it comes to environmentally sound production methods, and that money-back guarantees are not always ironclad.

If corporate references to honesty and trust have become cliché, consumers are more likely to simply accept these references as part and parcel of what advertising does. There is a peculiar process in capitalism that erases the meanings inherent in traditional symbols. Trust has become just another commodified thing, a concept invoked over and over again to the point of its ubiquity. But when we stop to consider *why* this particular phrase and this concept have become such a hallmark of contemporary advertising, we realize that this invocation has a history, one entirely contingent on cultural understandings of reputation developed by the white middle class in the early nineteenth century. The connection between brands and trust was not predetermined; rather, these ideas evolved over time in messy and uneven ways. Demonstrating one's commercial honesty and reputation was baked into the DNA of print advertising in the early nineteenth century specifically because economic instability cultivated anxieties about the trustworthiness of one's potential trading partners.

Nineteenth-century jurists strengthened the conceptual frameworks of virtue and reputation in policing the boundaries of legitimate commercial practice and fair competition. Again, these concepts evolved out of the cultural norms upheld by the antebellum middle class, and the judges' decisions in trademark cases represented an effort to prescribe moral standards for ethical business practice while restraining the unchecked forces of capitalism—greed and fraud—that threatened the downfall of American society. The century's many financial panics had demonstrated the structural and physical violence that could be wrought on American families, on the cities, and on artisanal laborers. While reformers throughout the century sought to curb these unchecked forces in their movements for the abolition of slavery, urban sanitation, the prohibition of alcohol, the elimination of child labor, and the education of the working classes (among other movements), jurists sought to curb these same forces by imposing moral standards on corporate and commercial actors. The efforts of reformers and jurists can thus be framed as two sides of the same coin—both stemmed from a revulsion toward the unsavory side effects of capitalist industrialization. One might call this an effort to reassert the importance of a moral economy, or, perhaps, an effort to inscribe the political economy with moral values.

In these ways, the political economy that enacted the 1905 trademark law was a result of disparate forces that sought to ensure that market competition operated according to culturally accepted moral values. Admen shamed the producers of imitation and counterfeit products, applying a cultural punishment that paralleled the legal punishments against trademark infringement enacted in the courts and the legislatures. Through these discursive mechanisms, American capitalists policed the boundaries of fair competition, marking as illegitimate the practices that failed to conform to their culturally established standards. Though they adapted and modified those standards and practices over the nineteenth century and into the twentieth, American advertisers and advertising professionals held tight to the principle that maintaining and protecting one's reputation was a key component in earning the public's trust, and thus their patronage. Advertisers, printers, and admen branded trust as an essential element of American capitalism—an element that was refined through advertising and communicated in print and other media.

Significantly, the continuities between the antebellum and postbellum periods in the United States outweigh many of the disruptions witnessed during the Civil War years, especially in the areas of consumption and advertising. Beginning in the 1830s and over the next century, advertising professionals learned how to navigate public relations by crafting consumer-oriented appeals that would build and maintain goodwill with the public—the necessary ingredient for protecting one's reputation, winning a larger market share, and growing profits. Advertisers in the early nineteenth century attempted to win public favor through the best method they knew: They demonstrated their character and class in printed advertisements that would speak to like-minded members of the white middle class. Through the middle decades of the century, market competition increased and pushed printers and advertisers to continually reframe, adapt, and innovate strategies to attract the viewer's eye and to gain his or her confidence. Entertainment aesthetics shaped advertising strategies in newspapers, trade cards, and other visual media. In trade characters such as the Franco-American Little Chef, corporations built upon the sentimental symbolism of Victorian visual culture and devised new strategies for communicating character in print. At the same time, manufacturers formulated ways to protect their brands from infringement, relying heavily on the courts to police the boundaries of fair and unfair competition. The moral stipulations that framed fair competition in the antebellum years would provide the foundation for the development of federal trademark law, first in 1870 and then in 1905. By that time, the terms "goodwill" and "branding" had come to replace the emphasis that admen had placed on reputation and trademark-centered advertising.

These interrelated developments in law, culture, and business practice are only visible when the historian takes a longer view of the nineteenth century, looking for patterns of continuity and transformation between the antebellum and postbellum periods. Demonstrations of character, protecting trademarks, and entertaining novelties in print came together at the end of the nineteenth century, cementing the legal importance of trademarks and goodwill together with the entertainment aesthetics of visual appeals. In these ways, visual media hold the key for understanding the development of America's modern consumption regime. Branding trust has become a central component of American capitalism, but that trust has been primarily imagined and established through trademarks, advertising imagery, and the visual rhetoric of commercial honesty.

Notes

The following abbreviations appear in the notes.

AAS	American Antiquarian Society, Worcester, MA
AC NMAH	Archives Center, National Museum of American History, Washington, DC
Ayer	N. W. Ayer Advertising Agency Records, Archives Center, National Museum of American History, Washington, DC (formerly, N. W. Ayer ABH International Collection 59)
BTC HL	Business Trade Cards Ephemera Collection, The Huntington Library, San Marino, CA
DCWL	Joseph Downs Collection of Manuscripts and Printed Ephemera, Henry Francis du Pont Winterthur Museum and Library, Winterthur, DE
Duke	John W. Hartman Center for Sales, Advertising, and Marketing History, David M. Rubenstein Rare Books and Manuscripts Library, Duke University, Durham, NC
JWTPC	J. Walter Thompson Company, Publications Collection, John W. Hartman Center for Sales, Advertising, and Marketing History, David M. Rubenstein Rare Books and Manuscripts Library, Duke University, Durham, NC
Last HL	Jay T. Last Collection of Printing and Publishing, The Huntington Library, San Marino, CA
LCP	Rare Books Collections, The Library Company of Philadelphia, Philadelphia, PA
LOCPP	Library of Congress Prints & Photographs Division, Washington, DC
RBWL	Rare Books Collection, Henry Francis du Pont Winterthur Museum and Library, Winterthur, DE
RRD	R. R. Donnelley & Sons Company Archive, Hanna Holborn Gray Special Collections Research Center, University of Chicago Library, Chicago, IL
USPTO	United States Patent & Trademark Office Archival Records, Washington, DC
Warshaw	Warshaw Collection of Business Americana (Col. 60), Archives Center, National Museum of American History, Washington, DC

Introduction

1. The cases in question were as follows: in New York, *Taylor v. Carpenter* (1844), 11 Paige Ch. 292; and *J. Coats et al. v. Holbrook, Nelson & Co.* (1845), 2 Sand. Ch. 586. In Massachusetts, *Taylor v. Carpenter* (1844), 23 Fed. Cas. 744; and *Coats, James et al. v. Thayer, Benjamin, and Bufford, John*, Oct. Term 1844 (unreported); U.S. Circuit Court for the District of Massachusetts; Case Files, 1790–1911; Record Group 21: Records of District Courts of the United States, 1685–2009; National Archives at Boston.

2. Jack Authelet, *Foxborough: Gem of Norfolk County* (Charleston, SC: Arcadia, 2001), 42, 76.

3. Historically, when trade journals spoke of "advertisers," they referred primarily to the individuals and firms placing advertisements in public media, which could include individual proprietors, agents for proprietors, distributors, retailers, or others. In general, the term "advertiser" did not refer to individuals involved in the advertising industry until after World War I, though as late as the 1920s advertising agents continued to use this term to refer to their clients. Throughout the nineteenth century, men involved in the advertising industry generally referred to themselves and each other as "agents," as "industry men," or by particular role in the industry, such as "copyists," "illustrators," "editors," and the like. In the following chapters, I have attempted to preserve this historical variance in terms and refer to individuals advertising their own wares or services as "advertisers" or "manufacturers" interchangeably, while using terms like "admen" (the industry's own slang term) or "agents" to refer to the group of professionals who acted on behalf of others to design, place, and distribute published advertisements.

4. Mira Wilkins, "The Neglected Intangible Asset: The Influence of the Trade Mark on the Rise of the Modern Corporation," *Business History* 34, no. 1 (1992): 66–68.

5. Lionel Bently, "The Making of Modern Trade Mark Law: The Construction of the Legal Concept of Trade Mark (1860–1880)," in *Trade Marks and Brands: An Interdisciplinary Critique*, ed. Jane C. Ginsburg et al. (New York: Cambridge University Press, 2008), 3; Teresa da Silva Lopes and Mark Casson, "Brand Protection and the Globalization of British Business," *Business History Review* 86, no. 2 (2012): 291; and David M. Higgins, "'Forgotten Heroes and Forgotten Issues': Business and Trademark History During the Nineteenth Century," *Business History Review* 86, no. 2 (2012): 283.

6. Nancy Koehn lays out these functions in *Brand New: How Entrepreneurs Earned Consumers' Trust from Wedgwood to Dell* (Boston: Harvard Business School Press, 2001), 328–329. Susan Strasser makes a similar argument about profit margins in *Satisfaction Guaranteed: The Making of the American Mass Market* (Washington, DC: Smithsonian Books, 1989), 28.

7. Ariel Katz, "Beyond Search Costs: The Linguistic and Trust Functions of Trademarks," *Brigham Young University Law Review* 2010, no. 5 (2010): 1566–1568.

8. I am building my analysis from the work of Ruth E. Iskin, who proposes an inversion to Walter Benjamin's notion of the diminishing aura, which she calls "auratization." See Iskin, *The Poster: Art, Advertising, Design, and Collecting, 1860s–1900s* (Hanover, NH: Dartmouth College Press, 2014), 27–29; and Walter Benjamin, "The Work of Art in the Age of Mechanical Reproduction," in *Illuminations* (New York: Schocken Books, 1969), 221–223.

9. While many scholars agree that the term "branding" became part of common advertising parlance after 1945, some trace its origins to the 1890s or earlier, especially Stefan Schwarzkopf, "Turning Trademarks into Brands: How Advertising Agencies Practiced and Conceptualized Branding, 1890–1930," in *Trademarks, Brands, and Competitiveness*, ed. Teresa da Silva Lopes and Paul Duguid (New York: Routledge, 2010), 166. See also Koehn, *Brand New*, 60; Paul Duguid, "Developing the Brand: The Case of Alcohol, 1800–1880," *Enterprise & Society* 4, no. 3 (2003): 433–436; Duguid, "French Connections: The International Propagation of Trademarks in the Nineteenth Century," *Enterprise & Society* 10, no. 1 (2009): 3–37; Andreas P. Zangger, "Chops and Trademarks: Asian Trading Ports and Textile Branding,

1840–1920," *Enterprise & Society* 15, no. 4 (2014): 759–790; and Ross D. Petty, "Pain-Killer: A 19th Century Global Patent Medicine and the Beginnings of Modern Brand Marketing," *Journal of Macromarketing* 39, no. 3 (2019): 287–303.

10. John R. Commons, *Legal Foundations of Capitalism* (1924; repr. Madison: University of Wisconsin Press, 1968), 199, 213, 263–265.

11. I thus refer to the confluence of meanings and reputation signified by the trademark and aura of the product as the "brand" and the process of constructing said meanings and reputation as "branding." This is a conscious language choice meant to reinforce the book's arguments that the roots of modern branding practice substantially predate the 1890s.

12. Frank Presbrey, *The History and Development of Advertising* (Garden City, NY: Doubleday, Doran & Co., 1929).

13. Related studies privilege the achievements of a select group of entrepreneurs, whose successes might provide models for future business leaders. See Douglas B. Holt, *How Brands Become Icons: The Principles of Cultural Branding* (Boston: Harvard Business School Press, 2004); and Koehn, *Brand New*.

14. Presbrey, *History of Advertising*, 236–240. Ann Douglas traces the interwar generation's rejection of Victorian value systems in *Terrible Honesty: Mongrel Manhattan in the 1920s* (New York: Farrar, Straus and Giroux, 1995).

15. Later scholars denounced advertising's role in manipulating individual desires in order to maintain corporate hegemony, especially Vance Packard, *The Hidden Persuaders* (New York: David McKay Co., 1957); and Stuart Ewen, *Captains of Consciousness: Advertising and the Social Roots of the Consumer Culture* (New York: Basic Books, 2001 [1976]). Others disputed the oppressive power of advertisements, especially Stephen Fox, *The Mirror Makers: A History of American Advertising and Its Creators*, 2nd ed. (Chicago: University of Illinois Press, 1997 [1984]); and Michael Schudson, *Advertising, the Uneasy Persuasion: Its Dubious Impact on American Society* (New York: Basic Books, 1984). Even still, subsequent scholars have tended to uphold Presbrey's periodization. Daniel Pope plays a key role in this literature, as his book, *The Making of Modern Advertising* (New York: Basic Books, 1983), provided a foundational reference for the next generation of advertising historians. See Strasser, *Satisfaction Guaranteed*; James D. Norris, *Advertising and the Transformation of American Society, 1865–1920* (Westport, CT: Greenwood Press, 1990); Regina Lee Blaszczyk, *American Consumer Society, 1865–2005: From Hearth to HDTV* (London: Wiley, 2009); and Edd Applegate, *The Rise of Advertising in the United States: A History of Innovation to 1960* (Lanham, MD: Scarecrow Press, 2012). Through Pope, Presbrey's work has also influenced adjacent studies, such as Michael Pettit, *The Science of Deception: Psychology and Commerce in America* (Chicago: University of Chicago Press, 2013); Joseph M. Gabriel, *Medical Monopoly: Intellectual Property Rights and the Origins of the Modern Pharmaceutical Industry* (Chicago: University of Chicago Press, 2014); Gary S. Cross and Robert Proctor, *Packaged Pleasures: How Technology & Marketing Revolutionized Desire* (Chicago: University of Chicago Press, 2014); and Benjamin R. Cohen, *Pure Adulteration: Cheating on Nature in the Age of Manufactured Food* (Chicago: University of Chicago Press, 2022).

16. Presbrey drew heavily from Henry Sampson's *The History of Advertising from Its Earliest Years* (London: Chatto and Windus, 1874); George Rowell, *Forty Years an Advertising Agent, 1865–1905* (New York: Printers' Ink Publishing Co., 1906); Joseph Herbert Appel and Leigh Mitchell Hodges, *Golden Book of the Wanamaker Stores: Jubilee Year, 1861–1911* (Philadelphia: John Wanamaker, 1911); Claude Hopkins, *My Life in Advertising* (New York: Harper & Row, 1927); and various other trade manuals and institutional histories. This genre continued to characterize most publishing on advertising and its history until the 1970s. See, especially, Ralph M. Hower, *The History of an Advertising Agency: N. W. Ayer & Son at Work, 1869–1939* (Cambridge, MA: Harvard University Press, 1939); John Gunther, *Taken at the*

Flood: The Story of Albert D. Lasker (New York: Harper, 1960); and David Ogilvy, *Confessions of an Advertising Man* (New York: Atheneum, 1963).

17. Pope, *Making of Modern Advertising*, 5, 8, 34, 119, 133.

18. Juliann Sivulka, *Soap, Sex, and Cigarettes: A Cultural History of American Advertising* (Belmont, CA: Wadsworth, 1998), 34–36, 81. See also Pamela Walker Laird, *Advertising Progress: American Business and the Rise of Consumer Marketing* (Baltimore: Johns Hopkins University Press, 1998), chap. 5; and T. J. Jackson Lears, *Fables of Abundance: A Cultural History of Advertising in America* (New York: Basic Books, 1994), chap. 3.

19. See, for example, Rowell, *Forty Years an Advertising Agent*; J. Walter Thompson, *Blue Book on Advertising* (1901), JWTPC, Duke; and "A Veteran Newspaper Man," *Elk County Advocate*, February 19, 1874. Later scholars would credit these agencies with the explosion of brand-name goods after 1945. See Tom Blackett, "What Is a Brand?" in *Brands and Branding*, ed. Rita Clifton (New York: Wiley, 2009), 15; John Mercer, "A Mark of Distinction: Branding and Trade Mark Law in the UK from the 1860s," *Business History* 52, no. 1 (2010): 33–35; and Pope, *Making of Modern Advertising*, 8, 111.

20. Montgomery Ward appeared in the late 1870s and Sears Roebuck in the 1890s. See William Cronon, *Nature's Metropolis: Chicago and the Great West* (New York: W. W. Norton, 1992), 318–340; and Strasser, *Satisfaction Guaranteed*, 77, 90–94, 212–222.

21. Several scholars have advocated for a top-down interpretation of trademark law, suggesting that changes in the law pushed corporate innovations to ensure novelty and a competitive advantage. See Mercer, "Mark of Distinction," 22, 35; Wilkins, "Intangible Asset," 82; Carma Gorman, "The Role of Trademark Law in the History of US Visual Identity Design, c.1860–1960," *Journal of Design History* 30, no. 4 (2017): 371–388; and Oren Bracha, "The Emergence and Development of United States Intellectual Property Law," in *The Oxford Handbook of Intellectual Property Law*, ed. Rochelle Cooper Dreyfuss and Justine Pila (New York: Oxford University Press, 2018), 264. In contrast, Paul Duguid argues that the law follows, rather than prescribes, business practice in "A Case of Prejudice? The Uncertain Development of Collective and Certification Marks," *Business History Review* 86, no. 2 (2012): 332.

22. Early Americanists have well-established America's early place in global trade and the effects of this on consumption and domestic industrialization. See Richard L. Bushman, *The Refinement of America: Persons, Houses, Cities* (New York: Vintage Books, 1993), 407; T. H. Breen, *The Marketplace of Revolution: How Consumer Politics Shaped American Independence* (New York: Oxford University Press, 2004); Ann Smart Martin, *Buying into the World of Goods: Early Consumers in Backcountry Virginia* (Baltimore: Johns Hopkins University Press, 2010); David Jaffee, *A New Nation of Goods: The Material Culture of Early America* (Philadelphia: University of Pennsylvania Press, 2012); Peter Andreas, *Smuggler Nation: How Illicit Trade Made America* (New York: Oxford University Press, 2013); Cary Carson, *Face Value: The Consumer Revolution and the Colonizing of America* (Richmond: University of Virginia Press, 2017); and Edward Cooke, *Inventing Boston: Design, Production, and Consumption* (New Haven, CT: Yale University Press, 2019).

23. In formulating a theory of brand-emergence, Koehn argues that periods of rapid industrialization help precipitate the emergence of name-brand goods; see Koehn, *Brand New*, 307. While her discussion largely overlooks the antebellum years, I would argue that such a period of rapid industrialization created a ripe situation for the growing use of trademarks in the United States before the Civil War. On the industrial development of the United States after 1800, see John Lauritz Larson, *The Market Revolution in America: Liberty, Ambition, and the Eclipse of the Common Good* (Cambridge: Cambridge University Press, 2009); and Stuart M. Blumin, *The Emergence of the Middle Class: Social Experience in the American City, 1760–1900* (New York: Cambridge University Press, 1989), 79. While the phrase "Market Rev-

olution" has become shorthand for the economic changes of this period, multiple scholars have problematized this concept, especially for the ways it obscures earlier developments. See, especially, Carson's arguments, first postulated in the 1980s, in *Face Value*, chap. 1.

24. In 1959, Alfred D. Chandler Jr. argued that the growth of the national market after the Civil War was a prerequisite for the rise of large, vertically integrated corporations in the United States (in "The Beginnings of Big Business in American Industry," *Business History Review* 33, no. 1 (1959): 1–31). Since then, several scholars have offered alternative criteria for the development of the American national market, but they tend to reinforce Chandler's original periodization. See, for example, Charles McCurdy, "American Law and the Marketing Structure of the Large Corporation, 1875–1890," *Journal of Economic History* 38, no. 3 (1978): 631–649; and note 15 in this chapter.

25. Rowena Olegario, *A Culture of Credit: Embedding Trust and Transparency in American Business* (Cambridge, MA: Harvard University Press, 2006), 15–35.

26. Edward J. Balleisen, *Navigating Failure: Bankruptcy and Commercial Society in Antebellum America* (Chapel Hill: University of North Carolina Press, 2001), 46.

27. Jessica M. Lepler, *The Many Panics of 1837: People, Politics, and the Creation of a Transatlantic Financial Crisis* (Cambridge: Cambridge University Press, 2013), 3–4.

28. Balleisen, *Navigating Failure*, 39.

29. Larson, *Market Revolution*, 8–10.

30. Larson, 9. On anonymity and class identity, see Karen Halttunen, *Confidence Men and Painted Women: A Study of Middle-Class Culture in America, 1830–1870* (New Haven: Yale University Press, 1982), 20–25; and David M. Henkin, *City Reading: Written Words and Public Spaces in Antebellum New York* (New York: Columbia University Press, 1998), 65. While Halttunen and Henkin connect class identity to language, others argue that Americans registered class identities through the consumption of durable goods, such as dishware and furniture. See Bushman, *Refinement*; Regina Lee Blaszczyk, *Imagining Consumers: Design and Innovation from Wedgwood to Corning* (Baltimore: Johns Hopkins University Press, 2000); and Kenneth Ames, *Death in the Dining Room and Other Tales of Victorian Culture* (Philadelphia: Temple University Press, 1992).

31. Halttunen, *Confidence Men*, 195; and Bushman, *Refinement*, xv–xvi. See also Norbert Elias, *The Civilizing Process, Volume 1: The History of Manners* (New York: Blackwell, 1978 [1939]); C. Dallett Hemphill, *Bowing to Necessities: A History of Manners in America, 1620–1860* (New York: Oxford University Press, 2002); and Catherine E. Kelly, *Republic of Taste: Art, Politics, and Everyday Life in Early America* (Philadelphia: University of Pennsylvania Press, 2016).

32. Halttunen, *Confidence Men*, xiv, 60–64, 195; John F. Kasson, *Rudeness & Civility: Manners in Nineteenth-Century Urban America* (New York: Hill and Wang, 1990), 216; and Jennifer L. Goloboy, *Charleston and the Emergence of Middle-Class Culture in the Revolutionary Era* (Atlanta: University of Georgia Press, 2016), 5–7.

33. Konstantin Dierks, *In My Power: Letter Writing and Communications in Early America* (Philadelphia: University of Pennsylvania Press, 2009), 283–284; and Thomas Augst, *The Clerk's Tale: Young Men and Moral Life in Nineteenth-Century America* (Chicago: University of Chicago Press, 2003), 16.

34. Kelly, *Republic of Taste*, 6–8. See also Michael Zakim, *Ready-Made Democracy: A History of Men's Dress in the American Republic, 1760–1860* (Chicago: University of Chicago Press, 2005); Tamara Plakins Thornton, *Handwriting in America: A Cultural History* (New Haven, CT: Yale University Press, 1996); Halttunen, *Confidence Men*; and Augst, *Clerk's Tale*.

35. See notes 30–34 in this chapter.

36. Koehn argues that brands help alleviate such information asymmetries in the market, in *Brand New*, 316, 329.

37. Edward J. Balleisen, *Fraud: An American History from Barnum to Madoff* (Princeton, NJ: Princeton University Press, 2017), 7.

38. McCurdy, "American Law," 642.

39. Richard R. John, "Ruling Passions: Political Economy in Nineteenth-Century America," *Journal of Policy History* 18, no. 1 (2006): 2. See also William J. Novak, "The Myth of the 'Weak' American State," *American Historical Review* 113, no. 3 (2008): 752–772.

40. Robert J. Gamble, "The Promiscuous Economy: Cultural and Commercial Geographies of Secondhand in the Antebellum City," in Brian P. Luskey and Wendy A. Woloson, eds., *Capitalism by Gaslight: Illuminating the Economy of Nineteenth-Century America* (Philadelphia: University of Pennsylvania Press, 2015), 31–52; and Corey Goettsch, "'The World Is But One Vast Mock Auction': Fraud and Capitalism in Nineteenth-Century America," in Luskey and Woloson, *Capitalism by Gaslight*, 109–126.

41. Stephen Mihm, *A Nation of Counterfeiters: Capitalists, Con Men, and the Making of the United States* (Cambridge, MA: Harvard University Press, 2007), 24, 51, 210.

42. Balleisen, *Navigating Failure*, 102–106, 130–132.

43. Olegario, *Culture of Credit*, 3–12; and Sharon Ann Murphy, *Investing in Life: Insurance in Antebellum America* (Baltimore: Johns Hopkins University Press, 2010), chap. 2. Lears shows how these ideals influenced admen's professionalization efforts in *Fables of Abundance*, 212.

44. Frank I. Schechter, "The Rational Basis of Trademark Protection," *Harvard Law Review* 40, no. 6 (1927): 831.

45. Several scholars have since disputed Presbrey's periodization of American consumer society, pushing its origin point back to at least the 1840s, if not earlier. See Neil McKendrick, John Brewer, and John Harold Plumb, *The Birth of a Consumer Society: The Commercialization of Eighteenth-Century England* (London: Europa Publications, 1982); Paul G. E. Clemens, "The Consumer Culture of the Middle Atlantic, 1760–1820," *William and Mary Quarterly* 62, no. 4 (2005): 577–624; Wendy A. Woloson, "The Rise of the Consumer in the Age of Jackson," in *A Companion to the Era of Andrew Jackson*, ed. Sean Patrick Adams (New York: Blackwell, 2013), 489–508; Joanna Cohen, *Luxurious Citizens: The Politics of Consumption in Nineteenth-Century America* (Philadelphia: University of Pennsylvania Press, 2017); Steven Carl Smith, *An Empire of Print: The New York Publishing Trade in the Early American Republic* (University Park: Pennsylvania State University Press, 2017); and Woloson, *Crap: A History of Cheap Stuff in America* (Chicago: University of Chicago Press, 2020).

46. Here, I take a methodological cue from Philip Scranton in *Figured Tapestry: Production, Markets, and Power in Philadelphia Textiles, 1855–1941* (New York: Cambridge University Press, 1989), 505.

47. Pamela Walker Laird advocates for such an approach in "The Business of Consumer Culture History: Systems, Interactions, and Modernization," in *Decoding Modern Consumer Societies*, ed. H. Berghoff and U. Spiekermann (New York: Palgrave Macmillan, 2012), 89–109. Related models include Sally H. Clarke, *Trust and Power: Consumers, the Modern Corporation, and the Making of the United States Automobile Market* (New York: Cambridge University Press, 2007); and Nan Enstad, *Cigarettes, Inc.: An Intimate History of Corporate Imperialism* (Chicago: University of Chicago Press, 2018). See also Bruno Latour, *Reassembling the Social: An Introduction to Actor-Network-Theory* (New York: Oxford University Press, 2005).

48. Since the 1990s, scholars of visual culture have proven the agency of images in precipitating change. Those particularly important for this study include Vanessa R. Schwartz, *Spectacular Realities: Early Mass Culture in Fin-de-Siècle Paris* (Berkeley: University of California Press, 1998); and Joshua Brown, *Beyond the Lines: Pictorial Reporting, Everyday Life, and the Crisis of Gilded Age America* (Berkeley: University of California Press, 2002).

49. Roland Marchand, *Advertising the American Dream: Making Way for Modernity, 1920–1940* (Berkeley: University of California Press, 1985); and Marchand, *Creating the Corporate Soul: The Rise of Public Relations and Corporate Imagery in American Big Business* (Berkeley: University of California Press, 1998), 3–5, 155. In a related study, Pamela Walker Laird traces manufacturers' promotion of consumption-as-progress. See Laird, *Advertising Progress*, 5, 109–113.

50. In particular, the sub-histories of readership and object use within the fields of literary and material-culture studies provide highly useful models for understanding reception. See, for example, Jennifer Wicke, *Advertising Fictions: Literature, Advertisement and Social Reading* (New York: Columbia University Press, 1988); Ellen Gruber Garvey, *The Adman in the Parlor: Magazines and the Gendering of Consumer Culture, 1880s to 1910s* (New York: Oxford University Press, 1996), esp. chap. 1; Brandon Graydon, "Marketing Fictions: Product Branding in American Literature and Culture, 1890–1915" (PhD diss., Vanderbilt University, 2008); and Henkin, *City Reading*, chaps. 3–4.

51. Throughout this book, I draw from the theories of iconographic analysis proposed by Erwin Panofsky and expanded by E. H. Gombrich, as well as the semiotic theories of Charles Saunders Peirce and Roland Barthes. See Panofsky, "Iconography and Iconology" (1939), in *Meaning in the Visual Arts* (New York: Doubleday, 1955), 26–54; Gombrich, *Symbolic Images* (London: Phaidon, 1972), chap. 1; Barthes, *Image, Music, Text*, trans. Stephen Heath (New York: Hill and Wang, 1977); and Keith P. F. Moxey, "Semiotics and the Social History of Art," *New Literary History* 22, no. 4 (1991): 985–999. Some contemporary practitioners suggest using semiotics to improve brand management; see Laura R. Oswald's *Marketing Semiotics: Signs, Strategies, and Brand Value* (New York: Oxford University Press, 2012). From material-culture studies, this book draws heavily on the methods offered by Bushman in *Refinement*; and E. McClung Fleming, "Artifact Study: A Proposed Model," in *Material Culture Studies in America*, ed. Thomas J. Schlereth (Nashville, TN: American Association for State and Local History, 1982), 162–173.

52. On the ban, see Daniel J. Boorstin, *The Americans: The Democratic Experience* (New York: Knopf Doubleday, 2010), 139; citing Frederic Hudson, *Journalism in the United States, from 1690–1872* (New York: Harper & Brothers, 1872).

53. Similarly, Susan V. Spellman credits rural grocers with innovating important currents in the trade around 1900. See *Cornering the Market: Independent Grocers and Innovation in American Small Business* (New York: Oxford University Press, 2016).

54. Iskin, *The Poster*, 26; Jennifer A. Greenhill, "Flip, Linger, Glide: Coles Phillips and the Movements of Magazine Pictures," *Art History* 40, no. 3 (2017): 595; and Jonathan E. Schroeder, *Visual Consumption* (New York: Routledge, 2005).

55. I elaborate further on this argument in "Exchange Cards: Advertising, Album Making, and the Commodification of Sentiment in the Gilded Age," *Winterthur Portfolio* 51, no. 1 (2017): 1–53.

Chapter 1

1. David M. Henkin, *City Reading: Written Words and Public Spaces in Antebellum New York* (New York: Columbia University Press, 1998), 28–29.

2. Lydia Maria Child, *Letters from New York* (New York: C. S. Francis & Company, 1845), 94–95.

3. Child, 97.

4. "July 2—Mock Auction Stores in Chatham Street," *New York Herald*, July 3, 1845. See also Corey Goettsch, "'The World Is But One Vast Mock Auction': Fraud and Capitalism in

Nineteenth-Century America," in *Capitalism by Gaslight: Illuminating the Economy of Nineteenth-Century America*, ed. Brian P. Luskey and Wendy A. Woloson (Philadelphia: University of Pennsylvania Press, 2015), 109–126.

5. Jessica M. Lepler, *The Many Panics of 1837: People, Politics, and the Creation of a Transatlantic Financial Crisis* (New York: Cambridge University Press, 2013), 3. See also Edward J. Balleisen, *Navigating Failure: Bankruptcy and Commercial Society in Antebellum America* (Chapel Hill: University of North Carolina Press, 2001), 102, 106; Sharon Ann Murphy, *Investing in Life: Insurance in Antebellum America* (Baltimore: Johns Hopkins University Press, 2010), 127; David R. Roediger, *The Wages of Whiteness: Race and the Making of the American Working Class* (New York: Verso, 1991); and Sean Wilentz, *Chants Democratic: New York City and the Rise of the American Working Class, 1788–1850* (New York: Oxford University Press, 2004).

6. Brian P. Luskey, *On the Make: Clerks and the Quest for Capital in Nineteenth-Century America* (New York: New York University Press, 2012), 56–57, 82. See also Sven Beckert, *The Monied Metropolis: New York City and the Consolidation of the American Bourgeoisie, 1850–1896* (New York: Cambridge University Press, 2001); and John Lauritz Larson, *The Market Revolution in America: Liberty, Ambition, and the Eclipse of the Common Good* (New York: Cambridge University Press, 2009).

7. Paul Staiti, "Character and Class," in *John Singleton Copley in America*, ed. Carrie Rebora (New York: Metropolitan Museum of Art, 1995), 53–78; and Kimberly S. Alexander, *Treasures Afoot: Shoe Stories from the Georgian Era* (Baltimore: Johns Hopkins University Press, 2018).

8. Richard L. Bushman, *The Refinement of America: Persons, Houses, Cities* (New York: Vintage Books, 1993), xvi. See also Catherine E. Kelly, *Republic of Taste: Art, Politics, and Everyday Life in Early America* (Philadelphia: University of Pennsylvania Press, 2016); and David Jaffee, *A New Nation of Goods: The Material Culture of Early America* (Philadelphia: University of Pennsylvania Press, 2012).

9. Peter John Brownlee, *The Commerce of Vision: Optical Culture and Perception in Antebellum America* (Philadelphia: University of Pennsylvania Press, 2018), 8–11; Kelly, *Republic of Taste*, 11; and John F. Kasson, *Rudeness and Civility: Manners in Nineteenth-Century Urban America* (New York: Hill and Wang, 1990), 72. Many tastemakers failed to acknowledge, however, the very tenuousness of the system they professed. See Karen Halttunen, *Confidence Men and Painted Women: A Study of Middle-Class Culture in America, 1830–1870* (New Haven, CT: Yale University Press, 1982), 101.

10. Katherine C. Grier, *Culture and Comfort: Parlor Making and Middle-Class Identity, 1850–1930* (Washington, DC: Smithsonian Institution Press, 1997), chap. 2; and Kenneth L. Ames, *Death in the Dining Room and Other Tales of Victorian Culture* (Philadelphia: Temple University Press, 1992). Jasmine Nichole Cobb asserts, in *Picture Freedom: Remaking Black Visuality in the Early Nineteenth Century* (New York: New York University Press, 2015), that middle-class identity was also performed by African Americans in similar ways.

11. Halttunen, *Confidence Men*, 90.

12. Linzy Brekke-Aloise, "'A Very Pretty Business': Fashion and Consumer Culture in Antebellum American Prints," *Winterthur Portfolio* 48, nos. 2–3 (2014): 206. See also Amy Sopcak-Joseph, "Fashioning American Women: *Godey's Lady's Book*, Female Consumers, and Periodical Publishing in the Nineteenth Century" (PhD diss., University of Connecticut, 2019), chap. 4.

13. Tamara Plakins Thornton, *Handwriting in America: A Cultural History* (New Haven, CT: Yale University Press, 1996), 35, 43, 53. See also John Hagge, "The Spurious Paternity of Business Communication Principles," *Journal of Business Communication* 26, no. 1 (Winter

1989): 46; Elizabethada A. Wright and S. Michael Halloran, "From Rhetoric to Composition: The Teaching of Writing in America to 1900," in James Jerome Murphy, ed., *A Short History of Writing Instruction: From Ancient Greece to Modern America* (Mahwah, NJ: Lawrence Erlbaum, 2001), 213–246; and Roger Chartier et al., *Correspondence: Models of Letter-Writing from the Middle Ages to the Nineteenth Century* (Princeton, NJ: Princeton University Press, 1997), 17.

14. David M. Henkin, *The Postal Age: The Emergence of Modern Communications in Nineteenth-Century America* (Chicago: University of Chicago Press, 2006), 95, 117. See also Deirdre M. Mahoney, "Bibliography of Nineteenth-Century Letter-Writing Manuals," in *Letter-Writing Manuals and Instruction from Antiquity to the Present: Historical and Bibliographic Studies*, ed. Carol Poster and Linda C. Mitchell (Columbia: University of South Carolina Press, 2007), 317–326. Many such manuals borrowed liberally from each other. See, for example, a passage discussing "phraseology" in Charles E. Sargent, *Our Home, or Influences Emanating from the Hearthstone* (Springfield, MA: King, Richardson, 1900), 217; reprinted from Orville J. Victor, *Beadle's Dime Letter-Writer* (New York: Beadle & Co., 1863), 20. See also *The Letter Writer* (Charlestown, MA: G. Davidson, 1827); *The New Parlor Letter Writer* (Buffalo: G. H. Derby & Co., 1849); and Florence Hartley, *The Ladies' Book of Etiquette, and Manual of Politeness* (Boston: G. W. Cottrell, 1860), 118.

15. Arthur Martine, *Martine's Sensible Letter-Writer* (New York: Dick & Fitzgerald, 1866), 25–40; and Victor, *Beadle's*, 20.

16. Konstantin Dierks, *In My Power: Letter Writing and Communications in Early America* (Philadelphia: University of Pennsylvania Press, 2009), 80–82; and Toby L. Ditz, "Formative Ventures: Eighteenth-Century Commercial Letters and the Articulation of Experience," in *Epistolary Selves: Letters and Letter-Writers, 1600–1945*, ed. Rebecca Earle (Brookfield, VT: Ashgate, 1999), 59–78.

17. T. H. Breen, *The Marketplace of Revolution: How Consumer Politics Shaped American Independence* (New York: Oxford University Press, 2004), 127, 137. See also Rowena Olegario, *A Culture of Credit: Embedding Trust and Transparency in American Business* (Cambridge, MA: Harvard University Press, 2006), chaps. 1–2.

18. Dierks, *In My Power*, 283–284; Halttunen, *Confidence Men*, 195. See also Thomas Augst, *The Clerk's Tale: Young Men and Moral Life in Nineteenth-Century America* (Chicago: University of Chicago Press, 2003), 16.

19. Julie Winch, "'A Person of Good Character and Considerable Property': James Forten and the Issue of Race in Philadelphia's Antebellum Business Community," *Business History Review* 75, no. 2 (2001): 261–296; and Eric Ledell Smith, "The End of Black Voting Rights in Pennsylvania: African Americans and the Pennsylvania Constitutional Convention of 1837–1838," *Pennsylvania History: A Journal of Mid-Atlantic Studies* 65, no. 3 (1998): 279–299.

20. Kelly, *Republic of Taste*, 5.

21. Joanna Cohen, *Luxurious Citizens: The Politics of Consumption in Nineteenth-Century America* (Philadelphia: University of Pennsylvania Press, 2017), 167–169.

22. Martin Robison Delany, *The Condition, Elevation, Emigration, and Destiny of the Colored People of the United States* (n.p., 1852), 56; and Erica Armstrong Dunbar, *A Fragile Freedom: African American Women and Emancipation in the Antebellum City* (New Haven, CT: Yale University Press, 2008), 132. On black activists' use of visual culture, see Maurice O. Wallace and Shawn Michelle Smith, *Pictures and Progress: Early Photography and the Making of African American Identity* (Raleigh, NC: Duke University Press, 2012); Cobb, *Picture Freedom*; John Stauffer et al., *Picturing Frederick Douglass* (New York: Liveright, 2015); and Aston Gonzalez, *Visualizing Equality: African American Rights and Visual Culture in the Nineteenth Century* (Chapel Hill: University of North Carolina Press, 2020). On the black press, see Benjamin Fagan, *The Black Newspaper and the Chosen Nation* (Atlanta: University

of Georgia Press, 2016), 29; Clint C. Wilson II, *Whither the Black Press?* (New York: Xlibris Corporation, 2014), 40–44; and Juliet E. K. Walker, *The History of Black Business in America: Capitalism, Race, Entrepreneurship, Volume 1, to 1865* (Chapel Hill: University of North Carolina Press, 2009), chap. 4.

23. Emma Jones Lapsansky, "'Since They Got Those Separate Churches': Afro-Americans and Racism in Jacksonian Philadelphia," *American Quarterly* 32, no. 1 (1980): 54–78.

24. Cohen, *Luxurious Citizens*, 167.

25. Lapsansky, "Separate Churches"; Elise Lemire, *"Miscegenation": Making Race in America* (Philadelphia: University of Pennsylvania Press, 2011), 90–92; and Bushman, *Refinement*, 438.

26. William Summers and Charles Hunt, "Life in Philadelphia: The New Shoes" (London, c. 1833), Library Company of Philadelphia Digital Repository, https://digital.librarycompany.org/islandora/object/Islandora%3A60231 (accessed 25 May 2022).

27. Summers and Hunt, "The New Shoes."

28. Brekke-Aloise, "Very Pretty Business," 210; and Samuel Otter, *Philadelphia Stories: America's Literature of Race and Freedom* (New York: Oxford University Press, 2013), 86.

29. Rev. Joshua Bates, *A Discourse, on Honesty in Dealing; Delivered at Middlebury, on the Annual Fast: April 15, 1818* (Middlebury, VT: J. W. Copeland, 1818), 4.

30. Bates, 10–11.

31. Keith L. Dougherty, *Collective Action Under the Articles of Confederation* (New York: Cambridge University Press, 2006), 173.

32. John Haven Dexter, *Mercantile Honor, and Moral Honesty* (Boston, 1855), 9; AAS.

33. Dexter, 14.

34. Kasson, *Rudeness and Civility*, 3–7.

35. Samuel Roberts Wells, *How to Do Business: A Pocket Manual of Practical Affairs, and Guide to Success in Life* (New York: Fowler and Wells, 1857), 13–14.

36. Wells, 24, 105.

37. Augst, *Clerk's Tale*, 263; and Luskey, *On the Make*, 3, 226.

38. Stuart M. Blumin, *The Emergence of the Middle Class: Social Experience in the American City, 1760–1900* (New York: Cambridge University Press, 1989), 67–68, 85, 92. Mona Domosh suggests that New York's retail district began to emerge as early as 1780, in "Shaping the Commercial City: Retail Districts in Nineteenth-Century New York," *Annals of the Association of American Geographers* 80, no. 2 (1990): 274.

39. Cohen, *Luxurious Citizens*, 154; Blumin, *Middle Class*, 92; and Grier, *Culture & Comfort*, 61.

40. Blumin, 80, 84, 102–103; and Cohen, 155–156.

41. Jocelyn and Annin Whitney, engravers, *Interior View of Appleton's Bookstore, 346 & 348 Broadway, New York* (1856), Art and Picture Collection, New York Public Library Digital Collections, online at http://digitalcollections.nypl.org/items/510d47e1-05db-a3d9-e040-e00a18064a99 (accessed 8 June 2018).

42. Grier, *Culture & Comfort*, 53.

43. Grier, 59, 63; and Cohen, *Luxurious Citizens*, 170.

44. Blumin, *Middle Class*, 91–92, 103. More recently, other historians have linked the iconography of paper money to corporate and regional identities. See Joshua R. Greenberg, *Bank Notes and Shinplasters: The Rage for Paper Money in the Early Republic* (Philadelphia: University of Pennsylvania Press, 2020); and Victoria Barnes and Lucy Newton, "Corporate Identity, Company Law and Currency: A Survey of Community Images on English Bank Notes," *Management & Organizational History* 17, no. 1–2 (2022): 43–75.

45. Olegario, *Culture of Credit*, 80–117; and Murphy, *Investing in Life*, 76. Likewise, the 1841 federal bankruptcy law established criteria for debt forgiveness using the same standards of character. See Balleisen, *Navigating Failure*, 102, 106.

46. Neil McKendrick, John Brewer, and John Harold Plumb, *The Birth of a Consumer Society: The Commercialization of Eighteenth-Century England* (London: Europa Publications, 1982), chap. 3. See also Bushman, *Refinement*, 410; Nancy F. Koehn, *Brand New: How Entrepreneurs Earned Consumers' Trust from Wedgwood to Dell* (Boston: Harvard Business School Press, 2001), 324; and Regina Lee Blaszczyk, *Imagining Consumers: Design and Innovation from Wedgwood to Corning* (Baltimore: Johns Hopkins University Press, 2000), 5–11.

47. Philip Syng, endorsement for Richard Humphreys's Goldsmith shop, in *Pennsylvania Gazette*, September 23, 1772, in Carl Robert Keyes et al., *The Adverts 250 Project*, blog, online at https://adverts250project.org/2022/09/23/september-23-7/ (accessed 23 September 2022).

48. See Henkin, *City Reading*, 40–65.

49. Rosemary Skinner Keller et al. use the term "witnessing" interchangeably with "testimony" and "testify" to refer to the physical displays of religious conversion (often by women) in the evangelical and revivalist traditions from the eighteenth century through the mid-twentieth century. See Keller et al., *Encyclopedia of Women and Religion in North America* (Bloomington: Indiana University Press, 2006), 227.

50. Olegario, *Culture of Credit*, 38–40, 49, 59.

51. Victor, *Beadle's*, 20.

52. Martine, *Letter-Writer*, 35–37; and Ingrid Jeacle and Tom Brown, "The Construction of the Credible: Epistolary Transformations and the Origins of the Business Letter," *Accounting, Business & Financial History* 16, no. 1 (2006): 40–41.

53. Wells, *How to Do Business*, 24, 105.

54. *The Letter Writer: Containing a Great Variety of Letters on the Following Subjects: Relationship—Business—Love, Courtship and Marriage—Friendship—and Miscellaneous Letters* (Boston: Charles Gaylord, 1831), 3.

55. While Olegario (in *Culture of Credit*) demonstrates the continued importance of concepts of virtue in credit reporting, Joanna Cohen argues that the cultural importance of public virtue was breaking down in the antebellum period, especially in the realm of consumer politics, as notions of individual fulfillment grew in popularity. See Cohen, *Luxurious Citizens*; and, for public virtue in the colonial period, Breen, *Marketplace of Revolution*.

56. "Testimony," in *Global Dictionary of Theology: A Resource for the Worldwide Church*, ed. William Dyrness et al. (Downer's Grove, IL: InterVarsity Press, 2008), 875–879. The practice of religious witnessing stems from the public displays of "New Birth" (often by female parishioners) in Puritan and Baptist congregations during the Great Awakening of the 1730s and 1740s. See Keller et al., *Encyclopedia of Women and Religion*, 227, 247. Conversely, in the Quaker tradition, "testimony" refers both to written traditions and to individual daily practice. See, for example, Society of Friends, *The Ancient Testimony of the Religious Society of Friends: Commonly Called Quakers, Respecting Some of Their Christian Doctrines and Practices* (Philadelphia: Society of Friends, 1870). At mid-century, testifying was common among Methodist and Baptist groups, while toward the end of the nineteenth century Pentecostal and Holiness groups took prominence in the revivalist movement. See George M. Thomas, *Revivalism and Cultural Change: Christianity, Nation Building, and the Market in the Nineteenth-Century United States* (Chicago: University of Chicago Press, 1989), esp. chap. 4.

57. Thomas, *Revivalism*, 74.

58. Though I use the terms "patent medicine" and "proprietary medicine" interchangeably to refer to the over-the-counter drug trade, the term "patent medicine" is actually a misnomer,

as many manufacturers did not register their formulas with the US Patent Office. For more on the early patent-medicine trade in the United States, see James Harvey Young, *The Toadstool Millionaires; a Social History of Patent Medicines in America Before Federal Regulation* (Princeton, NJ: Princeton University Press, 1961), 67–68.

59. Young, 139–140. Druggists received almanacs at the end of each year and distributed them free to their customers for use in the upcoming seasons.

60. *Jayne's Medical Almanac for 1847* (Philadelphia: Stavely & McCalla, 1846), Rare Books, LCP.

61. *Jayne's Medical Almanac and Guide to Health for 1849* (Philadelphia: Stavely & McCalla, 1848), Rare Books, LCP.

62. *Jayne's Medical Almanac and Guide to Health for 1852* (Philadelphia: Stavely & McCalla, 1851); and *Jayne's Medical Almanac and Guide to Health for 1859* (Philadelphia: J. S. McCalla, 1858); both Rare Books, LCP.

63. In the latter nineteenth century, it became common for manufacturers to represent their factories and offices on advertising material to, as Pamela Laird argues, demonstrate their commitment to the ideals of progress and modernity. See Laird, *Advertising Progress: American Business and the Rise of Consumer Marketing* (Baltimore: Johns Hopkins University Press, 1998), 311.

64. John Sharp Maginnis (1805–1852) was educated at Waterville College and Brown University, where he received his Doctor of Divinity in 1844. He was professor of Biblical Theology at Hamilton Theological Seminary from 1838 through 1850, before teaching at Rochester Theological Seminary and the University of Rochester (where he taught intellectual and moral philosophy) from 1850 through 1852. See Colgate University, *A General Catalogue, 1819–1919*, series 19, no. 4 (Hamilton, NY: Colgate University, 1919), 13. Reverend John Mason Peck (1789–1858) established the Rock Spring Seminary at Rock Spring, Illinois, in 1827. In 1831, the school was renamed Alton Seminary; it became Shurtleff College in 1836. See Austen Kennedy De Blois, *The Pioneer School: A History of Shurtleff College, the Oldest Educational Institution in the West* (New York: F. H. Revell Company, 1900). Shurtleff College closed in 1957. Although it remains difficult to validate the many testimonials that appeared in almanacs like this, I have found no evidence suggesting that anyone sued Jayne for slander or libel in state or federal court in the United States.

65. *Jayne's Medical Almanac for 1852*, 49. Swift served as mayor of Philadelphia intermittently through the 1830s and 1840s.

66. *Jayne's Medical Almanac for 1847*, 30–31.

67. See Henkin, *City Reading*, 40–65.

68. *Jayne's Medical Almanac for 1852*, 56. Henry Scrantom (1796–1868) was a merchant and the son of one of Rochester's early founders, Hamlet Scrantom (1772–1850). "Death of Henry Scrantom," *Rochester Evening Express*, December 14, 1868; and Rochester Public Library, Local History & Genealogy Division, "Rochester's First Settler, Hamlet Scrantom," *Local History Rocs!* Website (18 April 2017), https://rochistory.wordpress.com/2017/04/18/rochesters-first-settler-hamlet-scrantom-1-december-1772-10-april-1850/ (accessed 26 February 2021).

69. *Jayne's Medical Almanac for 1852*, 56.

70. See, for example, testimonials printed in *Jayne's Medical Almanac and Guide to Health for 1847* (Philadelphia: Owen & Fithian, 1846), 3, Rare Books, LCP.

71. *Jayne's Medical Almanac and Guide to Health, for 1850* (Philadelphia: Stavely & McCalla, 1849), 29, Rare Books, LCP.

72. *Jayne's Medical Almanac for 1852*, 33. The cultural emphasis placed on women's moral superiority is discussed by Ann Douglas in *The Feminization of American Culture* (New York: Knopf, 1977). This concept evolved out of the Revolutionary-era notion of Republican Moth-

erhood (see Linda K. Kerber, *Women of the Republic: Intellect and Ideology in Revolutionary America* [New York: W. W. Norton, 1986 (1980)]), and transformed in the latter nineteenth century into the concept of municipal housekeeping as Progressive-era reform took hold (see Maureen A. Flanagan, *America Reformed: Progressives and Progressivisms 1890s–1920s* [New York: Oxford University Press, 2007]).

73. *Jayne's Medical Almanac for 1847*, 3. Reverend Peck also echoed this personal endorsement of Jayne's character.

74. *Jayne's Medical Almanac for 1847*, 3.

75. Laird, *Advertising Progress*, 70–71. Yet, often, compositors in the print shop might have the final say on punctuation and spelling (as they physically composed the lines of type to print). See David Jury, *Graphic Design Before Graphic Designers: The Printer as Designer and Craftsman 1700–1914* (New York: Thames & Hudson, 2012), chap. 2. Given the large variety of conventions, language, and forms deployed in any particular newspaper, it seems unlikely that a clerk in the print shop had full autonomy over the advertising section (for, if he had, one would expect to see more uniformity, at least within the same newspaper). Moreover, few business manuals provided guidelines or templates for appropriate advertisements. A fairly exhaustive search of letter-writing manuals and guidebooks in this period yielded no substantial evidence of instruction or templates for writing advertisements. For these reasons, I believe the evidence supports the assumption that most advertisers wrote their own advertisements in this period (though Volney Palmer did offer to compose text for his clients' newspaper advertisements; this is discussed later in this chapter).

76. This research is based on a survey of advertisements published in the mainstream—white-owned—press in New York City between 1830 and 1900. Research conducted in the Library of Congress Chronicling America databases for the *New York Herald* and *New York Tribune*; and in ProQuest Historical Newspapers, *New York Times*. The sample set for the mainstream press was created through a random sampling of dedicated years and issues within each decade, resulting in a data set of 435 pages of advertisements. In tabulating data on the use of jargon in advertisements, I excluded public announcements related to local government, such as notices of taxes due and property for sale. Throughout this chapter and Chapter 3, I use the phrase "mainstream press" to refer to white-owned newspapers printed in various places throughout the United States. This is intended only for shorthand purposes, to distinguish developments that took a different trajectory in the black-owned (that is, African American) press. Wherever possible, I have attempted to make comparisons between these two newspaper genres.

77. Ad for Magne, Tailor, *New York Tribune*, July 1, 1841. Victor Magne also appears in *Longworth's Directory* (New York: Thomas Longworth, 1840), 424; in Irma and Paul Milstein Division of United States History, Local History and Genealogy, New York Public Library, online at https://digitalcollections.nypl.org/items/17e3e2c0-8a22-0136-1f25-4949c287a53f (accessed March 30, 2022).

78. Advertisements for Mrs. Peggy Williams, Richard Carrol, and the King Street Garden, in the *Colored American* (New York), July 11, 1840.

79. Ad for Ackerman & Miller, *New York Tribune*, January 8, 1845.

80. Ads for Rogers' Vegetable Pulmonic Detergent, *New York Tribune*, July 3–November 5, 1841.

81. "Important to the Public," *New York Tribune*, July 8, 1841. To the bottom left appears a code, likely added by the typesetter to keep track of the terms paid for by the subscriber. The ad contains the code "jy1 1m*", and when compared to other codes throughout the paper, it becomes clear that the first set of letters and numbers is the date the ad was placed, while the second set is the duration of the ad (i.e., 1w, 1m, etc.). In this case, Rogers paid for the ad on July 1, and asked that it run for a month.

82. Henkin, *City Reading*, chap. 3.

83. Cohen argues that shared visual experiences on the city streets helped to constitute an urban consuming public, in *Luxurious Citizens*, 161–164.

84. Ad for Purviance & Co., *Pennsylvania Gazette*, July 4, 1765; cited in Carl Robert Keyes, "Early American Advertising: Marketing and Consumer Culture in Eighteenth-Century Philadelphia" (PhD diss., Johns Hopkins University, 2008), 147 fig. 3.5.

85. For example, see *Letter Writer* (Davidson), 64–84; and *New Parlor Letter Writer*, 35–36.

86. *The Pocket Letter Writer* (Worcester, MA: S. A. Howland, 1852), 16–23; and Daniel Harrison Jacques and Samuel Roberts Wells, *How to Write* (New York: Fowler and Wells, 1857), 40. See also *New Parlor Letter Writer*, 35–36.

87. In the sample set, the most concentrated use of the word "respectfully" appeared in advertisements published in the 1840s and 1850s (84 percent of all hits for the word), with a dramatic reduction in use by the 1870s.

88. Survey using approximately 500 pages of advertising in African American newspapers published between 1828 and 1900, taken from semirural, rural, and urban locales. These samples all came from collections held or linked through the Library of Congress's Chronicling America database. The Library of Congress also maintains an index of all African American newspapers published in the United States, regardless of digitized status, which is available in its US Newspaper Directory (accessed 27 March 2022). Of the 500 pages in the sample set used for this study, 115 of these contained at least one advertisement using the word "respectfully" (aside from ads that quoted from testimonials, which was also a common practice at the time).

89. Ad for Powell House, *National Standard* (New York), October 28, 1871.

90. Ad for R. H. Bundy, *New York Freeman*, December 13, 1884.

91. For example, see ads in the *Savannah Tribune* (GA), June 4, 1887; ad for Smallwood & Duffield, *Washington Bee* (DC), November 16, 1889; and for William Ellis Jr., *Richmond Planet* (VA), February 23, 1895.

92. Glenda E. Gilmore, *Gender and Jim Crow: Women and the Politics of White Supremacy in North Carolina, 1896–1920* (Chapel Hill: University of North Carolina Press, 1996), xix; and Eurie Dahn, *Jim Crow Networks: African American Periodical Cultures* (Amherst: University of Massachusetts Press, 2021), 3, 21.

93. J. C. Ayer to various clients, 1852–1858, Warshaw Series I Patent Medicine, AC NMAH.

94. *Ayer's American Almanac* (1854), Rare Books Collection, Huntington Library, San Marino, CA.

95. Young, *Toadstool Millionaires*, 67–69; and Joseph M. Gabriel, *Medical Monopoly: Intellectual Property Rights and the Origins of the Modern Pharmaceutical Industry* (Chicago: University of Chicago Press, 2014), 26.

96. Tim P. Vos, "Explaining the Origins of the Advertising Agency," *American Journalism* 30, no. 4 (2013): 462–467.

97. Donald R. Holland, "Volney B. Palmer: The Nation's First Advertising Agency Man," *Pennsylvania Magazine of History and Biography* 98, no. 3 (1974): 358.

98. While Vos, in "Explaining the Origins," argues that Palmer aimed to boost revenues for canal operators (466–467), Holland suggests that he was trying to raise revenues for rural papers. See Holland, "Volney Palmer," 360.

99. Holland, 368; and Edd Applegate, *The Rise of Advertising in the United States: A History of Innovation to 1960* (Toronto, ON: Scarecrow Press, 2012), 31. In the UK, the first advertising agency was opened in the mid-1840s by Charles Mitchell. See Matthew J. Shaw, *An Inky Business: A History of Newspapers from the English Civil Wars to the American Civil War* (London: Reaktion Books, 2021), 209–210.

100. Holland, "Volney Palmer," 361. See also Frank Presbrey, *The History and Development of Advertising* (Garden City, NY: Doubleday, 1929), 261.

101. Ad for Palmer in the *New York Tribune*, March 21, 1846.

102. Holland, "Volney Palmer," 381, 371. See also Laird, *Advertising Progress*, 156.

103. Today, practitioners would characterize Palmer's services within a business-to-business (B-B) framework, such as when one business sells a particular service or product to another business, while B-B advertising facilitates these transactions. See Sean Brierley, *The Advertising Handbook*, 2nd ed. (New York: Routledge, 2002 [1995]), 16–17.

104. Ads for Volney Palmer, in the *New York Daily Tribune*, September 19, 1846; and the *New York Daily Tribune*, December 23, 1850.

105. "Newspaper Advertising," *Sunbury American and Shamokin Journal* (Sunbury, PA), March 7, 1846.

106. Augst, *Clerk's Tale*, 181; citing Rush Welter, *The Mind of America* (New York: Columbia University Press, 1975), 129; and Leonard Neufeldt, *The Economist* (New York: Oxford University Press, 1989), 31.

107. Laird, *Advertising Progress*, 311.

108. Ad for Volney Palmer, *New York Daily Tribune*, November 30, 1850.

109. Ads for Volney Palmer, in *New York Daily Tribune*, June 16, 1852; and *New York Daily Tribune*, December 23, 1850. It is difficult to verify Palmer's estimated reach through the newspapers he counted as clients, and it is worth noting that he may have exaggerated this number to further appeal to potential clients.

110. Ad for Palmer in the *New York Tribune*, March 21, 1846; and Holland, "Volney Palmer," 362, citing *V. B. Palmer's Business-Men's Almanac* (New York, 1849), 61.

111. Palmer ad, *New York Daily Tribune* December 23, 1850.

112. Susan V. Spellman notes this quality for small retail grocers in *Cornering the Market: Independent Grocers and Innovation in American Small Business* (New York: Oxford University Press, 2016), 23–24. On turnover in the newspaper trade, which partially resulted from comparatively low entry barriers, see S. N. D. North, *History and Present Condition of the Newspaper and Periodical Press of the United States, with a Catalogue of the Publications of the Census Year* (Washington, DC: US Government Printing Office, 1884), 93–94. See also Stephen Mihm, *A Nation of Counterfeiters: Capitalists, Con Men, and the Making of the United States* (Cambridge, MA: Harvard University Press, 2007), chap. 5.

113. A general history of sales agents and their work in this period can be found in Timothy B. Spears, *100 Years on the Road: The Traveling Salesman in American Culture* (New Haven, CT: Yale University Press, 1995), esp. chaps. 1–2. See also Susan V. Spellman, "Trust Brokers: Traveling Grocery Salesmen and Confidence in Nineteenth-Century Trade," *Enterprise & Society* 13, no. 2 (2012): 276–312.

114. Vos, "Explaining the Origins," 468; citing Archibald McElroy, *McElroy's Philadelphia Directory* (Philadelphia: Isaac Ashmead and Co., 1842), and "New Facilities to the Business Community," *Public Ledger* (Philadelphia, PA), March 17, 1842. On note depreciation as a factor requiring currency exchange, see Joshua Greenberg, "The Era of Shinplasters: Making Sense of Unregulated Paper Money," in Luskey and Woloson, *Capitalism by Gaslight*, 71.

115. Later in the century, advertising experts reminded firms to remain honest and to deliver high-quality goods so that consumers' experiences reflected advertising's promises. This is discussed later, in Chapter 6. Koehn provides a related discussion in *Brand New*, 332.

116. "To Businessmen of Philadelphia," *Jeffersonian Republican* (Stroudsburg, PA), February 27, 1845. See also "Palmer's Column," *New York Daily Tribune*, June 19, 1852; and "Newspaper Advertising," *Sunbury American and Shamokin Journal* (Sunbury, PA), March 7, 1846. Whether these remarks were unsolicited testimonials, as the context suggested, or were scripted by Palmer himself, remains to be discovered.

117. Henkin, *City Reading*, 104, 135, 173.

118. For example, see the *Jeffersonian Republican* (Stroudsburg, PA), February 27, 1845; *Lewisburg Chronicle* (Lewisburg, PA), June 27, 1851; *Mountain Sentinel* (Ebensburg, PA), January 1, 1852; and *New York Daily Tribune*, January 23, 1852.

Chapter 2

Note to epigraph: Ad for Orris Toothpaste, *New York Morning Herald*, December 31, 1839. Peine paraphrases Iago in Shakespeare's *Othello* (3.3.164–166).

1. Hugh Chisholm, ed., *The Encyclopedia Britannica: A Dictionary of Arts, Sciences, Literature, and General Information*, 11th ed. (New York: Encyclopedia Britannica Co., 1910), vol. 12, p. 23.

2. Ads for Joseph Gillott's Steel-Tip Pens, *New York Morning Herald*, July 3 and July 24, 1837.

3. Sharon Ann Murphy, *Investing in Life: Insurance in Antebellum America* (Baltimore: Johns Hopkins University Press, 2010); Jessica M. Lepler, *The Many Panics of 1837: People, Politics, and the Creation of a Transatlantic Financial Crisis* (New York: Cambridge University Press, 2013), chap. 1; and Rowena Olegario, *A Culture of Credit: Embedding Trust and Transparency in American Business* (Cambridge, MA: Harvard University Press, 2006). These developments are outlined in more detail in Chapter 1.

4. Stuart Banner, *American Property* (Cambridge, MA: Harvard University Press, 2011), 31.

5. On the rule of *caveat emptor* in the antebellum economy, see Max A. Geller, *Advertising at the Crossroads: Federal Regulation vs. Voluntary Controls* (New York: Garland, 1985), 253–254.

6. Mark P. McKenna argues that the "passing-off doctrine," or illegitimate attempts to divert trade away from genuine products toward counterfeit imitations, characterized most of the litigation around trademark protections in the nineteenth century. See McKenna, "The Normative Foundations of Trademark Law," *Notre Dame Law Review* 82, no. 5 (2007): 1859.

7. As early as 1825, state courts in the United States had recognized the necessity of protecting commercial goodwill from competitors who sought to defraud the public through deception or imitation or both, and extended such protections to newspaper editors. See *Snowden v. Noah* (1825), Hopkins Ch. R. 347, cited in Rowland Cox, *American Trade Mark Cases* (Cincinnati, OH: Robert Clarke & Co., 1871), 2–6. See also McKenna, "Normative Foundations," 1850; and Banner, *American Property*, 28–29, 31–32, 39.

8. Ad for Brandreth's Pills, *New York Morning Herald*, June 9, 1838.

9. Ads for Gillott's Pens, in *The Times* (London, UK), December 1, 1832; *The Times* (London, UK), March 4, 1841; and *New York Tribune*, July 16, 1841. While Gillott deployed similar strategies deriding imitation goods in both London and New York newspapers, the actual text and layout of the ads would need to change because of idiosyncratic editorial rules established by each publication. Such shifting rules will be further discussed in Chapter 3. Advertisements for a variety of household consumable goods, including medicines, soaps, clothing, shoes, and other goods, frequently referenced the celebrity/fame of the products as a sales tactic. See, for example, ads for Kent's Inks, *New York Tribune*, July 1, 1841; Walnut Oil Shaving Soap, *New York Herald*, May 2, 1847; J. & P. Coats Threads, *New York Herald*, July 1847; and Lea & Perrins' Worcestershire Sauce, *Evening Star* (Washington, DC), December 21, 1853.

10. Ad for Gillott's Pens, *New York Morning Herald*, April 26, 1839.

11. Neil McKendrick et al, *The Birth of a Consumer Society: The Commercialization of Eighteenth-Century England* (London: Europa Publications, 1982), 111. Such emulation is explored further by Richard L. Bushman, *The Refinement of America: Persons, Houses, Cities* (New York: Vintage Books, 1993).

12. Others deployed this strategy, too; see ads for Orris Tooth Paste, *New York Morning Herald*, April 26, 1838; and Lea & Perrins' Worcestershire Sauce, *Evening Star*, December 21, 1853.

13. David M. Henkin, *City Reading: Written Words and Public Spaces in Antebellum New York* (New York: Columbia University Press, 1998), 144; and Tamara Plakins Thornton, *Handwriting in America: A Cultural History* (New Haven, CT: Yale University Press, 1996), xi–xiii, 95. Stephen Mihm discusses the importance of signatures on paper money in *A Nation of Counterfeiters: Capitalists, Con Men, and the Making of the United States* (Cambridge, MA: Harvard University Press, 2007), 221.

14. On the connections between identity and labor, see, especially, E. P. Thompson, *The Making of the English Working Class* (New York: Pantheon, 1964); and Emma L. Greenwood, "Work, Identity and Letterpress Printers in Britain, 1750–1850" (PhD diss., University of Manchester, 2015), 68–70. For the US context, see Eric Foner, *Free Soil, Free Labor, Free Men: The Ideology of the Republican Party Before the Civil War* (New York: Oxford University Press, 1995 [1970]); Herbert G. Gutman, "Work, Culture, and Society in Industrializing America, 1815–1919," *American Historical Review* 78, no. 3 (1973): 531–588; Stuart M. Blumin, *The Emergence of the Middle Class: Social Experience in the American City, 1760–1900* (New York: Cambridge University Press, 1989); and Brian P. Luskey, *On the Make: Clerks and the Quest for Capital in Nineteenth-Century America* (New York: New York University Press, 2012).

15. Gillott's Pens (April 17, 1838, and July 16, 1841). Many manufacturers derided inferior competitors and raised up their own goods' celebrated qualities, including firms that made soaps, medicines, threads, and other household goods. See ads for Gouraud's Italian Medicated Soap, *New York Herald*, June 7, 1844; Orris Tooth Paste, *New York Morning Herald*, December 31, 1839; and J. & P. Coats, *South Carolina Standard*, April 16, 1845. Moral diatribes against imitations continue to shape copyright-infringement cases today; see Christopher Buccafusco and David Fagundes in "The Moral Psychology of Copyright Infringement," *Minnesota Law Review* 100 (2016): 2433–2507.

16. James Harvey Young, *The Toadstool Millionaires: A Social History of Patent Medicines in America Before Federal Regulation* (Princeton, NJ: Princeton University Press, 1961), chaps. 11–12. Mihm notes that the publishers of counterfeit currency manuals (called "counterfeit detectors") also shamed and discredited competitors to gain a larger market share (*Nation of Counterfeiters*, 251).

17. Edward J. Balleisen, *Fraud: An American History from Barnum to Madoff* (Princeton, NJ: Princeton University Press, 2017), 79–81.

18. For context on these developments, see Joanna Cohen, *Luxurious Citizens: The Politics of Consumption in Nineteenth-Century America* (Philadelphia: University of Pennsylvania Press, 2017); Mihm, *Nation of Counterfeiters*, 281; and Balleisen, *Fraud*.

19. Gillott sued several manufacturers for trademark infringement in the late 1860s. See, for example, *Gillott v. Esterbrook et al.*, 47 Barb. 455; 1867 N.Y. App. Div. LEXIS 23 (8 January 1867).

20. Per Mollerup, *Marks of Excellence* (London: Phaidon, 1998), 17–40; Edward S. Rogers, "Some Historical Matter Concerning Trade-Marks," *Michigan Law Review* 9, no. 1 (1910): 29–43; and Clayton Lindsay Smith, *The History of Trade-Marks* (New York: Priv. Pub., 1923), 9–16. Since Mira Wilkins's foundational article on trademarks ("The Neglected Intangible Asset: The Influence of the Trade Mark on the Rise of the Modern Corporation," *Business History* 34, no. 1 (1992): 66–96), scholars have complicated and expanded the history of trademarks. A useful overview of this literature appears in Patricio Sáiz and Rafael Castro, "Trademarks in Branding: Legal Issues and Commercial Practices," *Business History* 60, no. 8 (2018): 1105–1126.

21. Munroe Smith, foreword to *The Historical Foundations of the Law Relating to Trade-Marks*, by Frank I. Schechter (New York: Columbia University Press, 1925), x; and McKenna, "Normative Foundations," 1850. Recent scholars have given renewed attention to guild and merchants' marks as proto-brands; see, especially, Carlo Marco Belfanti, "Branding Before the Brand: Marks, Imitations and Counterfeits in Pre-Modern Europe," *Business History* 60, no. 8 (2018): 1127–1146; and Robert Fredona and Teresa da Silva Lopes, "Merchant Marks in Renaissance Italy and the Mediterranean: The Case of the Medici Wool Trade" (paper, Business History Conference 49th Annual Meeting, Mexico City, April 7, 2022).

22. Banner, *American Property*, 28–29.

23. Belfanti, "Branding Before the Brand," 1137, citing Nancy F. Koehn, *Brand New: How Entrepreneurs Earned Consumers' Trust from Wedgwood to Dell* (Boston: Harvard Business School Press, 2001), 4. On Samuel Lane, see Kimberly S. Alexander, *Treasures Afoot: Shoe Stories from the Georgian Era* (Baltimore: Johns Hopkins University Press, 2018), 26–27, 88. Also relevant are McKendrick, *Birth of a Consumer Society*, chap. 3; and John Styles, "Product Innovation in Early Modern London," *Past and Present* 168, no. 1 (2000): 148–158.

24. Siva Vaidhyanathan, *Copyrights and Copywrongs: The Rise of Intellectual Property and How It Threatens Creativity* (New York: New York University Press, 2003), 21.

25. In 1791, then Secretary of State Thomas Jefferson reported to Congress a petition from a Boston sail manufacturer, Samuel Breck, who requested the exclusive privilege to use a particular mark to designate his wares on the market. Jefferson agreed that such protections would be beneficial to domestic manufacturers, and he recommended that Congress consider developing a law to that effect (though no bills were introduced). Thomas Jefferson, "Report on the Petition of Samuel Breck and Others, 9 December 1791," in *The Papers of Thomas Jefferson* vol. 22 (August 6, 1791–December 31, 1791), ed. Charles T. Cullen (Princeton, NJ: Princeton University Press, 1986), 384–385, available online at Founders Online, National Archives, http://founders.archives.gov/documents/Jefferson/01-22-02-0354 (accessed 14 September 2015). This petition is also discussed in Arthur Philip Greeley, "Dissenting Report," in Francis Forbes et al., *Report of the Commissioners Appointed to Revise the Statutes Relating to Patents, Trade and Other Marks, and Trade and Commercial Names, Under the Act of Congress Approved June 4, 1898*, vol. 4031, Congressional Serial Set, Senate Doc. no. 20 (US Government Printing Office, 1902), 92; and Banner, *American Property*, 29.

26. Balleisen, *Fraud*, 69–70; and Richard R. John, "Ruling Passions: Political Economy in Nineteenth-Century America," *Journal of Policy History* 18, no. 1 (2006): 13.

27. Ross D. Petty, "From Label to Trademark: The Legal Origins of the Concept of Brand Identity in Nineteenth Century America," *Journal of Historical Research in Marketing* 4, no. 1 (2012): 132.

28. Luna Francis Lambert, "The Seasonal Trade: Gift Cards and Chromolithography in America, 1874–1910" (PhD diss., George Washington University, 1980), 94; and Paul Duguid, "Information in the Mark and the Marketplace," *Enterprise & Society* 15, no. 1 (2014): 18. Later practitioners advocated doing just this; see Oscar E. Binner, "Does Copyright Law Protect Advertisers?" *Profitable Advertising* 8, no. 8 (January 1898): 292–295; and "Copyrighted Pictures for Advertisers," *Printers' Ink* 14, no. 12 (March 1896): 38.

29. Petty, "From Label to Trademark," 138–140; and Thomas B. Hudson, "A Brief History of the Development of Design Patent Protection in the United States." *Journal of the Patent Office Society* 30 (1948): 380–384.

30. Petty, "From Label to Trademark," 149. While the 1842 revision allowed the filing of design patents (as Beverly Pattishall notes in "Two Hundred Years of American Trademark Law," *Trademark Reporter* 68 [1978]: 129), patents were not made available to the public broadly until after 1871. See Chauncey Smith, "A Century of Patent Law," *Quarterly Journal of Economics* 5, no. 1 (1890): 56; and USPTO, "History and Background of Patent and Trademark

Resource Centers," www.uspto.gov/learning-and-resources/support-centers/patent-and
-trademark-resource-centers-ptrc/history-and-0 (accessed 29 March 2020).

31. Carma Gorman, "The Arts & Crafts Knock-Off and US Intellectual Property Law," in
The Rise of Everyday Design: The Arts and Crafts Movement in Britain and America, ed. Monica Penick and Christopher Long (New Haven, CT: Yale University Press, 2019), 145–146.

32. Bill of complaint filed by B. Warburton in March 1843, in New York Chancery court;
cited in *J. & W. Taylor v. Carpenter* (1846), 2 Sand. Ch. 603, §6–7. Information about the dates
of Carpenter's use of the spurious labels was reported in the US Circuit Court appeal, October term 1846: *Taylor v. Carpenter* (1846), 23 Fed. Cas. 745.

33. B. Warburton in *Taylor* (1846), at §6–7. Emphasis added.

34. Lionel Bently, "The Place of *Scienter* in Trade Mark Infringement in Nineteenth
Century England: The Fall and Rise of *Millington v. Fox*," *Case Western Reserve Law Review*
71, no. 2 (2020): 531–532.

35. The longer history of British trademark protections before the mid-nineteenth century
is explored in Cox, *Trade Mark Cases* (1871); and Bently, "The Place of *Scienter*."

36. British standards for ethical behavior, honor, and transparency mirrored American
understandings of the same. See John Kasson, *Rudeness & Civility: Manners in 19th-Century
Urban America* (New York: Hill and Wang, 1990), chap. 1, drawing from Norbert Elias, *The
Civilizing Process: The History of Manners* (New York: Urizen Books, 1978 [1939]). Also relevant
is Geoffrey Russell Searle, *Morality and the Market in Victorian Britain* (New York: Oxford
University Press, 1998).

37. *Taylor* (1846), at §8.

38. Jack Authelet, *Foxborough: Gem of Norfolk County* (Charleston, SC: Arcadia Publishing, 2001), 42.

39. As Stephen Mihm notes, marginal personnel connected to legitimate enterprises often
exploited their connections to facilitate counterfeiting. See Mihm, *Nation of Counterfeiters*,
221–222, 283–285.

40. *Taylor* (1846), at §10–11.

41. On *caveat emptor*, see Balleisen, *Fraud*, 50.

42. *Taylor, John et al. v. Carpenter, Daniels*, Oct. Term 1844; US Circuit Court for the District of Massachusetts; Case Files, 1790–1911; Record Group 21: Records of District Courts of
the United States, 1685–2009; National Archives at Boston (hereafter NARA-B).

43. *Taylor v. Carpenter* (1844), 23 Fed. Cas. at 744, citing Act of Congress Sept. 24, 1789,
§11 (1 Stat. 78).

44. *Coats, James et al. v. Thayer, Benjamin, and Bufford, John*, Oct. Term 1844 (unreported);
NARA-B.

45. *Taylor v. Carpenter* (1844), 11 Paige Ch. at 298.

46. On the reciprocity between British and American courts, see Francis Henry Upton,
*A Treatise on the Law of Trade Marks: With a Digest and Review of the English and American
Authorities* (Boston: W. C. Little, 1860), 9–17.

47. Joseph Story (1779–1845) served on the US Supreme Court from 1812 through 1845
and was "riding circuit" for this particular case. Story is best remembered for his role in
United States v. Schooner Amistad, 40 U.S. (15 Pet.) 518 (1841). See James McClellan, *Joseph
Story and the American Constitution* (Oklahoma City: University of Oklahoma Press, 1971).

48. *Taylor v. Carpenter* (1844), 23 Fed Cas. at 744.

49. *Taylor* (1844), at 744. However, Story did note that *Snowden v. Noah* (1825) provided
ample precedent for protecting a firm's goodwill with the public. In his 1841 legal treatise, Story
argued that goodwill included the "advantage or benefit" beyond a firm's capital holdings,
which comes from public patronage and "habitual customers," owing to its "local position
or common celebrity, or reputation for skill or affluence, or punctuality," among other

things. Joseph Story, *Commentaries on the Law of Partnership: As a Branch of Commercial and Maritime Jurisprudence: With Occasional Illustrations from the Civil and Foreign Law* (Boston: Little & Brown, 1841), 139–140.

50. Edward Balleisen refers to Story's moral influences elsewhere, in *Navigating Failure: Bankruptcy and Commercial Society in Antebellum America* (Chapel Hill: University of North Carolina Press, 2001), 103–114.

51. Justice Woodbury for US Circuit Court of Massachusetts, October term, in *Taylor v. Carpenter* (1846), 23 Fed. Cas. at 747, 751.

52. *Taylor* (1846), at 749–750. In their decisions on the *Taylor* case, the appellate judges referenced several British cases establishing legal precedents for the protections granted to the Taylors, as was regular practice at the time (see *Taylor* [1846], 2 Sand. Ch. 603, §15).

53. E. I. du Pont de Nemours & Company took its cue from the *Taylor* case in bringing legal action against infringers upon their own goods. See E. I. du Pont de Nemours & Company records (Accession 0500.I), Manuscripts and Archives Department, Hagley Museum and Library, Wilmington, DE (hereafter "Hagley").

54. *J. and P. Coats et al. v. Holbrook, Nelson & Co.* (1845), 2 Sand. Ch. 586, §6.

55. This information appears in "Schedule F," in *Coats v. Thayer* (1844), NARA-B.

56. *Coats* (1845), at 586, §7–10.

57. *Coats* (1845), §15, 20–22.

58. Many scholars suggest that *caveat emptor* yielded to the notion of the "unwary purchaser" around 1900; as in Max A. Geller, *Advertising at the Crossroads: Federal Regulation vs. Voluntary Controls* (New York: Garland, 1985), 127–133; Michael Pettit, *The Science of Deception: Psychology and Commerce in America* (Chicago: University of Chicago Press, 2013), 122–130; and Banner, *American Property*, 33–34.

59. Pettit notes that the "unwary purchaser" doctrine emerged after 1870 to "limit personal responsibility and suspend the notion of *caveat emptor* in order to protect the interests of established businesses." See Pettit, *Science of Deception*, 17.

60. B. Andrew Coates (for James, Peter, and Thomas Coats), Bill of Complaint (8 August 1844), in *Coats v. Thayer* (1844), NARA-B.

61. Subsequently, printers would be called as witnesses to substantiate the fraudulent intent of defendants. See Cox, *Trade Mark Cases* (1871), 662.

62. S. F. Plimpton (for Benjamin W. Thayer and John H. Bufford), Answer (19 October 1844), in *Coats v. Thayer*, NARA-B. In one case, the customer requested plates be made but did not order subsequent prints.

63. Schedule F, *Coats v. Thayer* (1844), NARA-B. Average wages for printers in Massachusetts ranged from $8 through $10 per week between 1840 and 1845, thus about $468 per year. See Carroll D. Wright, *Comparative Wages, Prices, and Cost of Living (from the Sixteenth Annual Report of the Massachusetts Bureau of Statistics of Labor, for 1885)* (Boston: Wright & Potter Printing Co., 1889), 59.

64. Plimpton had helped Carpenter prepare his answer to the bill of complaint from the Taylors in February 1844 and later that year helped Thayer prepare his answer to the bill filed by Coats et al. in *Coats v. Thayer*, NARA-B.

65. Plimpton Answer, *Coats v. Thayer*, NARA-B.

66. Jay T. Last, *The Color Explosion: Nineteenth-Century American Lithography* (Santa Ana, CA: Hillcrest Press, 2006), 47–48; S. N. Dickinson, *Boston Almanac for the Year 1846* (Boston: Thomas Groom & Co., 1845), 77; and David Tatham, *John Henry Bufford, American Lithographer* (Worcester, MA: American Antiquarian Society, 1976), 57–58.

67. Balleisen, *Navigating Failure*, 43.

68. Benjamin Franklin, *Autobiography of Benjamin Franklin: 1706–1757* (Bedford, MA: Applewood Books, 2008), 91–92. On broader developments in the printing industry, see

Joseph M. Adelman, *Revolutionary Networks: The Business and Politics of Printing the News, 1763–1789* (Baltimore: Johns Hopkins University Press, 2019).

69. Mihm, *Nation of Counterfeiters*, 262, 278–298.

70. Mihm, 87–91.

71. Mihm, 210; and Balleisen, *Fraud*, 27–29, 32.

72. Holbrook sold McGregor's threads for $0.275/dozen for the first batch and $0.375/dozen for the second, taking a commission rate of 6 percent. This was a substantial discount from Coats's rates, at $0.45–$0.475/dozen. Given the low sales in this case, McGregor's profits only amounted to $130, making Holbrook's commission $7.80. See Holbrook's answer (dated November 6, 1844) in *Coats v. Holbrook* (1845), New York State Archives, Series JN315-17, Box 50, BM1084-C.

73. McGregor's order was accounted for in Schedule F, *Coats v. Thayer* (1844), NARA-B.

74. Ads for J. & P. Coats's Six Cord Thread, *New York Daily Tribune*, May 2, 1845; and *North Carolina Standard*, May 7, 1845. Similar ads also appeared in both newspapers in April of the same year.

75. See Ads for Coats's and Coates's threads, *New York Herald*, July 12, 1847; *New York Herald*, June 14, 1847; and *New York Tribune*, December 7, 1850.

76. Based on research conducted in the *New York Times* (1857–1900), Library of Congress Chronicling America (newspapers across the United States, 1830–1900), and *The Times* of London (1780–1900).

77. The Bank of England's restriction of credit in the late 1830s is best discussed by Lepler, *The Many Panics of 1837*, 57–59.

78. Agents often served as deputized police forces in uncovering frauds. See Teresa da Silva Lopes and Mark Casson, "Brand Protection and the Globalization of British Business," *Business History Review* 86, no. 2 (2012): 296; Ian Klaus, *Forging Capitalism: Rogues, Swindlers, Frauds, and the Rise of Modern Finance* (New Haven, CT: Yale University Press, 2014), 102; and Thomas Mollanger, "The Effects of Producers' Trademark Strategies on the Structure of the Cognac Brandy Supply Chain During the Second Half of the 19th Century: The Reconfiguration of Commercial Trust by the Use of Brands," *Business History* 60, no. 8 (2018): 1267.

79. On guilds, see Mollerup, *Marks of Excellence*, 33. On Wedgwood, see Belfanti, "Branding Before the Brand," 1137; and Koehn, *Brand New*. Cox (in *Trade Mark Cases*, 1871) provides a detailed discussion of the British legal precedents forming common-law protections for trademarks, from the first case in 1590. As Bently explains (in "The Place of *Scienter*"), the British courts had taken efforts to more clearly define trademark protections through the 1830s.

80. Paul Duguid traces similar efforts in the British alcohol industry, albeit somewhat later in the century, in "Developing the Brand: The Case of Alcohol, 1800–1880," *Enterprise & Society* 4, no. 3 (2003): 405–441.

81. "An Act to Punish and prevent frauds in the use of false stamps and labels," *Laws of the State of New York*, 68th Session (Albany, NY: C. Van Benthuysen, 1845), chap. 279, pp. 304–305.

82. Steven W. Usselman and Richard R. John argue that economic change often motivates legal reform, in "Patent Politics: Intellectual Property, the Railroad Industry, and the Problem of Monopoly" 18, no. 1 (2006): 99. A related discussion appears in Koehn, *Brand New*, 5.

83. Senator Lott, arguing against Carpenter's appeal in *Taylor* (1846), 2 Sand. Ch. at 613–616.

84. Balleisen, *Navigating Failure*, 72–73, 97–98. Such arguments helped shape commercial institutions such as credit reporting in the United States (see Olegario, *Culture of Credit*, chap. 3); and they can also be seen in movements to professionalize advertising agents at the

end of the nineteenth century, as T. J. Jackson Lears shows in *Fables of Abundance: A Cultural History of Advertising in America* (New York: Basic, 1994), 12, 212.

85. *Taylor* (1846), 2 Sand. Ch. at 617–618. Made in 1846, this statement most certainly refers to the physical mark itself (akin to one made with a branding iron on livestock) rather than the abstract concept of the commercial brand (such as Nike, Pepsi, etc.) most familiar to advertising historians today.

86. On the periodization of brands and branding to the 1890s and later, see Stefan Schwarzkopf, "Turning Trademarks into Brands: How Advertising Agencies Practiced and Conceptualized Branding, 1890–1930," in *Trademarks, Brands, and Competitiveness*, 165–193; and Regina Lee Blaszczyk, *American Consumer Society, 1865–2005: From Hearth to HDTV* (New York: Wiley, 2009), 117. Some legal scholars suggest that the trademark began to function as a repository of goodwill by the 1860s (as in Banner, *American Property*, 39); though most point to the 1920s, as in Oren Bracha, "The Emergence and Development of United States Intellectual Property Law," in *The Oxford Handbook of Intellectual Property Law*, ed. Rochelle Cooper Dreyfuss and Justine Pila (New York: Oxford University Press, 2018), 260.

87. Petty, "From Label to Trademark," 138, table I.

88. On the cotton trade, see Balleisen, *Fraud*, 72; and for alcohol, Paul Duguid, "Early Marks: American Trademarks Before US Trademark Law," *Business History* 60, no. 8 (2018): 1154–1158.

89. Ad for Lea & Perrins' Worcestershire Sauce, *New Orleans Daily Crescent*, morning ed., October 2, 1857.

90. Ads for Lea & Perrins' Worcestershire Sauce, *Daily Nashville Patriot* (TN), July 3, 1857; *Vermont Phoenix*, September 12, 1857; and *Memphis Daily Appeal* (TN), May 8, 1858.

91. Petty, "From Label to Trademark," 137.

92. Such cases are outlined in Rowland Cox, *A Manual of Trade-Mark Cases*, 2nd ed. (New York: Houghton Mifflin, 1892).

93. *Fetridge v. Wells* (1857), 4 Abb. Pr. R. 144, cited in Cox, *Trade Mark Cases* (1871), 184–185, 188.

94. Zvi S. Rosen, "In Search of the Trade-Mark Cases: The Nascent Treaty Power and the Turbulent Origins of Federal Trademark Law," *St. John's Law Review* 83, no. 3 (2012): 834; citing Paul Duguid, "French Connections: The International Propagation of Trademarks in the Nineteenth Century," *Enterprise & Society* 10, no. 1 (2009): 13–14, 28–29.

95. On the various provisions by state, see Rosen, "Trade-Mark Cases," 840–843. Charles McCurdy argues that such inconsistency was one factor pushing large industrial firms to lobby for federal laws that would override state laws regulating commerce, in "American Law and the Marketing Structure of the Large Corporation, 1875–1890," *Journal of Economic History* 38, no. 3 (1978): 642.

96. *Congressional Globe*, 36th Cong., 2nd Sess. 670 (1861); and *Congressional Globe*, 36th Cong., 2nd Sess. 798 (1861). See also Rosen, "Trade-Mark Cases," 832–833.

97. "Trade Marks," *Scientific American* 16, no. 8 (February 23, 1867): 125.

98. Rosen, "Trade-Mark Cases," 833–836. France was the first to develop domestic trademark protections and was instrumental in pushing other countries to engage in reciprocal agreements. See Duguid, "French Connections," 23–24.

99. "To Druggists," letter from Joseph Burnett & Co., in *New York Times*, December 22, 1858.

100. *Burnett v. Phalon* (1867), 5 Abb. Pr. R., N. S. 212, in Cox, *Trade Mark Cases* (1871), 376. Cox cites the 1860 ruling in New York Superior Court (19 How. Pr. 530), wherein Judge Edwards Pierrepont drew upon the precedents for protecting goodwill established by *Snowden v. Noah* (1825) and *Taylor v. Carpenter* (1845).

101. I'd like to thank Wendy Woloson for her thoughtful suggestion to consider the public nature of trademarks here.

102. Many legal historians suggest that the law predicted and shaped business practice. Paul Duguid argues convincingly against these assumptions in "Developing the Brand."

103. Rosen, "Trade-Mark Cases," 840–843. Pettit suggests that the 1870 law marked a moment when the federal government sought to increase its regulatory power to "control deceitful persons and things" (in *Science of Deception*, 5), though Usselman and John trace the consistency of such regulatory impulses from the founding generation, in "Patent Politics."

104. On the shifting relationship of the government to the people after 1860, see Eric Foner, *The Story of American Freedom* (New York: W. W. Norton, 1998), 106–107.

105. "US Statute Concerning the Registration of Trade Marks," §78 and 84, in Cox, *Trade Mark Cases* (1871), 722–725.

106. "US Statute Concerning Trade Marks," §77, 78, 79, 82, and 84.

107. Cox, *Trade Mark Cases* (1871), 775.

108. Rosen, "Trade-Mark cases," 840–843. Articles in *Scientific American* indicate the importance of trademark lawsuits for its readership. See "Trade-Marks at Law," *Scientific American* 14, no. 38 (May 28, 1859): 316; and "Trade Marks," *Scientific American* 16, no. 8 (February 23, 1867): 125.

109. Petty, "From Label to Trademark," 144; and Pamela Walker Laird, *Advertising Progress: American Business and the Rise of Consumer Marketing* (Baltimore: Johns Hopkins University Press, 1998), 189, 414 n. 13, citing *Statistical History of the United States from Colonial Times to the Present*, intro. Ben J. Wattenberg (New York: Basic Books, 1976), 956–959. See also Cox, *Trade-Mark Cases* (1892); and Susan Strasser, *Satisfaction Guaranteed: The Making of the American Mass Market* (Washington, DC: Smithsonian Books, 1989), 44–52.

110. Cox, *Trade Mark Cases* (1871), iii. Yet Cox's book doesn't account for unrecorded decisions, such as the one in *Coats v. Thayer*, likely because it was never recorded in a formal court reporter (the parties settled outside of court).

111. Cox, *Trade-Mark Cases* (1892). Oren Bracha argues that lawyers played an important role in the design and development of trademarks in the United States after the 1920s by cultivating a proprietary attitude toward trademarks and brands and by translating that proprietary attitude into specific practice (such as litigation, threats of litigation, etc.). Oren Bracha, "There's a Huge Corporate Asset Here: Brands & Trademark Law with Oren Bracha," Stories from the Stacks/Hagley Library (June 2019), https://www.hagley.org/there%E2%80%99s -huge-corporate-asset-here-brands-trademark-law-oren-bracha (accessed 30 May 2020).

112. *Colman v. Crump* (1877), 70 NY 578–580, in Cox, *Trade-Mark Cases* (1892), 325–326.

113. Cox (1892), 325. This case is also discussed by da Silva Lopes and Casson in "Brand Protection," 299. *McLean v. Fleming* 96 US 245 (1878) is often cited as the case that cast aside the requirement of the defendant's malicious and/or deceitful intent to determine infringement (as in Pettit, *Science of Deception*, 126). However, Lionel Bently (in "The Place of *Scienter*") has suggested that the rejection of the legal principle of *scienter* (malicious intent) can be traced to the British case *Millington v. Fox* 3 Myl. & Cr. 338 (1838); subsequent cases diverged by requiring malicious intent, and thus *Millington* existed as an outlier until the 1870s, when the strict liability principle rejecting *scienter* came into favor.

114. "All About a Bull's Head," *New York Herald*, February 1, 1872. See also "Fight Between Coleman's [*sic*] English Mustard Bull and American Bulls," *New York Sun*, February 1, 1872.

115. Here, I am building from the hypothesis that intellectual property law has evolved through and been shaped by rhetorical discourses related to culture, identity, and power. See Anjali Vats, *The Color of Creatorship: Intellectual Property, Race, and the Making of Americans* (Stanford, CA: Stanford University Press, 2020), 6–7, 27–28.

Chapter 3

1. Lewis Saxby, "The Genius of Pictorial Advertising," *Printers' Ink* 11, no. 19 (1894): 804.

2. Many histories suggest that consumer-oriented appeals did not emerge in American advertising until professional communications experts and marketing specialists entered the industry around 1900. See; for example, Stephen R. Fox, *The Mirror Makers: A History of American Advertising and Its Creators* (Chicago: University of Illinois Press, 1984), 13–39. Recent works also support this chronology, as in Edd Applegate, *The Rise of Advertising in the United States: A History of Innovation to 1960* (Lanham, MD: Scarecrow Press, 2012); Dawn Spring, *Advertising in the Age of Persuasion: Building Brand America 1941–1961* (New York: Palgrave Macmillan, 2011); Joseph M. Gabriel, *Medical Monopoly: Intellectual Property Rights and the Origins of the Modern Pharmaceutical Industry* (Chicago: University of Chicago Press, 2014); and Gary S. Cross and Robert Proctor, *Packaged Pleasures: How Technology & Marketing Revolutionized Desire* (Chicago: University of Chicago Press, 2014).

3. Carl Robert Keyes, "Early American Advertising: Marketing and Consumer Culture in Eighteenth-Century Philadelphia" (PhD diss., Johns Hopkins University, 2007), 283. See also T. H. Breen, *The Marketplace of Revolution: How Consumer Politics Shaped American Independence* (New York: Oxford University Press, 2004); and Joanna Cohen, *Luxurious Citizens: The Politics of Consumption in Nineteenth-Century America* (Philadelphia: University of Pennsylvania Press, 2017).

4. David Jury, *Graphic Design Before Graphic Designers: The Printer as Designer and Craftsman 1700–1914* (New York: Thames & Hudson, 2012), 11–13, 24.

5. Carl Keyes has written extensively on colonial advertising, especially in "Early American Advertising." More recently, Keyes has published his findings in "The Adverts 250 Project: An Exploration of Advertising in Colonial America 250 Years Ago This Week," blog (from 2016), online at https://adverts250project.org/ (accessed 23 June 2020). See, especially, Keyes, "John Head, *Supplement to the Boston Evening-Post*, April 30, 1770," Blog post, "The Adverts 250 Project" (30 April 2020), https://adverts250project.org/2020/04/30/april-30-5/ (accessed 23 June 2020).

6. Applegate, *Rise of Advertising*, 10.

7. Keyes, "Early American Advertising," 67; and Jury, *Graphic Design*, 60.

8. Carl R. Keyes, "Jolley Allen, *Boston Post-Boy* July 7, 1766" Blog post, "The Adverts 250 Project" (July 7, 2016), https://adverts250project.org/2016/07/07/july-7/ (accessed 21 May 2019); Keyes, "Jacob Treadwell, *New-Hampshire Gazette*, December 15, 1769" Blog post, "The Adverts 250 Project" (December 15, 2019), https://adverts250project.org/2019/12/15/december-15-4/ (accessed 8 June 2021); Keyes, "Early American Advertising," 279; and Jury, *Graphic Design*, 67. More on colonial-era printers can be found in Joseph M. Adelman, *Revolutionary Networks: The Business and Politics of Printing the News, 1763–1789* (Baltimore: Johns Hopkins University Press, 2019).

9. Jury, *Graphic Design*, 60–63.

10. Jury, 69–71.

11. Pamela Walker Laird, *Advertising Progress: American Business and the Rise of Consumer Marketing* (Baltimore: Johns Hopkins University Press, 1998), 71.

12. Jury, *Graphic Design*, chap. 2.

13. David Jury, "Artistry in Letterpress and Engraving," *Ephemera Journal* 16, no. 2 (2014): 4; and Daniel J. Boorstin, *The Americans: The Democratic Experience* (New York: Knopf Doubleday, 2010), 138.

14. See, for example, *New York Tribune*, July 21, 1941, p. 1.

15. Frank Presbrey, *The History and Development of Advertising* (Garden City, NY: Doubleday, 1929), 236–240.

16. John Nerone, "Newspapers and the Public Sphere," in *A History of the Book in America*, vol. 3, ed. Scott E. Casper et al. (Chapel Hill: University of North Carolina Press, 2007), 239; and Jury, *Graphic Design*, 67–69.

17. Boorstin, *The Americans*, 143.

18. Boorstin, 143.

19. Erika Piola, "The Rise of Early American Lithography and Antebellum Visual Culture," *Winterthur Portfolio* 48, no. 2/3 (2014): 126.

20. Joshua Brown, *Beyond the Lines: Pictorial Reporting, Everyday Life, and the Crisis of Gilded Age America* (Berkeley: University of California Press, 2002), 39; and Nerone, "Newspapers," 239. On stereotyping and electrotyping, see also Michael Winship, "Printing with Plates in the Nineteenth Century United States," *Printing History* 10, no. 2 (1983): 15–26.

21. This research is based on a survey of newspapers published in New York, Pennsylvania, Vermont, North Carolina, and Ohio from 1830 through 1900. From the *New York Times*, *New York Tribune*, and *New York Morning Herald*, I collected approximately 265 individual pages to form the sample set. From rural and semi-urban papers in the other aforementioned states, I collected approximately 100 pages at regular intervals to form the sample set. Taken together, these samples thus yielded information on approximately 18,000 advertisements.

22. Boorstin, *The Americans*, 138.

23. This is based on my observations of the advertisements in these papers and my analysis of the mainstream-press sample set used in researching this chapter.

24. *New York Herald*, June 9, 1838.

25. Ad for Hay's Liniment, *New York Herald*, September 29, 1838.

26. Jury, *Graphic Design*, 70–72.

27. On the manicule, see William H. Sherman, *Used Books: Marking Readers in Renaissance England* (Philadelphia: University of Pennsylvania Press, 2010), chap. 2.

28. Ad for F. W. & W. F. Gilley Dry Goods, *New York Tribune*, September 21, 1841.

29. "The Value of Blank Space," *Printing Art* 16, no. 4 (1910): 297–298.

30. Applegate, *Advertising*, 10.

31. Ad for Hovey's Trunk Repository, *New York Tribune*, August 10, 1841; and ad for Lee's Blacking, *New York Tribune*, July 1, 1841. See also ad for Magnolia Shaving Soaps, *New York Tribune*, June 9, 1841.

32. Keyes "Early American Advertising," 67. Trade cards featuring depictions of the firm's location were common in the nineteenth century; see, for example, the card for R. S. & P. Cushman, Importers (c. 1830), Col. 9, DCWL. Lee's logo also appears in *Longworth's American Almanac, New-York Register and City Directory for 1840/41* (New York: Thomas Longworth, 1840), 386; New York Public Library Digital Collections, online at https://digitalcollections.nypl.org/items/17e3e2c0-8a22-0136-1f25-4949c287a53f (accessed 11 July 2022). Skilled engravers earned higher wages than the apprentice boys who sorted type and operated the presses; therefore, custom images commanded a higher price. Georgia B. Barnhill, "Business Practices of Commercial Nineteenth-Century American Lithographers," *Winterthur Portfolio* 48, no. 2/3 (2014): 217–219, 223–224. As Barnhill notes, by the 1830s, lithographs could be commissioned from printing houses as well, but these were not yet suitable for use in newspaper advertising due to their higher cost.

33. Advertisement for C. B. Fisher, Dry Goods, *Columbia Democrat* (Bloomsburg, PA), December 23, 1837.

34. See, for example, a woodcut depicting ladies' bonnets in an ad for Rupert & Barton, Fancy Goods, *Columbia Democrat* (Bloomsburg, PA), December 9, 1837; and *Burlington Free Press* (Burlington, VT), May 1, 1846.

35. Ad for John Sillban's shoe store, *North-Carolinian* (Fayetteville, NC), May 3, 1845; ad for American Cooking Stoves, *Burlington Free Press* (Burlington, VT), September 11, 1846; and notice placed by Samuel W. Pearson, local tax collector, in the *Somerset Herald* (Somerset, PA), August 3, 1847.

36. Sillban's shoe store (1845).

37. Advertisement for C. C. Alvord, *Rutland Herald* (Rutland, VT), March 8, 1836.

38. Ads for Wistar's Balsam of Cherry, *Somerset Herald* (Somerset, PA), August 3, 1847, and in the *Cadiz Sentinel* (Cadiz, OH), December 3, 1845.

39. "Trust," *Printers' Ink* 10, no. 13 (1894): 354.

40. On agents, see Rowena Olegario, *A Culture of Credit: Embedding Trust and Transparency in American Business* (Cambridge, MA: Harvard University Press, 2006), 26; citing Glenn Porter and Harold Livesay, *Merchants and Manufacturers: Studies in the Changing Structure of Nineteenth-Century Marketing* (Baltimore: Johns Hopkins University Press, 1971).

41. Piola, "Early American Lithography," 129–131. On collecting chromos, see Katharine Martinez, "At Home with Mona Lisa: Consumers and Commercial Visual Culture, 1880–1920," in *Seeing High and Low: Representing Social Conflict in American Visual Culture*, ed. Patricia Johnston (Berkeley: University of California Press, 2006), 160–176. The visual turn in the 1840s is also discussed in Gregory M. Pfitzer, *Picturing the Past* (Washington, DC: Smithsonian Institution Press, 2002), 16–17.

42. Jury, *Graphic Design*, 70; and Presbrey, *History of Advertising*, 498–499.

43. Richard W. Flint, "A Great Industrial Art: Circus Poster Printing in America," *Printing History* 25 no. 2, orig. series no. 50 (2007): 18–43. See also Bradford R. Collins, "The Poster as Art: Jules Cheret and the Struggle for the Equality of the Arts in Late Nineteenth-Century France," *Design Issues* 2, no. 1 (1985): 41–50; Neil Harris, "American Poster Collecting: A Fitful History," *American Art* 12, no. 1 (1998): 11–39; and Ruth E. Iskin, *The Poster: Art, Advertising, Design, and Collecting, 1860s–1900s* (Hanover, NH: Dartmouth College Press, 2014).

44. Brown, *Beyond the Lines*, 23, 35–39; and Piola, "Early American Lithography," 133.

45. Katharine Morrison McClinton, *The Chromolithographs of Louis Prang* (New York: C. N. Potter, 1973), 59–60; and Jay T. Last, *The Color Explosion: Nineteenth-Century American Lithography* (Santa Ana, CA: Hillcrest Press, 2006), 244.

46. Last, *Color Explosion*, 22–26; Laird, *Advertising Progress*, 83.

47. Brown, *Beyond the Lines*, 14; David M. Henkin, *City Reading: Written Words and Public Spaces in Antebellum New York*, Popular Cultures, Everyday Lives (New York: Columbia University Press, 1998), 119; and Boorstin, *The Americans*, 139; citing Frederic Hudson (*Journalism in the United States, from 1690–1872* [NY: Harper & Brothers, 1872]). See also Antoinette Shryock, "Advertising in Its Infancy," *Judicious Advertising* 23, no. 2 (1925): 68.

48. Henkin, *City Reading*, 117. See also Patricia Cline Cohen, *The Murder of Helen Jewett* (New York: Vintage, 1999).

49. In some ways, this might be considered a rejection of the carnivalesque in favor of a "modern" professional or managerial aesthetic, though such moves are more typical of the end-of-the-century, rather than the antebellum, era. See T. J. Jackson Lears, *Fables of Abundance: A Cultural History of Advertising in America* (New York: Basic Books, 1994), 10–11.

50. See, for example, *New York Daily Tribune*, December 7, 1850.

51. A cursory examination of the London *Times* for the period 1840 through 1900 suggests that the paper adhered more rigidly to the Agate Rule than other papers even in the United States, and for longer. Research conducted in the *Times Digital Archive* database (Gale Group) (accessed 27 June 2022).

52. Ad for Longworth's Cincinnati Wines, *New York Times*, June 11, 1858.

53. Ad for the *New York Ledger*, in the *New York Times*, December 24, 1857. On Bonner, see Boorstin, *The Americans*, 140–141; and Presbrey, *History of Advertising*, 233–239.

54. Ads for Brady's Gallery, *New York Times*, August 21, 1856; and *New York Tribune*, October 27, 1856.

55. Ad for Imray's Domestic Medicine, *New York Times*, February 23, 1857.

56. Henkin, *City Reading*, 174.

57. David Waldstreicher, *In the Midst of Perpetual Fetes: The Making of American Nationalism, 1776–1820* (Chapel Hill: University of North Carolina Press, 1997), 293; Henkin, *City Reading*, 176; and Jason Hill and Vanessa R. Schwartz, eds., *Getting the Picture: The Visual Culture of the News* (New York: Bloomsbury Publishing, 2015), 7.

58. Phineas Taylor Barnum, *The Life of P.T. Barnum: Written by Himself* (London: Sampson Low, Son, & Co., 1855), 157.

59. Wendy A. Woloson, "The Rise of the Consumer in the Age of Jackson," in *A Companion to the Era of Andrew Jackson*, ed. Sean Patrick Adams (New York: Blackwell, 2013), 494–496. Woloson expands this discussion in *Crap: A History of Cheap Stuff in America* (Chicago: University of Chicago Press, 2020).

60. Examples include an ad for Dr. Hoofland's Celebrated German Bitters, *Mountain Sentinel* (Edensburg, PA), December 16, 1852; ads for Thomas Devine and Robert Davis, both in *Democrat and Sentinel* (Edensburg, PA), December 2, 1857; double-column ads in *Gallipolis Journal* (Gallipolis, OH), May 17, 1855; and illustrations included in *Tarborough Press* (Edgecombe Co., NC), August 3, 1850; *Western Democrat* (Charlotte, NC), August 3, 1855; and *Burlington Free Press* (Burlington, VT), September 5, 1856.

61. See the *Mountain Sentinel* (Edensburg, PA), December 2, 1852; and the *Democrat and Sentinel* (Edensburg, PA), December 2, 1857.

62. Presbrey, *History of Advertising*, 499–500; and Jury, *Graphic Design*, 69.

63. William Smith, *Advertise: How? When? Where?* (London: Routledge, Warne, and Routledge, 1863), 7.

64. Smith, 16, 36, emphasis in original.

65. Smith, 80.

66. Lawrence A. Kreiser Jr., *Marketing the Blue and Gray: Newspaper Advertising and the American Civil War* (Baton Rouge: Louisiana State University Press, 2019), chap. 1.

67. Laird, *Advertising Progress*, 73.

68. Brown, *Beyond the Lines*, 14–17, 23–35.

69. Ad for Ward's Shirts, *New York Times*, March 31, 1860.

70. Ad for Lewis's Shirts, *New York Times*, March 26, 1863.

71. Ads for Mrs. S. A. Allen's Hair Restorer, Smith & Brother Pale Ale, and Isaac Smith's Umbrellas, in *New York Times*, February 17, 1863.

72. See *Wyoming Democrat* (Tunkhannock, PA), for April 14, 1867; August 14, 1867; and December 18, 1867.

73. *Holmes County Republican* (Millersburg, OH), May 17, 1860. Subsequent issues followed suit.

74. Sandwich-board designs were common on trade cards at the time, see card for Elwood Irish Sewing Supplies (Adrian, MI) (c.1880), Col. 134, DCWL. While antebellum advertisers would have commonly duplicated their trade cards in newspaper advertisements, especially in rural settings, the ad for Koch's store predates the widespread use of chromolithographed trade cards by several years.

75. Ads for Lea & Perrins' Worcestershire Sauce, in *Daily Nashville Patriot*, July 3, 1857; *Vermont Phoenix*, September 12, 1857; *Memphis Daily Appeal*, May 8, 1858; *Evening Star* (Washington, DC), January 6, 1861; and *New York Times*, January 26, 1863. It is worth noting that

these examples are not an exhaustive representation of all of Lea & Perrins' advertising in the United States at the time.

76. Ads for Lea & Perrins' Worcestershire Sauce, in the *Polynesian* (Honolulu, HI), April 4, 1863; *Charleston Daily News* (Charleston, SC), December 7, 1866; *Ohio Statesman* (Columbus, OH), October 27, 1866; *Ohio Statesman* (Columbus, OH), October 26, 1867; *Nashville Union & Dispatch*, August 17, 1867; and *New York Times*, August 21, 1874.

77. In searching for ads for Lea & Perrins' Worcestershire Sauce in the London *Times*, I was not able to locate any examples using illustrations of the bottle or label, though the firm did use iteration copy in that paper by the 1860s. Because the London *Times* appears to have adhered more rigidly to the Agate Rule at this time, Lea & Perrins likely could not have deployed the same ads in that paper because images appear to have been excluded or prohibited in the *Times* until around 1900. Research conducted in Gale Group, the *Times Digital Archive*, online at https://www.gale.com/c/the-times-digital-archive (accessed 27 June 2022).

78. Research conducted in the Library of Congress Chronicling America database demonstrates that the brand went through several waves of coordinated advertising strategies, with clear design changes structuring each wave of ads.

79. While this is true for the United States, Neil McKendrick demonstrates that Josiah Wedgwood advertised his wares on a regional and continental scale in the late eighteenth century. See McKendrick et al., *The Birth of a Consumer Society: The Commercialization of Eighteenth-Century England* (Bloomington: Indiana University Press, 1982), 113–126.

80. Based on research conducted in LOCPP Chronicling America and ProQuest Historical Newspapers, *New York Times*.

81. Irvine Garland Penn, *The Afro-American Press and Its Editors* (Springfield, MA: Willey & Company, 1891), 62.

82. Ads for Wistar's Balsam of Wild Cherry, the *Republic* (Washington, DC), March 8, 1850; and the *National Era* (Washington, DC), June 6, 1850.

83. Ads for Wheeler & Wilson sewing machines, in the *Cincinnati Daily Press*, February 2, 1861; and in the *Colored Citizen* (Cincinnati, OH), May 19, 1866. See also ads for Aetna Insurance, in the *Colored Citizen* (Cincinnati, OH), May 19, 1866; the *Lancaster Gazette* (OH), May 10, 1866; and the *Delaware Gazette* (OH), June 15, 1866. By the 1880s, more brand-name goods could readily be found advertised in African American newspapers, in a range of locations, including Lydia Pinkham's Vegetable Tonic, Hostetter's Stomach Bitters, Hood's Sarsaparilla, Singer Sewing Machines, Ayer's Sarsaparilla, and Hires Root Beer. These observations are based on research collected from the Library of Congress Chronicling America database, comprising a dataset of approximately 500 newspaper pages of African American newspapers published between 1828 and 1900. These included samples from semirural and urban locales, including Georgia, Indiana, Louisiana, North Carolina, New York, Ohio, Pennsylvania, South Carolina, Tennessee, and the District of Columbia.

84. Brown, *Beyond the Lines*, 33–35, 234–236; and Neil Harris, *Cultural Excursions: Marketing Appetites and Cultural Tastes in Modern America* (Chicago: University of Chicago Press, 1990), 305–306. It is important to note, however, that halftone processes would not be used successfully in newspapers until the late 1890s.

85. Ad for Smith Bros. Pale Ale, *New York Herald*, December 15, 1876. No comparable ads appeared in the other New York papers for that day.

86. Laird, *Advertising Progress*, 72.

87. *New York Times*, May 17, 1874.

88. Ads for Hearn Clothiers, *New York Times*, March 31, 1878.

89. *New York Times*, December 20, 1885.

90. Ad for Hearn's Clothiers, *New York Tribune*, January 2, 1890, paralleling the ad for Hovey's Trunk Repository in 1841 discussed in the text above.

91. See, for example, ads for Royal Baking Powder, in the *New York Tribune*, May 20, 1882; for Castoria, in the *Gold Leaf* (Henderson, NC), April 4, 1895; and both in the *Freeland Tribune* (Freeland, PA), April 29, 1897. These two brand-name goods appeared regularly in the sample set from the 1880s forward.

92. *New York Times*, March 4, 1897; and *New York Times Illustrated Magazine*, February 27, 1898.

93. "New York Times Company Timeline," *Internet Archive* archived version, online at https://web.archive.org/web/20090313111252/http://nytco.com/company/milestones/timeline_1881.html (accessed 17 October 2019).

94. See, for example, ads for Wanamaker & Brown and National Silver Plating Co., in the *Centre Reporter* (Centre Hill, PA), December 6, 1877; and an ad for Barnum's Museum, *Gallipolis Journal* (Gallipolis, OH), September 16, 1875.

95. Ad for Dr. Warner's Coraline Corsets, *New York Tribune*, April 15, 1894. See also ads for O'Neill's Department Store, *New York Tribune*, January 6, 1890; Frear's Popular Bazar, *Bennington Banner* (Bennington, VT), May 7, 1891; Wanamaker's Store, *New York Times*, March 21, 1900; and Neuburger's Department Store, *Freeland Tribune* (Freeland, PA), December 15, 1902.

96. Regina Lee Blaszczyk suggests that advertising agencies began to generalize from one account to another, to form a theory of practice, by the 1920s. See *American Consumer Society, 1865–2005: From Hearth to HDTV* (Oxford, UK: Wiley, 2009), 135.

97. Jed Scarboro, "How to Make a Live Ad," *Printers' Ink* 9, no. 21 (1893): 541. See also Sam W. Hoke, "Not Made by a Trust," *Printers' Ink* 9, no. 11 (1893): 285.

98. George P. Rowell Agency, "To Catch the Eye," advertisement in *Printers' Ink* 4, no. 12 (1891): 418.

99. John Irving Romer, "The Greatest Newspaper Advertiser in the World," *Printers' Ink* 8, no. 26 (1893): 755–761; and Daniel Pope, *The Making of Modern Advertising* (New York: Basic Books, 1983), 234–235.

100. Untitled article (Maxims for Successful Advertising), *Printers' Ink* 10, no. 20 (1894): 600–601.

101. "Illustrations for Advertisements," *Printers' Ink* 1, no. 11 (1888): 260. See also "Illustrated Advertisements," *Printers' Ink* 1, no. 10 (1888): 235; and Henry Lewis Johnson, "Half-Tone Engravings: Their Use in Advertisements," *Printers' Ink* 6, no. 6 (1892): 179–180.

102. Charles A. Bates, "Posters," *Printers' Ink* 12, no. 10 (1895): 17.

103. Saxby, "Genius," 804.

104. Charles L. Benjamin, "Every Advertiser His Own Architect," *Printers' Ink* 6, no. 7 (1892): 230–232. See also Jury, *Graphic Design*, 202–208.

105. R. G. Ray, "Ethics of Advertising," *Printers' Ink* 11, no. 21 (1894): 904–906; and A. D. Hosterman, "The Advertising Agent," *Printers' Ink* 10, no. 7 (1894): 163–165. On the professionalization of the agencies, see Lears, *Fables of Abundance*, 212.

106. Robert Jay, *The Trade Card in Nineteenth-Century America* (Columbia: University of Missouri Press, 1987), 100–102; and Last, *Color Explosion*, 245.

107. Boudinot Muidetter, "Local Advertising in the Country Weeklies," *Printers' Ink* 6, no. 15 (1892): 477–478; and A. V. Isakovics, "Mail-Order Advertising," *Printers' Ink* 6, no. 20 (1892): 634–636. On the printers' perspective, see Thomas Donnelley, "The Application of Art, So Called, to Advertising," *Printers' Ink* 5, no. 14 (1891): 364–365.

108. Laird, *Advertising Progress*, 216; and "Company Advertising" (Series III), RRD.

109. "Elements of a Good Ad," *Printers' Ink* 14, no. 11 (1896): 44–45; and Jury, *Graphic Design*, 259–264.

110. Laird, *Advertising Progress*, 255. Such specialists paralleled the "fashion intermediaries" discussed by Regina Lee Blaszczyk in *Imagining Consumers: Design and Innovation from Wedgwood to Corning* (Baltimore: Johns Hopkins University Press, 2000).

111. David Jury notes that British newspapers were slow to adopt printing innovations, and they only did so after American papers had well-established the importance of inventive type and design. See Jury, *Graphic Design*, 68.

Chapter 4

1. Elizabeth Wills Vernon, "Centennial Scrapbook" (1876), Last HL. A related discussion appears in Jennifer Jolly, "History in the Making: A Columbian Exposition Scrapbook," in *The Scrapbook in American Life*, ed. Susan Tucker, Katherine Ott, and Patricia Buckler (Philadelphia: Temple University Press, 2006), 79–96.

2. Sections of this chapter previously appeared as Jennifer M. Black, "Exchange Cards: Advertising, Album Making, and the Commodification of Sentiment in the Gilded Age," *Winterthur Portfolio* 51, no. 1 (2017): 1–53. On the commodification of sentiment as a marker of class, see also Richard L. Bushman, *The Refinement of America: Persons, Houses, Cities* (New York: Vintage Books, 1993).

3. Stephen Fox, *The Mirror Makers: A History of American Advertising and Its Creators* (Chicago: University of Illinois Press, 1997), 13–25; Susan Strasser, *Satisfaction Guaranteed: The Making of the American Mass Market* (Washington, DC: Smithsonian Institution Press, 1989); and James D. Norris, *Advertising and the Transformation of American Society, 1865–1920* (New York: Greenwood Press, 1990), chap. 1. Stefan Schwarzkopf has argued that this teleological view has limited historians' interpretations of the industry, and thus presents a major problem for the future of the field. See Schwarzkopf, "The Subsiding Sizzle of Advertising History: Methodological and Theoretical Challenges in the Post Advertising Age," *Journal of Historical Research in Marketing* 3, no. 4 (2011): 528–548.

4. See, for example, Robert Jay, *The Trade Card in Nineteenth-Century America* (Columbia: University of Missouri Press, 1987), 1; Mona Domosh, *American Commodities in an Age of Empire* (New York: Routledge, 2006), 56–57; Pamela Walker Laird, *Advertising Progress: American Business and the Rise of Consumer Marketing* (Baltimore: Johns Hopkins University Press, 1998), 6, 98, 149; and Ellen Gruber Garvey, *The Adman in the Parlor: Magazines and the Gendering of Consumer Culture, 1880s to 1910s* (New York: Oxford University Press, 1996), 17, 26.

5. Jay T. Last, *The Color Explosion: Nineteenth-Century American Lithography* (Santa Ana, CA: Hillcrest Press, 2006), 15–21, 66–67. Whereas letterpress printing uses heavy rollers to press paper onto an inked tray filled with dye-cast letters, the lithographic process works by applying a grease or oil treatment to a porous stone, then inking the stone (the grease repels the ink, so that it only sticks to certain ungreased areas of the design) and using the stone as a printing plate to make an image on paper. Georgia Barnhill and Lauren Hewes, "Early American Prints," and "Chromolithography" (lectures, Center for Historic American Visual Culture (CHAViC) summer seminar, American Antiquarian Society, Worcester, MA, June 2010).

6. Harriet Beecher Stowe, "What Pictures Shall I Hang on My Walls?" in *Atlantic Almanac for 1869* (Boston: Ticknor & Fields, 1868), 41, 43–44; and "Mrs. Stowe on Prang's Chromos," in *Prang's Chromo: A Journal of Popular Art* 1, no. 1 (January 1868): 2. See also Cynthia Lee Patterson, "'A Taste for Refined Culture': Imag(in)Ing the Middle Class in the Philly Pictorials of the 1840s and 1850s" (PhD diss., George Mason University, 2005), 31–32.

7. Last, *Color Explosion*, 22–26; and Laird, *Advertising Progress*, 83. See also Laura Anne Kalba, *Color in the Age of Impressionism: Commerce, Technology, and Art* (University Park: Pennsylvania State University Press, 2017); and Peter C. Marzio, *The Democratic Art: Pic-*

tures for a Nineteenth-Century America: Chromolithography, 1840–1900 (Boston: D. R. Godine, 1979).

8. "Mrs. Stowe," 2.

9. Karen Halttunen, Confidence Men and Painted Women: A Study of Middle-Class Culture in America, 1830–1870 (New Haven, CT: Yale University Press, 1982), 88–89.

10. Nathaniel Currier, "The Drunkards Progress, from the first glass to the grave," (ca. 1846), lithograph, LOCPP (online at https://www.loc.gov/item/91796265/); and Currier & Ives, "The Bad Husband: The Fruits of Intemperance and Idleness," (1870), lithograph, LOCPP (online at https://www.loc.gov/item/90708868/).

11. Louis Prang, Prang's American Card Album (Boston: Louis Prang, 1864), Louis Prang Archive, Last HL.

12. "On Prang's American Chromos," reprinted from Forney's Philadelphia Press, in Prang's Chromo: A Journal of Popular Art 1, no. 1 (January 1868): 3, in LOCPP.

13. For more on the history of album-making, see Black, "Exchange Cards," 30–32.

14. Since the publication of Marzio's Democratic Art, advertising historians have attributed the invention of the trade card to Prang. Yet, while Prang was first to copyright his trade cards, other lithographic firms in Boston, New York, and Philadelphia had independently developed similar lithographed cards in the early 1870s and had marketed and distributed their cards to retailers and stationers along the East Coast. For a more detailed account of these developments, see Black, "Exchange Cards," 10.

15. "Illuminated Business and Advertising Cards Published by L. Prang and Company," Price List (Spring 1879), Louis Prang Archive, Last HL. See also Jay, Trade Card, chaps. 2–3; and Deborah A. Smith, "Consuming Passions: Scrapbooks and American Play," Ephemera Journal 6 (1993): 65.

16. Black, "Exchange Cards," 53. See also Laird, Advertising Progress, 79.

17. Trade cards for Linden Bloom Perfume, S. D. Sollers and Co., and Merrill and Mackintire's Stationers (c. 1885), all BTC HL.

18. James Carrier, Gifts and Commodities: Exchange and Western Capitalism Since 1700 (New York: Routledge, 1995), chap. 7. Carrier further argued that, as western societies industrialized and production processes (and, by extension, the commodities that resulted) became more impersonal, the home became a "beleaguered personal sphere," which caused anxious Americans to invest gifts with personal meaning and emotion (156). In response, Elizabeth White Nelson argues that middle-class men and women used sentimental ideals to resolve the contradictions of market culture, developing a "sentimental pragmatism" to define the market relations of both production and consumption in moral terms. See Nelson, Market Sentiments: Middle-Class Market Culture in Nineteenth-Century America (Washington, DC: Smithsonian Institution Press, 2004), 6.

19. Black, "Exchange Cards."

20. Camille Block album (1875–1887), doc. 35, DCWL; Charles Swain Papers (c. 1840–1865), col. 798, DCWL; trade card for Standard Screw Fastened Shoes showing annotation "For Leona" at top (c. 1880), Warshaw I Shoes, AC NMAH; Caroline Cowles Richards, diary entry for December 24, 1863, in Village Life in America 1852–1872, ed. Margaret E. Sangster (New York: Henry Holt, 1913), 161; and Isabella Maud Mayne, diary entry for December 27, 1883, in Maud, ed. Richard Lee Strout (New York: Macmillian, 1939), 262.

21. Black, "Exchange Cards," 14–17.

22. Louis Prang to undisclosed client(s), November 30, 1876, Louis Prang Archive, Last HL. See also Barry Shank, A Token of My Affection: Greeting Cards and American Business Culture (New York: Columbia University Press, 2004), 96.

23. Halttunen, Confidence Men, chaps. 2 and 4. The practice of exchanging calling cards originated in continental Europe in the eighteenth century. See Maurice Rickards,

The Encyclopedia of Ephemera: A Guide to the Fragmentary Documents of Everyday Life for the Collector, Curator, and Historian (New York: Routledge, 2000), 351.

24. Abby Buchanan Longstreet, *Cards: Their Significance and Proper Uses, as Governed by the Usages of New York Society* (New York: F. A. Stokes and Bros., 1889), 1–3.

25. Jed Scarboro, "How to Make a Live Ad," *Printers' Ink* 9, no. 21 (1893): 541–542. On traveling salesmen, see Susan V. Spellman, "Trust Brokers: Traveling Grocery Salesmen and Confidence in Nineteenth-Century Trade," *Enterprise and Society* 13, no. 2 (2012): 276–312. Media scholars J. David Bolter and Richard Grusin have proposed the term "remediation" to explain the ways in which new media adapt and transform older media forms, building upon public familiarity to ensure the success of the new medium. See Bolter and Grusin, *Remediation: Understanding New Media* (Cambridge, MA: MIT Press, 1999), 273; and Marshall McLuhan, *Understanding Media: The Extensions of Man* (New York: Signet, 1964).

26. Rickards, *Encyclopedia of Ephemera*, 351.

27. Garvey, *Adman*, 46.

28. Trade card for John Wanamaker (c. 1876–1880), Grossman Col. 838, DCWL.

29. Joseph Herbert Appel, John Wanamaker (Firm), and Leigh Mitchell Hodges, *Golden Book of the Wanamaker Stores: Jubilee Year, 1861–1911* (Philadelphia: John Wanamaker, 1911), 218.

30. Here I am building on the arguments made by Katherine C. Grier, in *Culture & Comfort: Parlor Making and Middle-Class Identity, 1850–1930* (Washington, DC: Smithsonian Institution Press, 1997), chap. 1.

31. Trade card for Bufford's Boston, 1885, Warshaw I Advertising Industry, AC NMAH. See also "Quaint Devices in Trade: The Extensive Growth of Picture-Card Advertising," *New York Times*, June 18, 1882; and George Enos Throop, "Uses of the Colored Pictures as a Circulation Raiser," *Printers' Ink* 10, no. 9 (1894): 227–228. Regina Blaszczyk also notes that content came to rule the day, in *American Consumer Society, 1865–2005: From Hearth to HDTV* (London: Wiley, 2009), 273.

32. Lewis Saxby, "The Genius of Pictorial Advertising," *Printers' Ink* 11, no. 19 (1894): 804. See also Laird, *Advertising Progress*, 69, 215.

33. Black, "Exchange Cards," 53.

34. This romanticization is documented in Steven Mintz, *Huck's Raft: A History of American Childhood* (Cambridge, MA: Belknap Press, 2004); and Claire Perry, *Young America: Childhood in Nineteenth-Century Art and Culture* (New Haven, CT: Yale University Press, 2006).

35. Jay, *Trade Card*, 93; and T. J. Jackson Lears, *No Place of Grace: Antimodernism and the Transformation of American Culture* (New York: Pantheon, 1981), 146–147. See also Jessica K. Dallow, "Treasures of the Mind: Individuality and Authenticity in Late Nineteenth-Century Scrapbooks" (Master's thesis, University of North Carolina at Chapel Hill, 1995), 43.

36. Gregory M. Pfitzer argues that such sentimental images proliferated in the decades following the war and fostered a form of "sentimental escapism" that diverted attention from the persistent sectional tensions following Reconstruction. See Pfitzer, *Picturing the Past: Illustrated Histories and the American Imagination, 1840–1900* (Washington, DC: Smithsonian Institution Press, 2002), 127–132.

37. Grier, *Culture and Comfort*, 25–43, 59.

38. "Lydia Pinkham's Grandchildren," trade card, Warshaw I Patent Medicine, AC NMAH.

39. Sarah Stage, *Female Complaints: Lydia Pinkham and the Business of Women's Medicine* (New York: W. W. Norton, 1979), chap. 1.

40. Based on a sample set of more than 3,000 trade cards viewed in DCWL, BTC HL, AC NMAH, and other repositories. For a more complete discussion, including methodology, see Black, "Exchange Cards," 19–23.

41. This language was especially popular in gift books; see Frederick W. Faxon, *Literary Annuals and Gift Books: A Bibliography, 1823–1903* (1923; repr., Pinner, UK: Private Libraries Association, 1973), xii; Ralph Thompson, *American Literary Annuals and Gift Books, 1825–1865* (New York: H. W. Wilson Co., 1936), 3–4; Jack Goody, *The Culture of Flowers* (Cambridge: Cambridge University Press, 1993), 235, 238; and Alison Klaum, "Seeing Botanically: Linnaean Influence in Popular Antebellum Flower Books and the Library Company of Philadelphia's Visual Collections," *Pennsylvania History: A Journal of Mid-Atlantic Studies* 79, no. 3 (2012): 298–314.

42. Trade card for Fleischmann's Yeast (c. 1880), no. 26, col. 669, DCWL.

43. My interpretation of the rosebud on this card draws from Robert Tyas, *The Language of Flowers* (London: George Routledge, 1875), x–xi; and Goody, *Culture of Flowers*, 235. It is worth noting, however, that in the absence of concrete reflections from the historical individuals who encountered these objects, it is difficult to be 100 percent certain of their responses.

44. While my research in trade card collections at AC NMAH, DCWL, BTC HL, and elsewhere has shown that ethnic stereotypes appeared on approximately 9 percent of trade cards circulating at the time, Marilyn Maness Mehaffy suggests that up to 40 percent of similar ephemera included such stereotypes. See Black, "Exchange Cards," 53; and Mehaffy, "Advertising Race/Raceing Advertising: The Feminine Consumer(-Nation), 1876–1900," *Signs: Journal of Women in Culture and Society* 23, no. 1 (1997): 133, 141. See also Dawn Schmitz, "The Humble Handmaid of Commerce: Chromolithographic Advertising and the Development of Consumer Culture, 1876–1900" (PhD diss., University of Pittsburgh, 2004), v.

45. Arthur Asa Berger, *Blind Men and Elephants: Perspectives on Humor* (New Brunswick, NJ: Transaction, 2010), 95–96.

46. Printers appropriated both the characters and the dialogue from popular Gilbert and Sullivan works such as *HMS Pinafore* (1878), *Patience* (1881), and *The Mikado* (1885). See Bella Clara Landauer, *Gilbert and Sullivan's Influence on American Trade Cards* (New York: private, 1936).

47. Trade card for Magnolia Hams, featuring character from *Pinafore* (c. 1880), BTC HL; trade card for Higgins' German Laundry Soap (1880), no. 27, col. 669, DCWL; and Sir Arthur Sullivan and William S. Gilbert, *H.M.S. Pinafore*, vocal score, ed. Ephraim Hammett Jones and Carl Simpson (1878; repr., London: Courier Dover, 2002), 16.

48. "Florence Nightingale vs. Bridget McBruiser," in Samuel R. Wells, *New Physiognomy: Or Signs of Character* (New York: Fowler & Wells, 1875 [1866]), 537. Beginning in the 1930s and accelerating after 1945, the Irish and other groups would be folded into the hegemonic category of "white" in American society. See Matthew Frye Jacobson, *Whiteness of a Different Color: European Immigrants and the Alchemy of Race* (Cambridge, MA: Harvard University Press, 1998); and Noel Ignatiev, *How the Irish Became White* (New York: Routledge, 1995).

49. Roland Marchand discusses these transformative properties in *Advertising the American Dream: Making Way for Modernity, 1920–1940* (Berkeley: University of California Press, 1985).

50. Here, I use the term "Other" to refer to a subject of difference that is almost the same, and which draws mimicry. Theoretical discussions on this point have been made widely by scholars of postcolonial and subaltern studies. A well-known and oft-cited example is bell hooks's chapter, "Eating the Other," in *Black Looks: Race and Representation* (Boston: South End Press, 1992), 21–40.

51. Like *Pinafore,* the popularity of Gilbert and Sullivan's *The Mikado* (1885) contributed to an avalanche of cards borrowing Japanese themes and characters from the play. See, especially, col. 108, DCWL. On nativism in California, see Alexander Saxton, *The Indispensable Enemy* (Berkeley: University of California Press, 1995).

52. In fact, disgust was a key component in late nineteenth-century advertising, as Kyla Wazana Tompkins argues in *Racial Indigestion: Eating Bodies in the 19th Century* (New York: New York University Press, 2012), 168.

53. Rudyard Kipling popularized this phrase in his 1899 poem, "The White Man's Burden," written specifically to celebrate US imperial efforts in the Philippines at the time. My interpretation here draws from the arguments made by Domosh, in *American Commodities*, 3; and Kristin L. Hoganson, in *Consumers' Imperium: The Global Production of American Domesticity, 1865–1920* (Chapel Hill: University of North Carolina Press, 2010), 11.

54. Mehaffy, "Advertising Race," 135; and Jo-Ann Morgan, "Mammy and the Huckster: Selling the Old South for the New Century," *American Art* 9, no. 1 (1995): 86–109. On the Lost Cause in American History, see David Blight, *Race and Reunion: The Civil War in American Memory* (Cambridge, MA: Harvard University Press/Belknap, 2001), 255–299.

55. Such caricatures drew from the antebellum tradition of blackface minstrelsy, which Joshua Brown dates to 1831 in his visual essay, "True Likenesses," in Eric Foner, *Forever Free: The Story of Emancipation and Reconstruction* (New York: Knopf, 2005), 37. See also Tompkins, *Racial Indigestion*, 157; and Elise Lemire, *"Miscegenation": Making Race in America* (Philadelphia: University of Pennsylvania Press, 2011), 92–98.

56. Ann McClintock, *Imperial Leather: Race, Gender, and Sexuality in the Colonial Context* (New York: Routledge, 1995), 130–143; Marilyn Kern-Foxworth, *Aunt Jemima, Uncle Ben, and Rastus: Blacks in Advertising Yesterday, Today, and Tomorrow* (Westport, CT: Greenwood Press, 1994); Jan Nederveen Pieterse, *White on Black: Images of Africa and Blacks in Western Popular Culture* (New Haven, CT: Yale University Press, 1992), chap. 13; and Tompkins, *Racial Indigestion*, 145–182.

57. "Darktown Fire Brigade, Hook and Ladder Practice," trade card for Clarence Brooks varnish, designed by Thomas Worth and published by Currier and Ives, BTC HL. Currier and Ives issued the prints from the mid-1870s to the early 1890s in various sizes, including trade cards, with many large prints sold for framing and household decoration. Each installment in the series sold in the tens of thousands—a sales record for the time. See Brown, "Countersigns," in Foner, *Forever Free*, 182; and Brian F. Le Beau, "African Americans in Currier and Ives's America: The Darktown Series," *Journal of American and Comparative Cultures* 23, no. 1 (2000): 74. In addition to "Darktown" prints, Brooks also used the "Blackville" series, published in *Harper's Weekly* from 1874 through 1880 and later reproduced as trade cards and calendar images by the American Bank Note Co. See Michael D. Harris, "Memories and Memorabilia, Art and Identity," *Third Text* 12, no. 44 (1998): 28; and Francis Martin, "To Ignore Is to Deny: E. W. Kemble's Racial Caricature as Popular Art," *Journal of Popular Culture* 40, no. 4 (2007): 662.

58. These standards of beauty are discussed and historicized by Nell Irvin Painter in *The History of White People* (New York: W. W. Norton, 2011), 43–71.

59. In the mid-seventeenth century, Thomas Hobbes argued for a "superiority theory" of humor, which, once elaborated by Henri Bergson in the nineteenth century, held that laughter can often be a "social gesture of mockery," extending from the realization of one's superiority over another person and resulting in a supposition of power over the ridiculed subject. See John Morreall, ed., *The Philosophy of Humor and Laughter* (New York: State University of New York Press, 1987), 19, 117, citing Thomas Hobbes, *The Elements of Law, Natural and Politic* (London: 1650–1651), chap. 9, pt. 13, available online at www.google.com/books/edition/The _Elements_of_Law/3hDSyx3tymIC?hl=en&gbpv=0 (accessed 26 July 2022).

60. Morreall, *Humor*, 188; and Joseph Boskin, "The Complicity of Humor: The Life and Death of Sambo," in Morreall, *Humor*, 254–259. Tompkins, in *Racial Indigestion*, argues that caricatures of blacks provoked desire and disgust among white audiences, particularly because of anxieties over political power, which was increasingly defined in terms of consumption. In-

terestingly, Tompkins suggests that caricatured cards showing blacks eating open a framework whereby blacks might actually be given political agency (vis-à-vis consumption), however uncomfortably (166, 172).

61. The Reconstruction Amendments, passed and ratified between 1865 and 1870, include the Thirteenth Amendment, which outlawed slavery; the Fourteenth Amendment, which guaranteed citizens equal protection under the law and established birthright citizenship for all individuals born within the borders of the United States; and the Fifteenth Amendment, which made it illegal to deny the right to vote based on race.

62. Jacobson, *Whiteness*, 68–75; and Tompkins, *Racial Indigestion*, 177.

63. Mehaffy, "Advertising Race," 151–152. In contrast, Tompkins asserts that black audiences may have been targeted as desired demographics as early as the 1870s (*Racial Indigestion*, 172, 178). By the twentieth century, African American firms had introduced consumer products made especially for black audiences. See Michelle Mitchell, *Righteous Propagation: African Americans and the Politics of Racial Destiny After Reconstruction* (Chapel Hill: University of North Carolina Press, 2004), chap. 6.

64. Catalogs produced by printers such as Prang demonstrate the typical issue of stock cards in series of four to eight designs and sold in sets of ten to twelve. Louis Prang Co., "Price List" (Boston: Prang, 1879), Louis Prang Archive, Last HL; and Caxton Printing Co., Sample Card Book (1883), doc. 403, DCWL.

65. Frank Luther Mott, *A History of American Magazines* (Cambridge, MA: Harvard University Press, 1938), vol. 1, p. 547; vol. 3, pp. 223–224, 399; and vol. 4, p. 118.

66. Jennifer Wicke argues that advertisers constructed advertisements within the genre of literature by appropriating familiar conventions, in *Advertising Fictions: Literature, Advertisement & Social Reading* (New York: Columbia University Press, 1988), 173.

67. Trade cards for Diamond Package Dyes (c. 1894), BTC HL. These same images were used in stock advertisements for retail stores. See trade cards for Peabody's, col. 548, DCWL.

68. *Pagliacci* premiered in the United States in 1893 and told the story of a jealous actor who killed his adulterous wife and her lover on stage while dressed as a clown. Konrad Dryden, *Leoncavallo: Life and Works* (Lanham, MD: Scarecrow Press, 2007), 61.

69. Brigham Young first declared polygamy part of Mormon official practice in 1852. As early as 1856, the issue reached national attention, and debates over the issue continued after the Civil War, until the Church of Latter-Day Saints banned polygamy as a sanctioned practice in 1890. Utah was admitted as a state in 1896. See Sarah Barringer Gordon, *The Mormon Question: Polygamy and Constitutional Conflict in Nineteenth-Century America* (Chapel Hill: University of North Carolina Press, 2002).

70. Frank Presbrey, *The History and Development of Advertising* (Garden City, NY: Doubleday, 1929), 499.

71. Presbrey, 500.

72. Anca I. Lasc, "The Power of Windows: Artistic Interventions in the Commercial World," conference paper, *Commercial Pictures and the Arts and Technics of Visual Persuasion* (Wilmington, DE: Hagley Museum & Library, November 8, 2019); William Leach, *Land of Desire: Merchants, Power, and the Rise of a New American Culture* (New York: Pantheon Books, 1993), chap. 11; and Rosalind H. Williams, *Dream Worlds: Mass Consumption in Late Nineteenth-Century France* (Berkeley: University of California Press, 1982), 58–106.

73. Richard W. Flint, "A Great Industrial Art: Circus Poster Printing in America," *Printing History* 25, no. 2, orig. series no. 50 (2007): 18–43. See also Laurence Senelick, "Signs of the Times: Outdoor Theatrical Advertising in the Nineteenth Century," *Nineteenth Century Theatre and Film* 45, no. 2 (2018): 173–211.

74. Ruth E. Iskin, *The Poster: Art, Advertising, Design, and Collecting, 1860s–1900s* (Hanover, NH: Dartmouth College Press, 2014), 179.

75. Iskin, 211.

76. This is a common trope in thread cards; see cards for Kerr, Willimantic, Merrick, Coats, and Clark's threads (c. 1880–1895), in col. 669, DCWL.

77. Trade card for Clark's Mile-End Thread (c. 1880), Warshaw I Thread, AC NMAH.

78. Louis Prang and Co., custom trade cards for Clark's O.N.T. Threads (1878), Louis Prang Archive, Last HL. Similar examples can be found for both Clark's Thread and J. & P. Coats Thread, in col. 9, col. 134, doc. 394, col. 548, and col. 669, all in DCWL.

79. Iskin, *The Poster*, 208–211.

80. "High Art on Card-Board," *New York Times*, December 3, 1882, 4; "Quaint Devices in Trade," 9; and "The Power of Art on Paper," *Paper World* 5, no. 4 (October 1882): 12.

81. "The Great Scrap-Book Maker," *Paper World* 4, no. 4 (April 1882): 21; "Queen Victoria's Scrap-Books," *Paper World* 32, no. 5 (May 1896): 185; and "The Advertising Card Business," *Paper World* 10, no. 4 (May 1885): 4–5. See also Anna Denov Rusk, "Collecting the Confederacy: The Civil War Scrapbook of Henry M. Whitney," *Winterthur Portfolio* 47, no. 4 (2013): 267–296; and Ellen Gruber Garvey, *Writing with Scissors: American Scrapbooks from the Civil War to the Harlem Renaissance* (New York: Oxford University Press, 2012).

82. Emma Osgood Carnes (d. 1886), diary entry for February 14, 1882, cited in Smith, "Consuming Passions," 66, and in Dallow, "Treasures of the Mind," 19 (original in the collections of the Olana State Historic Site, Hudson, NY).

83. The nineteenth-century albums we often call "scrapbooks" in archival collections today grew out of earlier practices related to friendship albums and commonplace books. See Tucker et al., *The Scrapbook in American Life*, 6–12; and Black, "Exchange Cards," 30–32. Several albums viewed for this study indicate collaboration, gift exchange, and bequest, as in Sarah and Sallie Mendinhall scrapbook (1877–1883), fol. 287, DCWL. On lost albums, see Cornelia Otis Hancock to her mother and sister, May 31, 1864, June 15, 1864, and July 14, 1864, in *Letters of a Civil War Nurse: Cornelia Hancock, 1863–1865*, ed. Henrietta Stratton Jaquette (Lincoln: University of Nebraska Press, 1998), 97, 105, and 127, respectively.

84. In a survey of 1,000 trade cards in BTC HL, 100 percent displayed evidence of former scrapbook use. See Black, "Exchange Cards," 34.

85. Raechel Elisabeth Guest, "Victorian Scrapbooks and the American Middle Class" (master's thesis, University of Delaware, 1996), 20; and Tucker et al., *Scrapbook in American Life*, 7–11.

86. I offer a more detailed literature review in "Gender in the Academy: Recovering the Hidden History of Women's Scholarship on Scrapbooks and Albums," *Material Culture* 50, no. 2 (Fall 2018): 38–52. Throughout this chapter, I use the words *album* and *scrapbook* interchangeably.

87. Beverly Gordon, "The Paper Doll House," in *The Saturated World: Aesthetic Meaning, Intimate Objects, and Women's Lives 1890–1940* (Chattanooga: University of Tennessee Press, 2006), 37–62; and E. Richard McKinstry, "Papered Dream Houses Offer Clues to Imagined Lives," *Ephemera News* 22, no. 3 (2004): 1, 13–16. Anne Higonnet argues that such albums used a form of bricolage that prefigured twentieth-century modern and postmodern artistic experiments. See Higonnet, "Secluded Vision: Images of Feminine Experience in Nineteenth-Century Europe," *Radical History Review* 38 (1987): 32–33.

88. Paper dollhouse album (c. 1885), fol. 371, DCWL.

89. Stock card produced by Major and Knapp, NY, as shown in fol. 393, p. 8, DCWL. Note that this card also appears in Thelma Seeds Mendsen Collection of Scrapbooks (hereafter, "Mendsen"), no. 39, col. 669, DCWL.

90. In her domestic manual intended for middle-class housewives, Mary Blake suggests that compiling and arranging found images would aid children in developing aesthetics and taste. See Blake, *Twenty-Six Hours a Day* (Boston: D. Lothrop and Company, 1883), 145–148.

91. Elsie Sargeant Abbot scrapbook (1893–1899), doc. 156, DCWL.

92. Abbot scrapbook, DCWL. This album is also examined by Guest, in "Victorian Scrapbooks," 27.

93. Stella Morris Osgood scrapbook (c. 1894), fol. 91, DCWL. It is unclear whether Stella had any relation to the aforementioned Emma Osgood Carnes.

94. In *Gifts and Commodities*, Carrier notes that handmade gifts took on higher importance as the United States industrialized in the nineteenth century (156).

95. Vernon scrapbook, Last, HL.

96. Lizzie Cadmus Autograph Album (1877–1882), doc. 447, DCWL; and Camille Block Album Souvenir (1875–1887), doc. 35, DCWL.

97. While Albert didn't sign his drawing in Lizzie's album directly, he is the most likely artist. In her discussion of early modern *album amicorum*, Margaret F. Rosenthal notes that signatories often included illustrations as supplementary gifts to the album owner, when asked to pen an inscription. See Rosenthal, "Fashions of Friendship in an Early Modern Illustrated *Album Amicorum*: British Library, MS Egerton 1191," *Journal of Medieval and Early Modern Studies* 39, no. 3 (2009): 622–624. An alternative explanation would have Cadmus doodling the drawing around Albert's name. In this case, the affection signified by the drawing would change direction (from Albert toward Lizzie, to Lizzie toward Albert), but the drawing would still serve to embellish the signature through the appropriation of cultural meanings associated with exchange cards.

98. Jay, *Trade Card*, 100–102; Neil Harris, "Iconography and Intellectual History: The Halftone Effect," in *Cultural Excursions: Marketing Appetites and Cultural Tastes in Modern America* (Chicago: University of Chicago Press, 1990), 304–317; and Joshua Brown, *Beyond the Lines: Pictorial Reporting, Everyday Life, and the Crisis of Gilded Age America* (Berkeley: University of California Press, 2002), 234–236.

99. Tucker et al., *Scrapbook in American Life*, 12. See also Douglas Collins, *The Story of Kodak* (New York: H. N. Abrams, 1990); Andrea L. Volpe, "Cheap Pictures: Cartes de visite Portrait Photographs and Visual Culture in the United States, 1860–1877" (PhD diss., Rutgers University, 1999); and Elizabeth Siegel, *Galleries of Friendship and Fame: The History of Nineteenth-Century American Photograph Albums* (New Haven, CT: Yale University Press, 2010).

100. Previous histories of advertising date this transition toward emotional advertising to the early twentieth century. See Blaszczyk, *American Consumer Society*, 120–122; and Fox, *The Mirror Makers*, 51.

101. As Sarah Banet-Weiser has argued (in *Authentic: Politics and Ambivalence in a Brand Culture* [New York: New York University Press, 2012]), contemporary branding practices seek to build relational connections between consumers and the brand, hoping that their brands will "evoke experience and stories . . . that are intimate and personal" (4). Banet-Weiser builds from the theories offered by Marc Gobé in *Brandjam: Humanizing Brands Through Emotional Design* (New York: Allworth Press, 2007); and in Gobé, *Emotional Branding: The New Paradigm for Connecting Brands to People* (New York: Allworth Press, 2009). Reputation, values, and emotional connections to the consumer remain top criteria for successful brands, according to the Forbes Agency Council, in "15 Top Trends That Will Impact Marketing in 2022," *Forbes*, January 14, 2022; online at www.forbes.com/sites/forbesagencycouncil /2022/01/14/15-top-trends-that-will-impact-marketing-in-2022/ (accessed 2 June 2022).

102. Most histories of the term "advertainment" root the practice in the 1930s, when marketers exploited connections to the film industry to sell goods. See Ross D. Petty, "Pain-Killer: A 19th Century Global Patent Medicine and the Beginnings of Modern Brand Marketing," *Journal of Macromarketing* 39, no. 3 (2019): 293; citing Cristel A. Russell, "Advertainment: Fusing Advertising and Entertainment," University of Michigan Yaffe Center

(2007), online at www.researchgate.net/profile/Cristel_Russell/publication/254351697 _Advertainment_Fusing_Advertising_and_Entertainment/links/0deec53a46ad354d 44000000/Advertainment-Fusing-Advertising-and-Entertainment.pdf. Of course, the most familiar form of "advertainment" from the nineteenth century would be the patent-medicine shows, which combined spectacle and selling in a unique form of traveling live entertainment. See Susan Strasser, "A Historical Herbal: Household Medicine and Herbal Commerce in a Developing Consumer Society," in *Decoding Modern Consumer Societies*, ed. H. Berghoff and U. Spiekermann (New York: Palgrave Macmillan, 2012), 221; and Ann Anderson, *Snake Oil, Hustlers and Hambones: The American Medicine Show* (Jefferson, NC: McFarland, 2005).

Chapter 5

1. Print advertisement for Franco-American Foods (1909), N. W. Ayer Advertising Agency Records, Col. 59 (hereafter Ayer), AC NMAH.

2. Susan V. Spellman, "Trust Brokers: Traveling Grocery Salesmen and Confidence in Nineteenth-Century Trade," *Enterprise & Society* 13, no. 2 (2012): 276–312.

3. Rowena Olegario, *A Culture of Credit: Embedding Trust and Transparency in American Business* (Cambridge, MA: Harvard University Press, 2006), 141, 153.

4. Shennette Garrett-Scott, *Banking on Freedom: Black Women in U.S. Finance Before the New Deal* (New York: Columbia University Press, 2019), 4–6. On general lending practices in the period, see Naomi R. Lamoreaux, *Insider Lending: Banks, Personal Connections, and Economic Development in Industrial New England* (New York: Cambridge University Press, 1994).

5. Andrew Carnegie, "The Road to Business Success: A Talk to Young Men," from an address to Curry Commercial College, Pittsburgh, June 23, 1885; in Carnegie, *The Empire of Business* (New York: Doubleday, Page, and Co., 1902), 3–18.

6. Judy Hilkey, *Character Is Capital: Success Manuals and Manhood in Gilded Age America* (Chapel Hill: University of North Carolina Press, 1997), 5, 7–8, 127–128. On the "crisis in masculinity" that prompted such discussions, see John F. Kasson, *Houdini, Tarzan, and the Perfect Man: The White Male Body and the Challenge of Modernity in America* (New York: Hill and Wang, 2001).

7. David M. Henkin, *The Postal Age: The Emergence of Modern Communications in Nineteenth-Century America* (Chicago: University of Chicago Press, 2006), 95. See also Lindsay O'Neill, *The Opened Letter: Networking in the Early Modern British World* (Philadelphia: University of Pennsylvania Press, 2015), 16–17.

8. L. Prang & Co. to undisclosed recipients, November 30, 1879; H. Maringin, Attorney for L. Prang & Co., to undisclosed recipients, Fall 1884; and L. Prang & Co. "Notices to the Press," November 1883, December 1884, and November 1887, in Louis Prang Papers, Last HL. Handwritten correspondence authenticates Prang's signature. See Louis Prang Papers, Temple University Libraries Special Collections Department.

9. Henkin, *Postal Age*, 117–118.

10. An incomplete set of Prang's "Weekly Letters," dating between 1885 and 1895, is available in the Louis Prang Papers at the American Antiquarian Society, Worcester, Massachusetts. See also Louis Prang to various recipients, 1877–1898, Louis Prang Papers, Last HL.

11. Like Prang, many other advertisers used representations of signatures in their communications with the public, including J. Walter Thompson, N. W. Ayer, and R. R. Donnelley & Sons. See Thompson, *The Red Ear* (1887), JWTPC; N. W. Ayer & Sons, "What Class of Things?" (1904), Ayer Series XIV, AC NMAH; and R. R. Donnelley & Sons, Series III: "Company Advertising," RRD.

12. Published rate guides and advertising manuals were common periodicals issued by advertising agents from the 1870s forward. Like Volney Palmer's collection of newspaper lists, rate guides offered a brief menu of services available from the advertising firm. The first published newspaper directories and rate guides came from George P. Rowell and N. W. Ayer & Son in the late 1860s and early 1870s. See Daniel J. Boorstin, *The Americans: The Democratic Experience* (New York: Knopf Doubleday, 2010), 147; and Stephen R. Fox, *The Mirror Makers: A History of American Advertising and Its Creators* (Chicago: University of Illinois Press, 1984), 20.

13. Donnelley, "Company Advertising"; and Spellman, "Trust Brokers."

14. Thompson, *The Red Ear*, 7. See also Charles A. Bates, "Picture Bargains," advertisement in *Printers' Ink* 16, no. 5 (1896): 26; and George P. Rowell, "Ad Space Has a Market Value," advertisement in *Printers' Ink* 22, no. 9 (1896): 7.

15. J. Walter Thompson Advertising Agency, *The Religious Press* (1887), 2–5, JWTPC.

16. J. Walter Thompson Advertising Agency, *J. Walter Thompson's Blue Book on Advertising* (1911), 8, JWTPC.

17. Thompson, *The Red Ear*, 8.

18. Thompson, *The Religious Press*, 1–5; and J. Walter Thompson Agency, *Thompson's Battery* (1889), 11, JWTPC.

19. J. Walter Thompson Agency, *The Thompson Blue Book on Advertising* (1901), JWTPC.

20. Handbill for N. W. Ayer Agency (1871), Ayer Series I, AC NMAH; and "Lakeside Press" (1921), in Donnelley, Series III: "Company Advertising," RRD.

21. G. A. Gaskell, *Gaskell's Compendium of Forms: Educational, Social, Legal and Commercial* (New York: Fairbanks & Palmer Publishing Co., 1882), 230.

22. Marlis Schweitzer and Marina Moskowitz, eds., *Testimonial Advertising in the American Marketplace: Emulation, Identity, Community* (New York: Palgrave Macmillan, 2009), 1–22.

23. Michael Pettit argues that the testimonials of local celebrities helped ensure the success of P. T. Barnum's various exhibitions initially and, when certain hoaxes crumbled, the reputations of local endorsers fell dramatically. See Pettit, "The Testifying Subject: Reliability in Marketing, Science, and the Law at the end of the Age of Barnum," in *Testimonial Advertising*, 55–59.

24. "Eminent Physicians," print ad for Just's Food (1896), Ayer Series II, AC NMAH.

25. *Bristol's Illustrated Almanac for California* (1866), 13, Rare Books, The Huntington Library, San Marino, CA (hereafter "HL"). Celebrity and expert endorsements could also be purchased by the manufacturer, as muckrakers would discover in the early twentieth century. See James Harvey Young, *The Toadstool Millionaires: A Social History of Patent Medicines in America Before Federal Regulation* (Princeton, NJ: Princeton University Press, 1961), 187–189.

26. *Prang's Chromo: A Journal of Popular Art* 1, no. 1 (1868): 2–4, LOCPP. See also *Ayer's American Almanac* (1854); *Bristol's Illustrated Almanac* (1873), Rare Books, HL; and G. G. Green, *Green's Diary Almanac* (1882–1883), Ephemera Collections, HL. This was also a tactic deployed by the manufacturers of sewing threads in the 1880s and for face creams and soaps by the early twentieth century. See Sandra and Gary Baden Collection of Celebrity Endorsements in Advertising, 1897–1979, AC NMAH; and Daniel D. Hill, *Advertising to the American Woman, 1900–1999* (Columbus: Ohio State University Press, 2002).

27. H. H. Hitchcock to unnamed Sears patrons, January 27, 1898, printed in Sears Roebuck & Co., "Consumer's Guide no. 107" (Chicago: Sears Roebuck & Co., 1898), 6. Other catalog retailers echoed Sears's strategy in printing verification letters from local bankers; see Boston Store, "Catalog no. 70" (Chicago: Boston Store, 1905); and Butler Bros., "Our Drummer no. 455" (New York: Butler Bros., 1903), all RBWL. Ian Klaus traces this strategy to

financial institutions, in *Forging Capitalism: Rogues, Swindlers, Frauds, and the Rise of Modern Finance* (New Haven, CT: Yale University Press, 2014), 134.

28. Gaskell, *Compendium*, 230.

29. *New Orleans Time-Democrat* (1901), reprinted in *Druggists' Circular* 45, p. xi, cited in Young, *Toadstool Millionaires*, 188. The notion that every man could be an expert directly contradicts a trend toward professionalism and bureaucratization in the Gilded Age explored by scholars such as Robert Wiebe, in *The Search for Order, 1877–1920* (New York: Hill and Wang, 1967); Alan Trachtenberg, in *The Incorporation of America* (New York: Hill and Wang, 1982); and Alfred Chandler Jr., in *The Visible Hand* (Cambridge, MA: Harvard University Press, 1977); and it speaks to the debates on Populism and anti-modernism as discussed by Richard Hofstadter, in *The Age of Reform* (New York: Vintage, 1995 [1955]); and T. J. Jackson Lears, in *Fables of Abundance: A Cultural History of Advertising in America* (New York: Basic Books, 1994).

30. *Ayer's American Almanac* (1854), Rare Books, HL.

31. G. G. Green, *August Flower and German Syrup Almanac* (1878), 16, Ephemera Collections, HL.

32. *Bristol's Illustrated Almanac* for 1866, 1869, and 1875, in Rare Books, HL. Some manufacturers were known to reprint testimonials even after the writer had died. See Young, *Toadstool Millionaires*, 189.

33. Green, *August Flower*, 16.

34. Publisher's note, *Ayer's American Almanac* (1854), Rare Books, HL.

35. Several experts recommended tailoring the advertising message to fit audience preferences. See J. E. Kennedy, "Fitting the Ad to the Locality," *Printers' Ink* 10, no. 15 (1894): 434–437; and Sherwin Cody, *Success in Letter Writing: Business and Social* (Chicago: A. C. McClurg & Company, 1906), 126–128. Claude Hopkins developed initial methods for studying and targeting specific markets of consumers and gathering feedback to improve advertising techniques in the 1890s. See Pamela Walker Laird, *Advertising Progress: American Business and the Rise of Consumer Marketing* (Baltimore: Johns Hopkins University Press, 1998), 284–289.

36. Lydia E. Pinkham Co., *Treatise on the Diseases of Women* (Lynn, MA: Lydia E. Pinkham Medicine Co., 1901), 43, in Warshaw, Series I Patent Medicine, AC NMAH.

37. *Ayer's American Almanac* (1880, 1896), Rare Books, HL.

38. *Warner's Safe Cure* (1892, 1896), Rare Books, HL. Underneath each of these testimonies, the signature of the writer is reprinted (though it is nearly impossible to verify whether these portraits and signatures depicted the actual speakers and/or their signatures).

39. Pinkham Co., *Treatise*, 51.

40. On signatures and bank notes, see Stephen Mihm, *A Nation of Counterfeiters: Capitalists, Con Men, and the Making of the United States* (Cambridge, MA: Harvard University Press, 2007), 221; and David M. Henkin, *City Reading: Written Words and Public Spaces in Antebellum New York* (New York: Columbia University Press, 1998), 144. Gregory Pfitzer notes that artists often included self-portraits with their illustrations for pictorial histories as a way of indicating the authenticity of the work. See Pfitzer, *Picturing the Past* (Washington, DC: Smithsonian Institution Scholarly Press, 2002), 107. Likewise, Aston Gonzalez makes a similar argument for the authenticating power of frontispiece portraits in the autobiographies of escaped slaves. See Gonzalez, *Visualizing Equality: African American Rights and Visual Culture in the Nineteenth Century* (Chapel Hill: University of North Carolina Press, 2020), 56.

41. Gonzalez, *Visualizing Equality*, chap. 2.

42. Benedict Anderson first explored the power of print to create "imagined communities" rooted in shared experience in *Imagined Communities: Reflections on the Origin and Spread of Nationalism* (New York: Verso, 2006 [1983]).

43. *Bristol's Illustrated Almanac* (1875), Rare Books, HL. This regional appeal may have worked especially well in California in the last decades of the century when nativists protested the increased immigration of workers from China and Japan to the western United States. On nativism in California, see Alexander Saxton, *The Indispensable Enemy* (Berkeley: University of California Press, 1995).

44. Marina Moskowitz argues that testimonial advertising helped to re-personalize commercial exchange by creating a community of users among the readers and writers of testimonials. See Moskowitz, "'After a Season of War': Sharing Horticultural Success in the Reconstruction-Era Landscape," in Schweitzer and Moskowitz, *Testimonial Advertising*, 79–94.

45. Market divisions are discussed in Richard S. Tedlow, *New and Improved: The Story of Mass Marketing in America* (New York: Basic Books, 1990), 3–6; and Charles McGovern, *Sold American: Consumption and Citizenship, 1890–1945* (Chapel Hill: University of North Carolina Press, 2006), 31–33.

46. Young, *Toadstool Millionaires*, 187–189, 205. The Federal Trade Commission launched an investigation in the 1930s into the use of false, fabricated, and purchased testimonials, targeting the J. Walter Thompson Company for regularly using fabricated statements and paying prominent individuals for their endorsements of products. See Schweitzer and Moskowitz, *Testimonial Advertising*, 9.

47. Joseph M. Gabriel, *Medical Monopoly: Intellectual Property Rights and the Origins of the Modern Pharmaceutical Industry* (Chicago: University of Chicago Press, 2014), 90; and Young, *Toadstool Millionaires*, 111. On addiction after the Civil War, see David T. Courtwright, *Dark Paradise: A History of Opiate Addiction in America* (Cambridge, MA: Harvard University Press, 2001), 54–55.

48. Paul Duguid recognizes the function of testimonials to build brand loyalty in "Information in the Mark and the Marketplace," *Enterprise & Society* 15, no. 1 (2014): 1–30. See also Ross D. Petty, "Pain-Killer: A 19th Century Global Patent Medicine and the Beginnings of Modern Brand Marketing," *Journal of Macromarketing* 39, no. 3 (2019): 287–303.

49. Print ad for Wanamaker's (1878–1880), Ayer Series I, AC NMAH, published in the *Christian Recorder*, January 1, 1880.

50. Though uncommon, this style of ad was used by other advertisers, including Royal Baking Powder (in the *New York Tribune*, April 17, 1894) and the N. W. Ayer & Son Advertising Agency ("Yours for Trade Next Year," 1893), Ayer Series XIV, AC NMAH.

51. Nancy F. Koehn offers additional discussion about novelty in Heinz's early twentieth-century advertising, in *Brand New: How Entrepreneurs Earned Consumers' Trust from Wedgwood to Dell* (Boston: Harvard Business School Press, 2001), 74.

52. B. Phillips, "Defining Trade Characters and Their Role in American Popular Culture," *Journal of Popular Culture* 29, no. 4 (1996): 146. The trade character paralleled shipper cards in the nineteenth-century Asian textile market, according to Andreas P. Zangger, "Chops and Trademarks: Asian Trading Ports and Textile Branding, 1840–1920," *Enterprise & Society* 15, no. 4 (2014): 759–790.

53. Phillips, 149–151; and McGovern, *Sold American*, 90–93.

54. Judith Garretson and Ronald W. Niedrich, "Spokes-Characters: Creating Character Trust and Positive Brand Attitudes," *Journal of Advertising* 33, no. 2 (2004): 25–36; and Margaret Falwell Callcott, "The Spokes-Character in Advertising: An Historical Survey and Framework for Future Research" (PhD diss., University of Texas at Austin, 1993). See also Phillips, "Defining Trade Characters," 147.

55. Phillips, 153.

56. Earnest Elmo Calkins dates the emergence of trade characters to about 1900 in *Modern Advertising* (New York: Garland, 1905), 317–322.

57. Laird, *Advertising Progress*, 96–97.

58. According to trademark registrations, Pinkham's portrait and signature were first used in commerce in 1881, though historians have dated the icon's use to the 1870s. See Sammy R. Danna, *Lydia Pinkham: The Face That Launched a Thousand Ads* (Lanham, MD: Rowman and Littlefield, 2015), 37–43. The earliest trademark registrations available are dated 1905. See Lydia Pinkham Co. trademark reg. 45,785, filed April 19, 1905 (reg. August 29, 1905), USPTO.

59. Sarah Stage, *Female Complaints: Lydia Pinkham and the Business of Women's Medicine* (New York: Norton, 1979), chap. 1.

60. Lydia E. Pinkham Co., "To the Women of America" (c. 1900): 2–3, Warshaw Series I Patent Medicine, AC NMAH.

61. Pinkham Co., *Treatise*, 34.

62. Young, *Toadstool Millionaires*, 214.

63. Lydia E. Pinkham Co. to Mrs. E. R. Holden, December 11, 1897, Warshaw Series I Patent Medicine, AC NMAH.

64. Print ads for Pinkham products (1896–1898), in Warshaw I Patent Medicine, AC NMAH.

65. Mrs. I. C. Dale, Claremont, VA, to Lydia E. Pinkham Co., April 4, 1900, in Pinkham Co., *Treatise*, 47.

66. Pinkham's community of women is a theme pursued in detail by Elysa Ream Engelman in "'The Face That Haunts Me Ever': Consumers, Retailers, Critics, and the Branded Personality of Lydia E. Pinkham" (PhD diss., Boston University, 2003).

67. Engelman, 20; and Stage, *Female Complaints*, 108.

68. Pinkham Co., *Treatise*, 34.

69. Most design historians have suggested that Visual Identity Design (VID), which prescribed consistent rules for trademark use across media, did not emerge until the post–World War II period in the United States. See, for example, Johanna Drucker and Emily McVarish, *Graphic Design History: A Critical Guide* (Upper Saddle River, NJ: Pearson, 2009), 262. Carma Gorman places this development in the 1930s, in "The Role of Trademark Law in the History of US Visual Identity Design, c.1860–1960," *Journal of Design History* 30, no. 4 (2017): 372.

70. Stage, *Female Complaints*, 105; Engelman, "The Face That Haunts Me Ever," chap. 1; Susan Strasser, "Commodifying Lydia Pinkham: A Woman, a Medicine, and a Company in a Developing Consumer Culture," in *Cultures of Consumption Working Paper Series* 32, (2007), 6, online at www.consume.bbk.ac.uk/publications.html#workingpapers (accessed 5 October 2011); and Danna, *Lydia Pinkham*, 54.

71. Engelman, "The Face That Haunts Me Ever," 21–22.

72. Engelman, 32.

73. Pinkham Co., *Treatise*, 43–53.

74. Thompson, *Blue Book on Advertising* (1911), 8.

75. Trademark registrations for Mennen Co., no. 121,288 filed December 7, 1917 (reg. April 23, 1918); and no. 123,623 filed December 7, 1917 (reg. November 19, 1918); USPTO. For Smith Bros., see Ernst Lehner, *American Symbols: A Pictorial History* (New York: W. Penn Pub. Co., 1957), 41; "Business and Finance: Cough Drops' Part," *Time*, September 24, 1934; and trademark reg. no. 50,947 filed May 16, 1905 (reg. April 3, 1906), USPTO.

76. Strasser, "Commodifying Lydia Pinkham."

77. Roland Marchand, *Creating the Corporate Soul: The Rise of Public Relations and Corporate Imagery in American Big Business* (Berkeley: University of California Press, 1998), chap. 1.

78. Similar trade characters also emerged in Europe around 1900. See Stephen L. Harp, *Marketing Michelin: Advertising and Cultural Identity in Twentieth-Century France* (Baltimore: Johns Hopkins University Press, 2001).

79. The Quaker Mill Company was founded in 1877 in Ravenna, Ohio. The original business failed and was resold in 1881; it merged with other mills in 1885 and 1888 and, finally, reorganized in 1891 to form the American Cereal Co. See "Quaker Oats Oatmeal," in *Encyclopedia of Consumer Brands*, vol. 1, ed. Janice Jorgensen (Detroit: St. James Press, 1994), 472–473; and Harrison John Thornton, *The History of the Quaker Oats Company* (Chicago: University of Chicago Press, 1933), 45–70. On the evolution of the Quaker Oats man, see "News Behind the Ads," *Changing Times: The Kiplinger Magazine* (December 1959): 38; and Arthur F. Marquette, *Brands, Trademarks, and Good Will: The Story of the Quaker Oats Company* (New York: McGraw-Hill, 1967), 31. Though Marquette cites the first trademark registration for the Quaker Oats man in 1877, records at the USPTO suggest the first commercial use of the Quaker Oats man occurred in either 1867 or 1877. See trademark reg. 26,254, filed January 22, 1895 (reg. March 19, 1895), USPTO; and trademark reg. 768,464, filed May 13, 1963 (reg. April 21, 1964), USPTO.

80. Jennifer Connerley, "Friendly Americans: Representing Quakers in the United States, 1850–1920" (PhD diss., University of North Carolina, 2006), 3–5.

81. Connerley, 208–209.

82. On nostalgia for the American Revolution, see Mike Wallace, *Mickey Mouse History and Other Essays on American Memory* (Philadelphia, PA: Temple University Press, 1996), 6–9.

83. Connerley, "Friendly Americans," 210–211.

84. Micki McElya, *Clinging to Mammy: The Faithful Slave in Twentieth-Century America* (Cambridge, MA: Harvard University Press, 2007), 15–16; and JoAnn Morgan, "Mammy and the Huckster: Selling the Old South for the New Century," *American Art* 9, no. 1 (1995): 96.

85. James Harvey Young, *Pure Food: Securing the Federal Food and Drugs Act of 1906* (Princeton, NJ: Princeton University Press, 1989), 36–38; and Donna J. Wood, "The Strategic Use of Public Policy, Business Support for the 1906 Food and Drug Act," *Business History Review* 59, no. 3 (1985): 405.

86. Wood, "Strategic Use," 410–412; and Frank Presbrey, *The History and Development of Advertising* (Garden City, NY: Doubleday, 1929), 531–535.

87. Koehn, *Brand New*, 62.

88. Print ad for Quaker Oats (1902), Ayer Series II, AC NMAH.

89. "The Food That Tells" (1902), Ayer Series II, AC NMAH.

90. Lauren Alex O'Hagan, "Blinded by Science? Constructing Truth and Authority in Early Twentieth-Century Virol Advertisements," *History of Retailing and Consumption* 7, no. 2 (2021): 162–192.

91. Calkins, *Modern Advertising*, 317–322.

92. Research in the N. W. Ayer Advertising Agency collection (Ayer AC NMAH) substantiates the popularity of children as trade characters in this period. See also Hal Morgan, *Symbols of America* (New York: Viking, 1986); and Warren Dotz, *Meet Mr. Product: The Art of the Advertising Character* (San Francisco: Chronicle Books, 2003).

93. Print ads for Franco-American Foods (1906–1910), Ayer Series II, AC NMAH.

94. Factory tours were a popular pastime between 1880 and 1950, as Allison C. Marsh notes in "The Ultimate Vacation: Watching Other People Work, a History of Factory Tours in America, 1880–1950" (PhD diss., Johns Hopkins University, 2008).

95. Donnelley, "Company Advertising." See also the Record Publishing Co. (Philadelphia), "Valuable Testimony," advertisement in *Printers' Ink* 23, no. 13 (1898): 1; and Ayer & Son, advertising pamphlet (1908), Ayer Series XIV, AC NMAH. In a similar investigation, Pamela Walker Laird suggests that illustrating the exterior of the factory was a demonstration of wealth and technological progress in the 1880s and 1890s. See Laird, *Advertising Progress*, 94–150.

96. Ad for Franco-American Soups (1906), Ayer Series II, AC NMAH.

97. "A Revelation to Visitors" (1906), Ayer Series II, AC NMAH.

98. "A Revelation to Visitors."

99. Neil Harris first posited the importance of an operational aesthetic for the antebellum period in *Humbug: The Art of P. T. Barnum* (Boston: Little, Brown, 1973).

100. "More Than Legal Purity" (1907), "My Standard Is High" (1909), and "Take No Chances with Food" (1909); all Ayer Series II, AC NMAH.

101. In this way, Franco-American "responded to consumers' changing priorities" just as later corporations would do in the twentieth century. See Koehn, *Brand New*, 320.

102. Print ads for Hires Root Beer (1909–1927), Ayer Series II, AC NMAH.

103. Print ad for Hires Root Beer (1912), Ayer Series II, AC NMAH.

104. "Dead for a Drink?" (1915), Ayer Series II, AC NMAH.

105. Margaret Young, "On the Go with Phoebe Snow: Origins of an Advertising Icon," *Advertising & Society Review* 7, no. 2 (2006), online through *Project MUSE*: https://doi.org/10.1353/asr.2006.0029 (accessed 28 December 2020).

106. Young, "Phoebe Snow."

107. Print ads for Fleischmann's Yeast (1913–1916), Ayer Series II, AC NMAH.

108. P. Christiaan Klieger, *Images of America: The Fleischmann Yeast Family* (Chicago: Arcadia, 2004), 16–17, 54.

109. Print ads for Fleischmann's Yeast (1913–1916), Ayer Series II, AC NMAH.

110. Klieger, *Fleischmann*, 54.

111. *Oxford English Dictionary* cites 1768 as the first use of this name, to signify an anonymous plaintiff in legal proceedings (with "Richard Roe" signifying a like defendant). By 1942, the term came to signify any "typical" man or unidentified male. *Oxford English Dictionary Online*, "John Doe," http://www.oed.com.libproxy.usc.edu/view/Entry/101505?redirectedFrom=John%20Doe#eid40416766 (accessed 17 January 2013).

112. "The Landing of the Pilgrims" (1916), Ayer Series II, AC NMAH.

113. On assimilation debates at the turn of the century, see Matthew Frye Jacobson, *Barbarian Virtues: The United States Encounters Foreign Peoples at Home and Abroad, 1876–1919* (New York: Hill and Wang, 2000); and David R. Roediger, *The Wages of Whiteness: Race and the Making of the American Working Class* (New York: Verso, 2007).

114. E. Melanie DuPuis discusses the symmetry between reformers' arguments for food purity and racial purity in *Dangerous Digestion: The Politics of American Dietary Advice* (Berkeley: University of California Press, 2015), 75–94.

115. Presbrey, *History of Advertising*, 382. See also Neil Harris, *Cultural Excursions: Marketing Appetites and Cultural Tastes in Modern America* (Chicago: University of Chicago Press, 1990), chap. 14.

116. Connerley, "Friendly Americans," 210–211. See also Isabell Cserno, "Race and Mass Consumption in Consumer Culture: National Trademark Advertising Campaigns in the United States and Germany, 1890–1930" (PhD diss., University of Maryland, College Park, 2008), chap. 3; and McElya, *Clinging to Mammy*, chap. 1.

117. In the 1910s, Life Savers candies crafted a stick-figure made from stacked candies, in a representation that closely resembled early iterations of Michelin's tire-man "Bibendum." See print ads for Life Savers candies (1919), Ayer Series II, AC NMAH; and print ads for Michelin Tires, in *Daily Gate City* (Keokuk, IA), May 18, 1910; *Birmingham Age Herald* (Birmingham, AL), June 18, 1916; and *Evening Missourian* (Columbia, MO), June 14, 1919. Likewise, Zephyr Flour created a flour-sack man with spikey wheat-stalk arms and legs to compete with John Dough, while Pettijohn Wheat's bearded Mennonite man seems to be a close approximation of the Quaker Oats man. See print ads for Zephyr Flour (1913), Ayer Series II, AC NMAH; and for Pettijohn's Breakfast Food, *Saturday Evening Post*, May 5, 1906.

118. Presbrey, *History of Advertising*, 384.

119. Dotz, *Meet Mr. Product*, 32.

120. N. W. Ayer & Son Advertising Agency, "Character," full-page print advertisement (1920), AC NMAH. This was slated for publication in the *Saturday Evening Post* and *Literary Digest*.

Chapter 6

1. Joshua Bates, *A Discourse, on Honesty in Dealing: Delivered at Middlebury, on the Annual Fast: April 15, 1818* (Middlebury, VT: J. W. Copeland, 1818); and Rev. Henry Mandeville Denison, *Lectures to Business Men: Delivered in St. Peter's Church, Charleston* (Charleston, SC: Walker, Evans, 1858).

2. Edward J. Balleisen, *Fraud: An American History from Barnum to Madoff* (Princeton, NJ: Princeton University Press, 2017), 183–186.

3. Grafton Dulany Cushing, "On Certain Cases Analogous to Trade-Marks," *Harvard Law Review* 4, no. 7 (1891): 332.

4. J. Walter Thompson, *Catalog of Magazines* (1887), 14, JWTPC.

5. Rowena Olegario, *A Culture of Credit: Embedding Trust and Transparency in American Business* (Cambridge, MA: Harvard University Press, 2006); and Sharon Ann Murphy, *Investing in Life: Insurance in Antebellum America* (Baltimore: Johns Hopkins University Press, 2010). For other applications in the modern regulatory state, see Balleisen, *Fraud*.

6. Edd Applegate, *The Rise of Advertising in the United States: A History of Innovation to 1960* (Lanham, MD: Scarecrow Press, 2012), 35–36.

7. Juliann Sivulka, *Soap, Sex, and Cigarettes: A Cultural History of American Advertising* (Belmont, CA: Wadsworth, 1998), 34–36, 81.

8. Applegate, *Rise of Advertising*, 149–170.

9. T. J. Jackson Lears, *Fables of Abundance: A Cultural History of Advertising in America* (New York: Basic Books, 1994), chap. 3.

10. Lears, 62–65.

11. Judy Hilkey, *Character Is Capital: Success Manuals and Manhood in Gilded Age America* (Chapel Hill: University of North Carolina Press, 1997), 5; and Lears, *Fables of Abundance*, 89. Warren Susman also examines the legacy of concepts of character in "Personality and the Making of Twentieth-Century Culture (1979)," in *Culture as History* (Washington, DC: Smithsonian Institution Press, 2003), 271–286.

12. Joseph Story and William Fisher Wharton, *Commentaries on the Law of Partnership as a Branch of Commercial and Maritime Jurisprudence with Occasional Illustrations from the Civil and Foreign Law*, 7th ed. (Boston: Little, Brown, 1881). Story's definition of goodwill is often the place where many later scholars begin their discussion of the concept and its case law. See A. S. Biddle, "Good-Will," *American Law Register*, new series 14, 23, no. 1–12 (1875): 1–11, 329–341, 649–659, 713–725; and Gabriel A. D. Preinreich, "The Law of Goodwill," *Accounting Review* 11, no. 4 (1936): 317–329.

13. "Trade Marks," *Scientific American* 16, no. 8 (1867): 125.

14. Biddle, "Good-Will," 6, 339. Many legal historians note that the two branches of law governing trademarks—torts, which govern civil infractions, and equity, which govern property—had been in tension when it came to trademark protections in nineteenth-century US jurisprudence, and only came together with the passage of the 1946 Lanham Act, which, in turn, spurred further trademark development and use. See Oren Bracha, "The Emergence and Development of United States Intellectual Property Law," in *The Oxford Handbook of Intellectual Property Law*, ed. Rochelle Cooper Dreyfuss and Justine Pila (New York: Oxford University Press, 2018), 257–262.

15. Biddle, "Good-Will," 651; and W. Henry Smith, "Good-Will," *Nebraska Law Journal* 1, no. 14 (1891): 590.

16. Frank Presbrey, *The History and Development of Advertising.* (Garden City, NY: Doubleday, 1929), 303.

17. See Edward S. Rogers, "The Expensive Futility of the United States Trade-Mark Statute," *Michigan Law Review* 12, no. 8 (1914): 661. This case is discussed in greater detail in Zvi S. Rosen, "In Search of the Trade-Mark Cases: The Nascent Treaty Power and the Turbulent Origins of Federal Trademark Law," *St. John's Law Review* 83, no. 3 (2012): 827–904; and Susan Strasser, *Satisfaction Guaranteed: The Making of the American Mass Market* (Washington, DC: Smithsonian Books, 1989), 45.

18. Rosen, "Trade-Mark Cases," 827, 873.

19. Charles F. Benjamin, "Trademarks for Advertisers," *Printers' Ink* 4, no. 14 (1891): 471–472.

20. "The Registration of Trade Marks," *Scientific American* 41, no. 24 (1879): 376; and Rosen, "Trade-Mark Cases," 904.

21. Rosen, 873–875.

22. Francis Forbes, Peter Stenger Grosscup, and Arthur Philip Greeley, *Report of the Commissioners Appointed to Revise the Statutes Relating to Patents, Trade and Other Marks, and Trade and Commercial Names, Under the Act of Congress Approved June 4, 1898*, vol. 4031, Congressional Serial Set, Senate Doc. no. 20 (Washington, DC: U.S. Government Printing Office, 1902), 104.

23. Debates over H.R. 125, 10 Cong. Rec. H78–79 (daily ed. December 11, 1879). See also debates over S. 846, 4 Cong. Rec. S4234–4235 (daily ed. June 29, 1876); and discussion of H.R. 5088, 10 Cong. Rec. H2701–2708 (daily ed. April 23, 1880).

24. H.R. Rep. No. 46-561 (1880); and discussion of H.R. 5088, 10 Cong. Rec. H2805–2807 (daily ed. April 27, 1880).

25. Rosen, "Trade-Mark Cases," 889. By this point, the United States had also signed trademark treaties with Austria-Hungary (1871); Germany (1871); Great Britain (1877); Brazil (1878); and, in 1883, Serbia, Spain, Italy, and the Netherlands.

26. Pamela Walker Laird, *Advertising Progress: American Business and the Rise of Consumer Marketing*, (Baltimore: Johns Hopkins University Press, 1998), 189. See also Ross D. Petty, "From Label to Trademark: The Legal Origins of the Concept of Brand Identity in Nineteenth Century America," *Journal of Historical Research in Marketing* 4, no. 1 (2012): 143–146.

27. J. M. Battle, "The Present Condition of the Trademark Law in the United States," *Iron Age* 52 (1893): 760; and Eberhard Faber, "Trade-Marks from the Manufacturer's Point of View," *Iron Age* 52 (1893): 761.

28. Joel Benton, "Barnum in Relation to the Press and Printers' Ink," *Printers' Ink* 4, no. 22 (1891): 727–728.

29. Tim Thrift, "Using Direct-Mail Advertising to Make Good-Will Pay Bigger Dividends," *Layman Printer* 7, no. 12 (1923): 1–5.

30. Susan V. Spellman, "Trust Brokers: Traveling Grocery Salesmen and Confidence in Nineteenth-Century Trade," *Enterprise & Society* 13, no. 2 (2012): 293.

31. Gregg Boorman, "The Power of Advertising," *Printers' Ink* 13, no. 9 (1895): 8.

32. J. Walter Thompson Co. (hereafter, JWT), *J. Walter Thompson Advertising* (1897), 19–21, JWTPC. See also Ross Petty, "The Co-Development of Trademark Law and the Concept of Brand Marketing in the United States Before 1946," *Journal of Macromarketing* 31, no. 1 (2011): 91; and Stefan Schwarzkopf, "Turning Trademarks into Brands: How Advertising Agencies Practiced and Conceptualized Branding, 1890–1930," in *Trademarks, Brands, and Competitiveness*, ed. Teresa da Silva Lopes and Paul Duguid (New York: Routledge, 2010), 166.

33. Henry Lewis Johnson, "Half-Tone Engravings: Their Use in Advertisements," *Printers' Ink* 6, no. 6 (1892): 179–180; and "Pictures in Advertising," *Advertising Experience* 4, no. 2 (1896): 11.

34. Lewis Saxby, "The Genius of Pictorial Advertising," *Printers' Ink* 11, no. 19 (1894): 804; and Sam W. Hoke, "Not Made by a Trust," *Printers' Ink* 9, no. 11 (1893): 285.

35. "Pictures in Advertising," 11.

36. James H. Collins, "The Economy of Symbolism," *Printers' Ink* 34, no. 12 (1901): 3–4; and S. Roland Hall, "Advertising Illustration," *Ad Sense* 20, no. 5 (1906): 452. See also "Designing and Designs," *Profitable Advertising* 12, no. 2 (1902): 121–125; "The Value of the Repeated Ad," *Ad Sense* 21, no. 1 (1906): 59; and W. Stanley Britton, "Views of Prominent Advertisers on Illustration," *Ad Sense* 20, no. 6 (1906): 483–487.

37. JWT, *Medical Journals* (1887), 2; JWT, *Catalog of Magazines* (1887), 4; and JWT, *J. Walter Thompson Advertising* (1897), 11; all JWTPC.

38. Collins, "Economy of Symbolism," 3–4.

39. David Jury, *Graphic Design Before Graphic Designers: The Printer as Designer and Craftsman 1700–1914* (New York: Thames & Hudson, 2012), 210; Ellen Mazur Thomson, "Early Graphic Design Periodicals in America," *Journal of Design History* 7, no. 2 (1994): 119; and Laird, *Advertising Progress*, 261. See also Charles L. Benjamin, "Every Advertiser His Own Architect," *Printers' Ink* 6, no. 7 (1892): 230–232; A. E. Hoyt, "Art in Advertising—Some Phases," *Printers' Ink* 12, no. 1 (1895): 26; and "Elements of a Good Ad," *Printers' Ink* 14, no. 11 (1896): 44–45.

40. Col. F. A. Seely, "Some Hints on Selecting a Trade-Mark," *Printers' Ink* 1, no. 14 (1889): 340–341.

41. "To Have, or Not to Have, a Trademark," *Layman Printer* 3, no. 4–5 (1912): 52. See also Frank Schechter, "The Rational Basis of Trademark Protection," *Harvard Law Review* 40, no. 6 (1927): 831.

42. JWT, *J. Walter Thompson Advertising* (1897), 11–15, JWTPC.

43. JWT, 11–15.

44. Pamela Walker Laird explores these connections between science and modernity in *Advertising Progress*, 6, 310–321.

45. JWT, *J. Walter Thompson Advertising* (1897), 11.

46. Trade card for Solar Tip Shoes, with patented trademark dated 1878, in Warshaw I Shoes, AC NMAH. See also trademark reg. no. 4,457, filed December 1, 1878 (reg. December 25, 1877); and reg. no. 5,970, filed April 22, 1878 (reg. April 30, 1878); USPTO.

47. Standard Tip Shoes trade card, with patented trademark dated 1882 and 1884. Warshaw I Shoes, AC NMAH. See also trademark reg. no. 9,620, filed June 19, 1882 (reg. August 22, 1882); and reg. no. 11,466, filed July 5, 1884 (reg. September 9, 1884); USPTO.

48. In approximately eighty-five trade card and newspaper advertisements found for Solar Tip Shoes in the archives of the BTC HL, Last HL, DCWL, and Warshaw AC NMAH, only thirteen (or 15 percent) included close-up images of the shoes themselves, while nearly every ad included the logo. It is, therefore, difficult to ascertain whether the two shoe brands would have appeared nearly identical to the uninformed customer. The practice of stamping one's logo or name on the sole of the shoe was commonplace, however, and frequently was pointed out to consumers in trade-card advertising.

49. To date, I have found no evidence to suggest that Mundell ever brought suit against Harris for infringement.

50. Thomas Warwick, "The Devil's Advertising," *Printers' Ink* 7, no. 5 (1892): 109–110; and John Z. Rogers, "The Confidence Man in Advertising," *Printers' Ink* 6, no. 5 (1892): 151–152.

51. "To Punish Pirates," *Printers' Ink* 13, no. 3 (1895): 15.

52. "To Punish Pirates," 15–16. See also "Sidelights on Substitution," *Printers' Ink* 21, no. 4 (1897): 17–19; Thomas Gibson, "Fake Financial Advertising," *Ad Sense* 20, no. 2 (1906): 122–125; and R. G. Ray, "Ethics of Advertising," *Printers' Ink* 11, no. 21 (1894): 904–906.

53. "To Punish Pirates," 15–16.

54. *National Biscuit v. Baker* 95 Fed. 135 (1899). See also *National Biscuit Co. v. Swick* 121 Fed. 1007 (1903).

55. Cushing, "Cases Analogous to Trade-Marks," 321, 332.

56. Rowland Cox, "The Prevention of Unfair Competition in Business," *Harvard Law Review* 5, no. 3 (1891): 142; and Bracha, "Emergence of US Intellectual Property Law," 258. For a different perspective, see Mark McKenna, "The Normative Foundations of Trademark Law," *Notre Dame Law Review* 82, no. 5 (2007): 1868, 1898.

57. Elysa Ream Engelman, "'The Face That Haunts Me Ever': Consumers, Retailers, Critics, and the Branded Personality of Lydia E. Pinkham" (PhD diss., Boston University, 2003), 60–61, 86.

58. Engelman, 74–76, 83–84. See also Balleisen, *Fraud*, 103.

59. Engelman, 91.

60. Engelman, 93.

61. "Commissioner Duell on Trade Marks," *Scientific American* 81, no. 20 (1899): 306–307.

62. Forbes et al., *Report of the Commissioners*.

63. Forbes et al., 40–48, 123.

64. On the connections between consumerism and empire in the United States, see Mona Domosh, *American Commodities in an Age of Empire* (New York: Routledge, 2006).

65. Forbes et al., *Report of the Commissioners*, 108–109.

66. Forbes et al., 60.

67. Forbes et al., 118, 125.

68. Paul Duguid, "A Case of Prejudice? The Uncertain Development of Collective and Certification Marks," *Business History Review* 86, no. 2 (2012): 316.

69. Geoffrey Russell Searle, *Morality and the Market in Victorian Britain* (London: Clarendon Press, 1998), chap. 2; and R. Daniel Wadhwani, "Moral Economy in Business History: The Question of Value and the Evolution of Firms and Markets," unpublished paper (Business History Conference, Portland, OR, 2016).

70. Munn & Co., *Trademarks*, sec. 2, 8–10.

71. Qualified marks included unique (i.e., nondescriptive) names, designs, or portraits that would not be confused with the mark of a direct (registered) competitor. See "An Act to Authorize the Registration of Trade-Marks," 33 Stat. 724–731 (1905), online at https://www.ipmall.info/sites/default/files/hosted_resources/lipa/trademarks/PreLanhamAct_086_Act_of_1905.htm (accessed 23 January 2023).

72. Clowry Chapman, "Why Register a Trademark?" *Ad Sense* 20, no. 1 (1906): 55; and Munn & Co., *Trademarks*, sec. 2, 8–25. See also Bracha, "Emergence of US Intellectual Property Law," 259. Legally, trademarks could only be tied to actual products under the 1905 statute. The ability to create a trademark associated with a particular corporation came under the extended protections offered by the 1946 Lanham Act. See Beverly Pattishall, "Two Hundred Years of American Trademark Law," *Trademark Reporter* 68 (1978): 121–147.

73. Trademark registrations for the years 1881–1904 totaled more than 36,000. See *Statistical History of the United States from Colonial Times to the Present*, intro. Ben J. Wattenberg (New York: Basic Books, 1976), 956–959; cited in Laird, *Advertising Progress*, 414 n. 13.

74. Mira Wilkins, "The Neglected Intangible Asset: The Influence of the Trade Mark on the Rise of the Modern Corporation," *Business History* 34, no. 1 (1992): 75.

75. Schechter, "Rational Basis," 813–815; "To Have, or Not," 49–50; Ferdinand Goss, "Trade Marks and Unfair Competition," *Ad Sense* 21, no. 1 (1906): 17–20; and "Trade-Marks and Trade-Names, Protection Apart from Statute, Use of Trade-Mark on Genuine Goods," *Harvard Law Review* 35, no. 5 (1922): 625. See also Paul Duguid, "Early Marks: American Trademarks Before US Trademark Law," *Business History* 60, no. 8 (2018): 1160.

76. Edward J. Balleisen, "Private Cops on the Fraud Beat: The Limits of American Business Self-Regulation, 1895–1932," *Business History Review* 83, no. 1 (2009): 115–120. See also Richard R. John, "Robber Barons Redux: Antimonopoly Reconsidered," *Enterprise & Society* 13, no. 1 (2012): 35; and Archie B. Carroll et al., *Corporate Responsibility: The American Experience* (New York: Cambridge University Press, 2012), 105–110.

77. On consumer protection measures within the Progressive movement, see Lorine Swainston Goodwin, *The Pure Food, Drink, and Drug Crusaders, 1879–1914* (Jefferson, NC: McFarland, 1999), 5–10; and James Harvey Young, *Pure Food: Securing the Federal Food and Drugs Act of 1906* (Princeton, NJ: Princeton University Press, 1989), chap. 8.

78. See Michael Pettit, *The Science of Deception: Psychology and Commerce in America* (Chicago: University of Chicago Press, 2013), 127–135.

79. Donna J. Wood, "The Strategic Use of Public Policy: Business Support for the 1906 Food and Drug Act," *Business History Review* 59, no. 3 (1985): 413. See also Xaq Frohlich, "Making Food Standard: The U.S. Food and Drug Administration's Food Standards of Identity, 1930s–1960s," *Business History Review* 96, no. 1 (2022): 145–176.

80. On the 1905 trademark statute as part of a regulatory and Progressive reform agenda, historians have been largely silent. Notable exceptions include Strasser, *Satisfaction Guaranteed*, 268; and Robert A. Rabe, "The Origins of Federal Regulation of Advertising: A Bibliographic Essay," unpublished paper.

81. On the consumer movement at the end of the nineteenth century, see Lawrence B. Glickman, *Buying Power: A History of Consumer Activism in America* (Chicago: University of Chicago Press, 2009), chap. 5; Balleisen, *Fraud*, chaps. 5 and 7; and Inger L. Stole, *Advertising on Trial: Consumer Activism and Corporate Public Relations in the 1930s* (Chicago: University of Illinois Press, 2006).

82. "Trade-Marks Registered," *Washington Post*, September 15, 1907; "Trade-Mark Office Busy," *Washington Post*, September 23, 1905; and "More Space for Patents," *Washington Post*, October 20, 1906.

83. Floyd A. Wright, "Nature and Basis of Legal Goodwill," *Illinois Law Review* 24 (1929–1930): 27, emphasis added. See also Charles A. Bates, "Some of America's Advertisers," *Printers' Ink* 12, no. 1 (1895): 27–35; Henry P. Williams, "Truthfulness as a Force in Business," *Ad Sense* 14, no. 6 (1903): 462–464; W. Stanley Britton, "The Aim of the Advertising Man," *Ad Sense* 20, no. 4 (1906): 378–379; Britton, "Individuality in Advertising," *Ad Sense* 20, no. 5 (1906): 433–434; Gibson, "Fake Financial Advertising"; and William M. Landes and Richard A. Posner, "Trademark Law: An Economic Perspective," *Journal of Law and Economics* 30, no. 2 (1987): 269.

84. "To Have, or Not," 52; and JWT, *Things to Know About Trademarks* (1911), 52, JWTPC.

85. Edward S. Rogers, *Good Will, Trade-Marks and Unfair Trading* (Chicago: A. W. Shaw Company, 1914), chap. 9; Goss, "Trade Marks," 18; and Frank S. Moore, *Legal Protection of Goodwill* (New York: Ronald Press, 1936), chap. 16.

86. National Biscuit emerged out of several mergers in 1889, 1890, and 1898, and took its home office in Chicago. See Melvin J. Grayson, *42 Million a Day: The Story of Nabisco Brands* (East Hanover, NJ: Nabisco Brands, 1986), 20–21; and William Cahn, *Out of the Cracker Barrel: The Nabisco Story, from Animal Crackers to Zuzus* (New York: Simon and Schuster, 1969), 29–32.

87. Cahn, 25, 30–32, 69–71.

88. Ayer Series II, AC NMAH.

89. Print ad for National Biscuit (1899), Ayer Series II, AC NMAH. A survey of *New York Times* advertisements for 1898 and 1899 indicates that advertising for the Uneeda brand did not commence (in this paper) until March 13, 1899. The "Uneeda" name was first registered as a trademark in December 1898, and, though this registration notes that it was first used in

commerce in September 1898, I have not been able to find advertisements to corroborate this claim. See trademark reg. 32, 301, filed November 18, 1898 (reg. December 27, 1898), USPTO.

90. Cahn, *Nabisco Story*, 92.

91. Print ads for National Biscuit (1899–1905), Ayer Series II, AC NMAH.

92. According to the trademark registration for Nabisco dated March 15, 1960, the cross and oval logo was first used in commerce on March 1, 1900. See trademark reg. 694,645, filed May 27, 1959 (reg. March 15, 1960), USPTO.

93. Grayson, *42 Million*, 21; Cahn, *Nabisco Story*, 82. Cahn appears to quote from an interview with Green published in James H. Collins, "National Biscuit," *Printers' Ink* 55, no. 3 (1906): 6.

94. Collins, "National Biscuit," 6. Per Mollerup offers evidence of this logo as a printer's mark and suggests that it symbolized the world and the Christian faith; see Mollerup, *Marks of Excellence* (London: Phaidon, 1998), 36.

95. Thomas Balmer notes that the mark symbolically gestures to the moisture-proof packaging of Nabisco, in "Why Textile Goods Should Be Advertised," *Textile World Record* 27 n.s., no. 1 (1904): 91.

96. See Tom Blackett, "What Is a Brand?" in Rita Clifton, ed., *Brands and Branding* (New York: Wiley, 2009), 15–18; and Sarah Banet-Weiser, *Authentic: Politics and Ambivalence in a Brand Culture* (New York: New York University Press, 2012), 4.

97. "What Does This Mean?" quarter-page ad (1900), and "Behind the In-Er-Seal Package," quarter-page ad (1900), Ayer Series II, AC NMAH.

98. "The Link Between You and the Baker," 8-sheet poster (1901), Warshaw I Bakers, NMAH.

99. "Bakers' Marks," quarter-page ad (1905); and "Sign Language," full-page ad (1904); both Ayer Series II, AC NMAH.

100. "Bakers' Marks."

101. "O.K.," quarter-page ad (1905), Ayer Series II, AC NMAH; and "What the National Biscuit Co. Stands For," quarter-page ad (1906), Ayer Series II, AC NMAH.

102. "Building Up Store Character," quarter-page ad (1915), Ayer Series II, AC NMAH.

103. Schechter, "Rational Basis," 149–150. See also Nancy F. Koehn, *Brand New: How Entrepreneurs Earned Consumers' Trust from Wedgwood to Dell* (Boston, MA: Harvard Business School Press, 2001), 6.

104. "John Doe," quarter-page ad (1905), Ayer Series II, AC NMAH.

105. Ruth E. Iskin, *The Poster: Art, Advertising, Design, and Collecting, 1860s–1900s* (Hanover, NH: Dartmouth College Press, 2014), 211.

106. Hotel Times Square (W. 43rd Ave.), view from 7th Ave. showing advertisements on the east wall of the building (1915), Outdoor Advertising Association of America Archives, ROAD Collection, Hartman Center, Duke University Special Collections.

107. Here, I draw from Iskin's theory of the consecration of the aura through reproductions in print. See, Iskin, *The Poster*, 27–28.

108. "Your Grandpa Knows Us," print ad for Smith Bros. Cough Drops (1917), Ayer Series II, AC NMAH; and print ads for Lea & Perrins' Worcestershire Sauce (1917), Ayer Series II, AC NMAH. See also Ian Klaus, *Forging Capitalism: Rogues, Swindlers, Frauds, and the Rise of Modern Finance* (New Haven, CT: Yale University Press, 2014), 134.

109. Such efforts are outlined in John Mercer, "A Mark of Distinction: Branding and Trade Mark Law in the UK from the 1860s," *Business History* 52, no. 1 (2010): 33.

110. Several scholars credit the law in motivating new business practices, especially branding. See Joseph M. Gabriel, *Medical Monopoly: Intellectual Property Rights and the Origins of the Modern Pharmaceutical Industry* (Chicago: University of Chicago Press, 2014), 206; Carma Gorman, "The Role of Trademark Law in the History of US Visual Identity Design, c. 1860–1960," *Journal of Design History* 30, no. 4 (2017): 371–388; and Thomas Mollanger, "The Ef-

fects of Producers' Trademark Strategies on the Structure of the Cognac Brandy Supply Chain During the Second Half of the Nineteenth Century: The Reconfiguration of Commercial Trust by the Use of Brands," *Business History* 60, no. 8 (2018): 1255–1276.

111. Roland Marchand, *Creating the Corporate Soul: The Rise of Public Relations and Corporate Imagery in American Big Business* (Berkeley: University of California Press, 1998), 2–3.

112. Collins, "Economy of Symbolism," 4.

113. Collins, 4.

114. Collins, "National Biscuit," 4–6.

115. National Biscuit Co., *Trade Mark Litigation: Opinions, Orders, Injunctions and Decrees Relating to Unfair Competition and Infringement of Trade Marks*, 5th ed. (priv. pub, 1915); and Cahn, *Nabisco Story*, 111–115.

116. See Charles McCurdy, "American Law and the Marketing Structure of the Large Corporation, 1875–1890," *Journal of Economic History* 38, no. 3 (1978): 631–649; Wood, "The Strategic Use of Public Policy"; and Richard S. Tedlow, "From Competitor to Consumer: The Changing Focus of Federal Regulation of Advertising," *Business History Review* 55, no. 1 (1981): 35–58.

117. *National Biscuit Co. v. Pacific Biscuit Co. et al.* (1914) 83 NJ Eq. 369.

118. *National Biscuit*, 83 NJ Eq. at 375.

119. As in the case of *Burnett v. Phalon* (1867), 5 Abb. Pr. R., N. S. 212, the law of trademarks still privileged the rule of first use in cases of simultaneous adoption.

120. *National Biscuit*, 83 NJ Eq. at 380.

121. The injunction against the sixteen products in question took effect in January 1915. Pacific Biscuit did not survive the economic crash of 1929, despite having recorded profit gains throughout the 1920s. In 1930, National Biscuit acquired the company's assets, earning an extra million dollars in net profits that year, even with the onslaught of the Depression. See "Pacific Biscuit Earnings Gain," *Los Angeles Times*, August 2, 1928; "Pacific Biscuit Votes Extra Disbursement," *Los Angeles Times*, May 3, 1929; "Pacific Biscuit Approves Merger," *Baltimore Sun*, June 10, 1930; and "National Biscuit Co. Nets $6,732,017 for September Quarter Against $5,791,645 Year Ago," *Wall Street Journal*, October 24, 1930.

122. Balleisen, *Fraud*, 110.

123. Edward S. Rogers, "Some Historical Matter Concerning Trade-Marks," *Michigan Law Review* 9, no. 1 (1910): 43.

Epilogue

1. Vachel Lindsay, *The Art of the Moving Picture*, rev. ed. (New York: Macmillan, 1922), book I, np. Available online at www.gutenberg.org/files/13029/13029-h/13029-h.htm#Page_1 (accessed 19 February 2021).

2. Frank I. Schechter, *The Historical Foundations of the Law Relating to Trade-Marks* (New York: Columbia University Press, 1925), 147–148.

3. Schechter, 150.

4. The issue of goodwill would be addressed in more detail in the Lanham Act. See Mira Wilkins, "The Neglected Intangible Asset: The Influence of the Trade Mark on the Rise of the Modern Corporation," *Business History* 34, no. 1 (1992): 70.

5. James A. Henretta et al., *America's History*, 5th ed. (New York: Bedford/St. Martin's, 2004), 668.

6. Michele Helene Bogart, *Artists, Advertising, and the Borders of Art* (Chicago: University of Chicago Press, 1995); and Juliann Sivulka, *Soap, Sex, and Cigarettes: A Cultural History of American Advertising* (Belmont, CA: Wadsworth, 1998), chaps. 3–4.

7. This slogan, created by the Benton & Bowles agency in the 1940s, was ranked number 85 in the top 100 advertising campaigns of the twentieth century. See Bob Garfield, "Advertising Age Ad Century: Top 100 Campaigns," *Advertising Age Online* (March 29, 1999), https://adage.com/article/special-report-the-advertising-century/ad-age-advertising-century-top-100-campaigns/140918 (accessed 1 February 2013).

8. Sarah Banet-Weiser, *Authentic: Politics and Ambivalence in a Brand Culture* (New York: New York University Press, 2012), 8–10.

9. Midas Muffler Shops, "About Midas," www.midas.com/aboutmidas/tabid/55/default.aspx (accessed 19 February 2021). This slogan, first used in the 1980s, was a product of collaboration between two agencies: DDB Chicago and Ogilvy & Mather Toronto. See *The Auto Channel*, "New Campaign Returns to Heritage of 'Trust the Midas Touch,'" www.theautochannel.com/news/2004/03/04/183456.html (accessed 19 February 2021). Ironically, in Greek mythology the "Midas touch" was a curse—finding everything he touched turned to gold became a horrifying experience for King Midas. Nathaniel Hawthorne popularized the tale in his *A Wonder Book for Girls and Boys* (Boston: Houghton Mifflin, 1892 [1851]).

10. Alan Feldman, quoted in *The Auto Channel*, "New Campaign."

Index

Acknowledgments

After roughly fifteen years of researching and studying character, trust, and personal relationships, one would think that I'd be an expert on how to convey my inner sentiments clearly in print. Yet I have struggled to organize these acknowledgments according to standard academic custom, grouping individuals together by relationship, role, or level of importance. I suppose the myriad debts I have incurred while writing this book are just as messy and uneven as the collaborations and developments I have traced within its pages. I hope my many creditors will forgive my clumsy attempts to thank them below. The book's successes are also theirs, but any errors are my responsibility alone.

Over the past two decades, I have been fortunate to receive advice and reinforcement from an exceptional group of scholars whose mentorship was formative in my own intellectual development. From these dedicated scholar-teachers, I learned the value of humility, of celebrating my students' insights, and of pushing my students to dig deeper—principles that have improved my own approach as a writer. While a master's student at Western Michigan University, Bruce Haight, Barbara Havira, Dick Keaveny, Judith Stone, Mary-Louise Totton, and the late Nora Faires encouraged me to find my voice and pursue a PhD. At the University of Southern California, I had the great fortune to work with Elinor Accampo, Daniela Bleichmar, Bill Deverell, Richard Fox, Paul Lerner, Peter Mancall, Steve Ross, and Brett Sheehan—all of whom left their mark on my professionalization, my identity as a scholar, and this book. Deb Harkness and Karen Halttunen backed this project from its earliest stages, offering writing advice that I've only now truly begun to appreciate. During a History of the Book seminar taught at the Huntington Library, Deb asked me to consider how advertisements might work as "corporate calling cards." That seminar paper launched this project and the core research in Chapter 4, and Deb's special skills in picking catchy titles helped me land on *Branding Trust* for this book. I want to thank Karen for her guidance in navigating the world of character and sentiment, which provided a sturdy foundation for my analysis of commercial activity. Most important, however, I especially want to thank her for her compassion and patience during the last year of my PhD program, when family hardships and illness threatened to derail my progress. Beyond any intellectual debts I owe, I am deeply appreciative of her for that.

The research featured within these pages was completed with generous support from several institutions. Fellowships granted by the Henry Francis DuPont Winterthur Museum & Library, the Huntington Library, and the Smithsonian Institution's National Museum of American History helped fund a full year of research early in the project. The University of Southern California, especially the History Department, the Visual Studies Program, and the Dornsife College of Arts and Sciences, provided funding that aided my completion of the dissertation. At Misericordia University, I especially want to thank the Faculty Research Grants committee, who sustained my continued research and writing over the past nine years. The Department of History and Government, as well as the offices of the dean of the College of Arts and Sciences, and the vice president for Academic Affairs, together provided a generous subvention for costs related to producing the book's many images. I am therefore grateful for the support of Chris Stevens, Heidi Manning, and David Rehm. Jennifer Delmar and Michelle Donato were instrumental in solving various procedural questions related to this funding.

Early in my studies, someone once advised me to consult with and listen to archivists, for "they will become your best friends." That was perhaps some of the best advice I've received, for certainly archivists, librarians, and others provided invaluable assistance while I researched this book. Early in the project, I profited tremendously from conversations with Cathy Cherbosque, Dave Mihaly, and Alan Jutzi at the Huntington Library; and from Emily Guthrie, Rosemary Krill, Greg Landry, Rich McKinstry, Laura Parrish, Helena Richardson, Jeanne Solensky, and Ann Wagner at the Winterthur Museum, Garden & Library. As a fellow in the Archives Center of the Smithsonian Institution's National Museum of American History, I was lucky to work with Vanessa Broussard-Simmons, Helena Wright, Richard Doty, Katherine Ott, and Deborra Richardson. For making short research trips fruitful and efficient, I'd like to recognize Lauren Hewes, Elizabeth Pope, and Paul Erickson (American Antiquarian Society); Jim Green, Sarah Weatherwax, and Connie King (Library Company of Philadelphia); Marge McNinch and Lucas Clawson (Hagley Museum and Library); Stefan Firtko (Lehigh University); Marianne Hansen (Bryn Mawr University Special Collections); Andrew Begley (National Archives and Records Administration at Boston); Joan Yamrick (Misericordia University); and the reference desk staffs at the Library of Congress Prints and Photographs Room, the New York State Archives, the University of Chicago Special Collections, the Public Search Facility of the US Patent and Trademark Office, Temple University's Special Collections, and the John W. Hartman Center for Sales, Advertising, and Marketing History at Duke University. For their help in obtaining permission to reprint the images in this book, I'd like to thank Carley Altenburger, Sheila Jain Kaushik, Joshua Larkin Rowley, Kay Peterson, Krystle Satrum, and Emily Smith. Moreover, I have been fortunate to work with several undergraduate research assistants—Alyssa Grieco, Kaitlin Hall, Erin McGee, Rebecca Schnable-Kozloski, Briana Scorey, Sara Shields, and Hope Spangler—whose efforts are greatly appreciated. My colleague and physicist-extraordinaire, Jeff Stephens, provided valuable skills in running some data sets through Python for further analysis. Finally, I owe a great debt to the staff who maintain the National Digital Newspaper Program's Chronicling America database housed at the Library of Congress, which facilitated my deep dive into the world of nineteenth-century newspaper advertising. This book couldn't have been written without the unparalleled resources made available there.

As a junior scholar, I was lucky to be welcomed into two intellectual communities that nurtured my research through the subsequent decade. While a faculty member at Misericordia University, I have benefited from a dedicated, thoughtful, and genuine community of scholars who challenged me intellectually, cheered me on, and generously offered comments as I expanded and revised this project. For their collegiality and encouragement, past and present, I'd like to thank Allan Austin, Scott Blanchard, Brian Carso, Maureen Cech, Joe Cipriani, Joe Curran, Patrick Danner, Thom Hajkowski, Rich Hancuff, Patrick Hamilton, Matt Hinton, Sue Lazur, Jennifer Luksa, Rebecca Padot, Russ Pottle, Chris Stevens, Patricia Thatcher, and David Wright. One of the true benefits of teaching at a small liberal arts school has been the camaraderie among the varied departments in the College of Arts and Sciences. To my third-floor colleagues, and all those not named here: thank you for your sharp wit, your intellectualism, and all you do.

I've often talked about this project with other scholars, and I know that the book has been made better through that discourse, even if it's hard to pinpoint exactly whose advice shaped what. My gratitude therefore goes to those students and fellows I interacted with through various channels early in the project, especially Joe Adelman, Matt Amato, Nicole Belolan, Michael Block, Annie Johnson, David and Helen LaCroix, Kate LaPrad, and Emily Pawley. Others kindly shared their time and thoughts as I mulled over the research, including Andrew Bell, Pete Daniel, Dick Flint, Jennifer Greenhill, Jason Hill, Carl Robert Keyes, Michael Leja, Justin Nordstrom, Dael Norwood, Robert Rabe, Susan Strasser, and the many #twitterstorians who have answered my random queries. I'd also like to recognize the audiences who provided much needed feedback as I workshopped the book's narrative at various conferences, including meetings hosted by the Popular Culture Association (2009); the Pacific Coast Branch of the American Historical Association (2010); the Emerging Scholars Symposium at the Winterthur Library (2010); the American Antiquarian Society (2011); the Organization of American Historians (2014); the Visual Studies Research Institute at the University of Southern California (2015); the National Council of Public History (2015); the Society for Historians of the Early American Republic (2017); the Nineteenth-Century Studies Association (2017); the Center for the History of Business, Technology, and Society Conferences held at the Hagley Library and Museum (2019 and 2021); and the Business History Conference (BHC) (2013–2018 and 2020–2022).

The BHC is a wonderful organization of dedicated scholars; it has opened doors and helped to launch my career in productive ways. This book wouldn't be what it is without the genuine and spontaneous support and feedback that I have received from various individuals I've met through the BHC. I especially want to thank Ed Balleisen, Steve Campbell, Mandy Cooper, Alicia Dewey, Barbara Hahn, Will Hausman, Justene Hill Edwards, Eric Hintz, Roger Horowitz, Vicki Howard, Carol Lockman, Stephen Mihm, Amanda Mushal, Lucy Newton, the late Ed Perkins, Andrew Popp, Teresa da Silva Lopes, Susan Spellman, Dan Wadhwani, Karen Ward Mahar, Wendy Woloson, and Mary Yeager.

Many friends and colleagues lent their time and expertise in reading various drafts as I wrote and revised this book, and I am forever indebted to them for their generosity in offering careful notes and suggestions. My deepest thanks thus go to Allan Austin, Gigi Barnhill, Brian Carso, Amanda Caleb, Kara Carmack, Catherine Clark, Kate Danner, Sarah Fried-Gintis, the late Karin Higa, Karin Huebner, Chera Kee, Sarah Keyes, Elisa Korb, Jonathan Kuiken, Anca Lasc, Allison Lauterbach, Ryan Linkof, Laine Little, Annie Manion, Casey Riffel, Noelia Saenz, George Shea, Akira Shimizu, Amy Sopkak-Joseph, Raphaelle Steinzig, Ericka Swensson, Jia Tan, Ben Uchiyama, Ryan Watson, Diana Williams, R. Lucas ("Luke") Williams, and Yanqiu Zheng. I am very fortunate that this book landed at the University of Pennsylvania Press, where I have benefited from Bob Lockhart's editorial expertise and thoughtful feedback. Special thanks are also due to my series editors, Andrew Cohen, Shane Hamilton, Kimberly Phillips-Fein, Elizabeth Tandy Shermer, as well as Alex Gupta and Noreen O'Connor-Abel, who provided expert assistance with production. I am grateful for the very helpful comments offered by the book's anonymous reviewers, especially their advice to refine my arguments about the long history of branding.

An earlier version of Chapter 4 appeared as "Exchange Cards: Advertising, Album-Making, and the Commodification of Sentiment in the Gilded Age," in *Winterthur Portfolio* 51, no. 1 (2017): 1–53, © 2017 by The Henry Francis du Pont

Winterthur Museum, Inc. Special thanks go to the journal and to the Winterthur, for permission to republish some of that material, and to Amy Earls and the anonymous reviewers who helped me expand my arguments about scrapbooks.

At various stages in my career, three exceptional scholars shaped my research agenda for the better, pushing me to identify and explain the broader and deeper histories undulating beneath many of the currents in this story. Shortly after we met, Sharon Murphy sent me hunting for a few footnotes about the history of business letters. Falling down what would later become a very productive rabbit hole, I uncovered research for three new chapters that reshaped the entire book's framework. I deeply appreciate Sharon's honest criticism, which has challenged me to think more critically and historiographically about my work. I am so glad to have had the opportunity to meet her during a women's luncheon at the BHC in 2013. Coincidentally, that same luncheon introduced me to Pamela Walker Laird, whose work I knew well and who left me, admittedly, a little starstruck. She graciously accepted my invitation to coffee, however, and listened enthusiastically as I must have rambled on and on about trade cards and logos. Since then, I have been privileged to count her as a great champion of my work, one who generously read my first draft and then chapter drafts as they evolved. This book profited from Pam's expansive knowledge of the literature, her pointed questions about the role of printers, and her mentorship through the revisions process. Her aid has advanced my career and my research in more ways than one. Finally, Vanessa Schwartz was instrumental in bringing me to the University of Southern California—an experience that reshaped the course of my life—and she subsequently played a formative role in helping me conceptualize this project. Vanessa tirelessly pushed me to think more deeply about the images I encountered, challenging me to better articulate what images "do," rather than simply what they "show." This lesson carried my work forward in new and productive ways over the last decade, framing how I've analyzed the evidence in this book as well as improving my teaching. I'm sure I must have frustrated her at times, but her patience and measured critiques have made me a better scholar. I'm very grateful for her faith in this project, for her honest feedback on so many things, and for her continued mentorship and support over the past sixteen years.

Finally, I have the very difficult task of thanking my family, those by relation and those by choice, for sustaining me through the long haul. For lunches, dinners, and drinks past and present, I especially want to thank Amanda Caleb, Kara Carmack, Jackie Conway, Nicky Edwards, Sarah Fried-Gintis, Jess Garner, Marnie Hiester, Mary Kay Kimelewski, Laine Little, Holly McBroom, Genna Nichols Perugini, Noreen O'Connor, Alicia Nordstrom, Marguerite Roy, Noelia Saenz, Melanie Shepherd, Becky Steinberger, Rachel Urbanowicz, and Matilda Zakian.

During various research trips, several friends and family members opened their homes to me, including Cindy and Mike Domanowski, Lesley and Wes Skinner, Sue and Skip Tornow, and Jonathon and Kara Petriches. I've been lucky to have an extended family whose warmth and positivity made life a little easier, even though we've lived far apart. For this, I'd like to recognize my relatives in the Black, Gauthier, and Petriches families—especially Patricia Gordon Petriches, George Black, Jeff Black, Jeanne Black, Shirley Brown, Sandy Kivela, Beverley Pare Black, Jonathon Petriches, and Kara Petriches. My parents, Jeff Petriches and Anne Marie Gauthier Petriches, showed me what it meant to be a smart, empowered young woman who knew her voice. They impressed upon me, from an early age, the value of education and the importance of integrity. They also worked incredibly hard so that I (and my brother) might be successful, and I am who I am today for their efforts. My father has been a tireless supporter of my intellectual pursuits, sharing in my joy and excitement when I succeeded, and reassuring me when disappointed. Thanks, Dad, for everything. My mother was a treasured adviser, confidant, and friend, whose optimism and faith pushed me to be a better person. I was heartbroken when she died, but I know she would have been proud to see me finish this book. She passed on much of her sparkle to my son, daughter, nieces, and nephew; I miss her dearly, but I cherish the gifts she left behind.

A colleague once told me (half in jest) that being a working mother offers a special opportunity—to fail at both motherhood and academia all at once. She wasn't lying: I, like many of my female colleagues with children, have often felt as though I were shortchanging my children or my career because there simply weren't enough hours in the day. I regret having missed many dinnertime conversations and bedtime stories because there was work to be done. But I hope that one day my children will look back, hopefully with pride, and take inspiration from knowing that their mother managed to research, write, and finish a book while working full time. Mine are genuinely two of the kindest, sweetest, and funniest kids, whose joy never ceases to bring a smile to my face. To Oliver and Lucy: I love you both more than you know, and I count myself lucky to be your mom.

Finally, to my husband and partner, Travis Black, I owe everything. Over the past twenty years, he encouraged me to continue pursuing my professional goals and this book, even when the circumstances must have made it difficult to do so: through two bouts of cancer; multiple losses; moving across the country and back again; expanding our family; and dealing with the weekly challenges of work, children, and professional life. It's nearly impossible to quantify that support. A true partner, he has unquestioningly stepped in to manage any number of household and family tasks at various moments over the past decade, not because he had to, or because I wouldn't, but because he cared and that's what good partners do. My career has been better because he stood behind me and beside me, and for that, and so many other things, I am grateful beyond words. It has become somewhat cliché for academics to thank their spouses in their book acknowledgments, speaking of love and devotion (and sometimes typing skills). Let me set the record straight: Travis didn't type a word of this book (though he did teach me Excel!). Nevertheless, he deserves my unending praise and love because he saw me not as a wife but as a friend who was working incredibly hard to pursue her goal and because he wanted to help me achieve it. Thank you, from the bottom of my heart.